MW01630352

Afghanistan

A DARKNESS VISIBLE

Seamus Murphy

With essays by Nancy Hatch Dupree and Anthony Loyd

SAQI

This edition first published in 2008
by Saqi Books
26 Westbourne Grove, London W2 5RH, UK
825 Page Street, Suite 203, Berkeley, California 94710
Tabet Building, Mneimneh Street, Hamra, Beirut
www.saqibooks.com

Design by Henrietta Molinaro
Printed in Italy by EBS

A full CIP record for this book is available from the British Library
A full CIP record for this book is available from the Library of Congress

ISBN 978-0-86356-620-2

for binkie and jimmie

There are in Afghanistan vistas of incomparable beauty, where the massive grandeur and stark strength of its mountain ranges intimidate the soul. In the valleys, the villages, fields and orchards glow like jewels beside springs and along the riverbanks, giving the lie to a nation besieged by threat.

Afghanistan is the pivotal axis where four great civilisations meet. It is the northern-most extension of the Indian subcontinent, the southern limit of Central Asia, the eastern periphery of the Iranian Plateau, and the western-most extension of China.

Peoples from those far regions have traversed the land for millennia. Some came as conquering empire builders, others as political exiles who eventually founded their own sumptuous kingdoms. They inevitably attracted marauding Central Asian nomads who, in their turn, were soon seduced by the glitter of city life and created empires of their own. Trader caravans have criss-crossed the landscape for 5,000 years, bringing in their wake artisans as well as men of intellect, missionaries and pilgrims.

Kindred ethnic groups straddle the borders that were drawn by the British and the Russians at the turn of the nineteenth century. Pushtun are found in Pakistan as well as Afghanistan, Baluch live in the south western corner of Afghanistan as well as in Iran and Pakistan. Tajik, Uzbek, Turkoman and Kirghiz occupy their own Central Asian states in addition to enclaves throughout northern Afghanistan. Similarities exist between these adjacent populations, but the Afghan groups are noticeably distinct – and proud of their uniqueness.

Arrian, the chronicler of Alexander the Great's sojourn in Afghanistan in the fourth century BC, Chinese Buddhist pilgrims in the fifth and seventh centuries AD, and a long line of interlopers since the Middle Ages have written copiously of the medley of lifestyles among these disparate groups. But there are social values that bind Afghan society with intense feelings of national identity. They are a paramount regard for family, meticulous attention to rules of hospitality and etiquette, individual and group honour, a positive pride in independence that rises from a love of self-reliance, tolerance towards others, respect for the elderly, respect for women, abhorrence of fanaticism and dislike for ostentation.

Years of discord have stretched taut the fabric of this society, and many once-respected national traits have been compromised. While no innate animosity divides the ethnic groups, competition for resources and political power has always existed, causing social discrimination. It is these tensions that are being exploited today in the name of ethnicity.

To say that inciting divisiveness along the lines of ethnicity is a terrorist tactic is not to exaggerate. Equally offensive is the fostering of sectarian conflict. Throughout its history different religions have mingled harmoniously in this land. Superlative silver coins minted by the Bactrians of the north in the fourth century BC bore images of Greek deities such as Zeus, Hercules and Athena, while Mitras of Iran was also present.

In the early centuries AD the Kushans, who replaced the Bactrians, were even more eclectic. Their most famous king, Kanishka, displayed a pantheon of twenty-three gods and goddess of Greek, Persian, Central Asian and Hindu origins on his copper coins, including the first human figure of the Buddha.

The summer capital of the Kushans was at Bagram, north of Kabul, near the present US military base. The Kushan citizens of this ancient city were passionately fond of the many luxurious goods brought to them by traders along the fabled Silk Route. These included exquisite painted glassware from Egypt, bronzes and erotic plaques from Rome, and sensuous ivories from India. Despite their love of luxury, however, these sybaritic Kushans generously patronised the many Buddhist establishments clustered around the countryside. This patronage inspired artists whose creativity produced masterpieces in stone and stucco, now called Gandhara Art, that are renowned to this day. In the serene valley of Bamiyan, at the very heart of the country, a large caravan city catered to travellers moving north from India. Here they stopped to rest before pushing on through the rugged mountains to the bustling depot at Balkh on the Oxus River, midway on the Silk Route between Rome and China. In the cliffs above Bamiyan's caravanserais Buddhist artists and devotees created the world's largest standing Buddha images that inspired artists throughout South Asia.

Hindu kings came to rule as the Kushan Empire waned, and then they too gave way to the splendid Islamic empires of the Ghaznavid, Timurids and Moghuls of the tenth – seventeenth centuries. There are no practising Buddhists in Afghanistan today, but dynamic Hindu communities thrive. Every year Shi'a, together with Sunni, joyously celebrate the coming of the New Year, Naoroz, at two famous Shi'a shrines in Mazar-i-Sharif and Kabul.

But recent sectarian power-plays threaten to let loose a spiral of animosity between these communities that is as shocking as the political manipulation of ethnicity. The attempt to impose austere Islam on these tolerant people is another political manoeuvre of grave concern, for the coercive aspects of the Taliban brand of Islam are widely deplored by most Afghans, to whom extremism and fanaticism are anathema. Nevertheless the ultraconservative messages appeal to some in part because they reinforce acceptable patriarchal norms. The Taliban did not invent the burqa, for instance, for the veil was adopted from the Persians many centuries ago. Honour is central to this society; and women are the embodiment of that honour. The veil, seclusion and curtailment of movement outside the home are safeguards that more easily guarantee chastity, respect for women and the respectability of the household. Afghan governments since 1959 have encouraged the voluntary removal of the veil and the end of seclusion. This movement progressed steadily until the Taliban attacked it so violently. Now it regains momentum. To see women in Parliament sitting with quiet aplomb next to male colleagues in this nation where tradition decrees politics an unsuitable pastime for honourable women is a positive measure of change. Change, for good or ill, is most evident in Kabul. The once placid charm of this city, now swollen to over two million – four times its population in 1978 – is threatened. The city is awash with displaced persons, returning refugees, job-seekers and opportunists. There is poverty to a degree unknown in the past, as the beggars roaming the streets attest; they were until recently unknown in Kabul.

Beside the skeletal remains of bombed-out buildings ostentatious new structures proclaim an unprecedented growth in the narcotics trade and rampant corruption. Ugly concrete barriers defacing once elegant neighbourhoods are reminders of the ongoing insurgency. Patience with the influx of foreigners living behind these barricades is wearing thin, since their promised improvements have proved few and far between.

Still a remarkable vitality is palpable throughout the city. The faces of the Afghans seldom reflect despondency. The resilient fortitude of the Afghan people remains and their admirable culture – battered and distorted as it may be – survives.

Nancy Hatch Dupree

If there is a Paradise on earth, it is this, it is this, it is this.

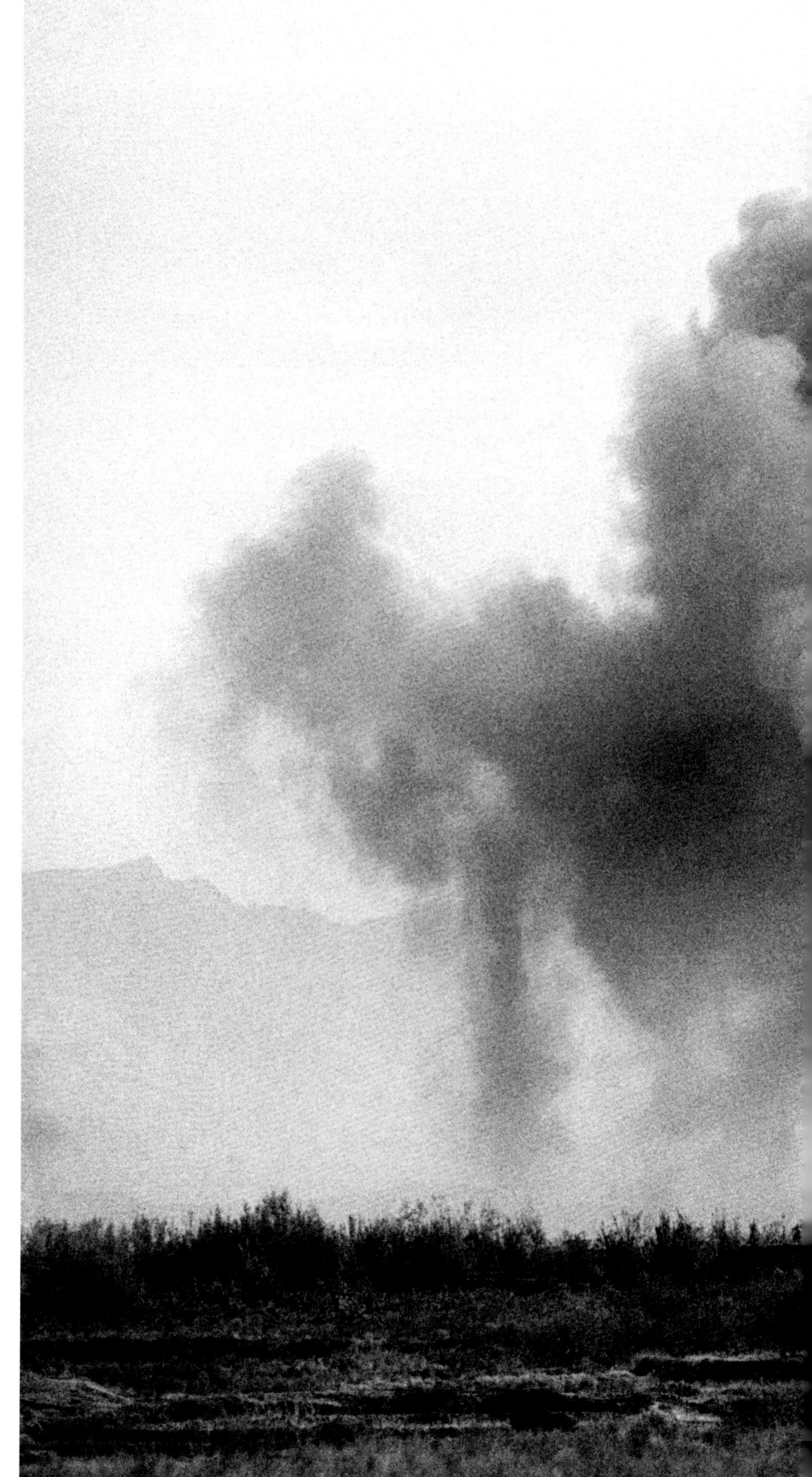

Shamali Plain, Parwan Province: November 2001
A US airstrike on Taliban frontlines north of
Kabul, using a 'Daisy Cutter' bomb.

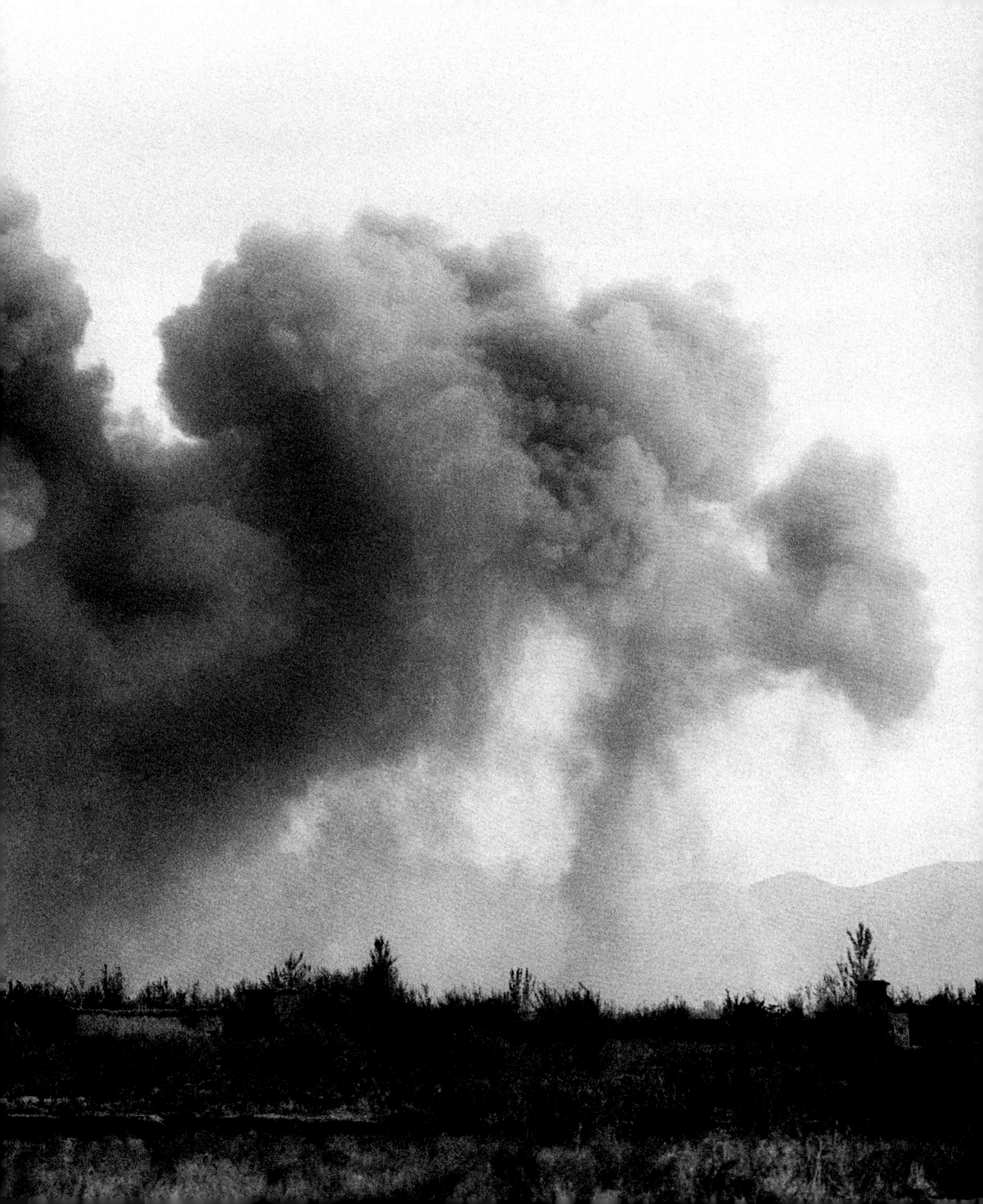

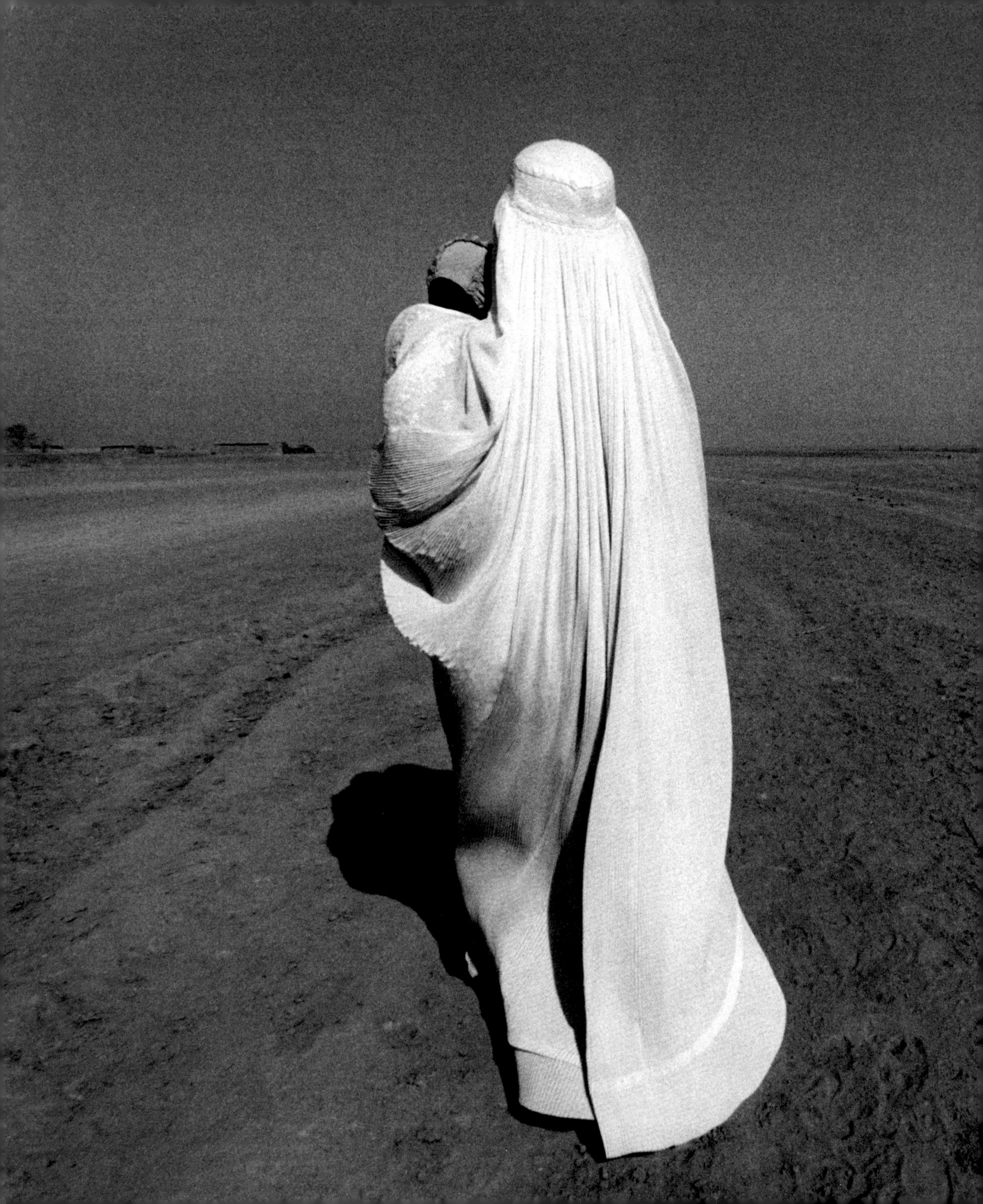

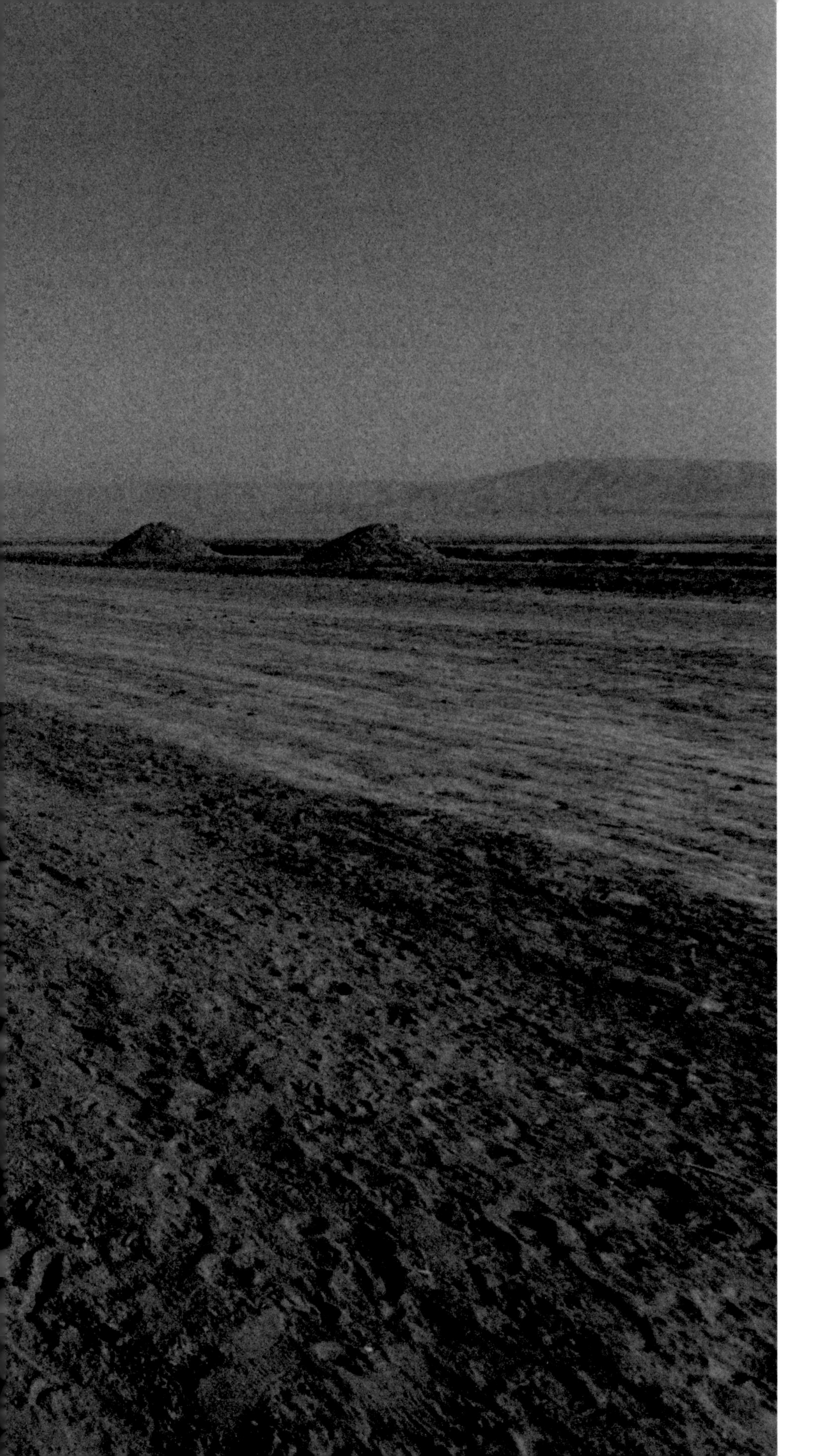

KHWAJA BAHAUDDIN, TAKHAR PROVINCE:
NOVEMBER 2000
The burqa had long been traditional for women
in Afghanistan before the arrival of the Taliban.

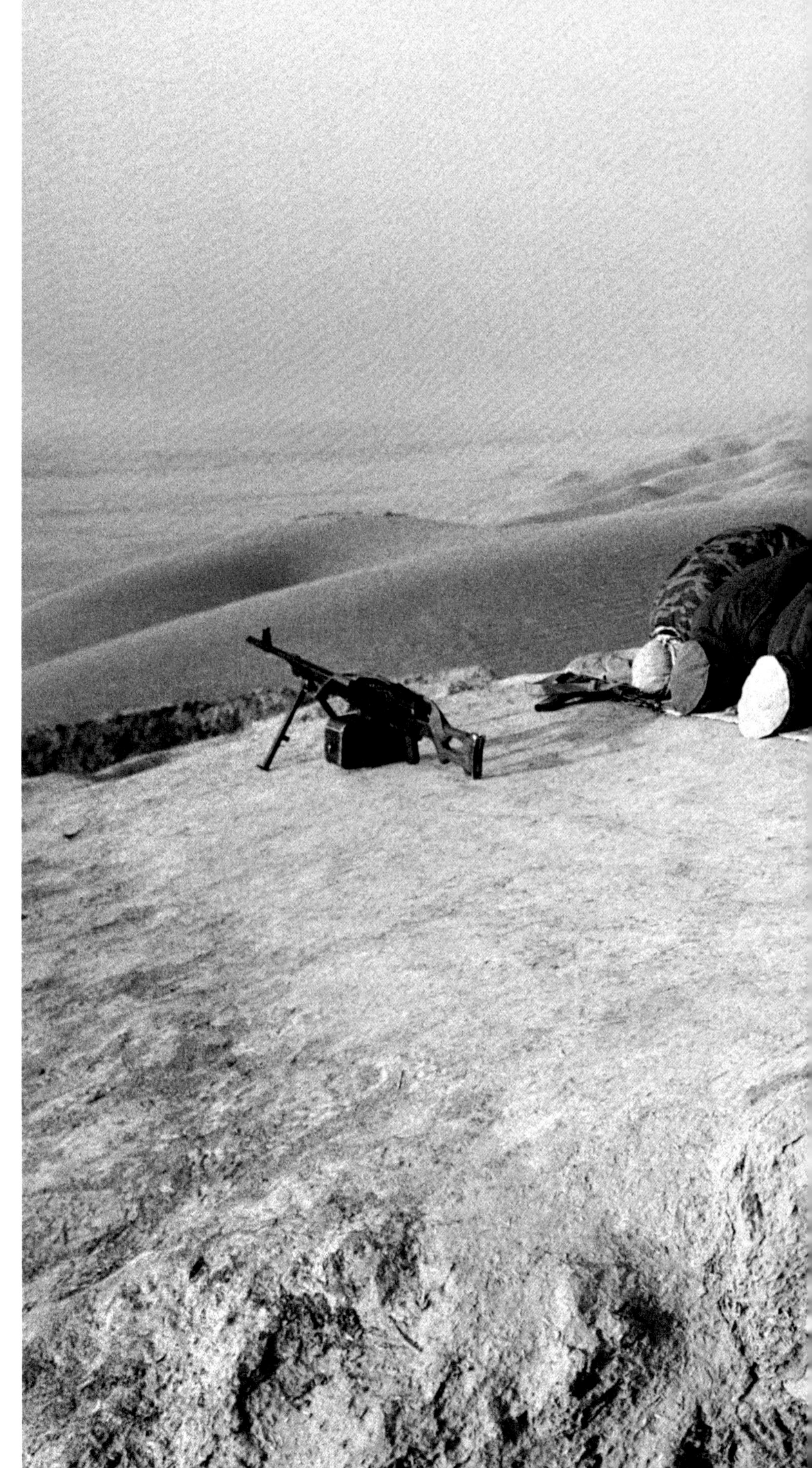

DASHT-E-QALA, TAKHAR PROVINCE: NOVEMBER 2000
Ahmad Shah Massoud leads evening prayers with
members of the Northern Alliance at the front
above Dasht-e-Qala.

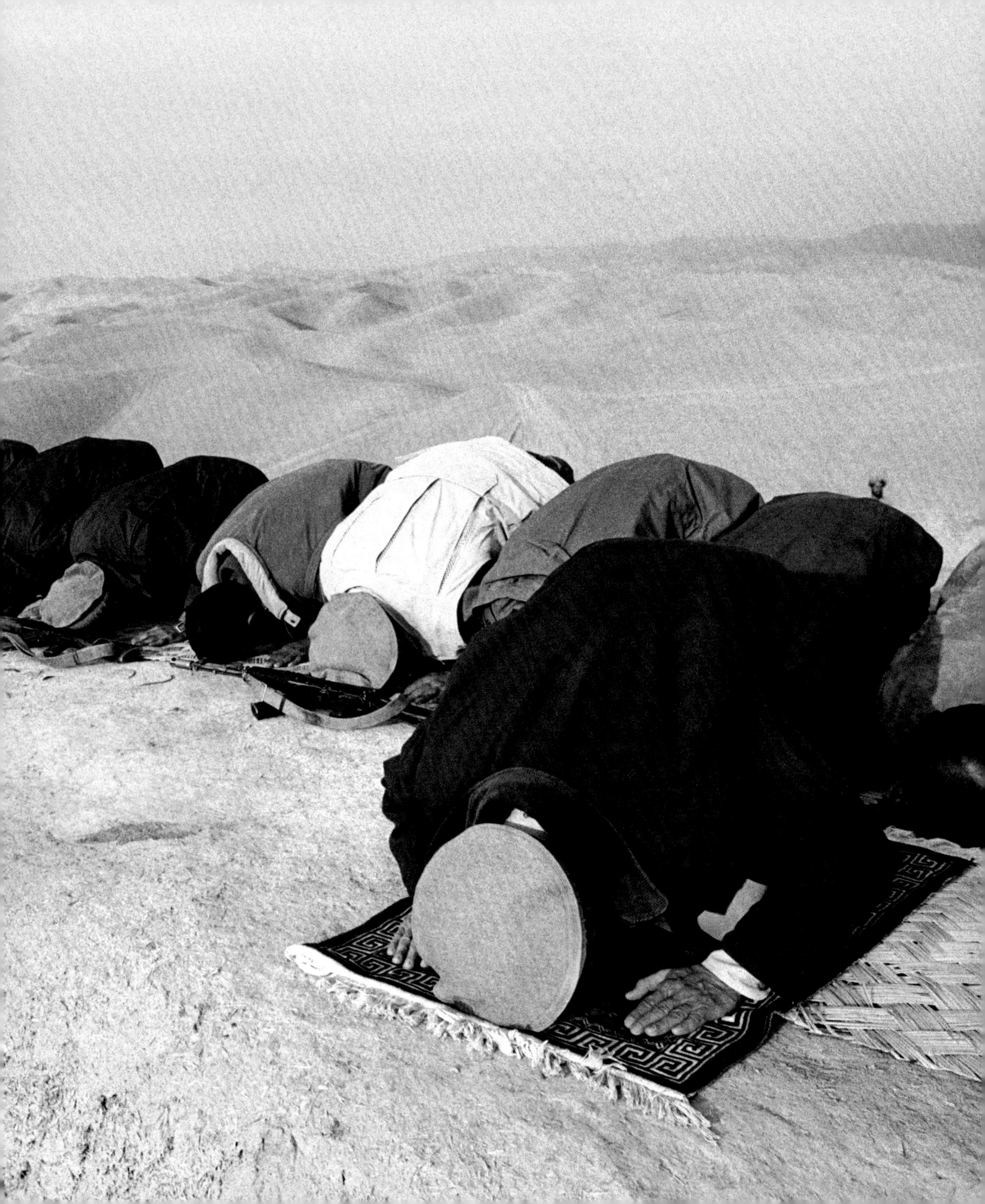

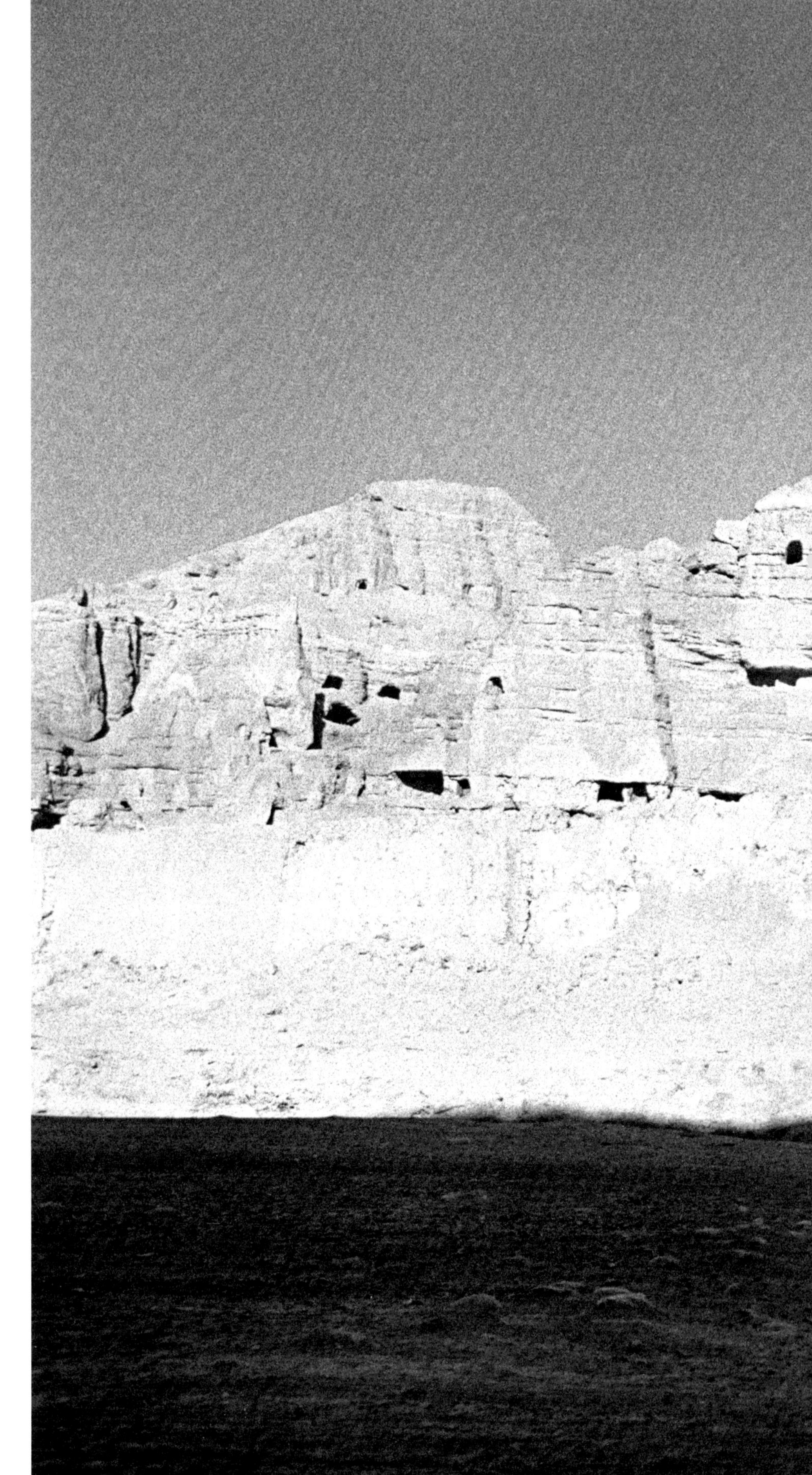

Bamiyan, Bamiyan Province: June 2003
A Hazara victim of the war passes the rock-face that housed the Buddhas of Bamiyan. The Hazara, as Shi'a Muslims, suffered particular tyranny under the Taliban. The statues were destroyed by the Taliban in 2001.

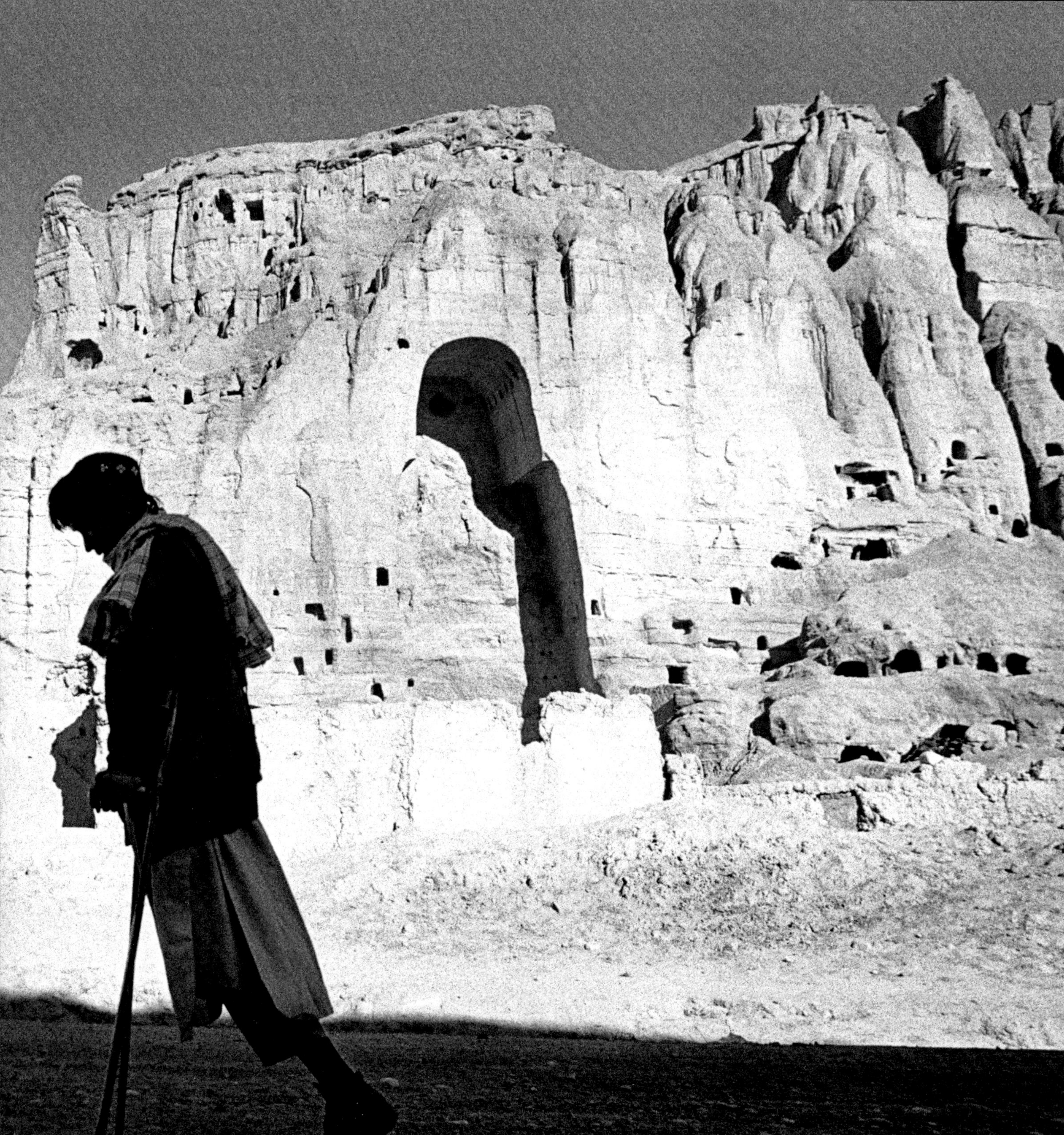

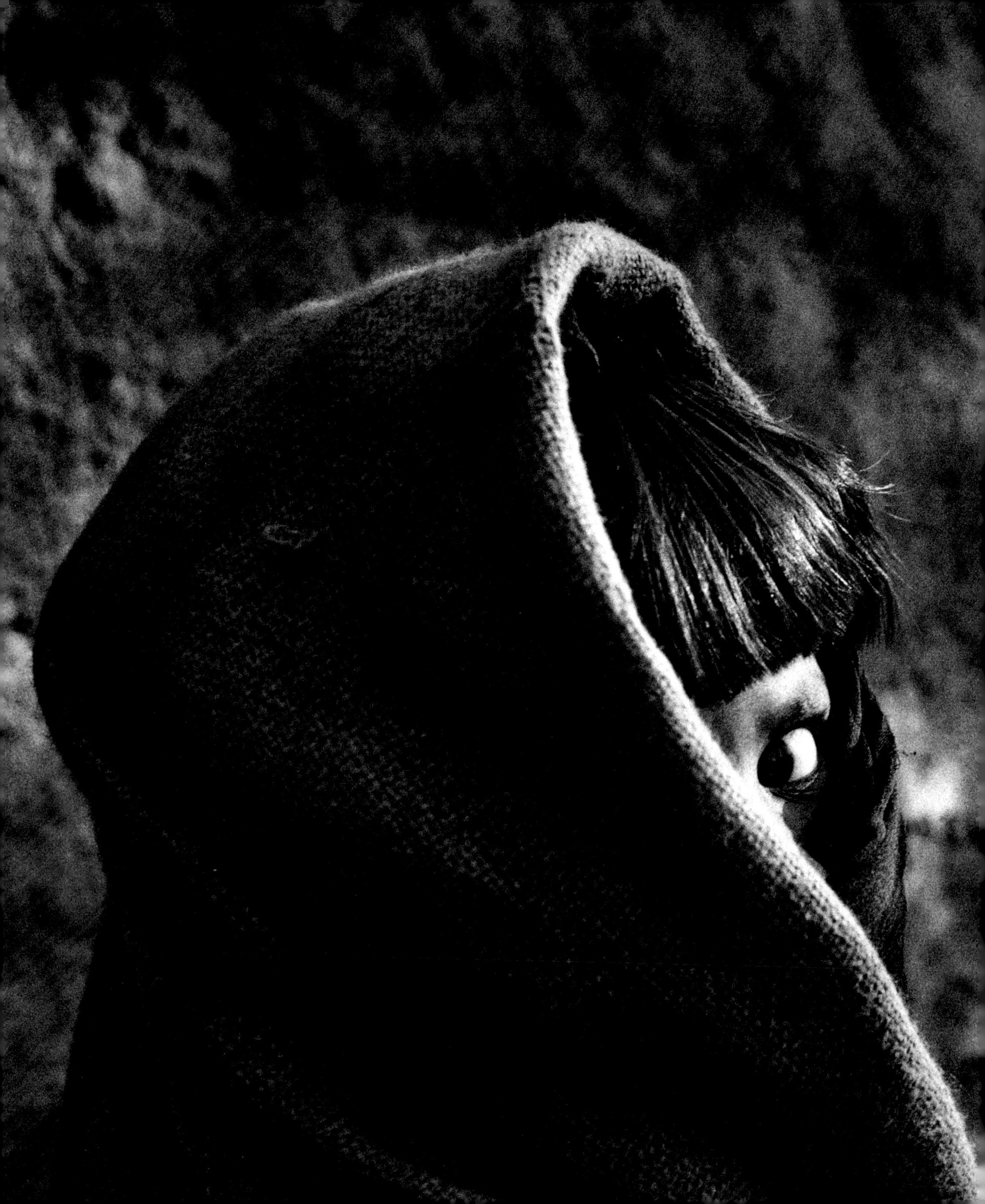

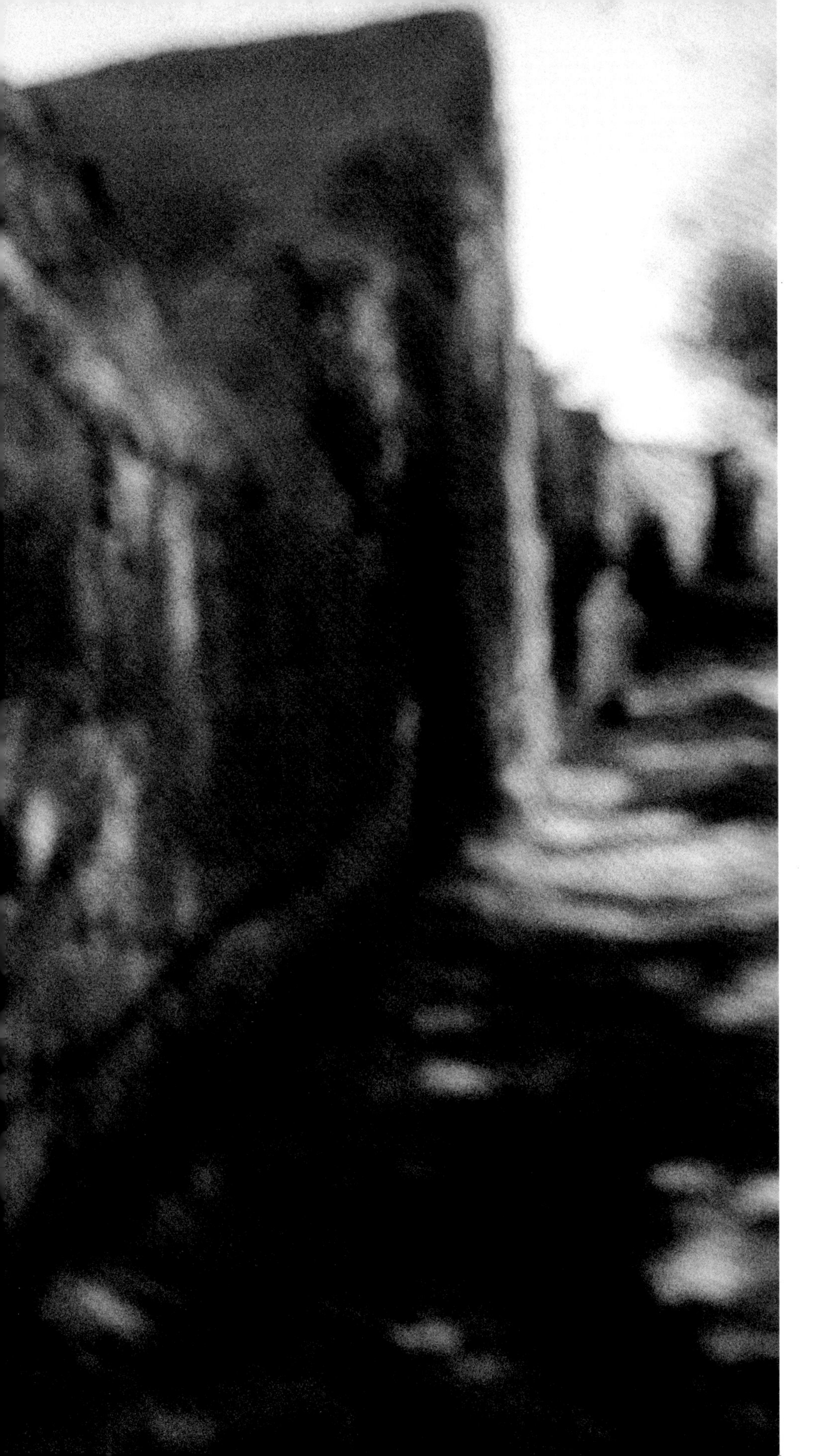

A young girl soon after dawn in the village of Ghulam Ali on the Shamali Plain. Fighting between the Northern Alliance and the Taliban, along with massive US airstrikes, made the plain a critically dangerous place to live.

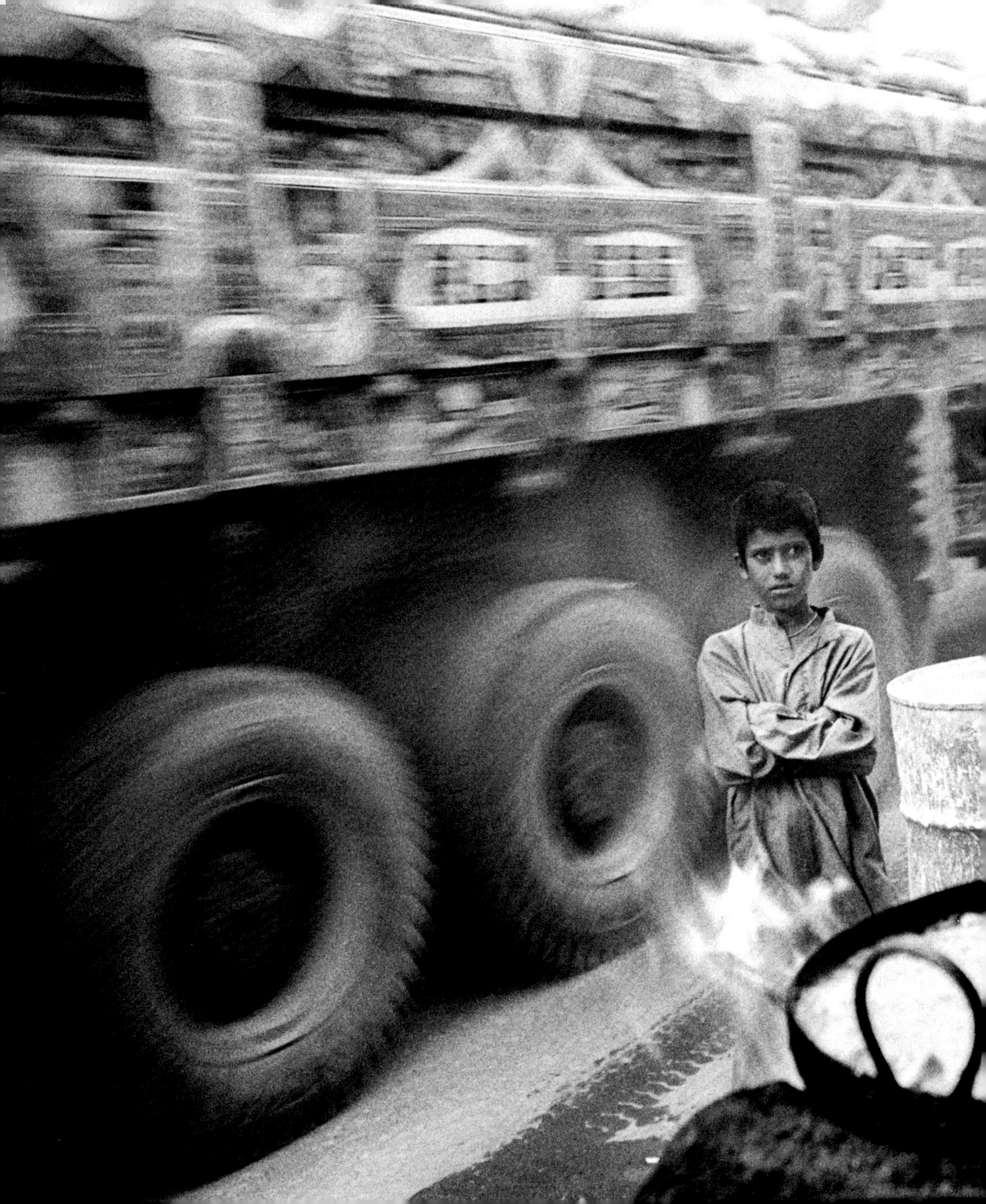

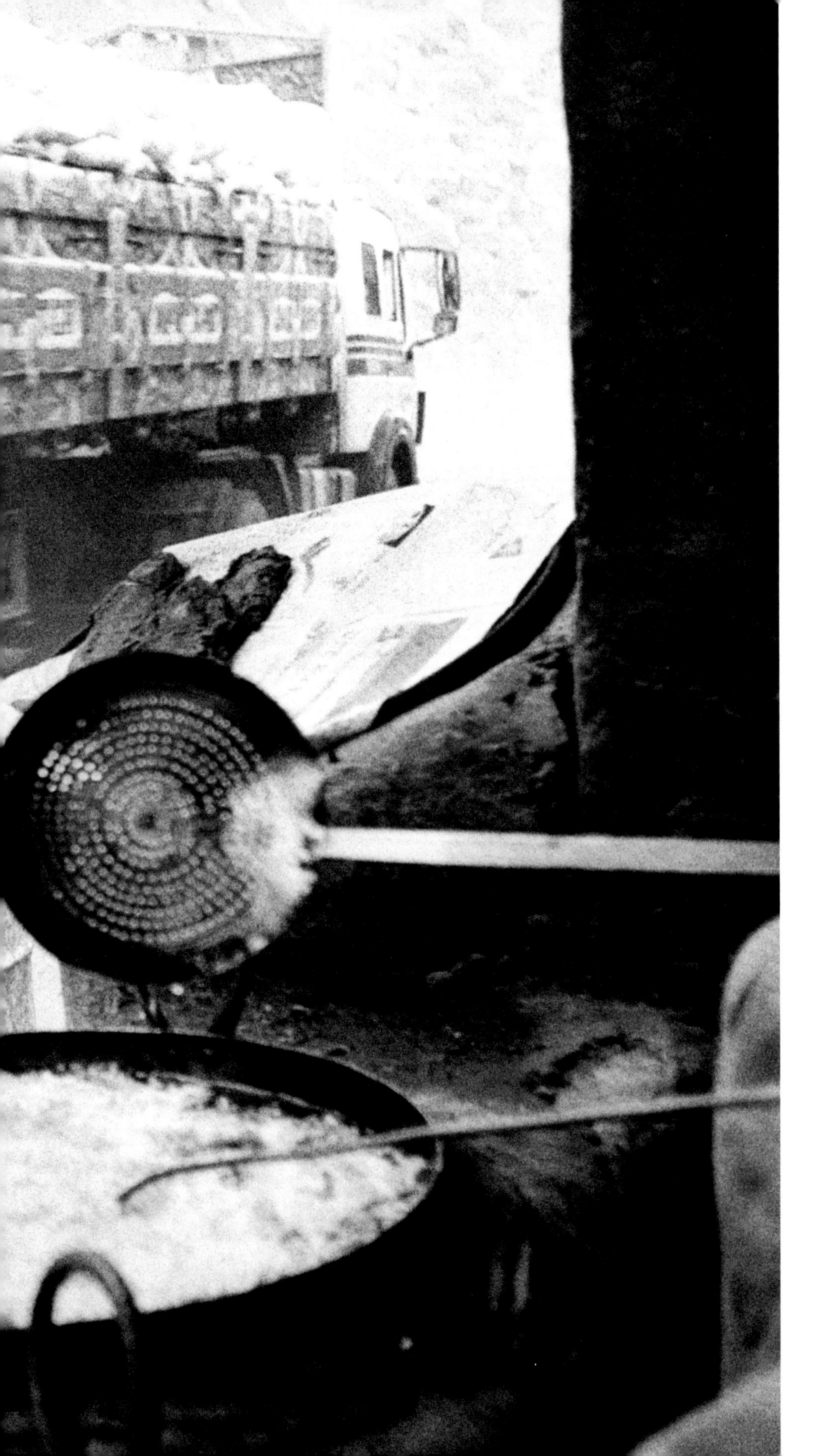

DARONTA, NANGRAHAR PROVINCE: OCTOBER 2004
A boy watches freshly-caught fish being fried at
the roadside.

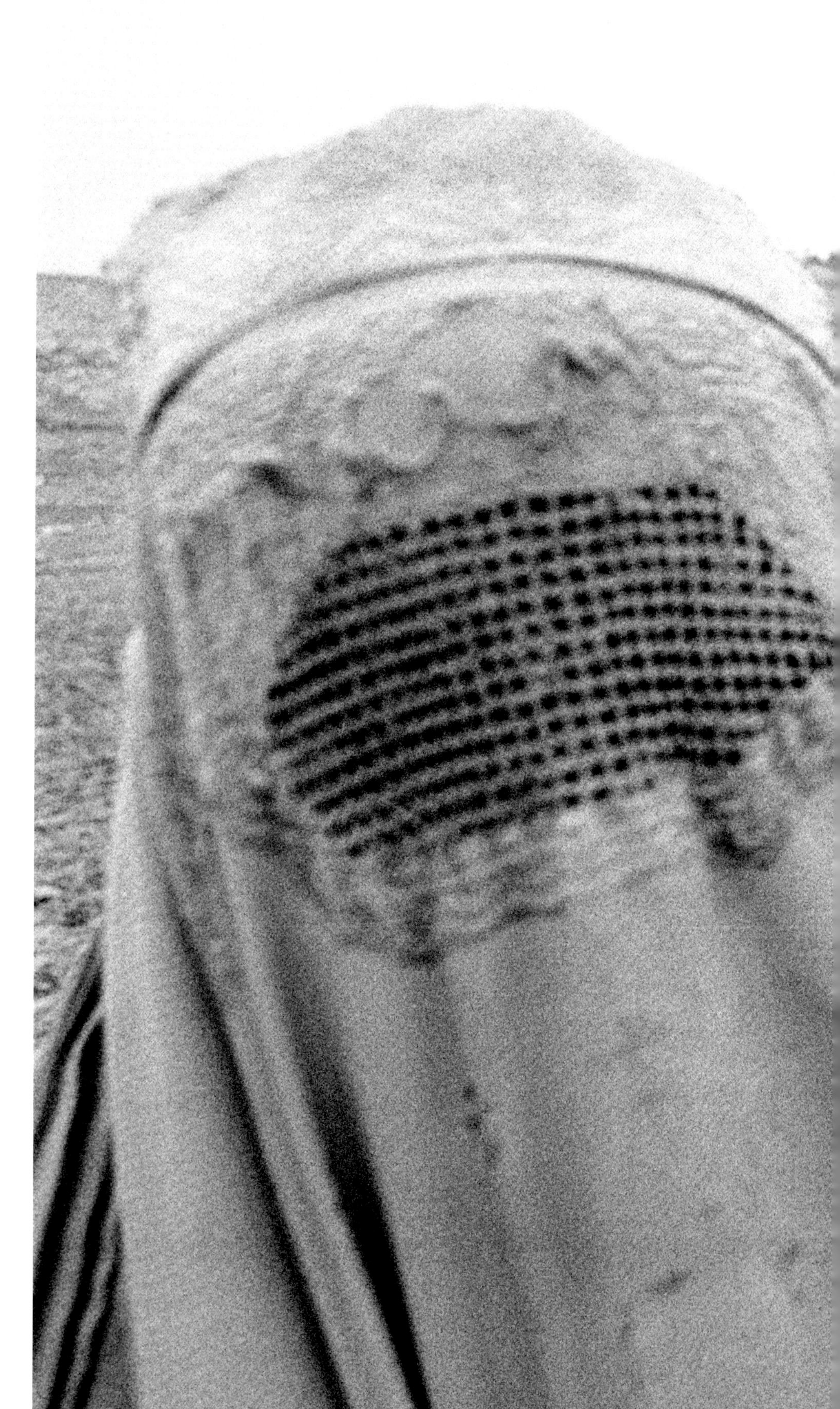

ISHKASHEM, BADAKHSHAN PROVINCE: NOVEMBER 2004
A mother and daughter returning home from
work in the fields.

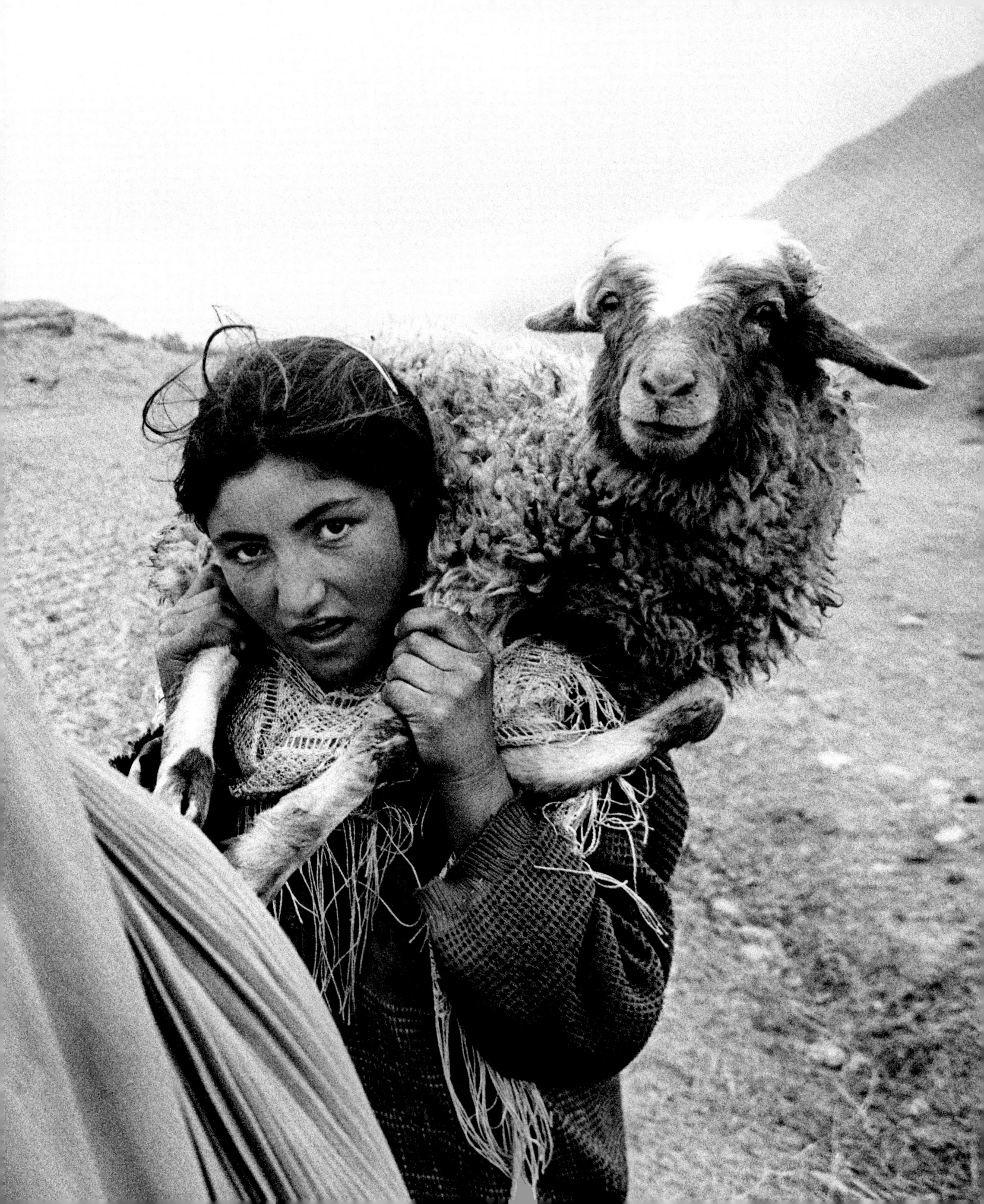

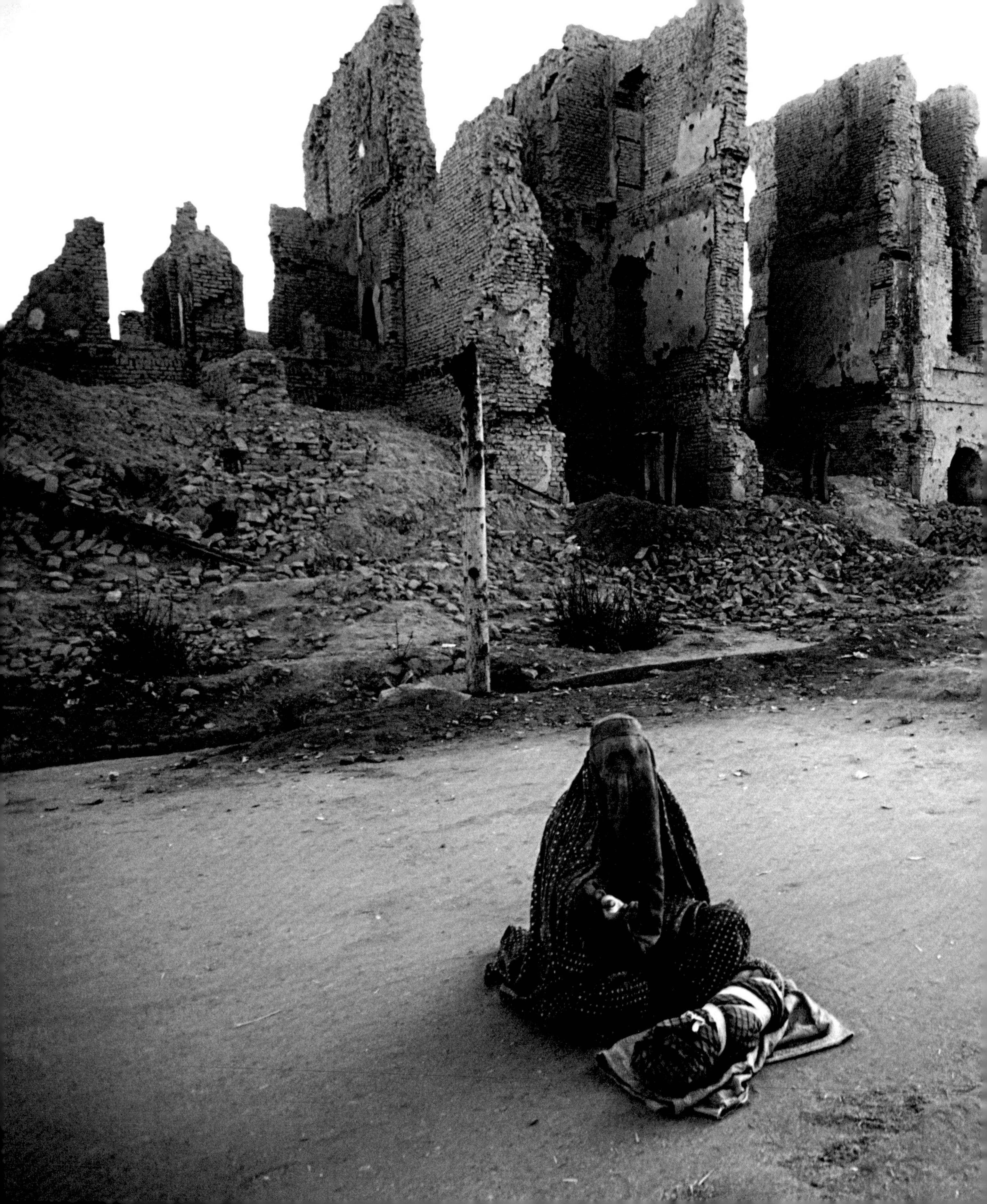

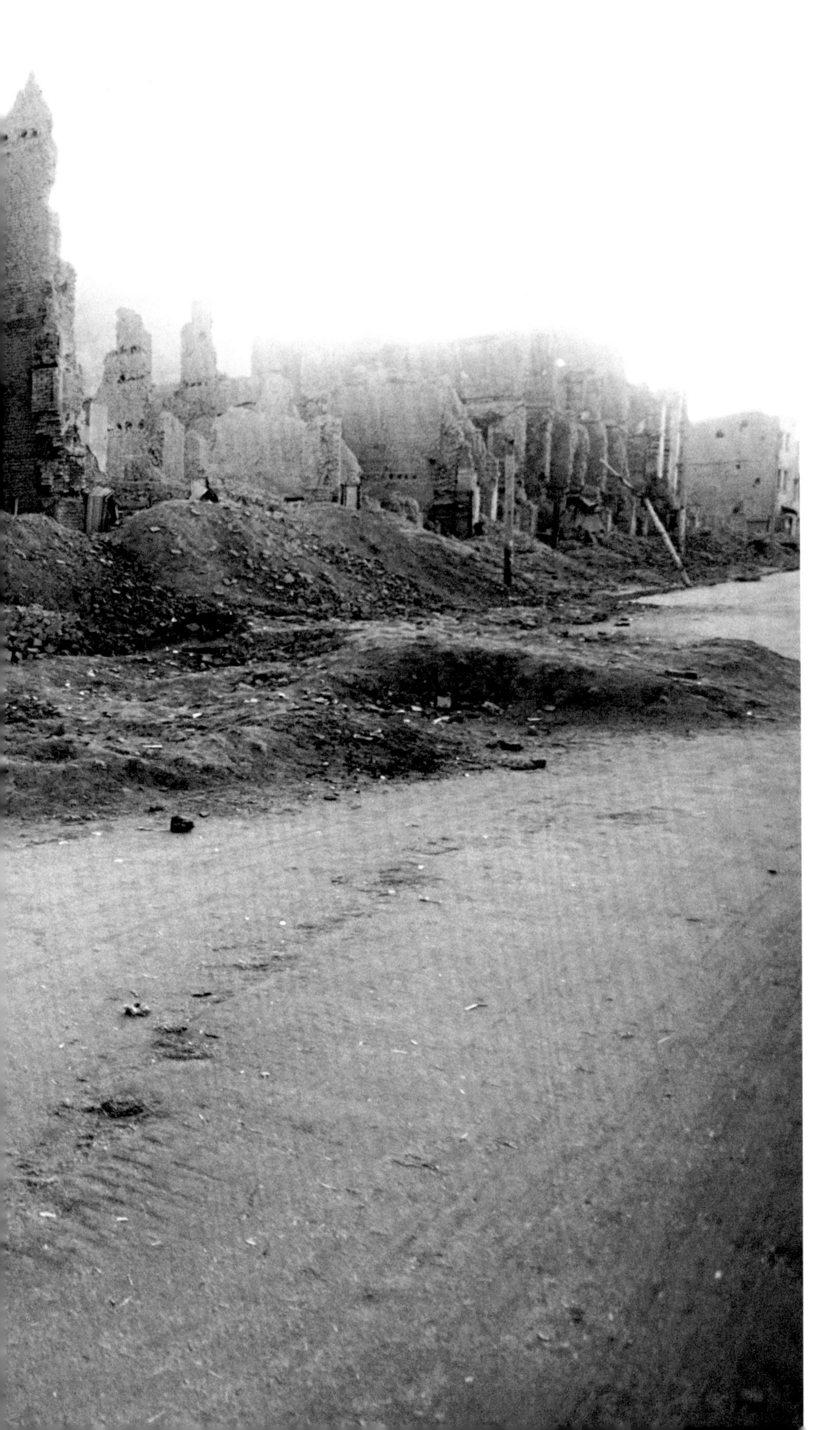

JADE MAIWAND, KABUL: NOVEMBER 1996
Widowed by war and unable to work under the
laws of the recently-arrived Taliban, women are
forced to beg.

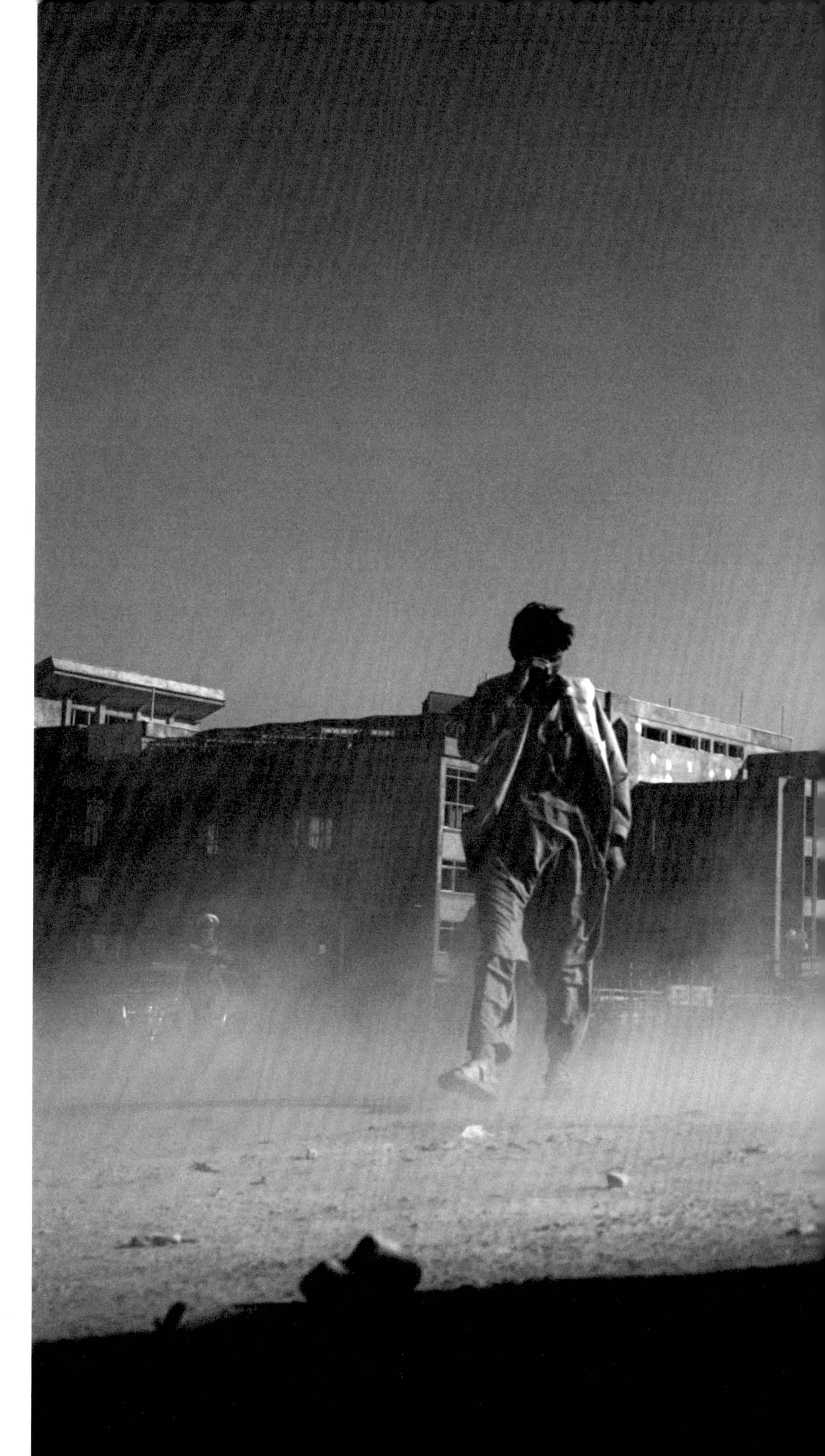

KABUL: JULY 2006
A replica of the Eiffel Tower advertises a nearby
wedding hall, the Sham-e-Paris.

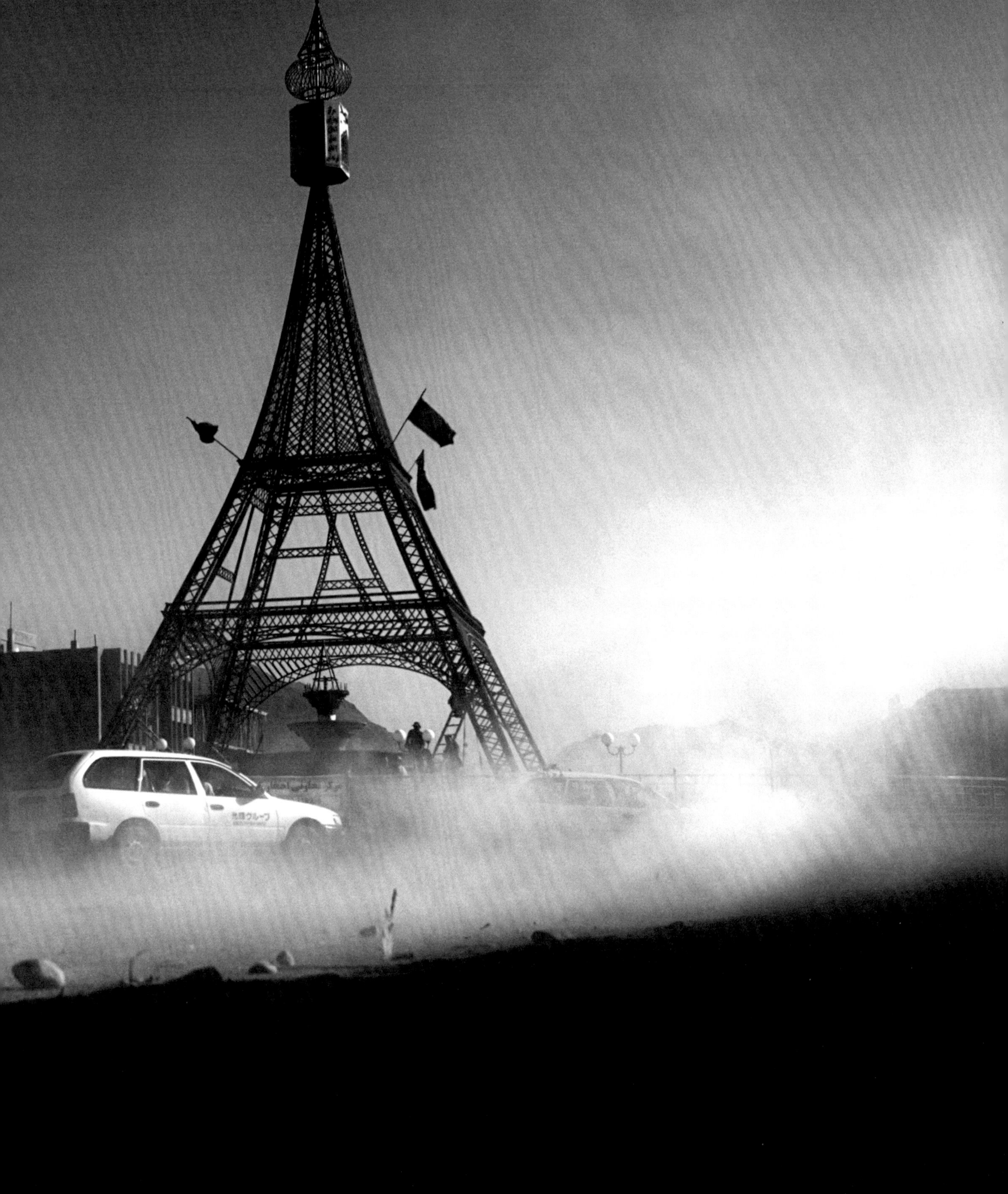

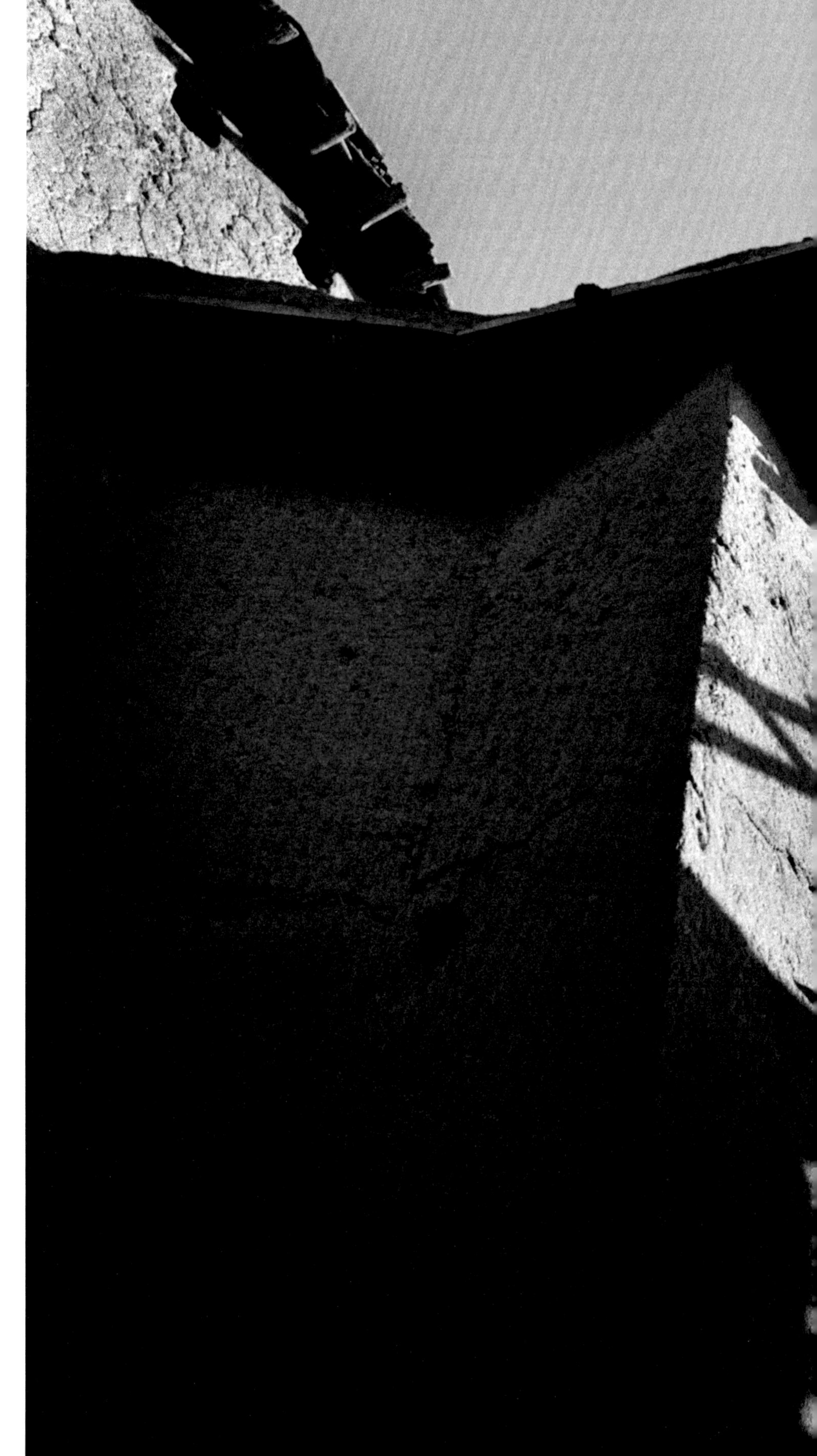

Considered the most skilful birdman in the
region, Agha Reza on his roof playing Kaftar Bazi
with his pigeons. Kaftar Bazi is a competitive
sport in which neighbours pit their birds against
each other. The flocks are released and fly over
the neighbourhood, deliberately crossing paths to
create confusion. When the owners signal them
home, the hope is that some of their opponents'
birds end up in their flock. The loser must then
pay to have the birds returned.

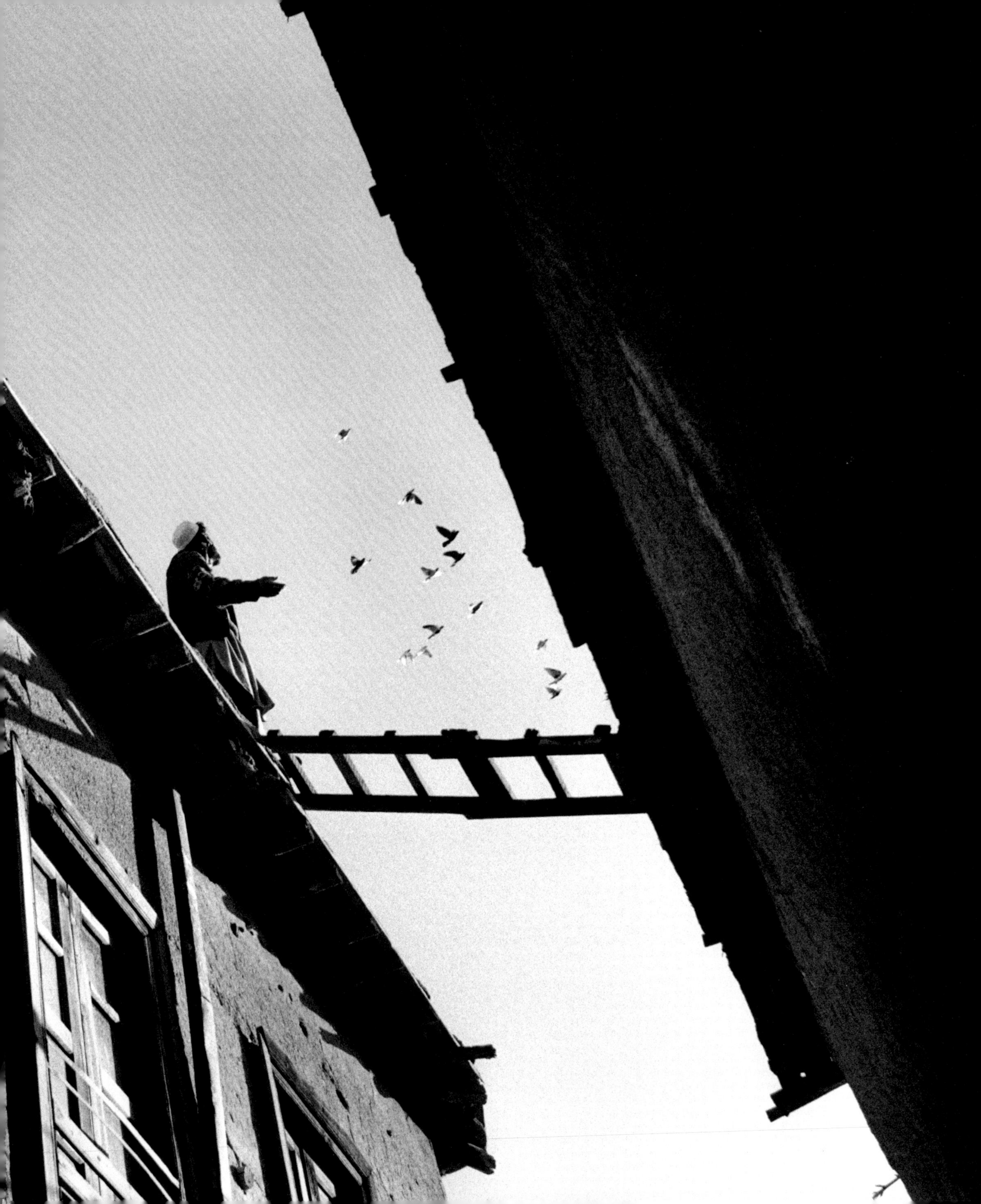

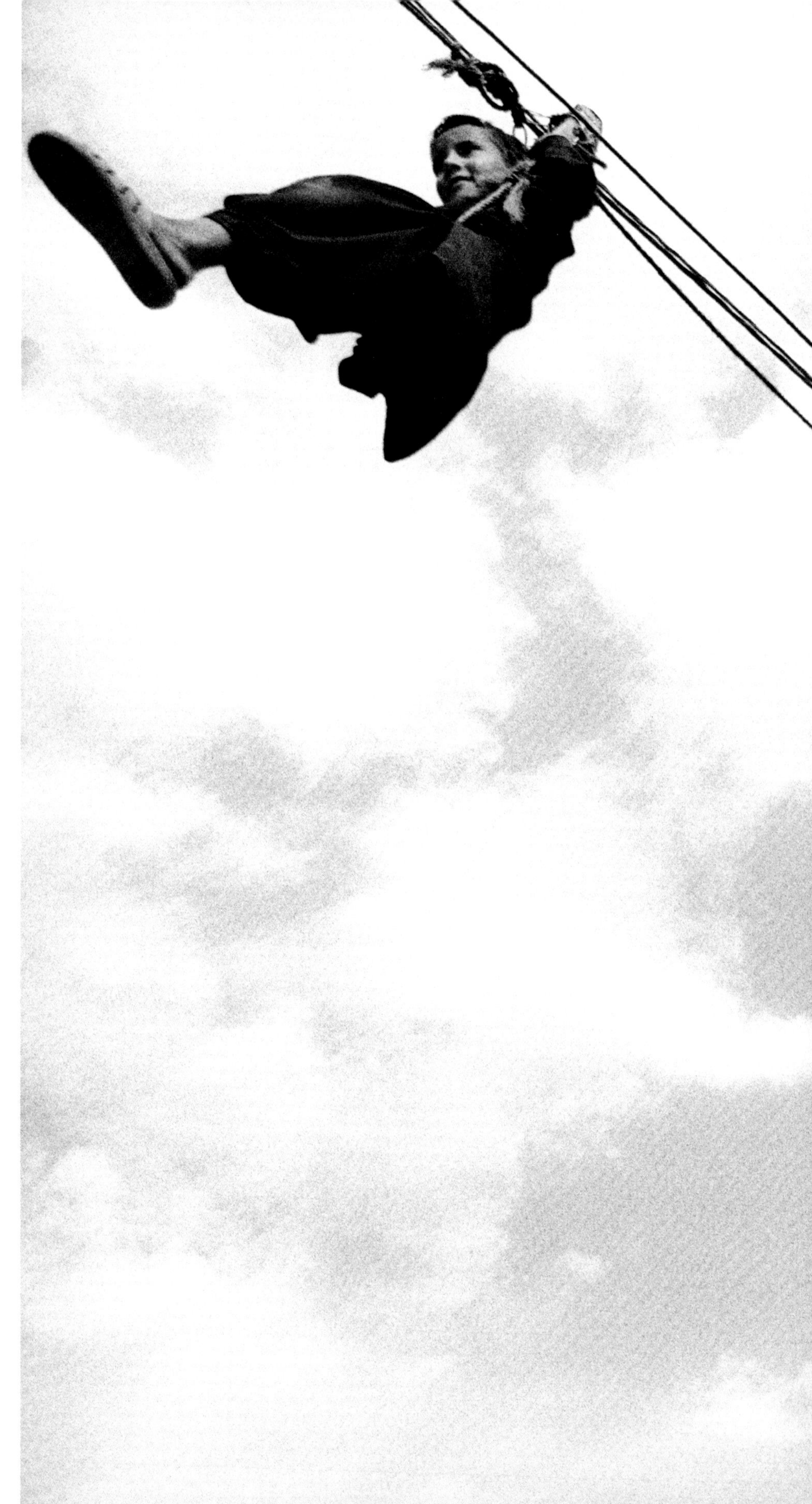

A boy uses a pulley system to cross the Hari Rud River beside the Minar-e-Jam (Minaret of Jam). It is the second tallest brick tower in the world after Qutub Minar in New Delhi, itself inspired by the Minaret of Jam. Ancient monuments of this type mostly escaped war damage, deterioration from neglect and inexperienced renovations. Plundering of archaeological sites was and remains a disaster.

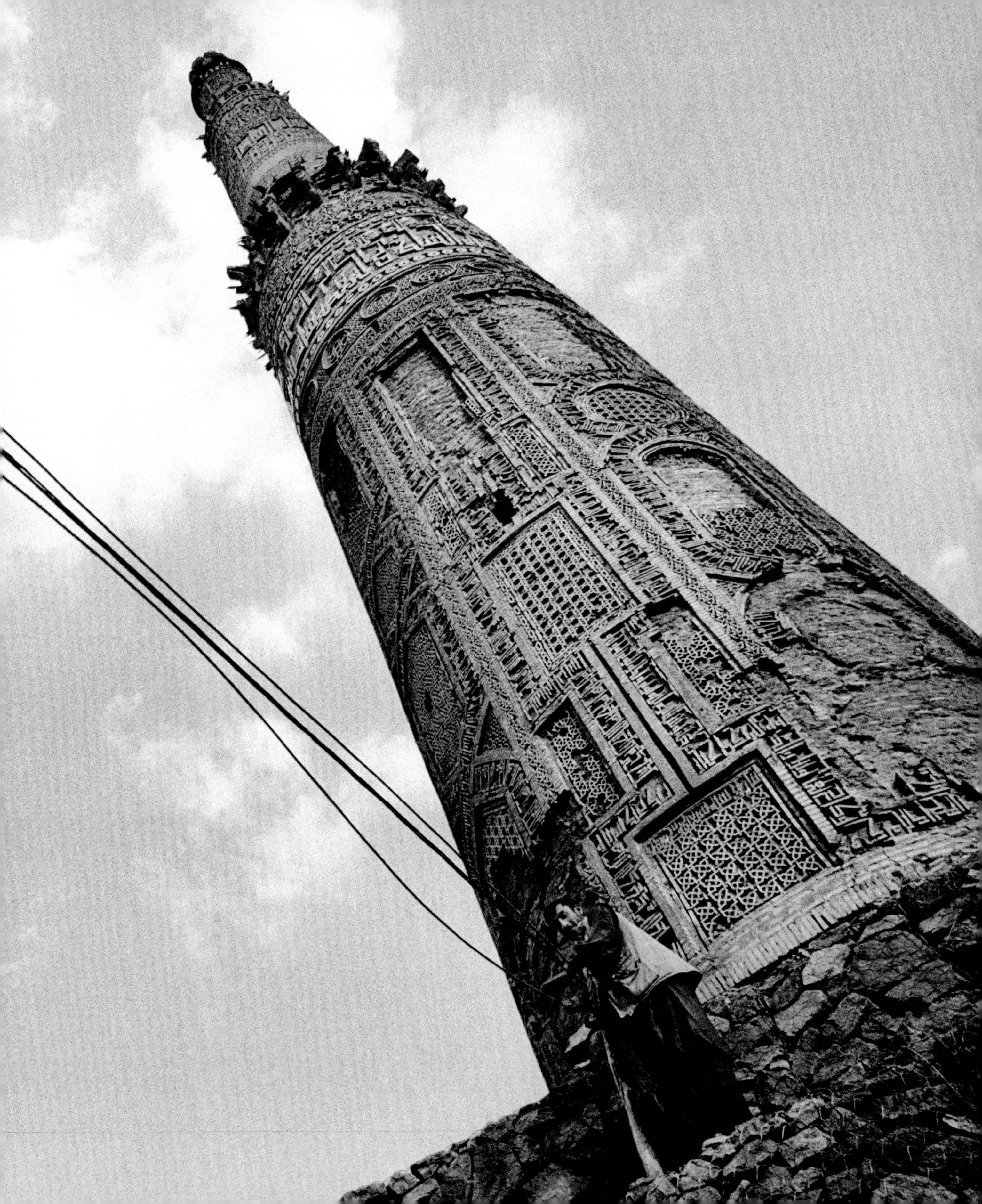

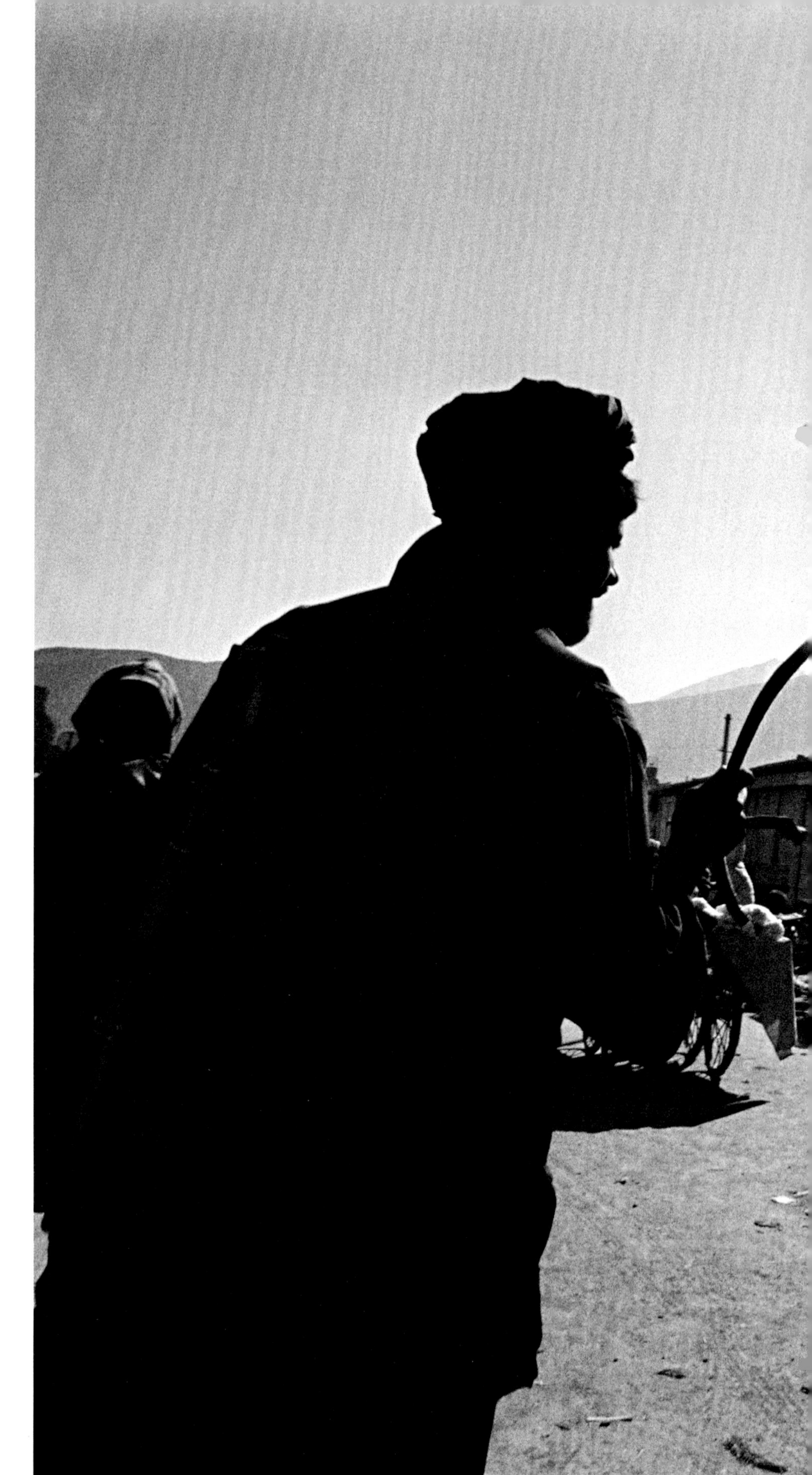

KABUL: OCTOBER 1996
A Talib threatens stallholders with a rubber whip
as prayer time approaches on Shor Bazaar in
Kabul's Old City.

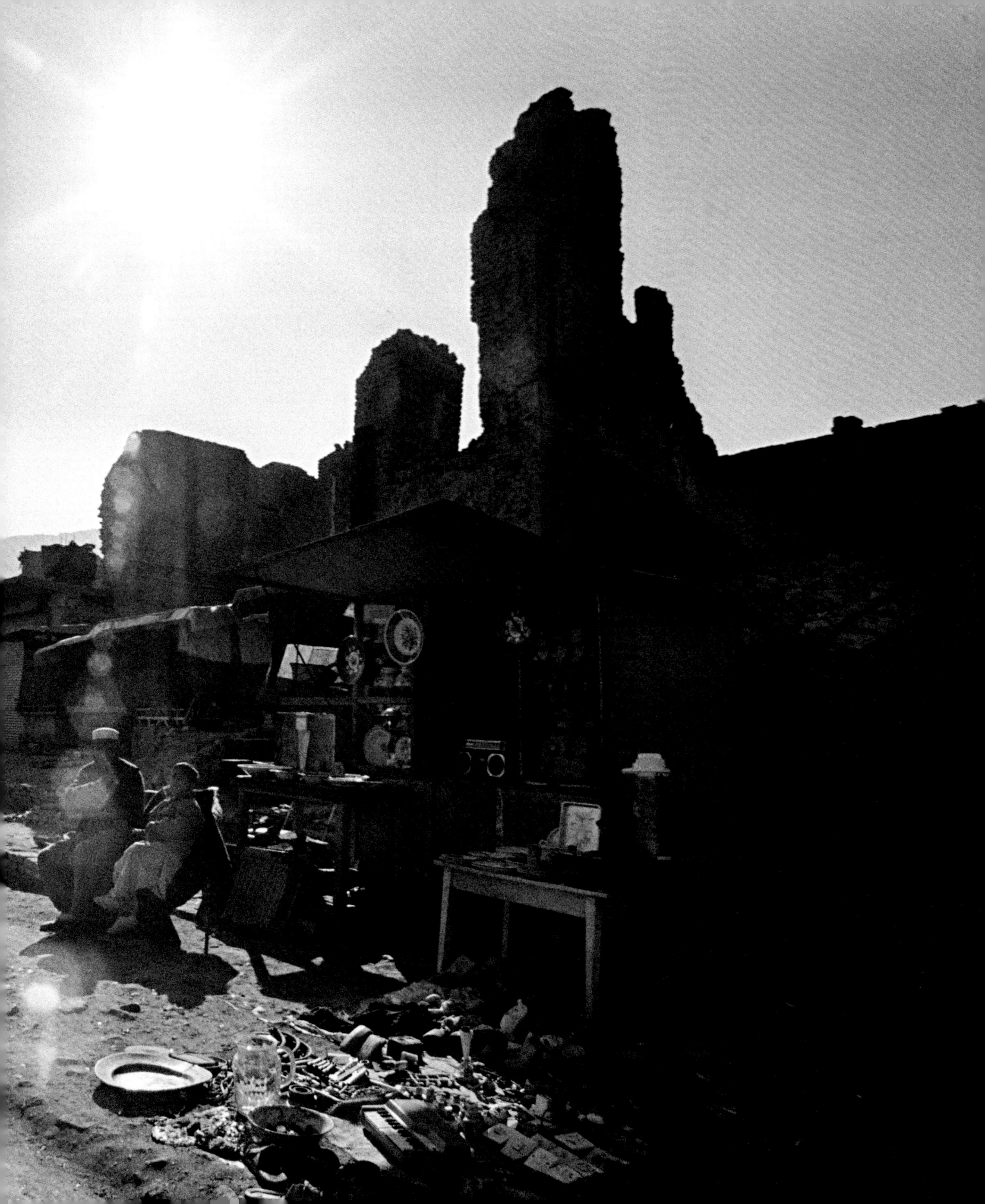

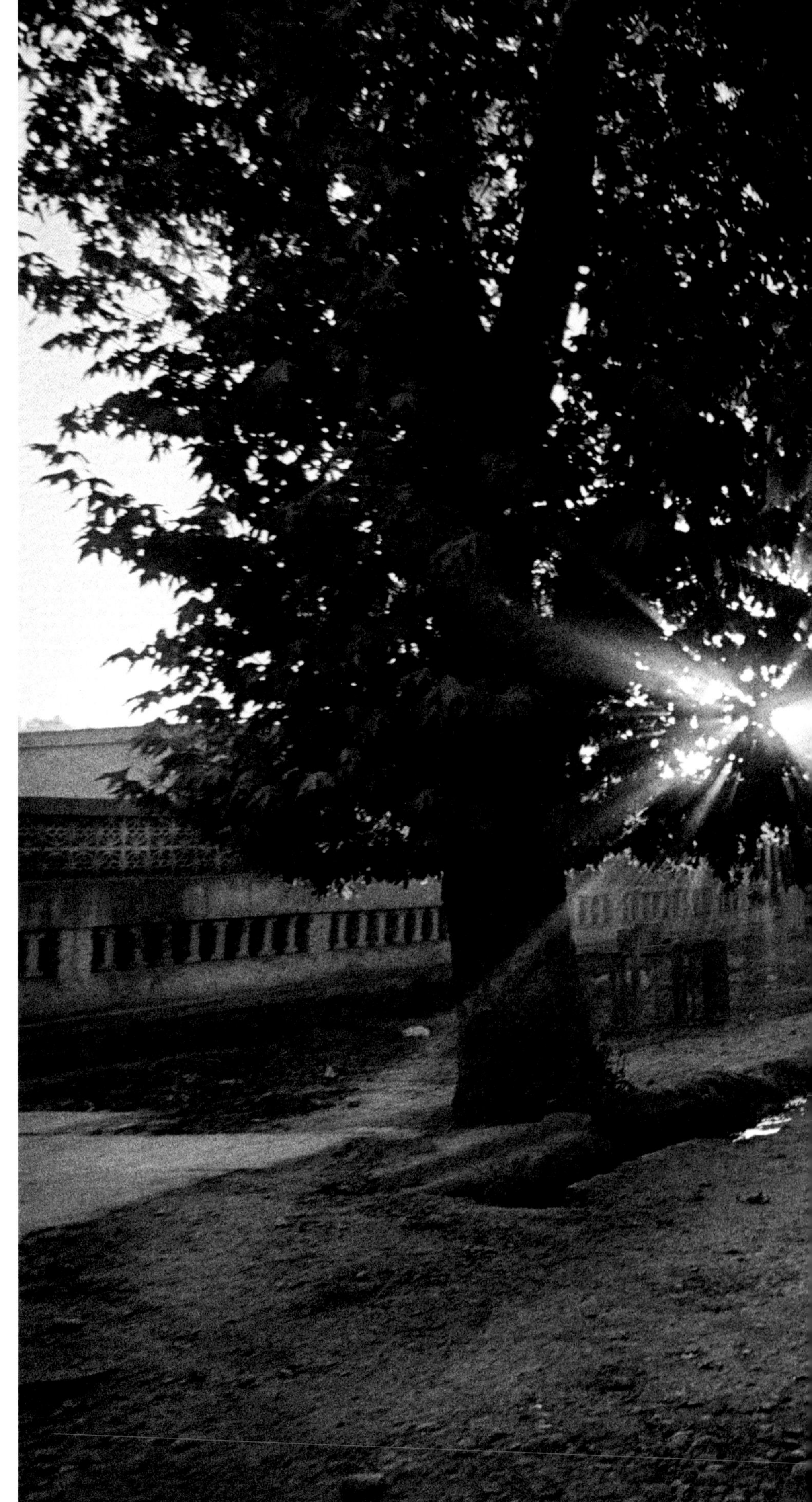

Taloqan, Takhar Province: November 2004
Running home before night falls.

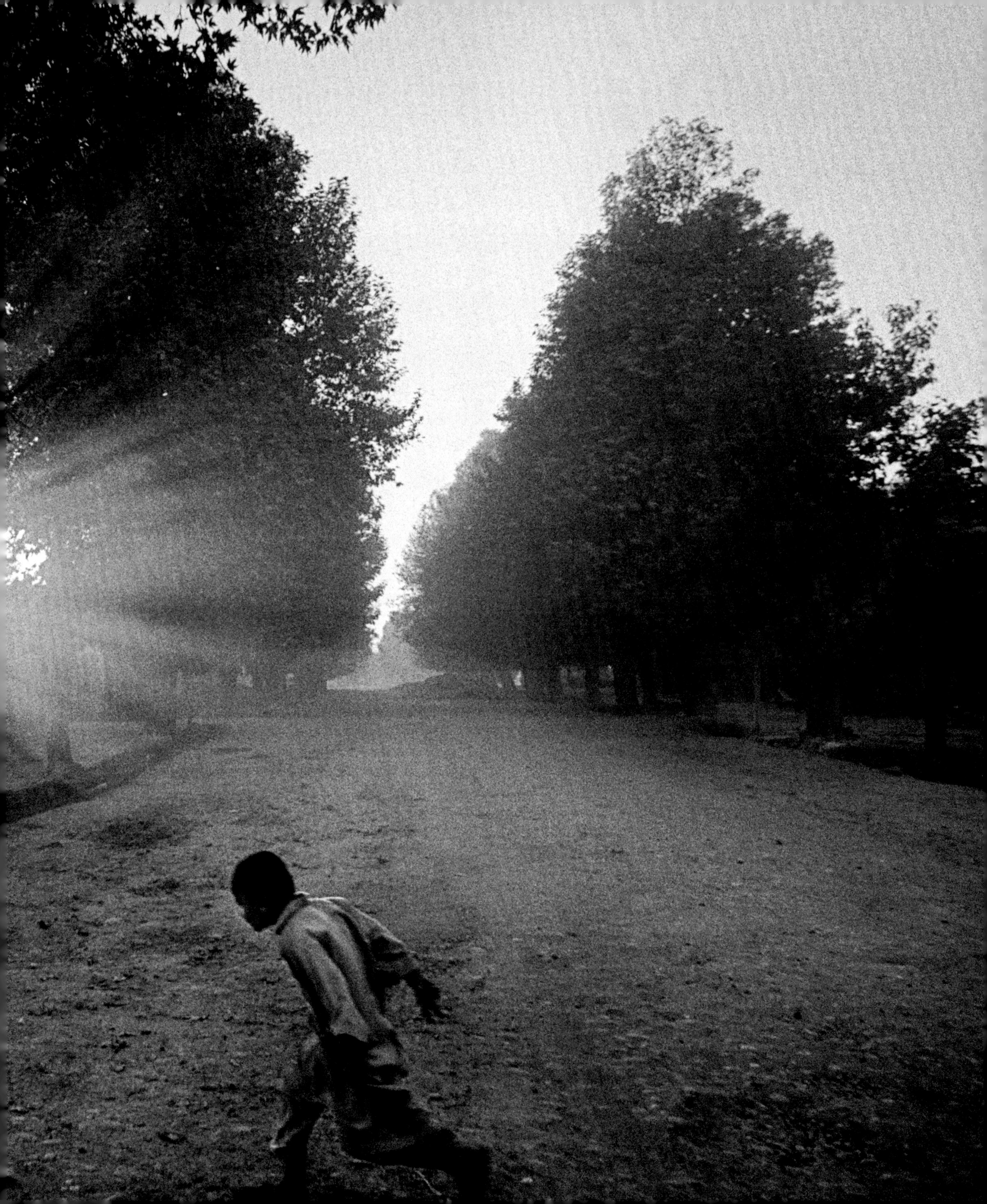

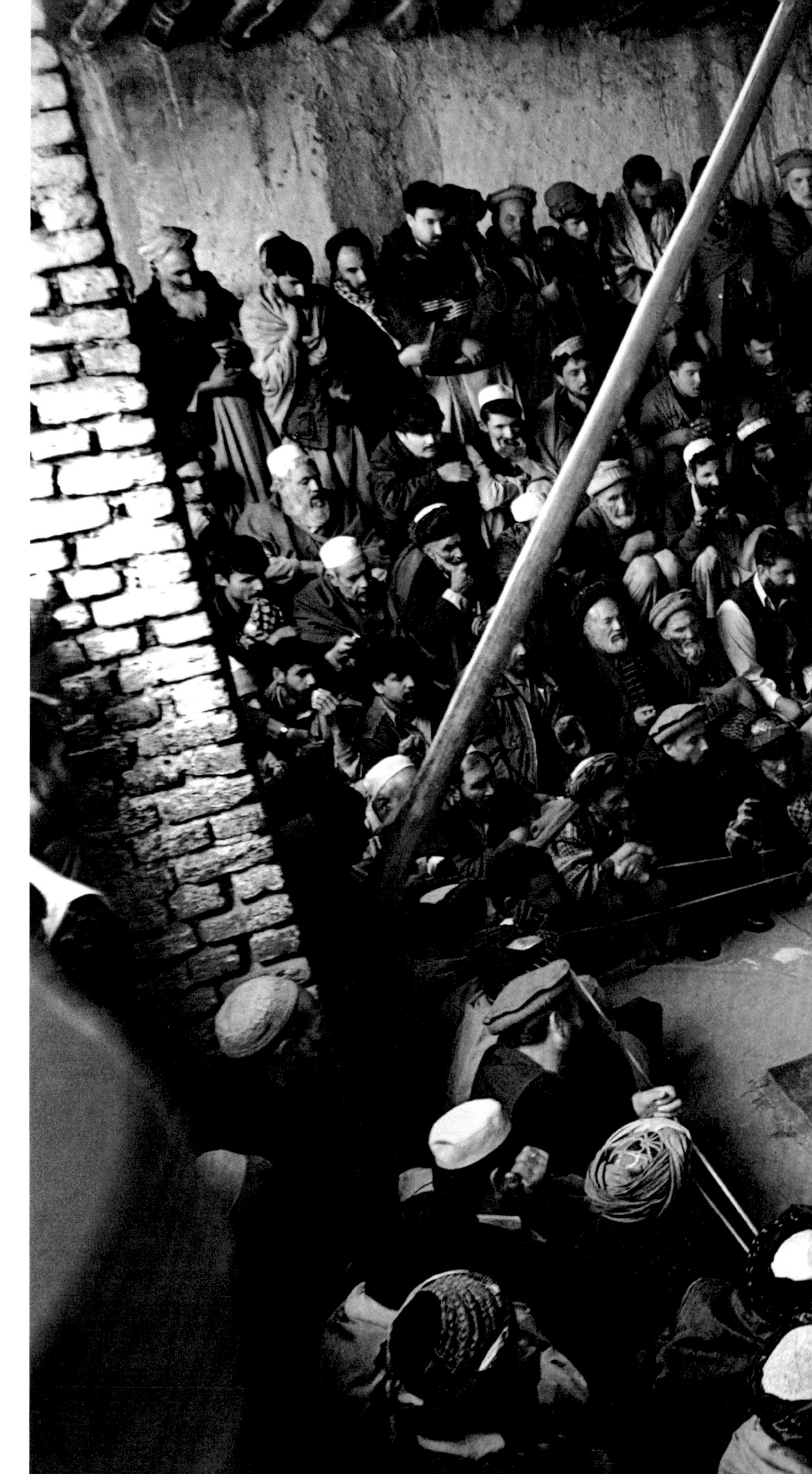

KABUL: NOVEMBER 2004
A bird fight on Friday morning behind a teahouse in the Old City. The birds are small quail, called bodahna. The contest attracts heavy gambling but the fights are never to the death.

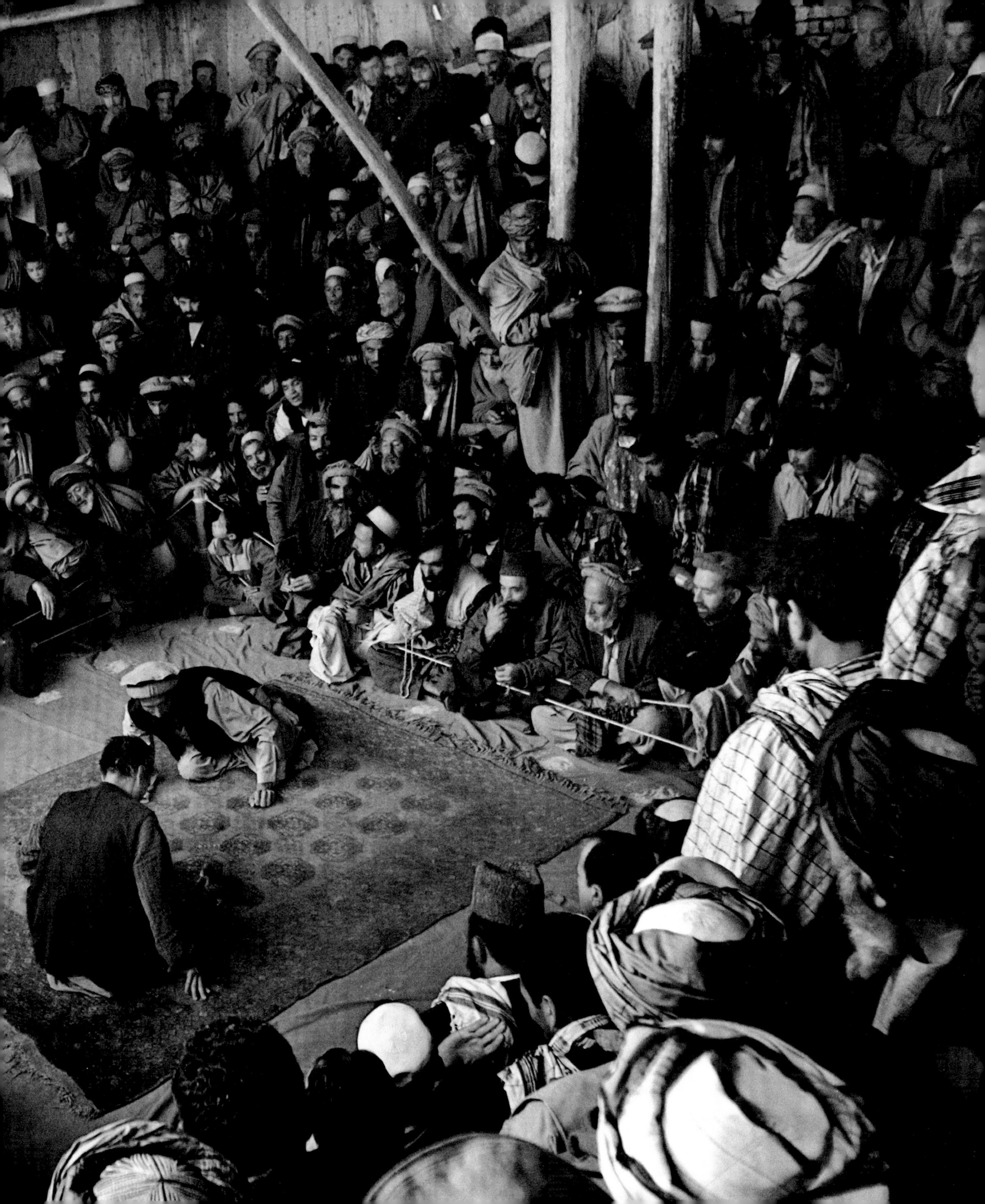

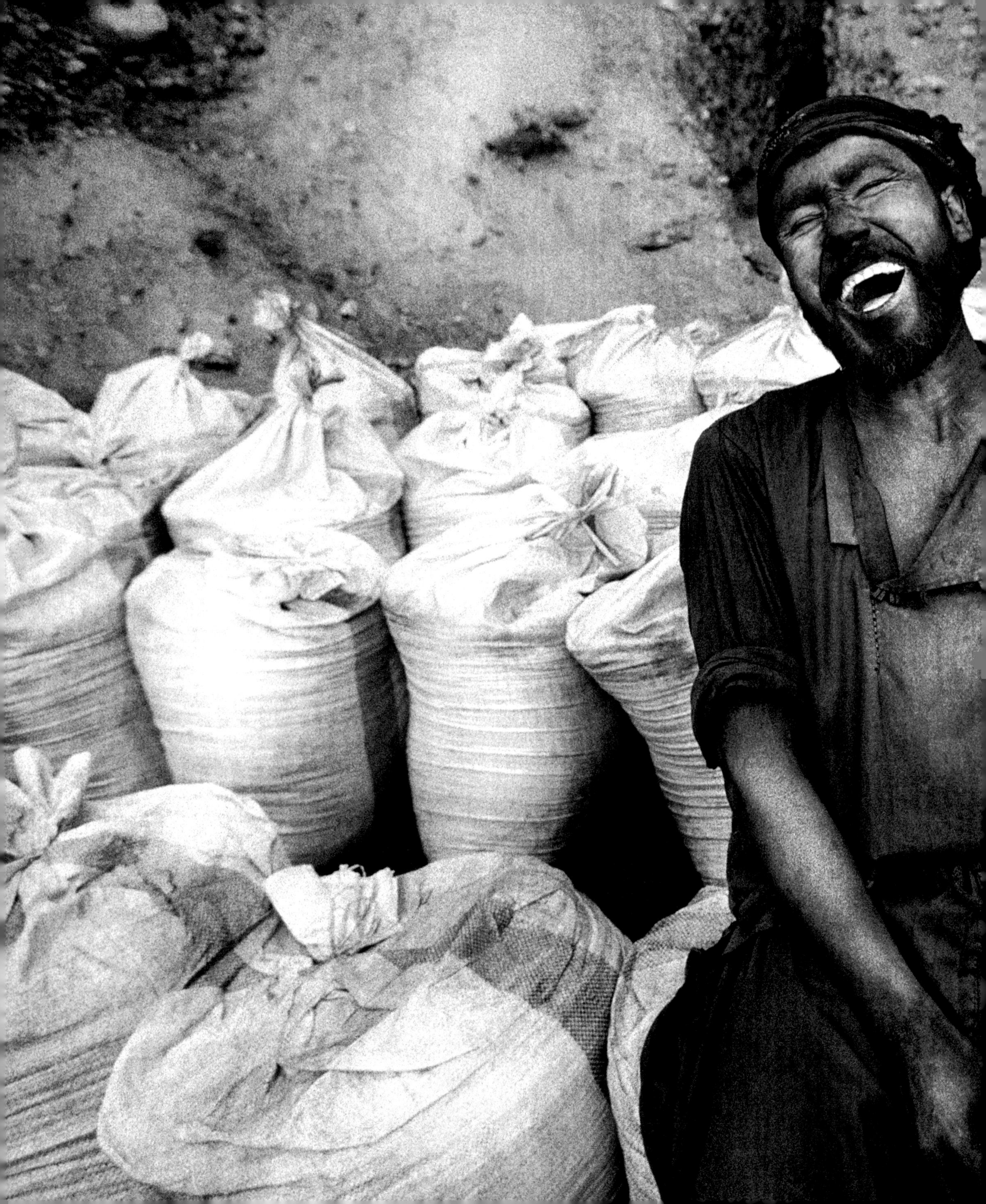

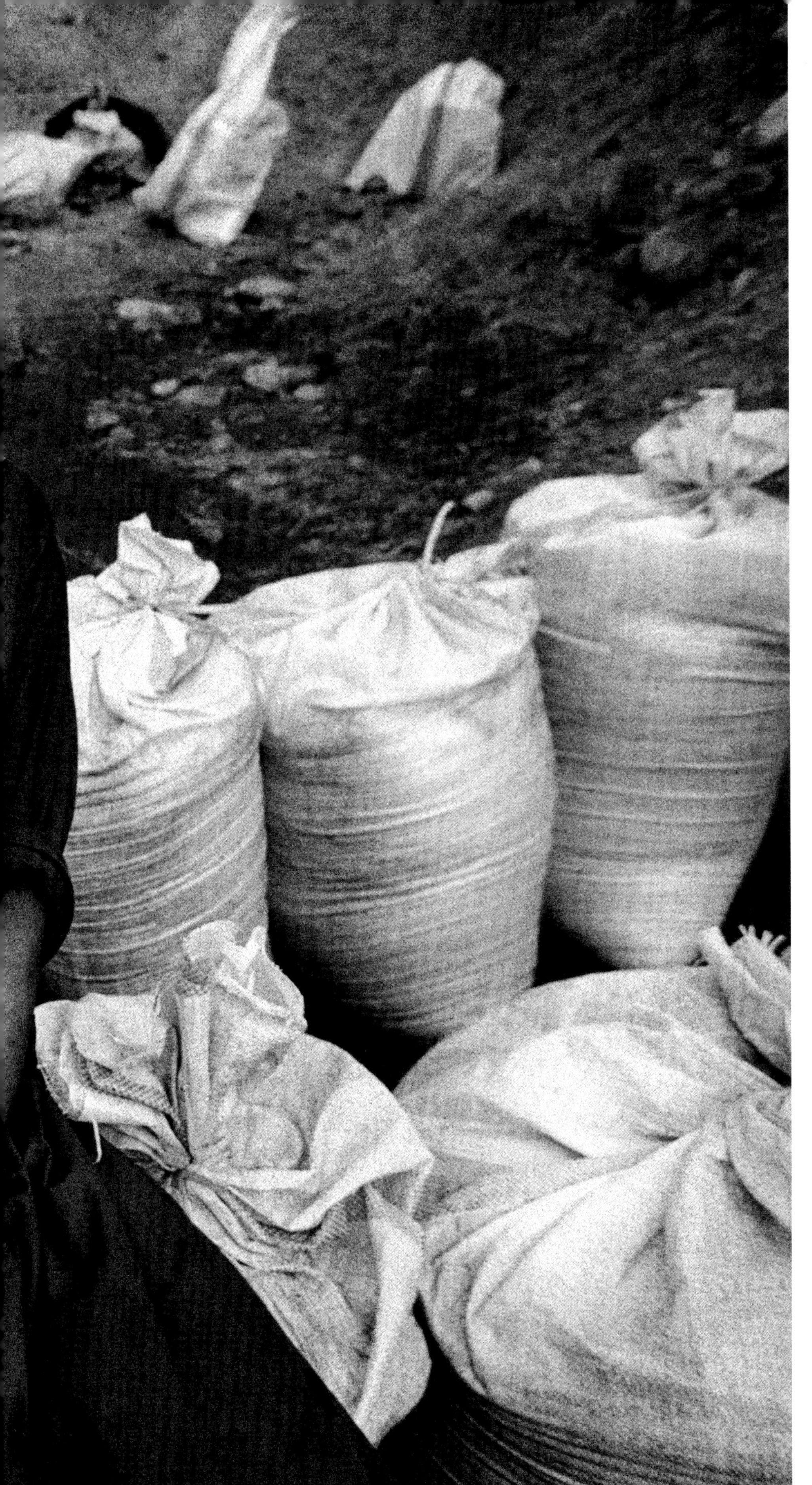

GAZASTAN, TAKHAR PROVINCE: NOVEMBER 2004
A miner takes a break from work.

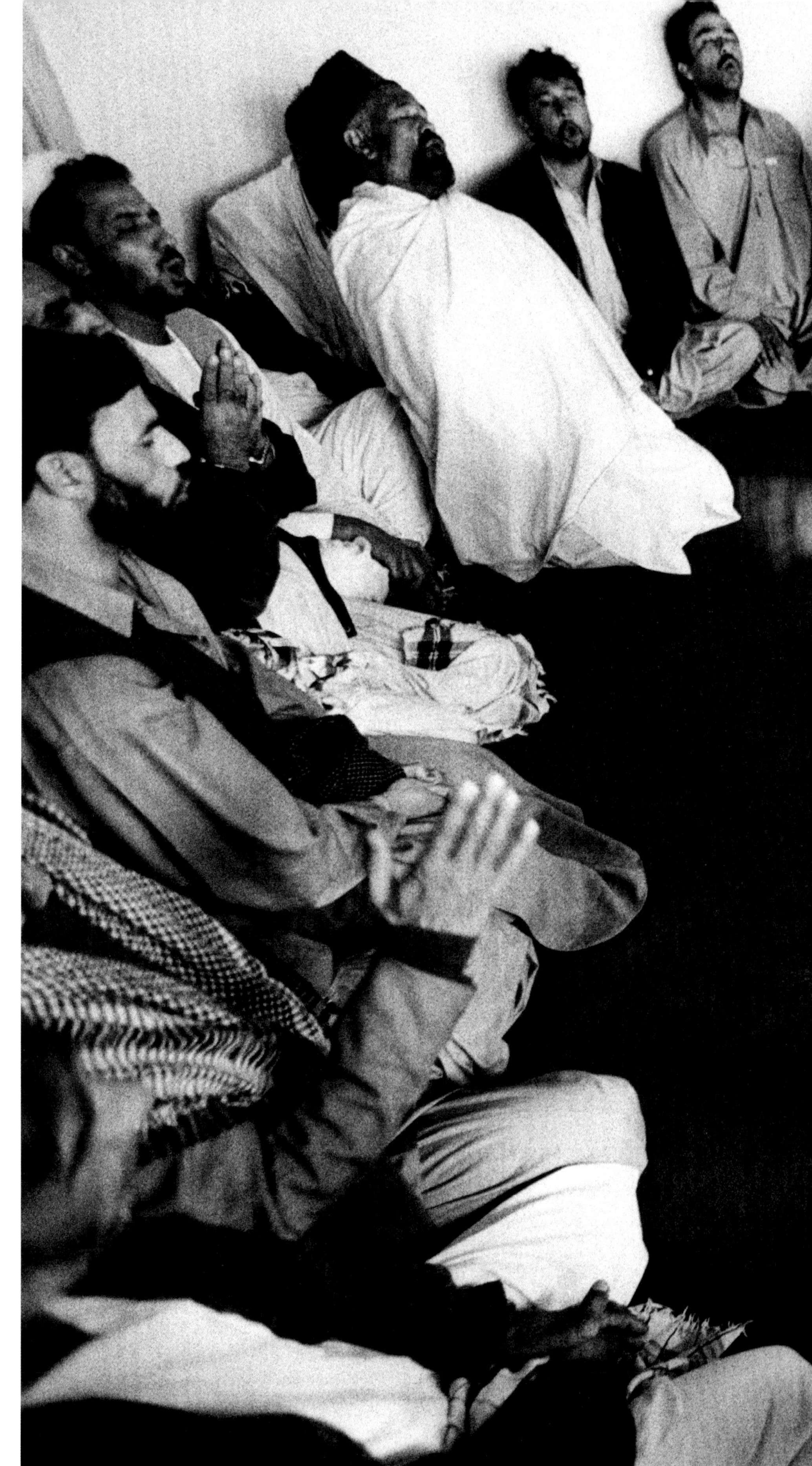

KABUL: OCTOBER 2004
A celebrant at a Sufi ceremony that has lasted
throughout the night in the Old City.

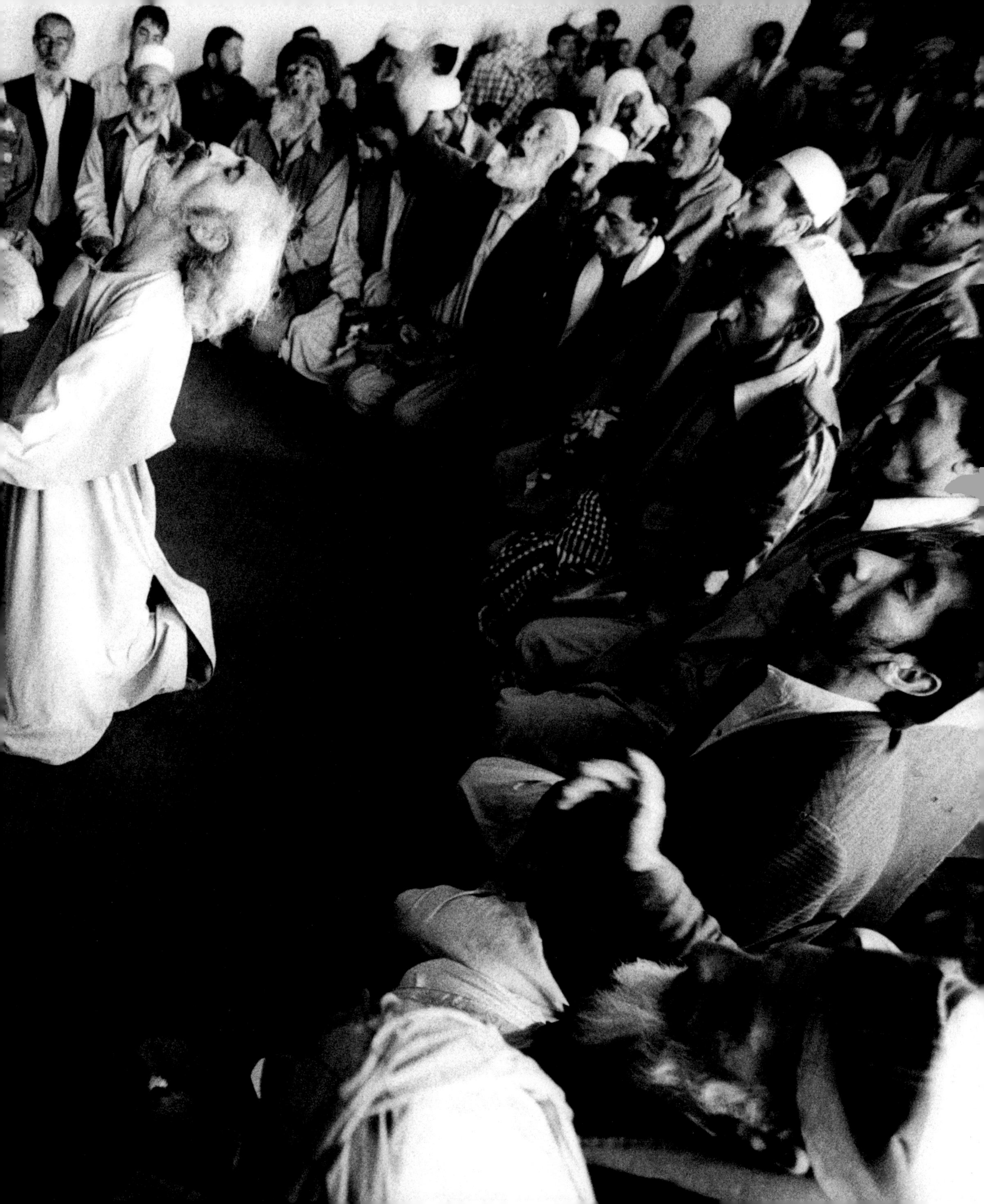

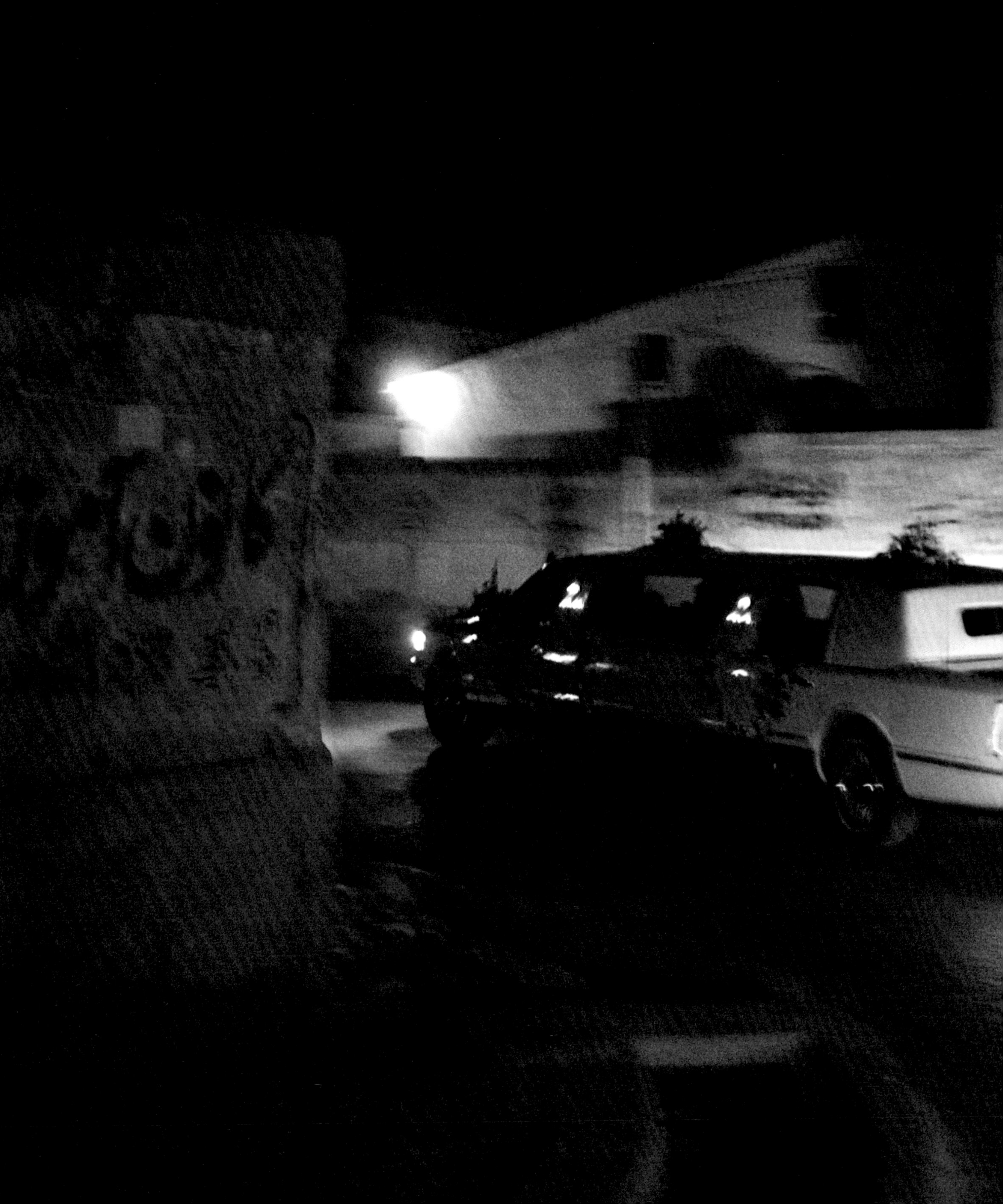

Kabul: July 2006
District of Shahr-e-Naw in the early hours of
the morning.

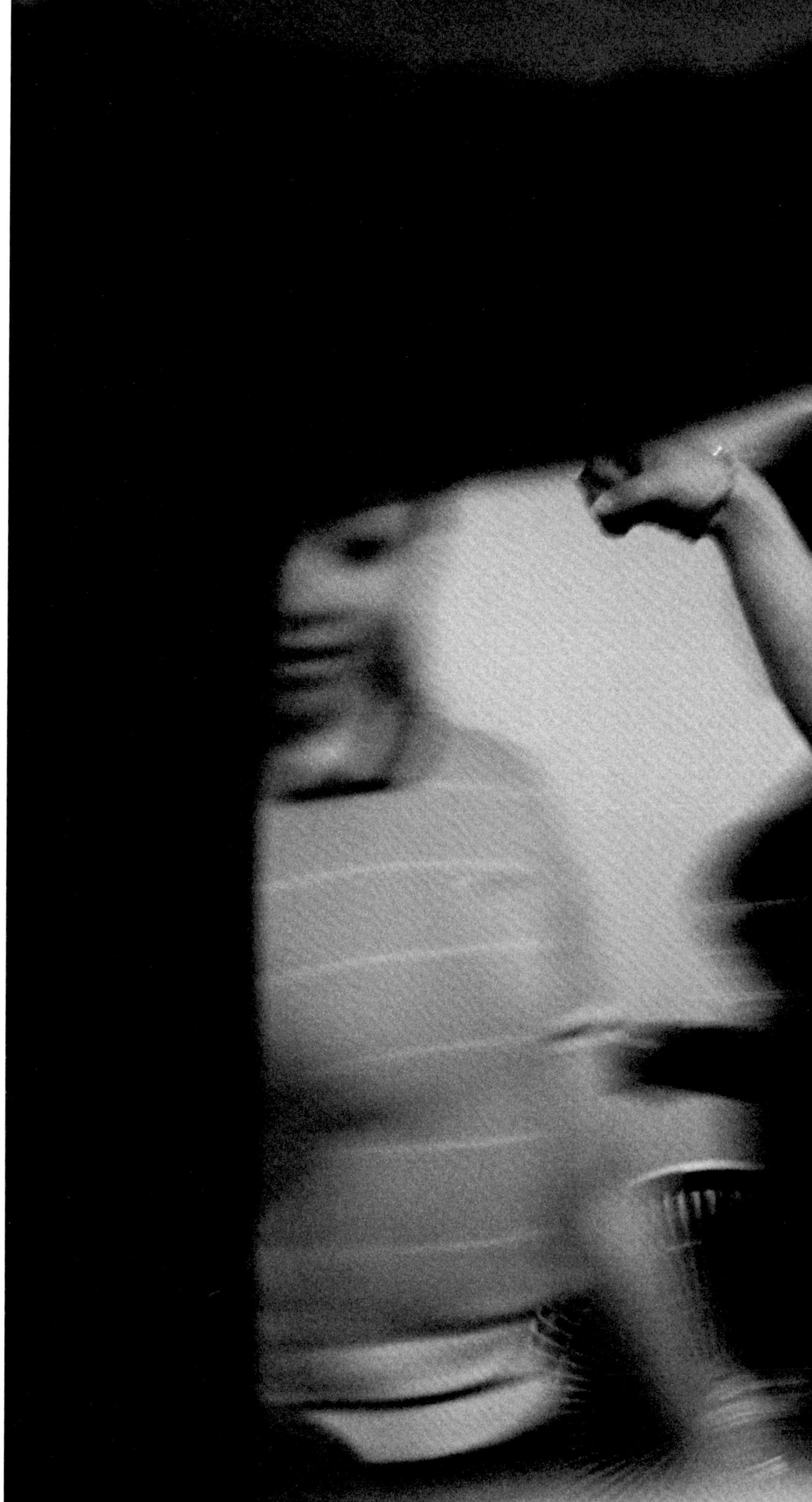

Kabul: July 2006
Chinese prostitutes entertaining clients in one
of the city's brothels, catering mainly to foreign
contractors and workers.

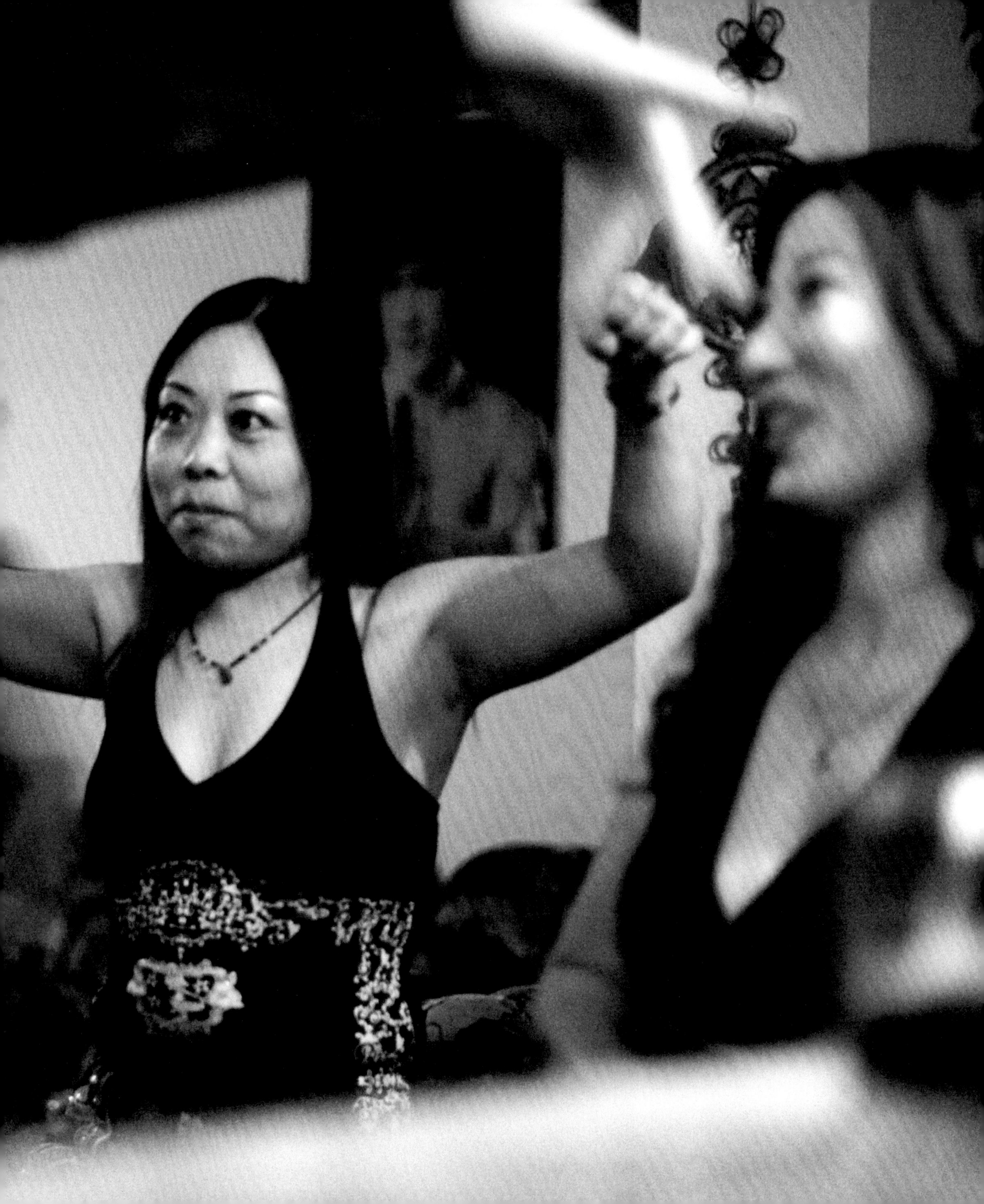

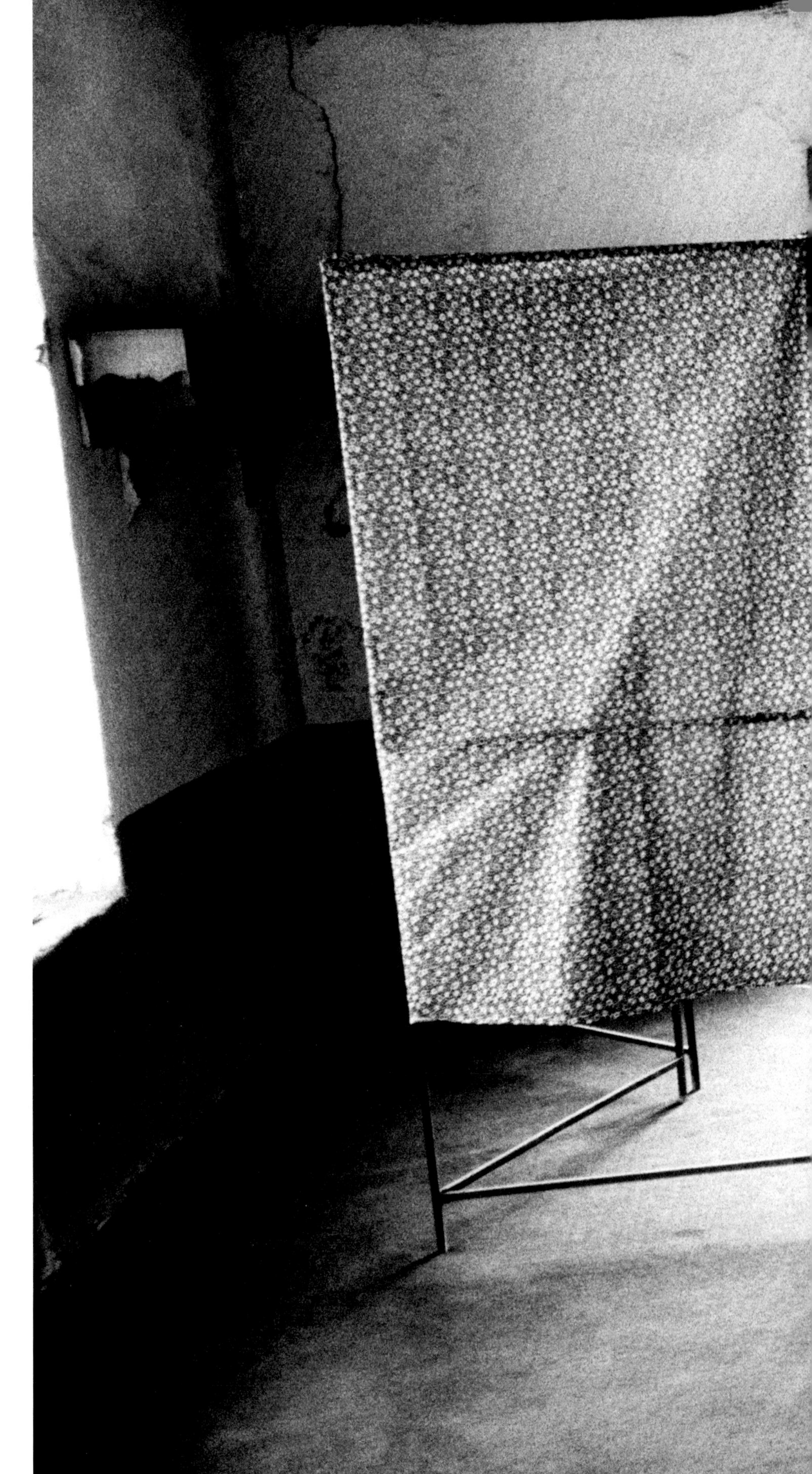

Kabul: October 2004
A man casts his vote at a mosque in the Old City
during Afghanistan's presidential election. Hamid
Karzai became Afghanistan's first democratically-
elected head of state.

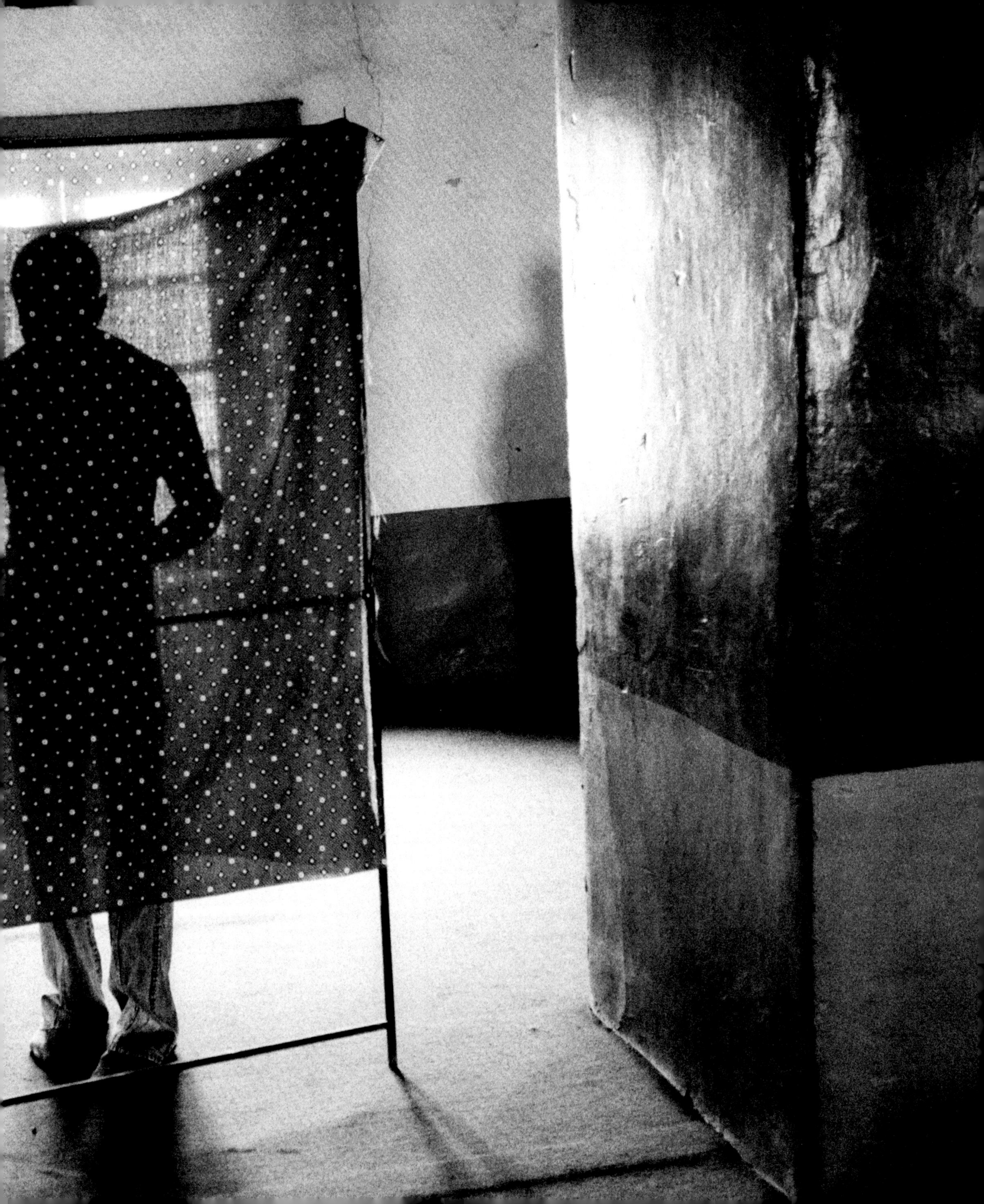

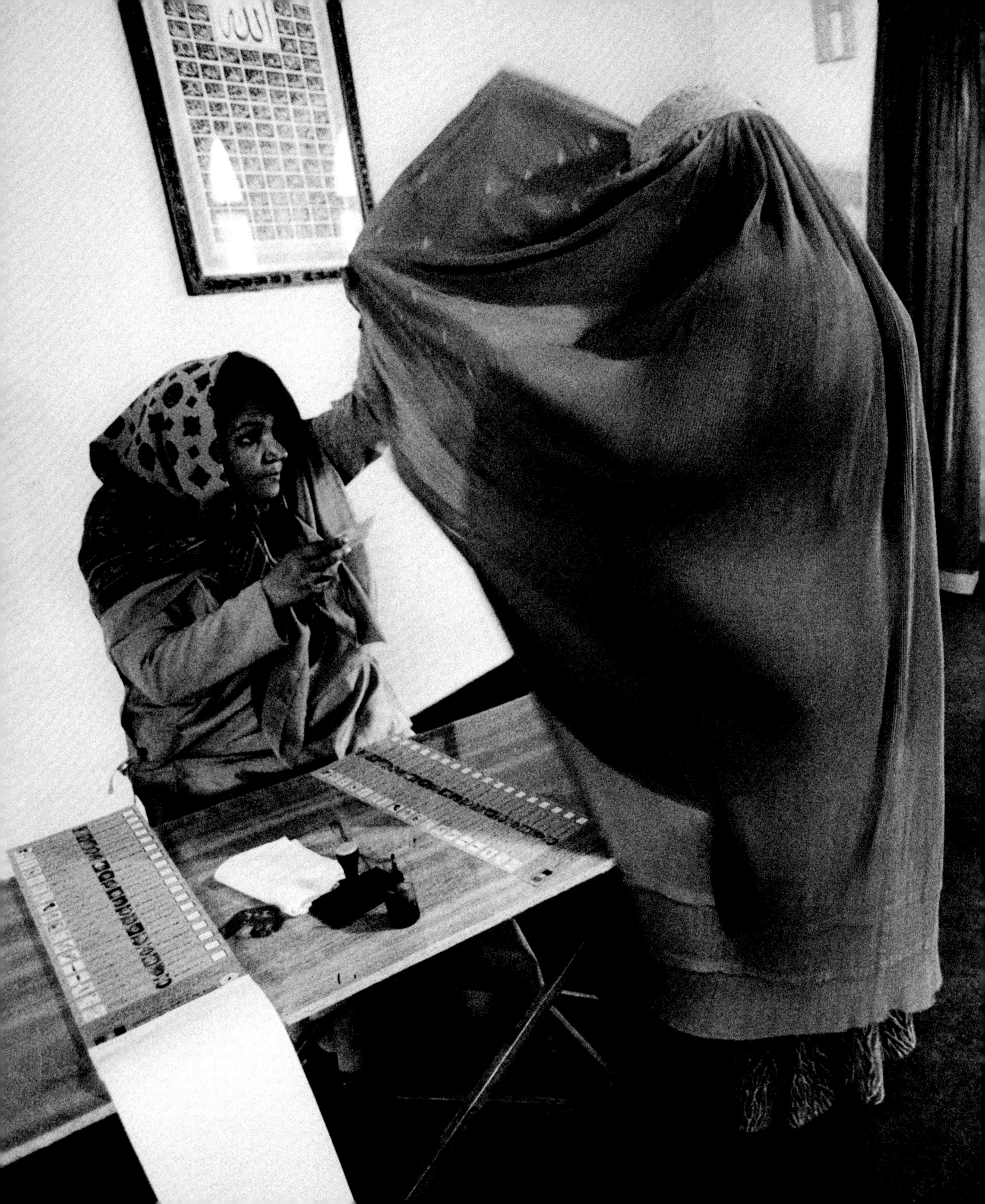

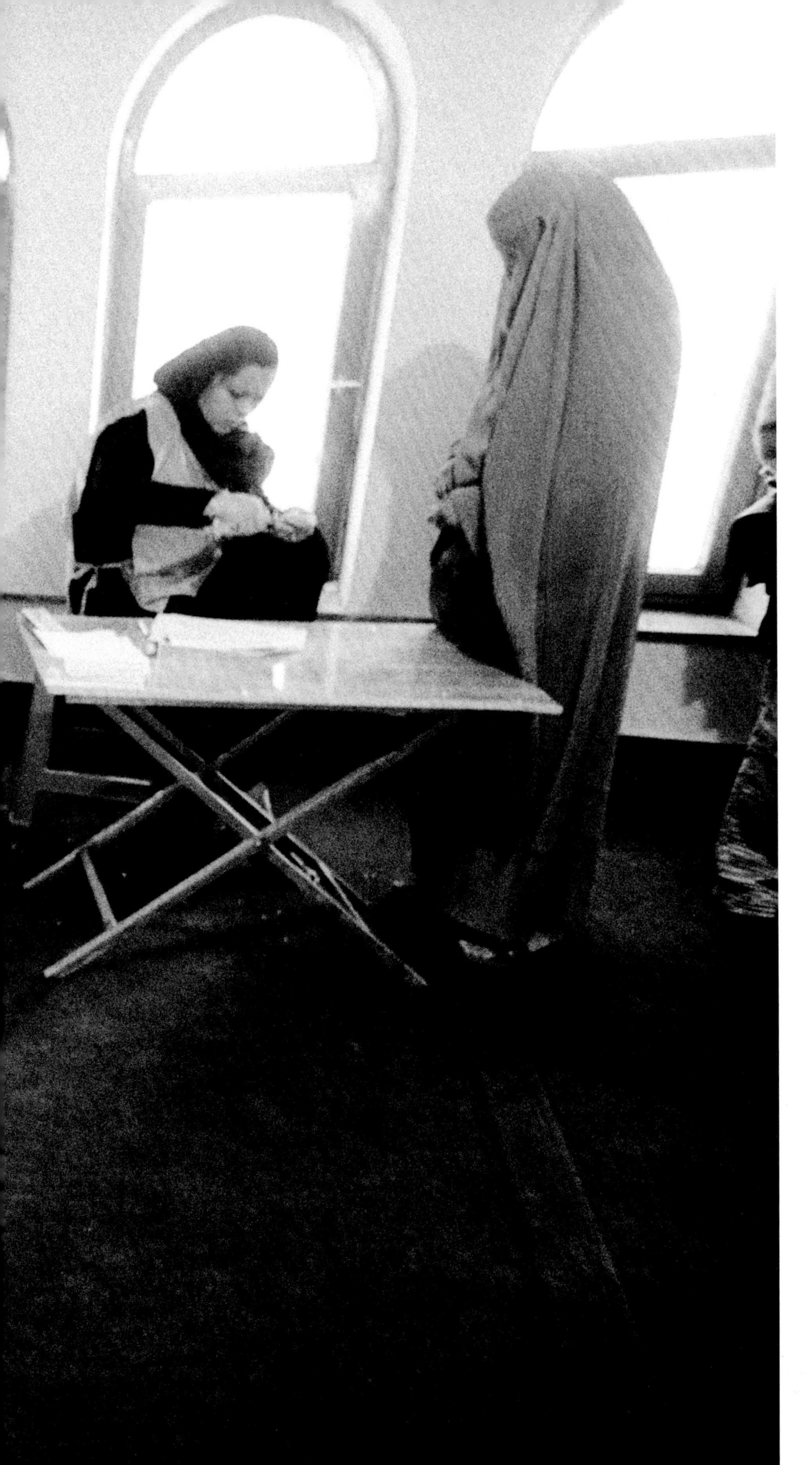

Kabul: October 2004
An election worker checks the identity of a voter
against her voting card at a polling station in a
school during Afghanistan's presidential election.

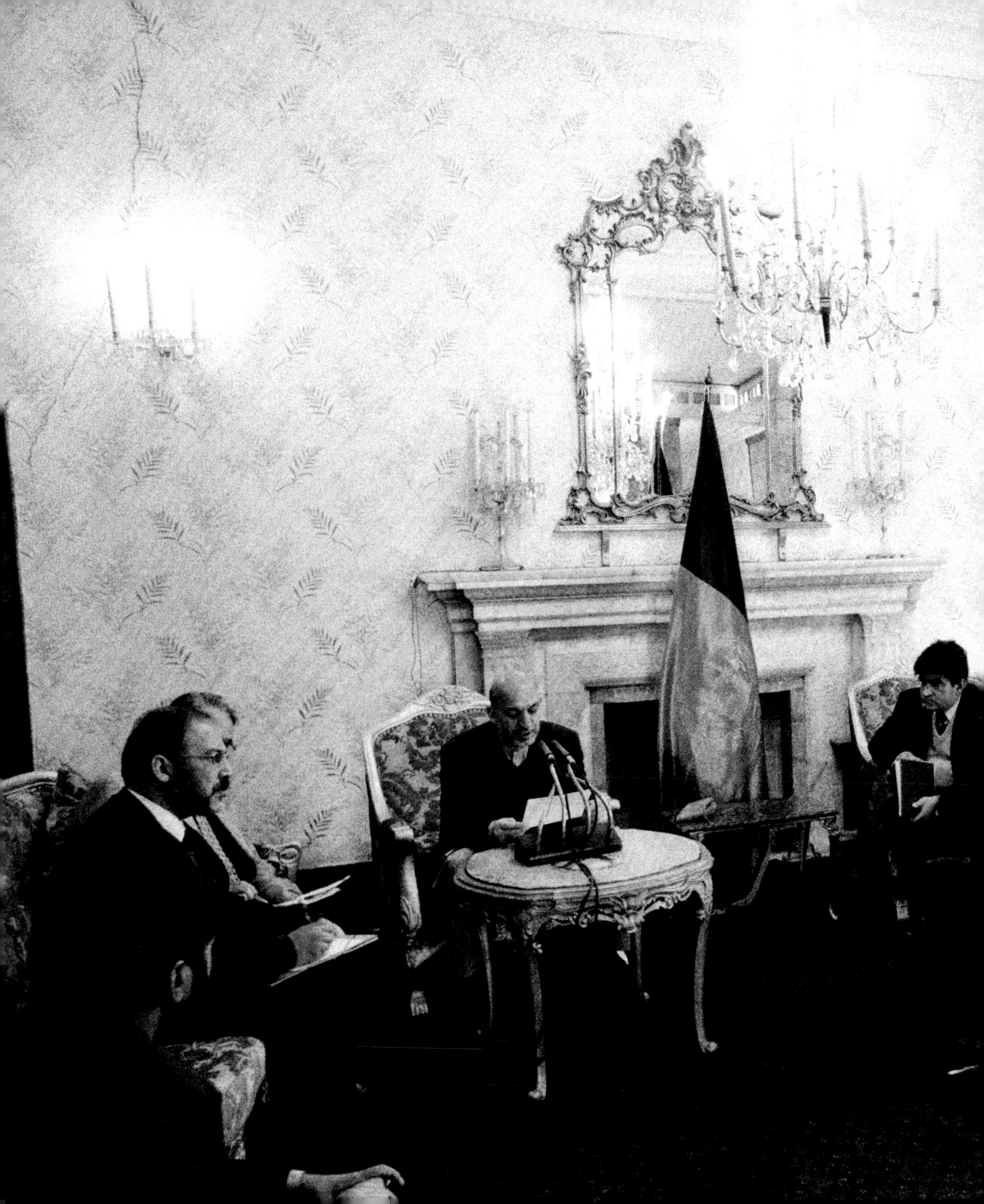

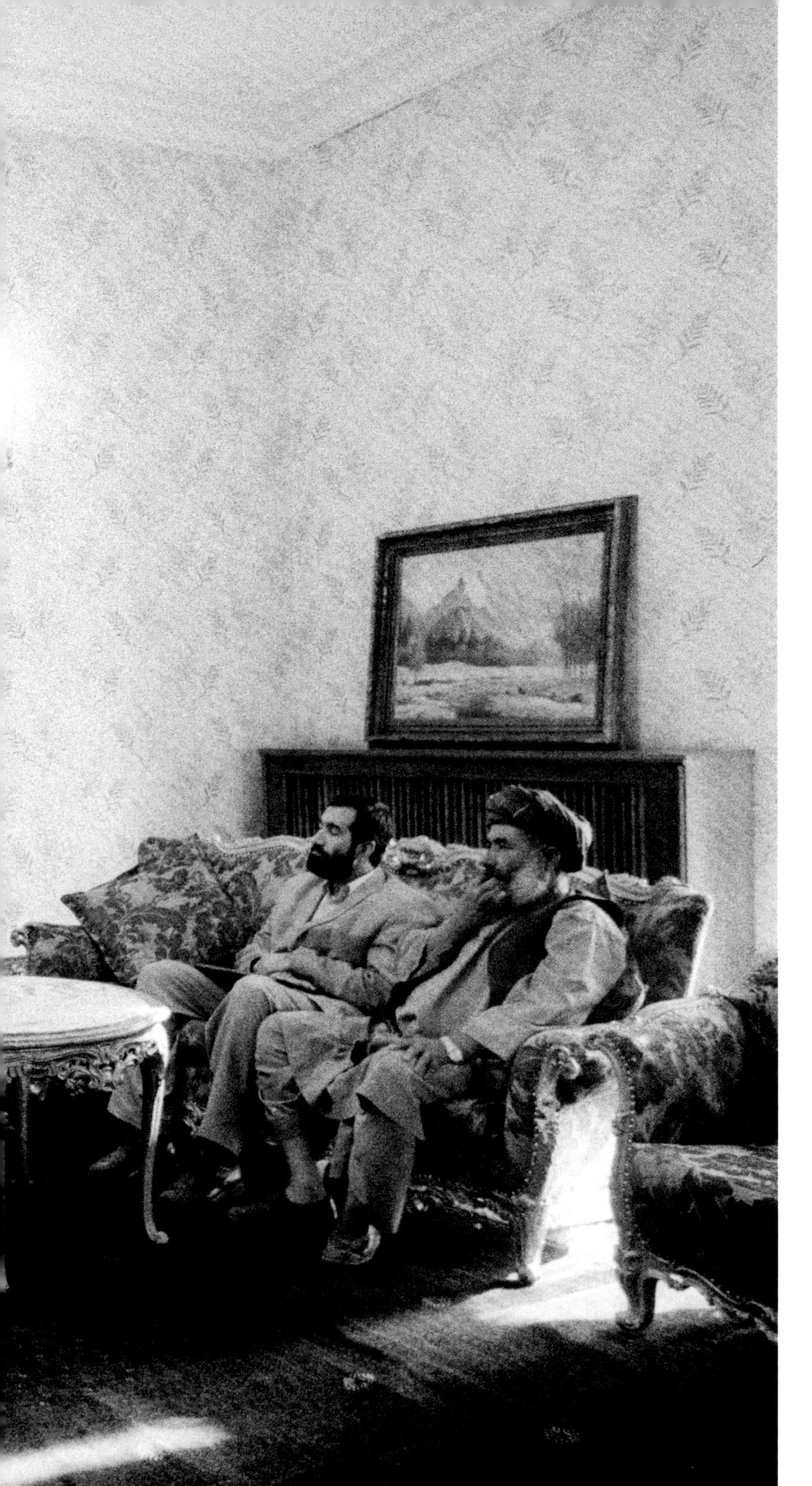

ARG PALACE, KABUL: NOVEMBER 2002
President Hamid Karzai making his weekly radio
speech addressing the nation.

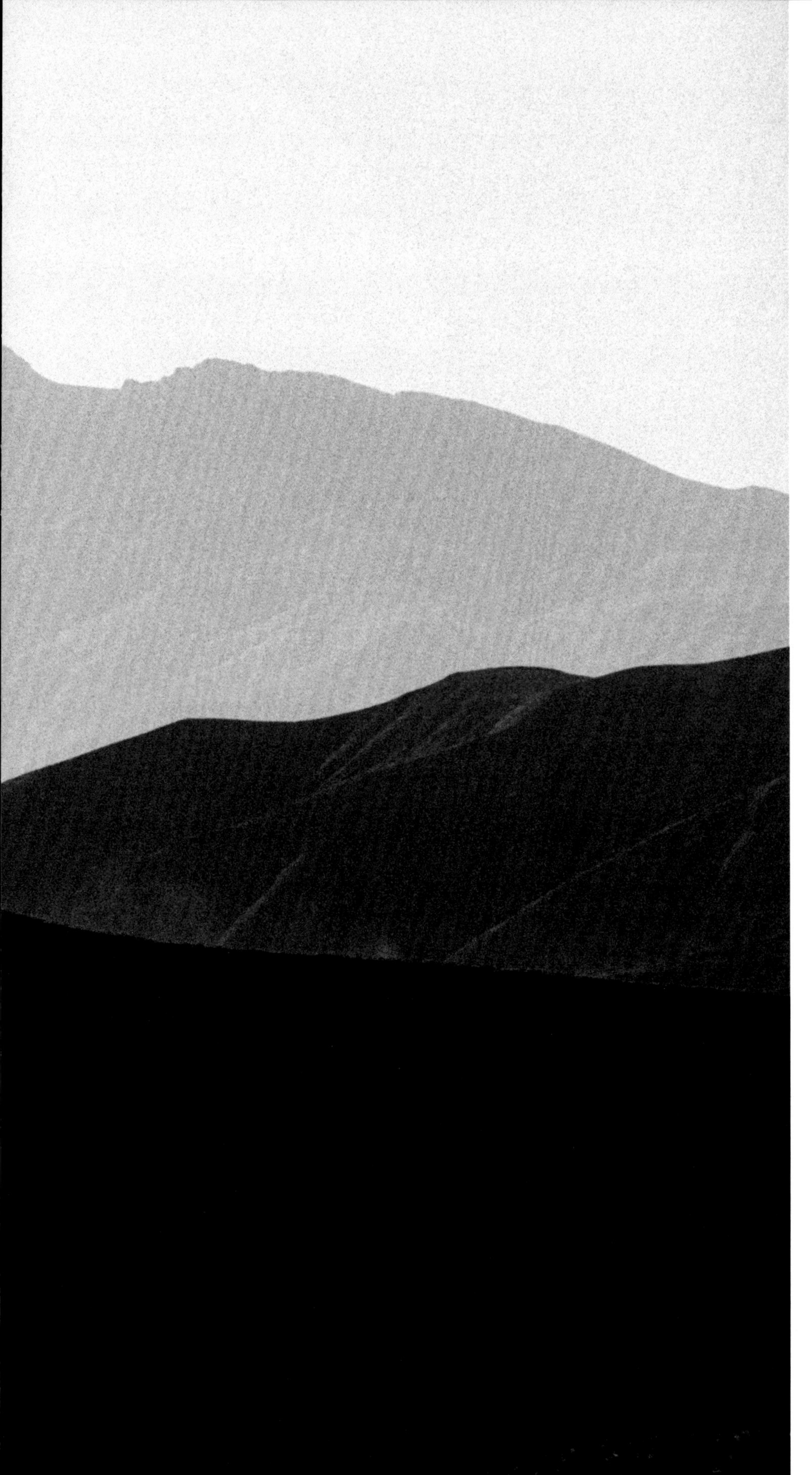

IBAR, TAKHAR PROVINCE: NOVEMBER 2000
Mujahideen fighters loyal to Ahmad Shah
Massoud defend a hilltop against Taliban advances.

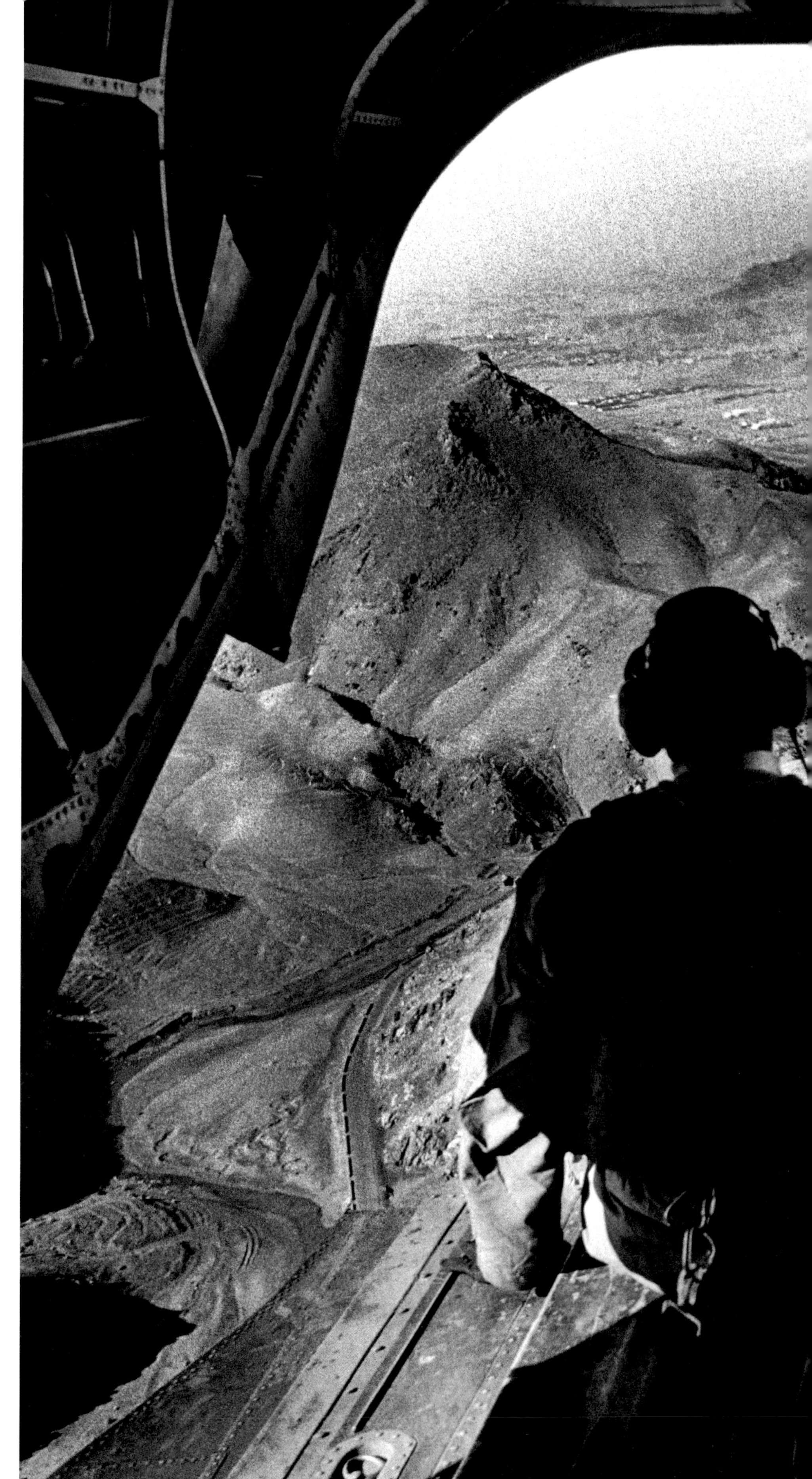

Kohe Safi Mountains: November 2002
American troops from the 82nd Airborne on a
mission searching for arms caches and remnants
of the Taliban.

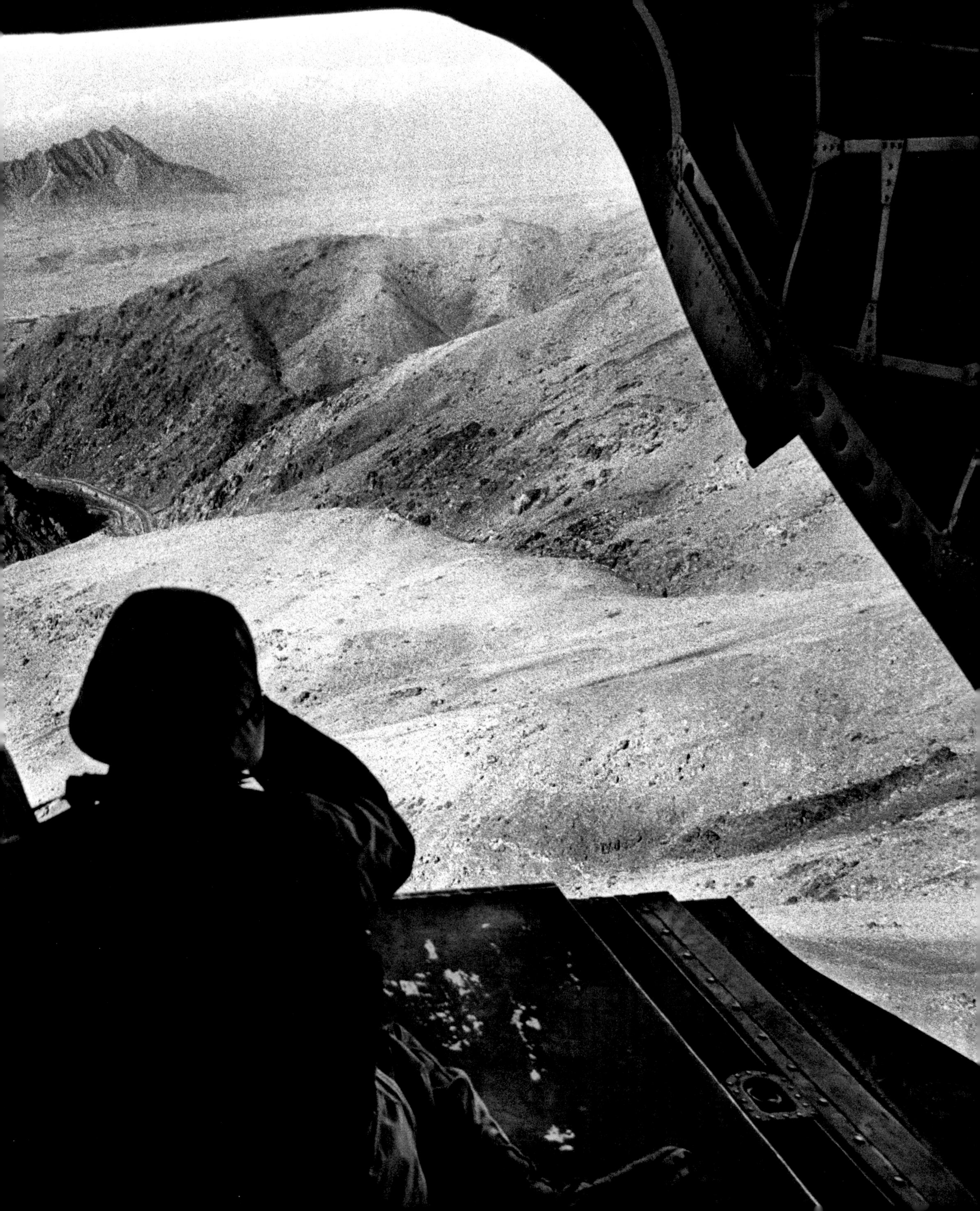

JABUL SERAJ, PARWAN PROVINCE: NOVEMBER 2001
Northern Alliance tanks below the Hindu Kush
mountains during preparations for the major
offensive to oust the Taliban from Kabul.

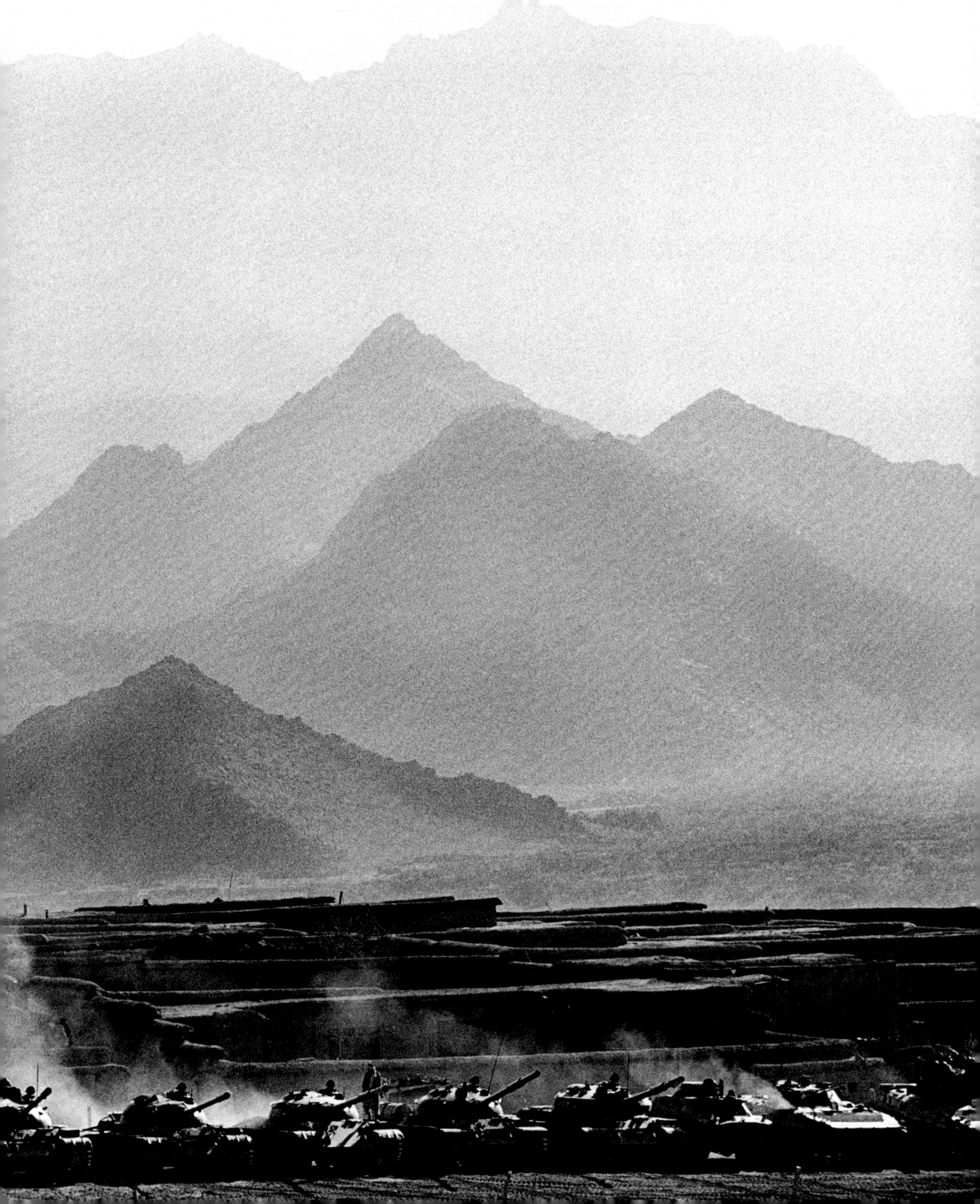

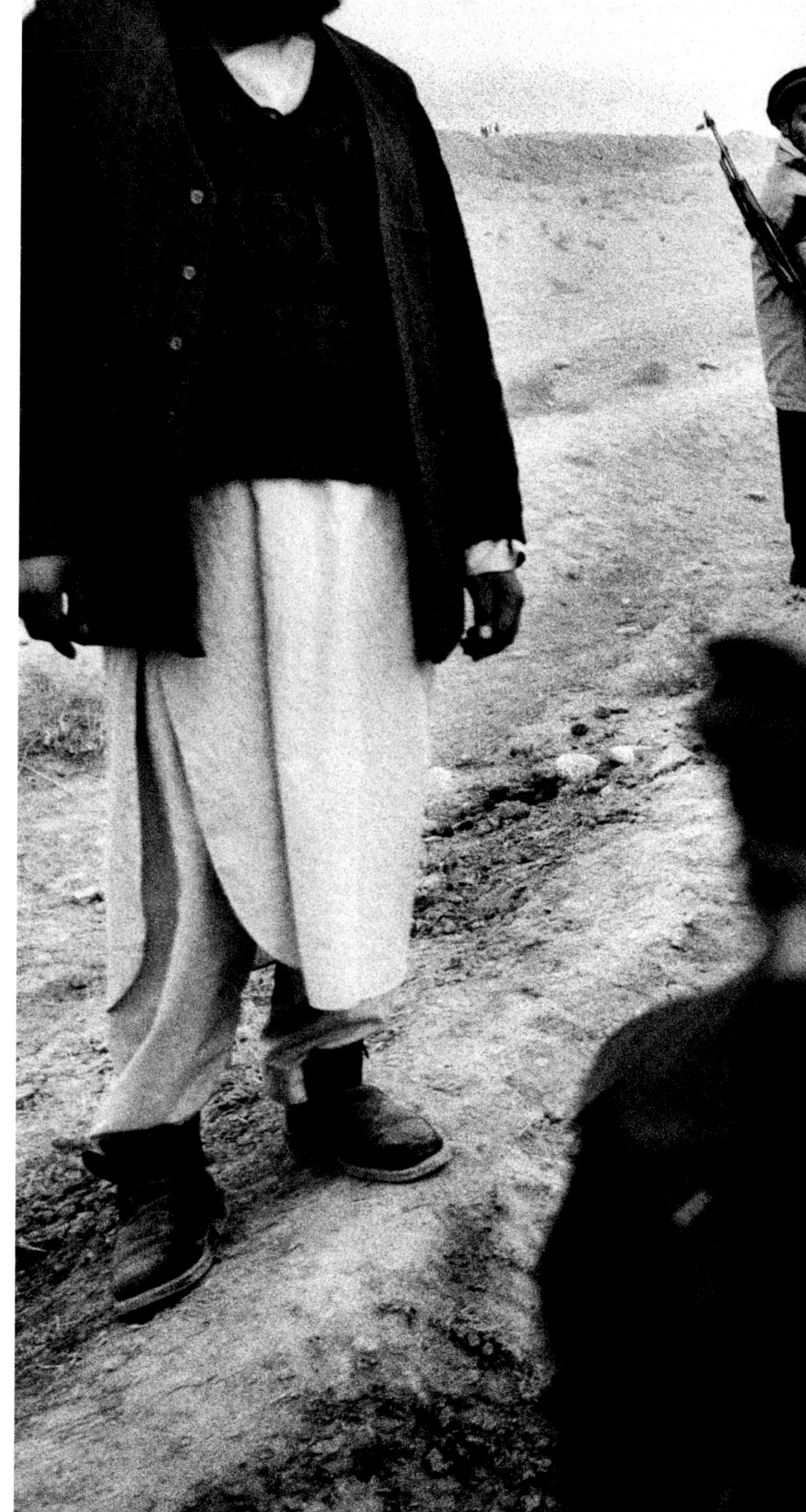

Dasht-e-Qala, Takhar Province: November 2000
Northern Alliance trenches on their defensive line.

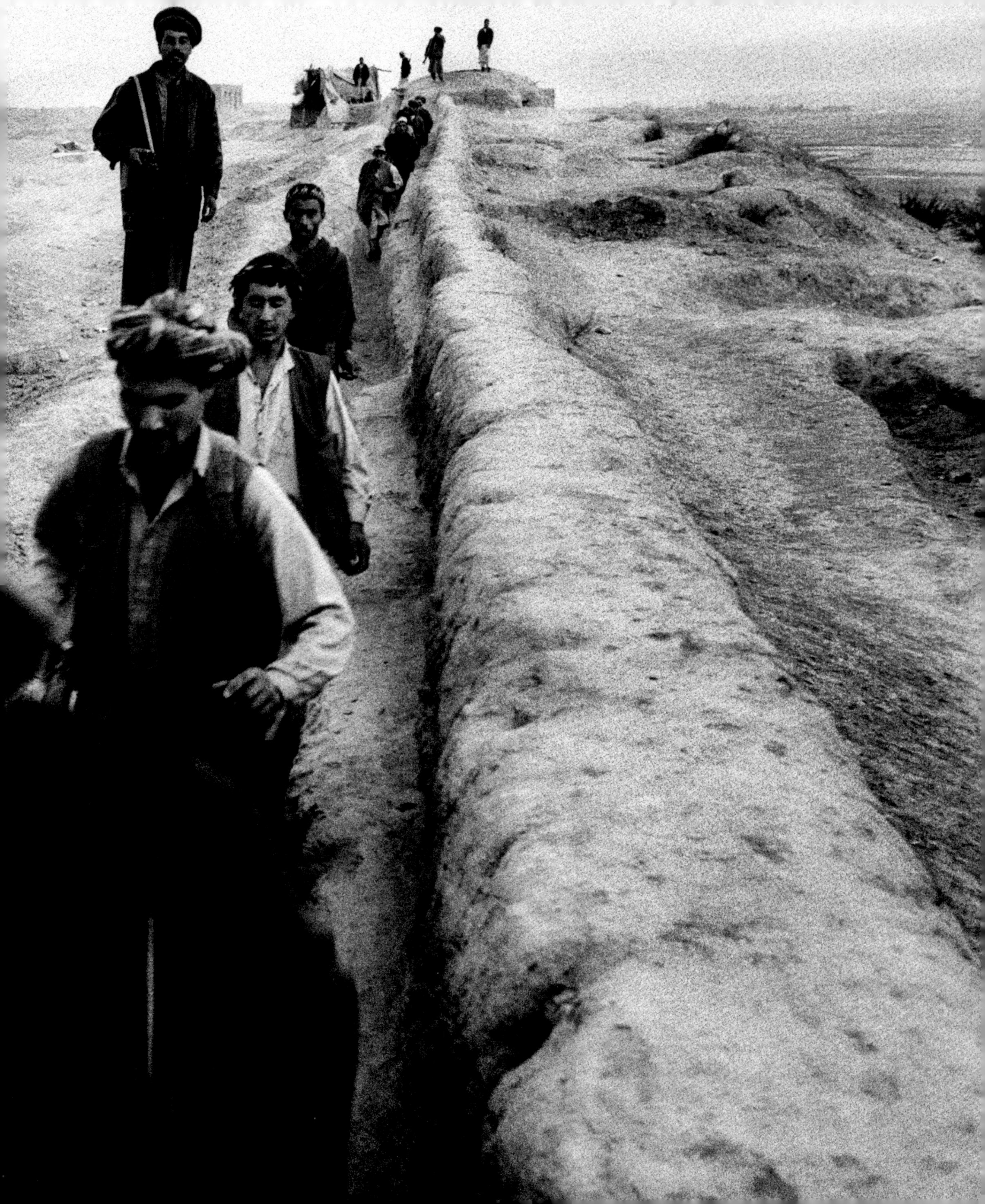

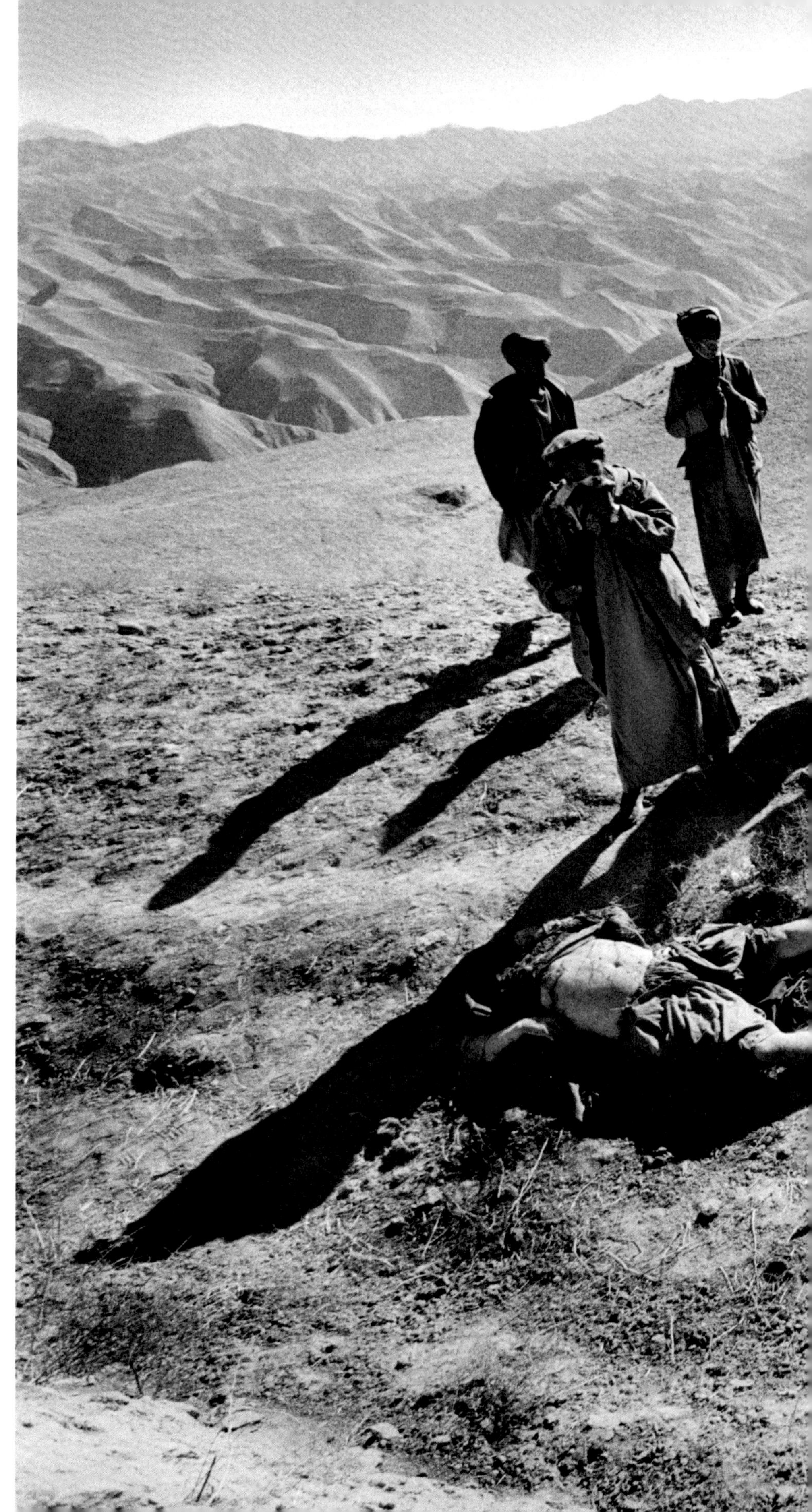

IBAR, TAKHAR PROVINCE: NOVEMBER 2000
Slain Taliban fighters after a failed ambush on a
Northern Alliance position.

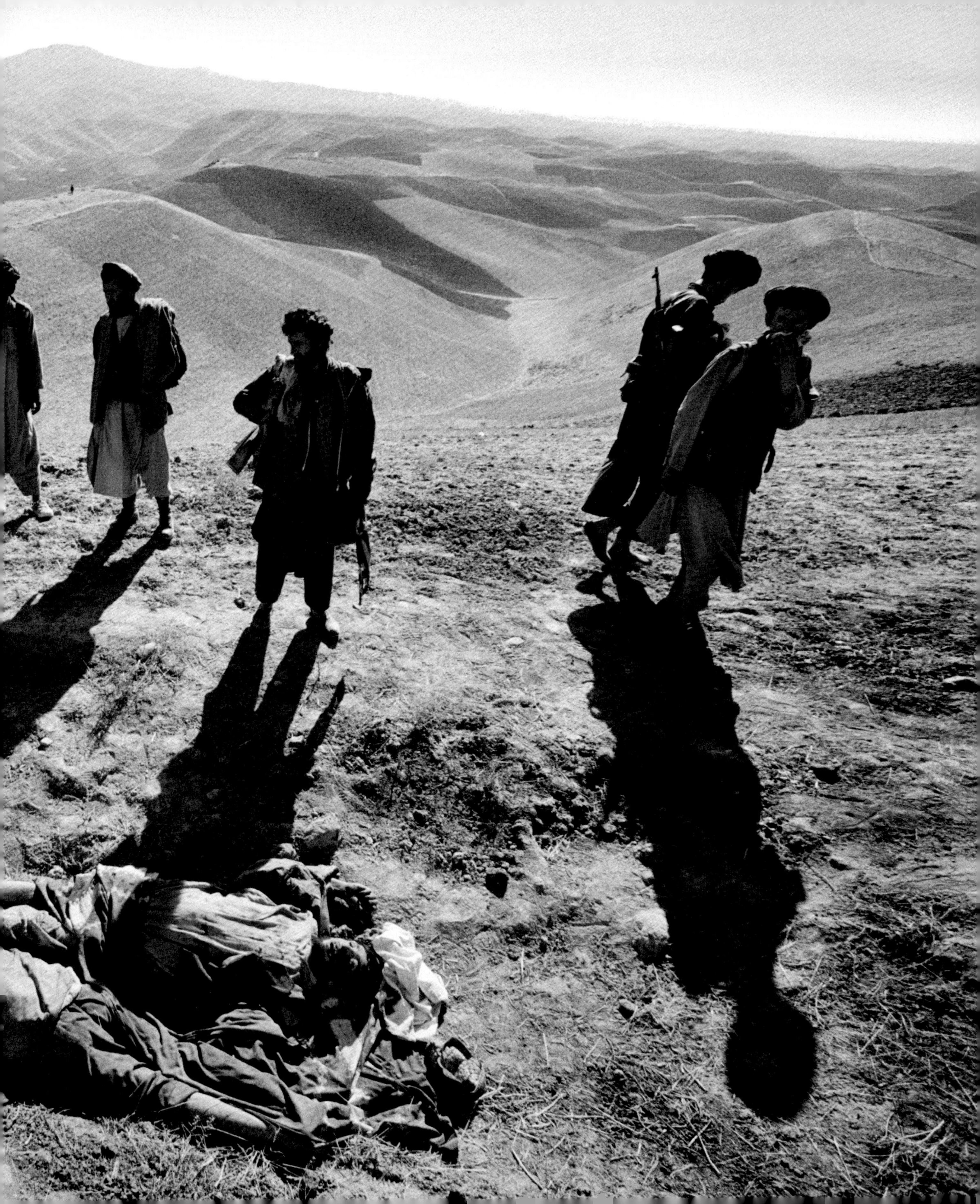

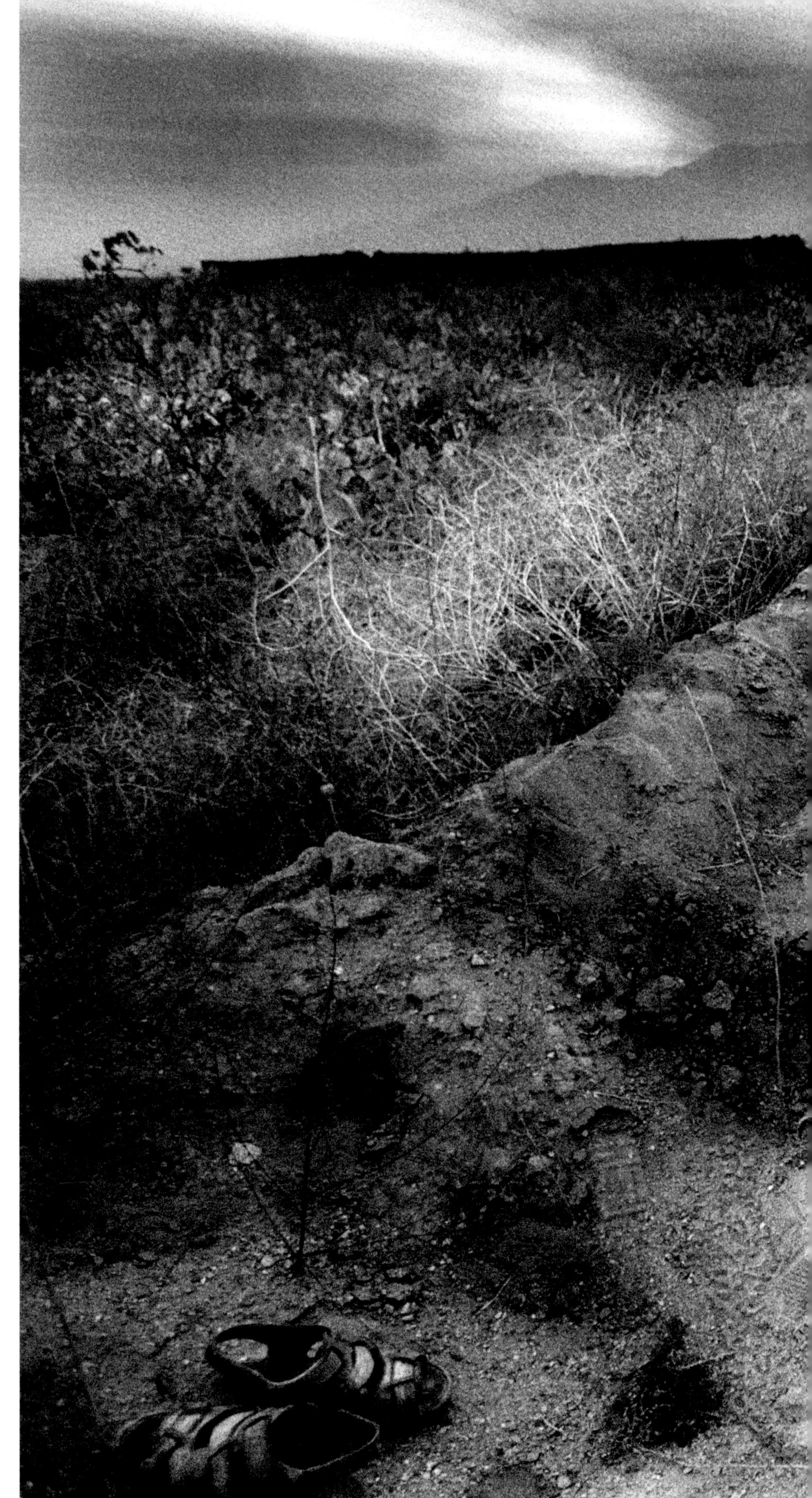

Shamali Plain, Kabul: 12 November 2001
A Taliban fighter who died defending the final
front before Kabul.

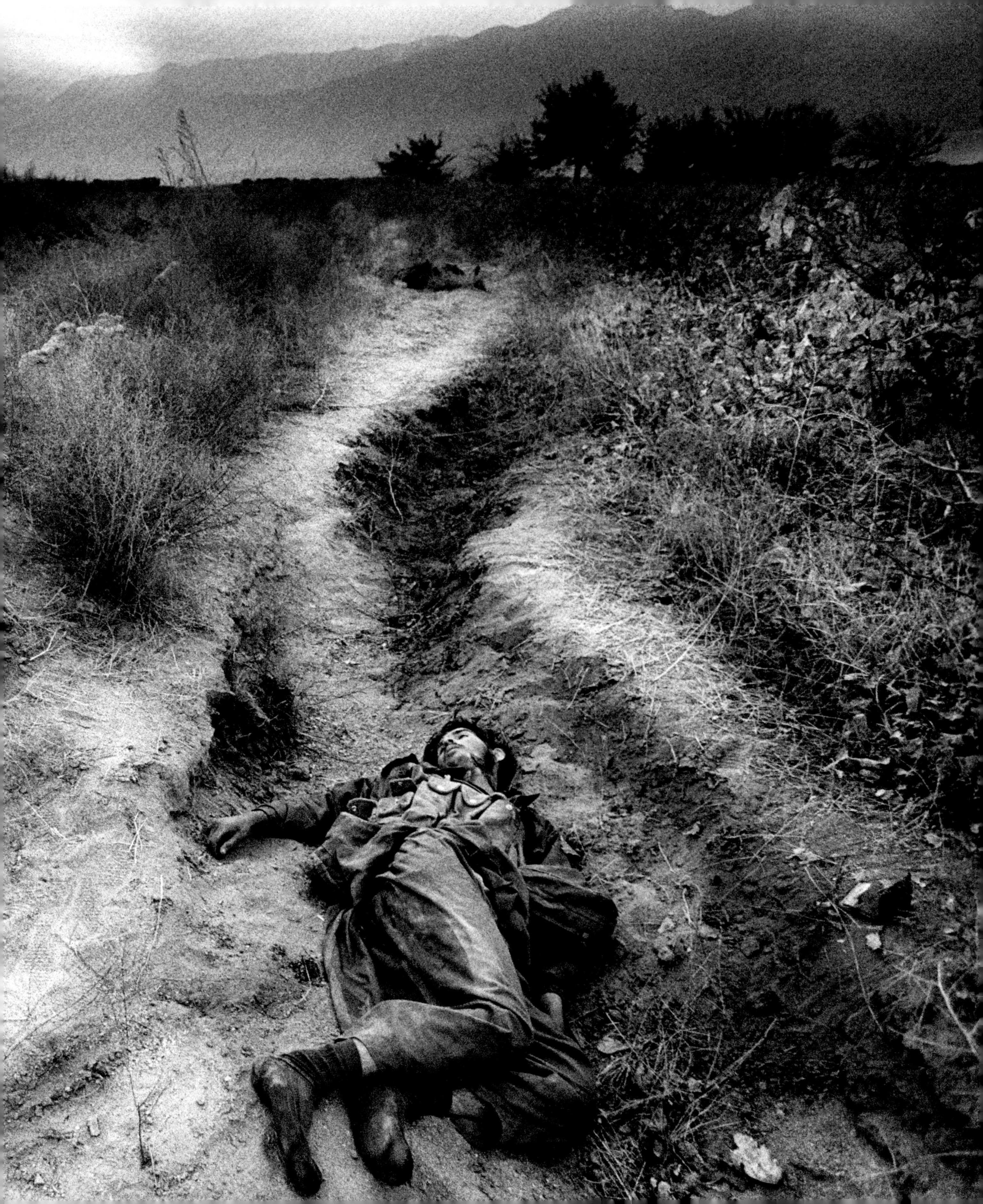

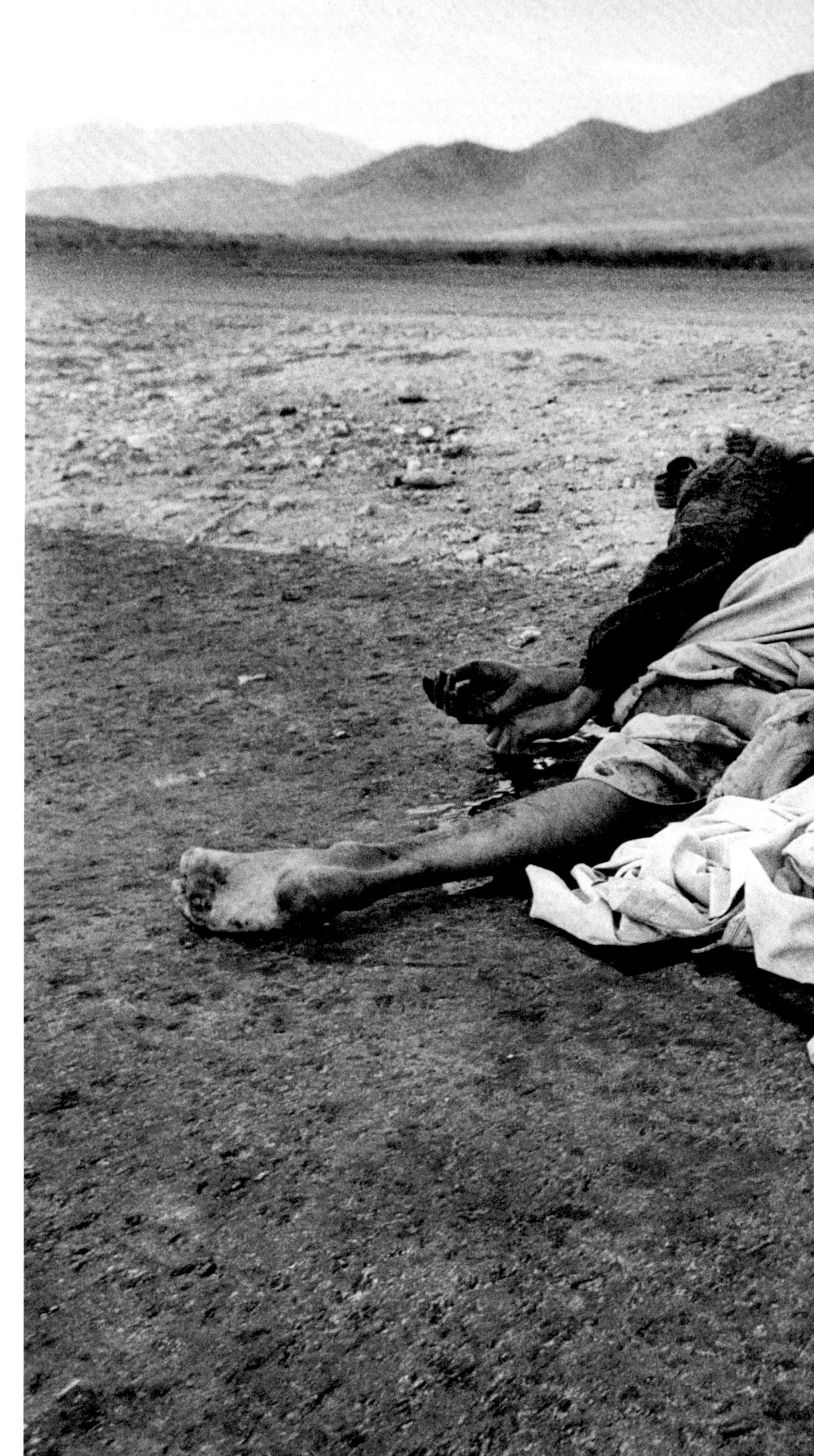

OLD ROAD TO KABUL, SHAMALI PLAIN:
13 NOVEMBER 2001
The bodies of Taliban fighters early on the day
the regime fled Kabul.

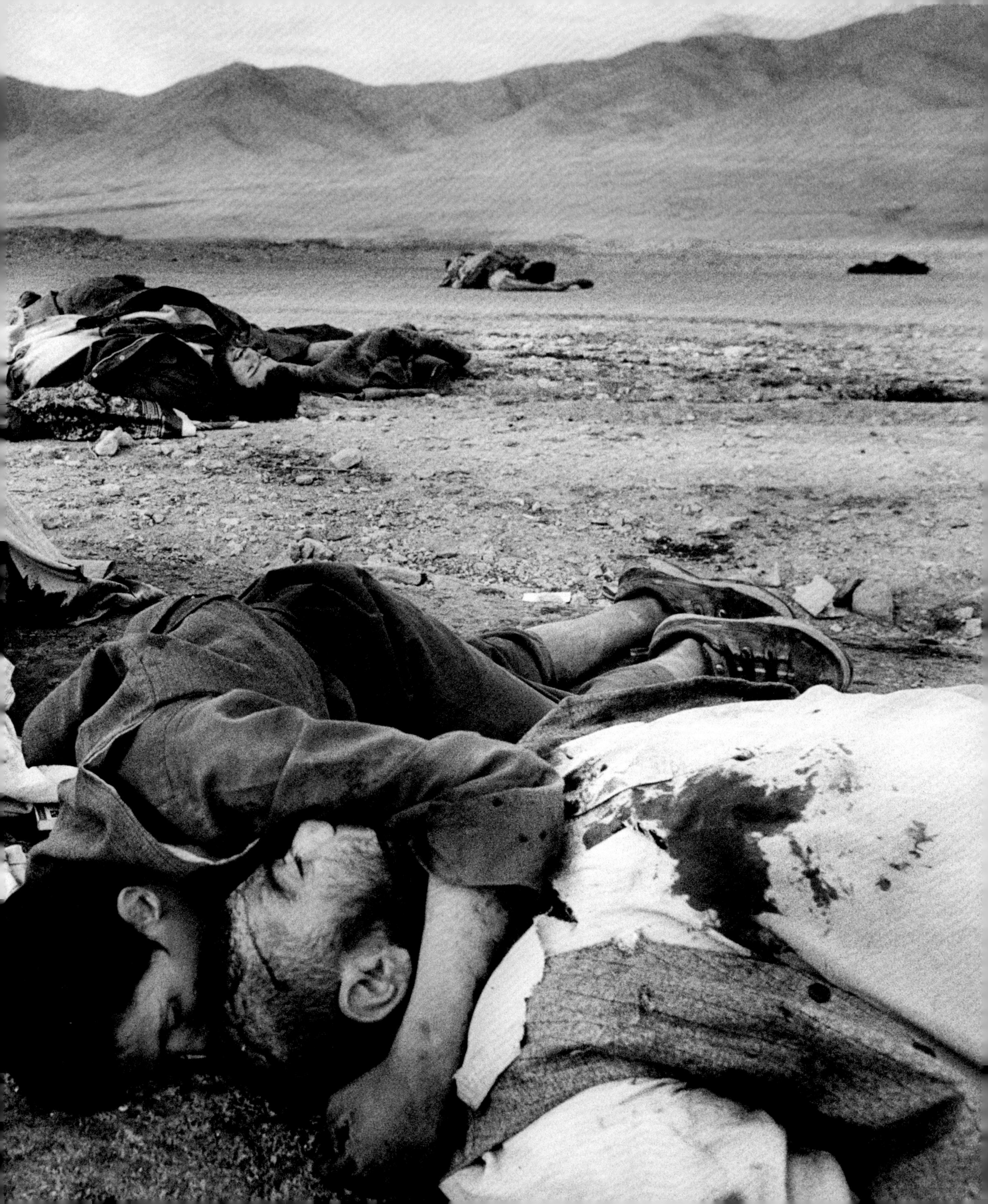

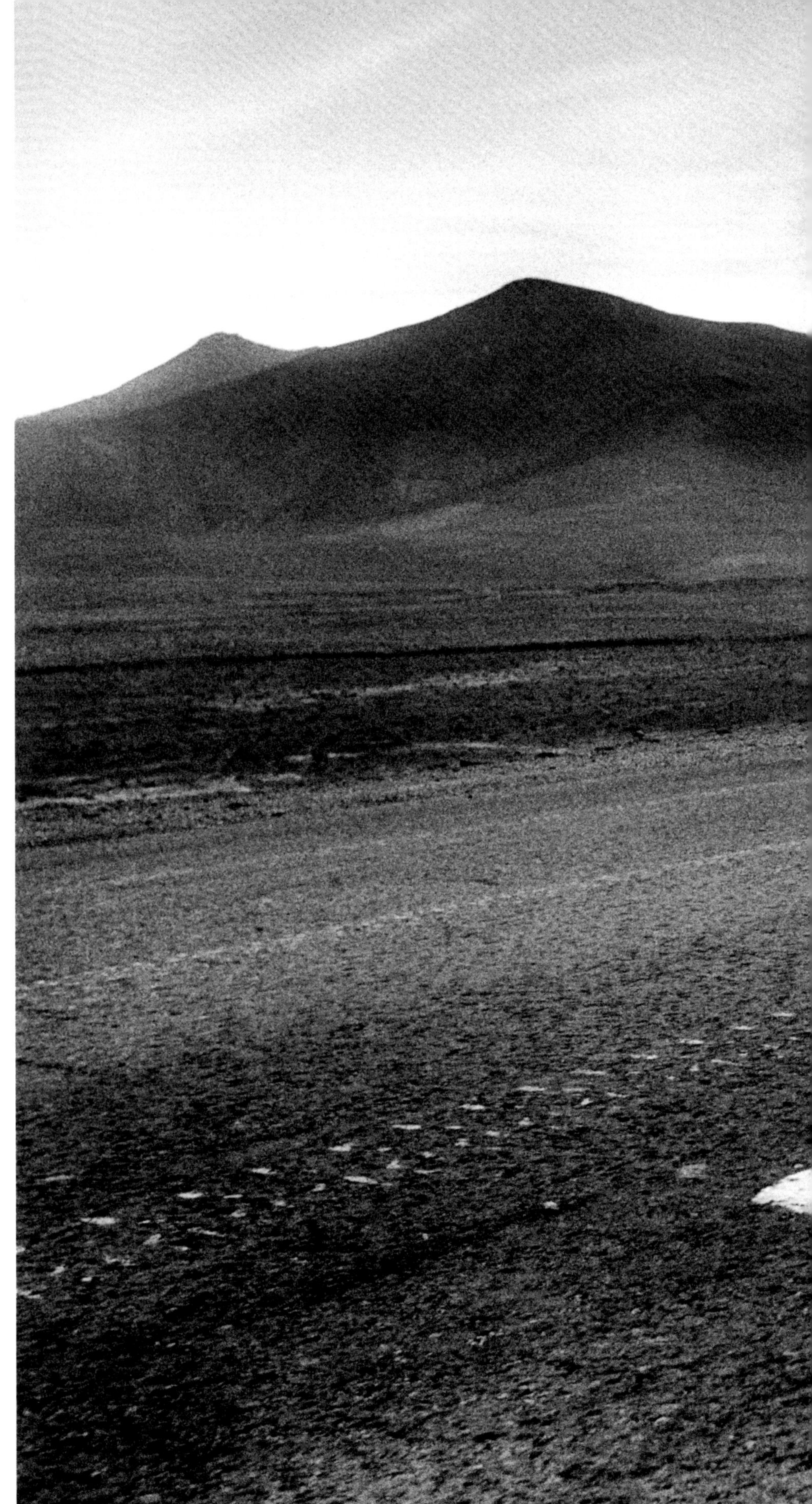

Old Road to Kabul, Shamali Plain:
13 November 2001
An executed Taliban fighter at dawn.

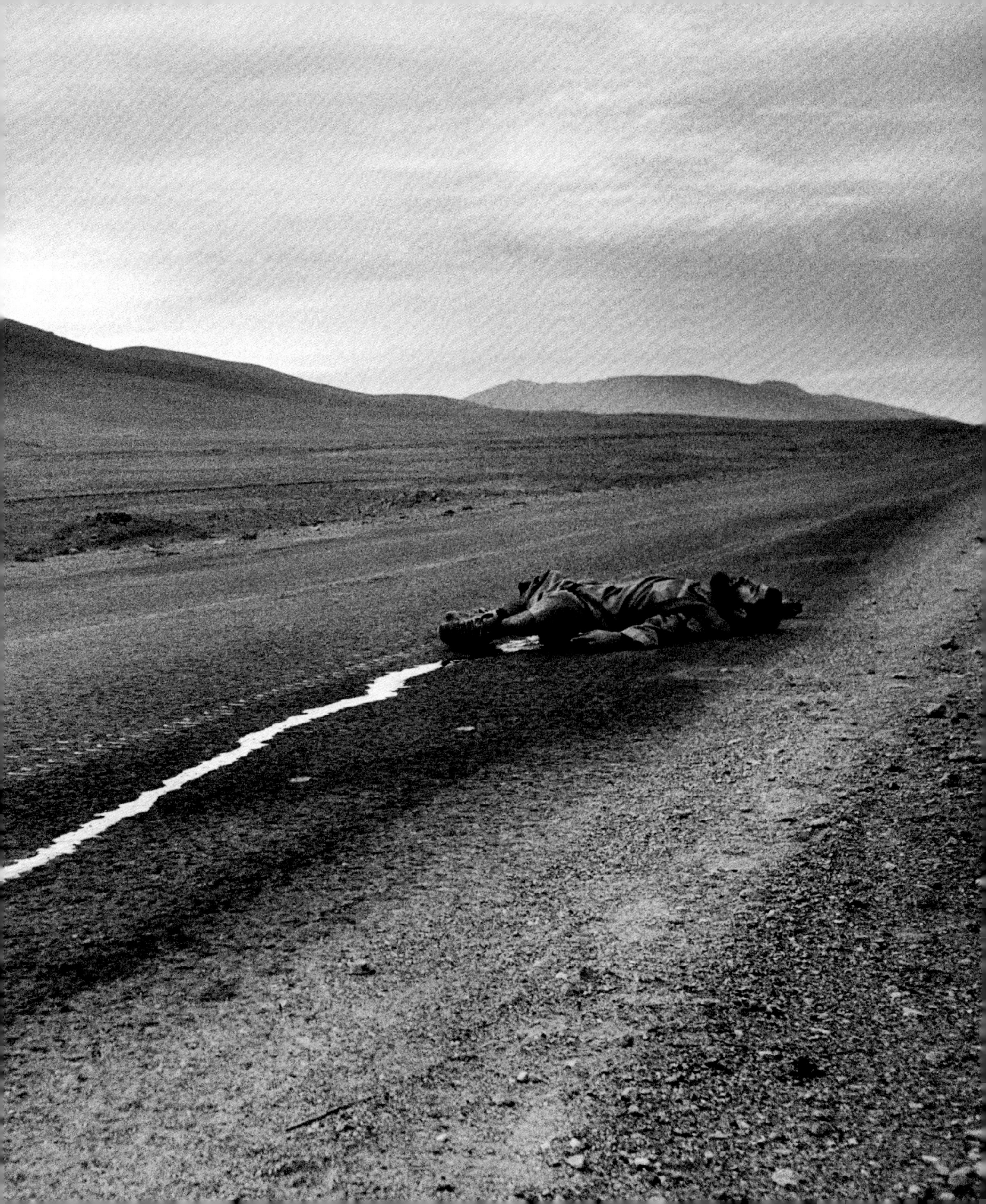

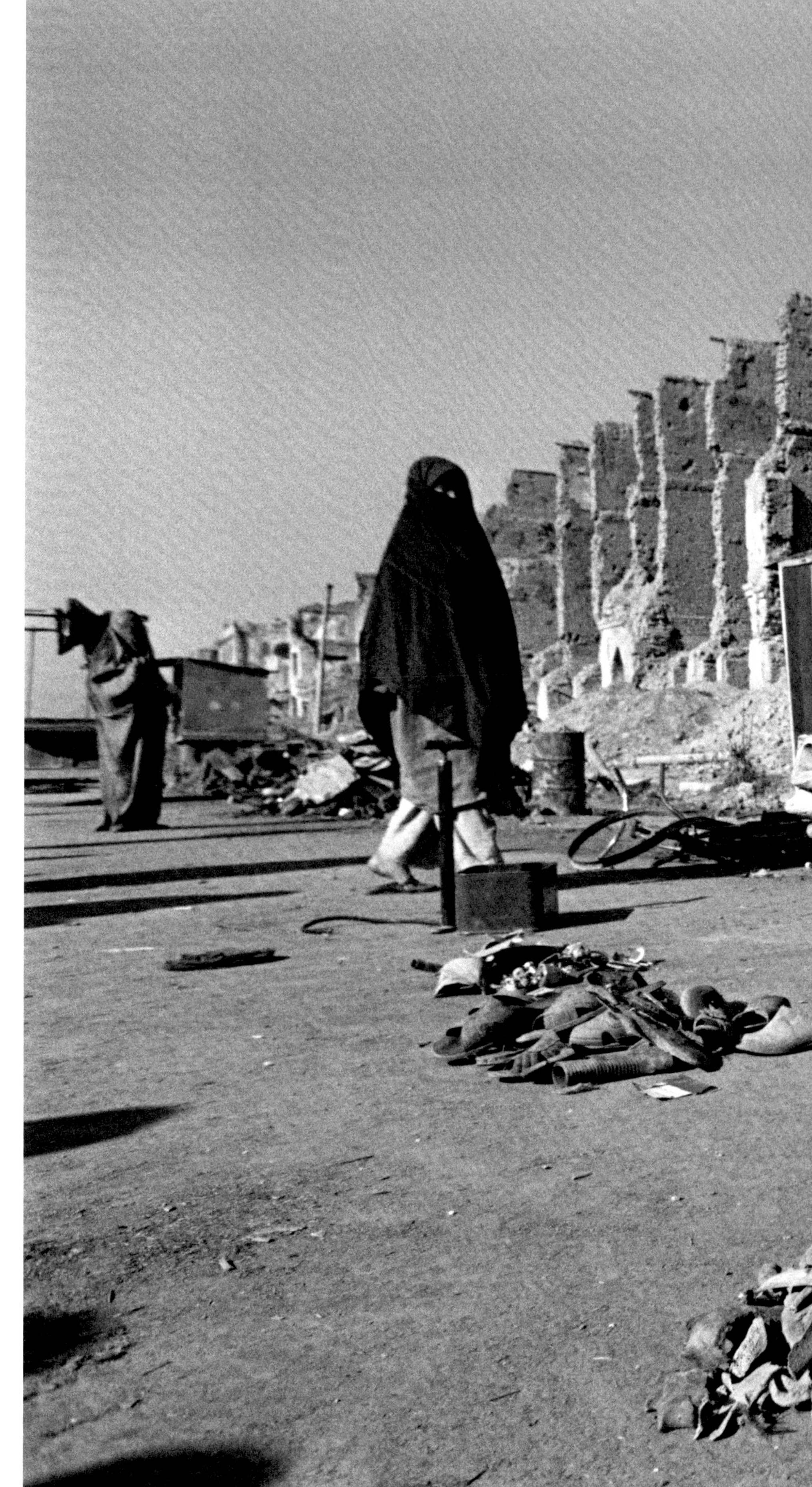

A bone merchant on Jade Maiwand. After the Taliban banned the scrap metal trade and other commercial activities on religious grounds, people in Kabul resorted to the trading of bones, animal and human. Children were especially active, rifling bones from the graves unearthed by constant bombing and shelling. The bones were warehoused by bigger merchants and eventually transported in trucks to Pakistan, where they were used in the manufacture of cooking oil, soap and buttons.

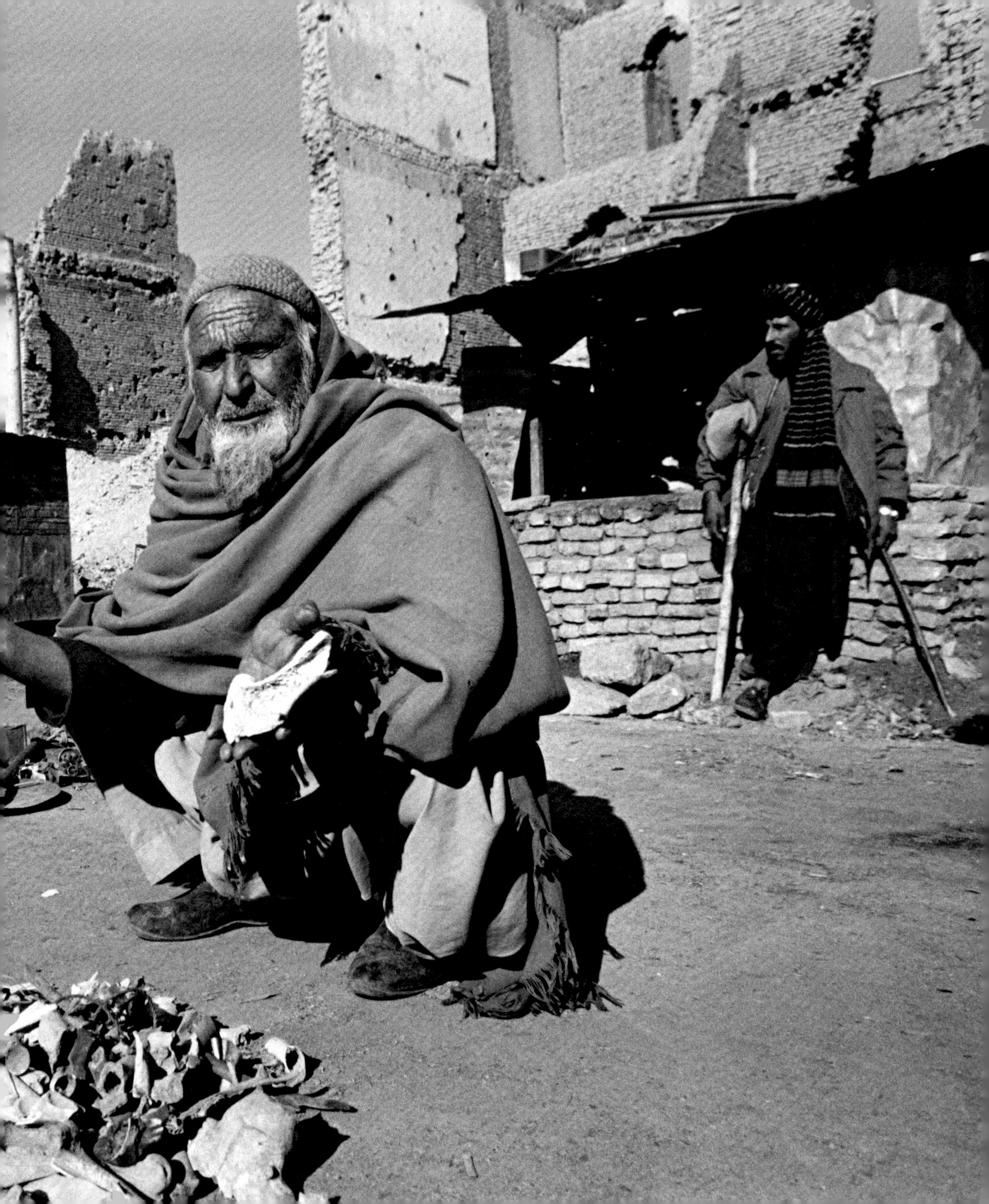

A Northern Alliance commander holds his radio aloft awaiting further orders. The Northern Alliance had promised to halt their advance at the front and not enter Kabul, conscious not to repeat the looting and murders that occured in 1992 after liberation. However, later in the day they took control of the capital.

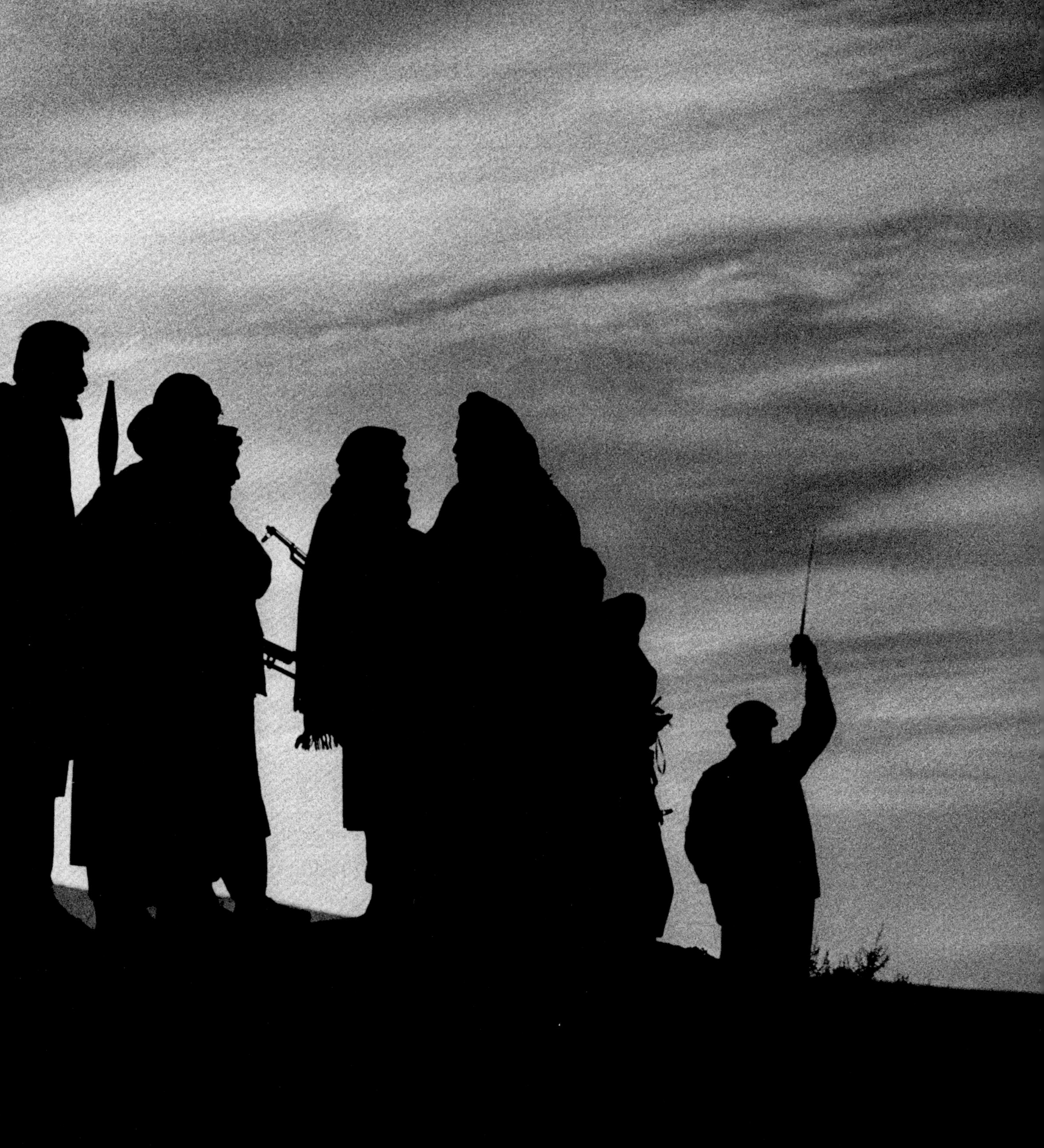

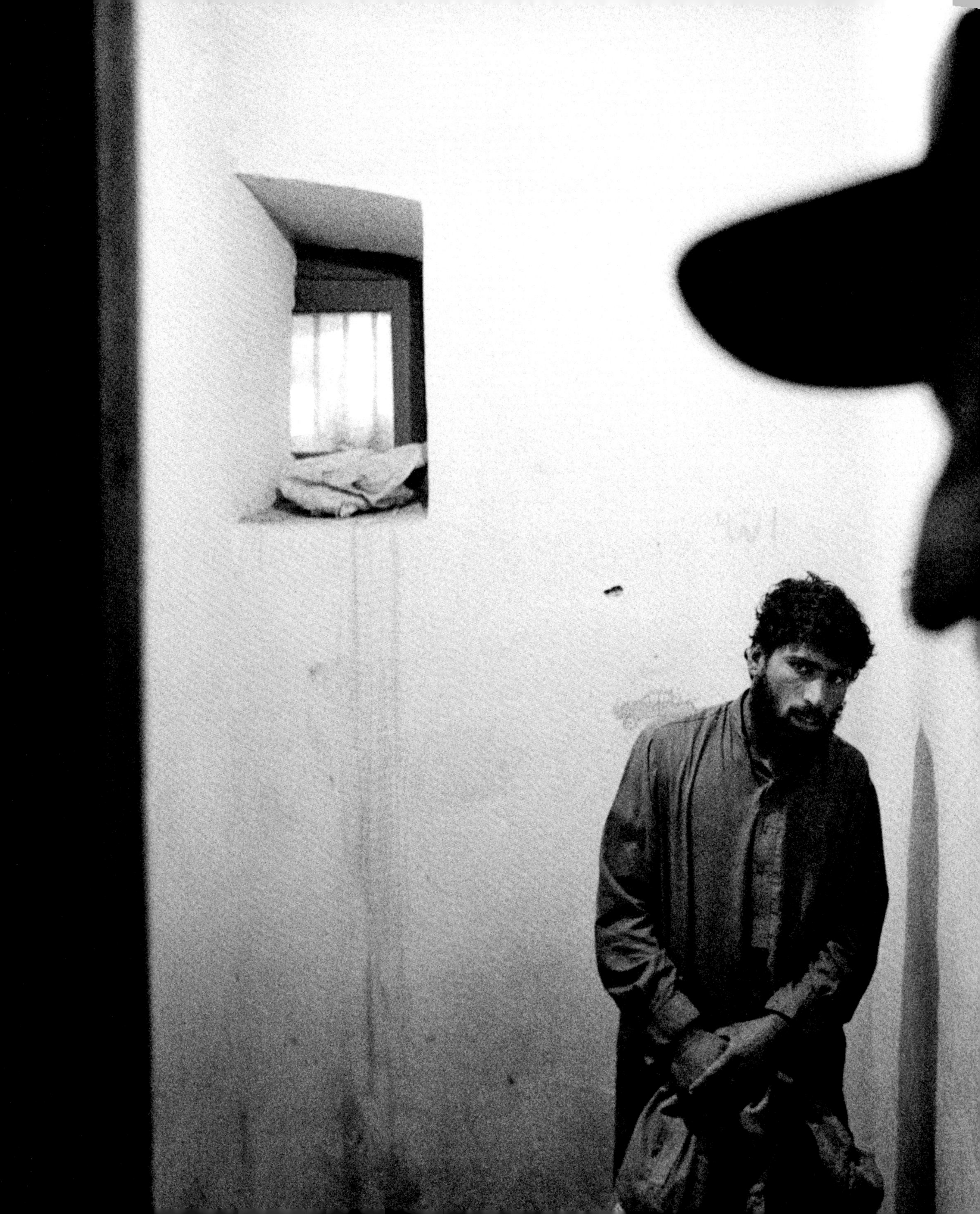

KABUL: 13 NOVEMBER 2001
A Taliban prisoner is held by Northern Alliance
forces on the day Kabul is taken.

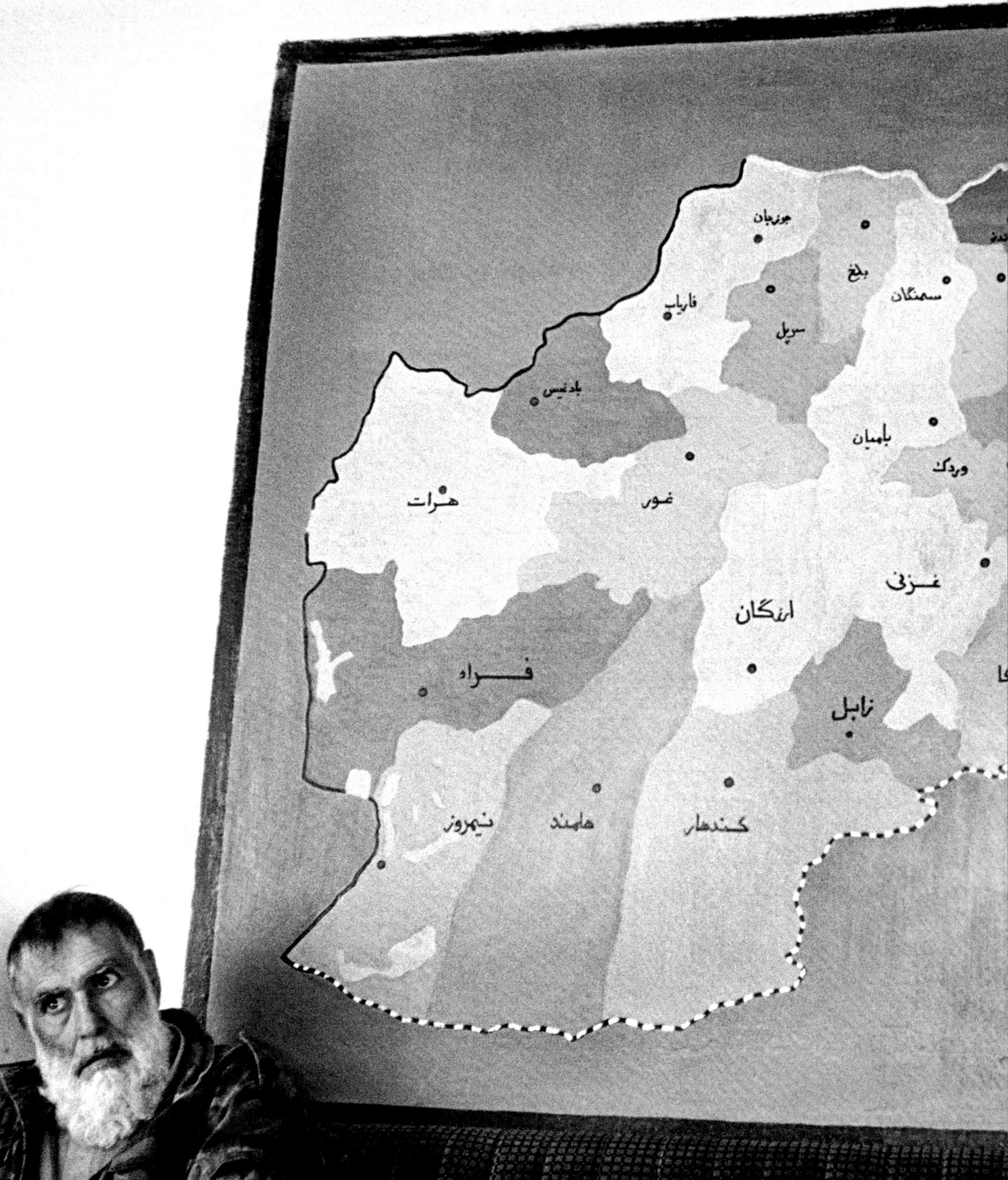

جوزجان
بلخ
سمنگان
فارياب
سرپل
بادغيس
باميان
وردك
هرات
غور
غزنی
ارزگان
فراه
زابل
نيمروز
هلمند
کندهار

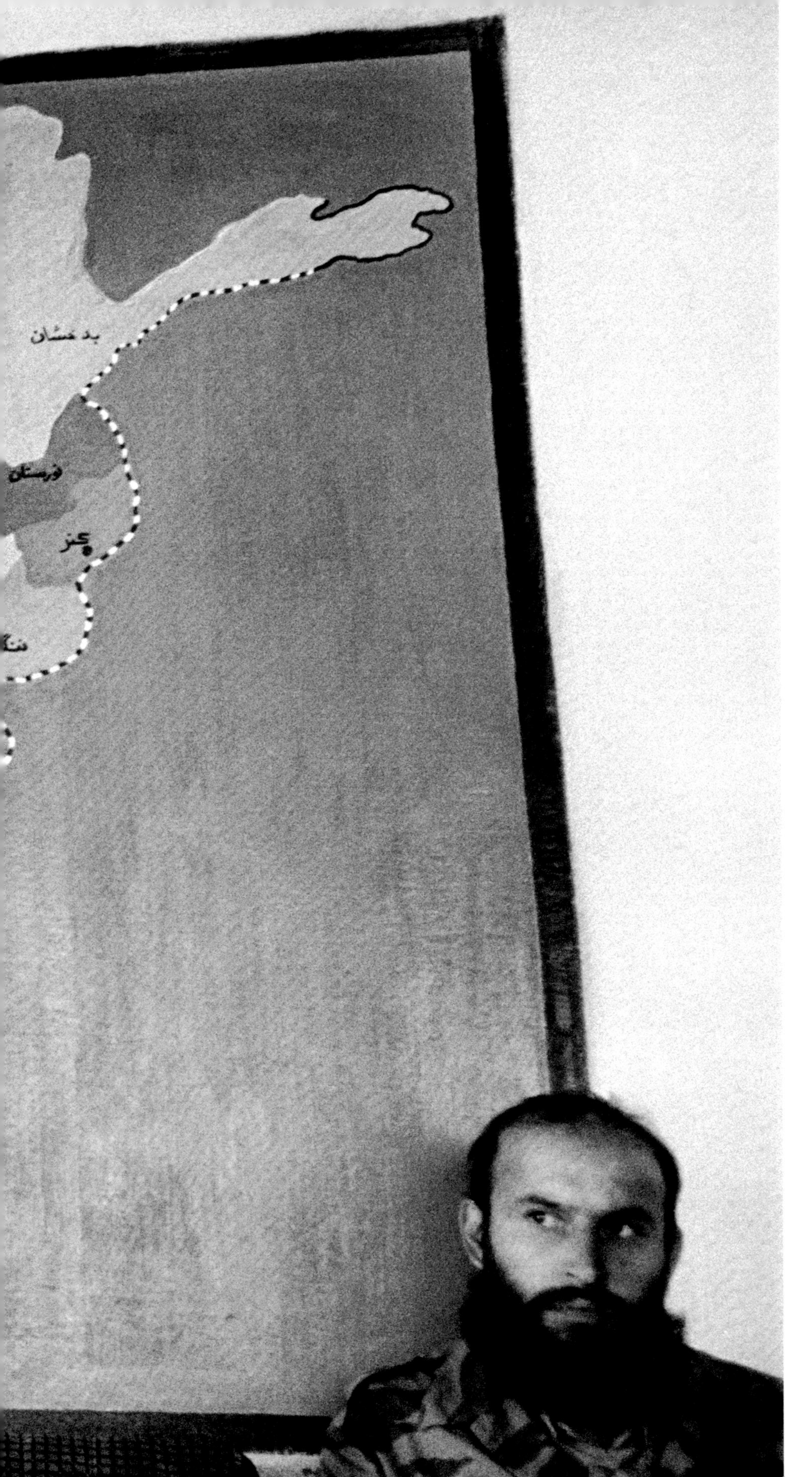

PARAKH, PANJSHIR VALLEY: OCTOBER 2001
Northern Alliance fighters under a map
of Afghanistan.

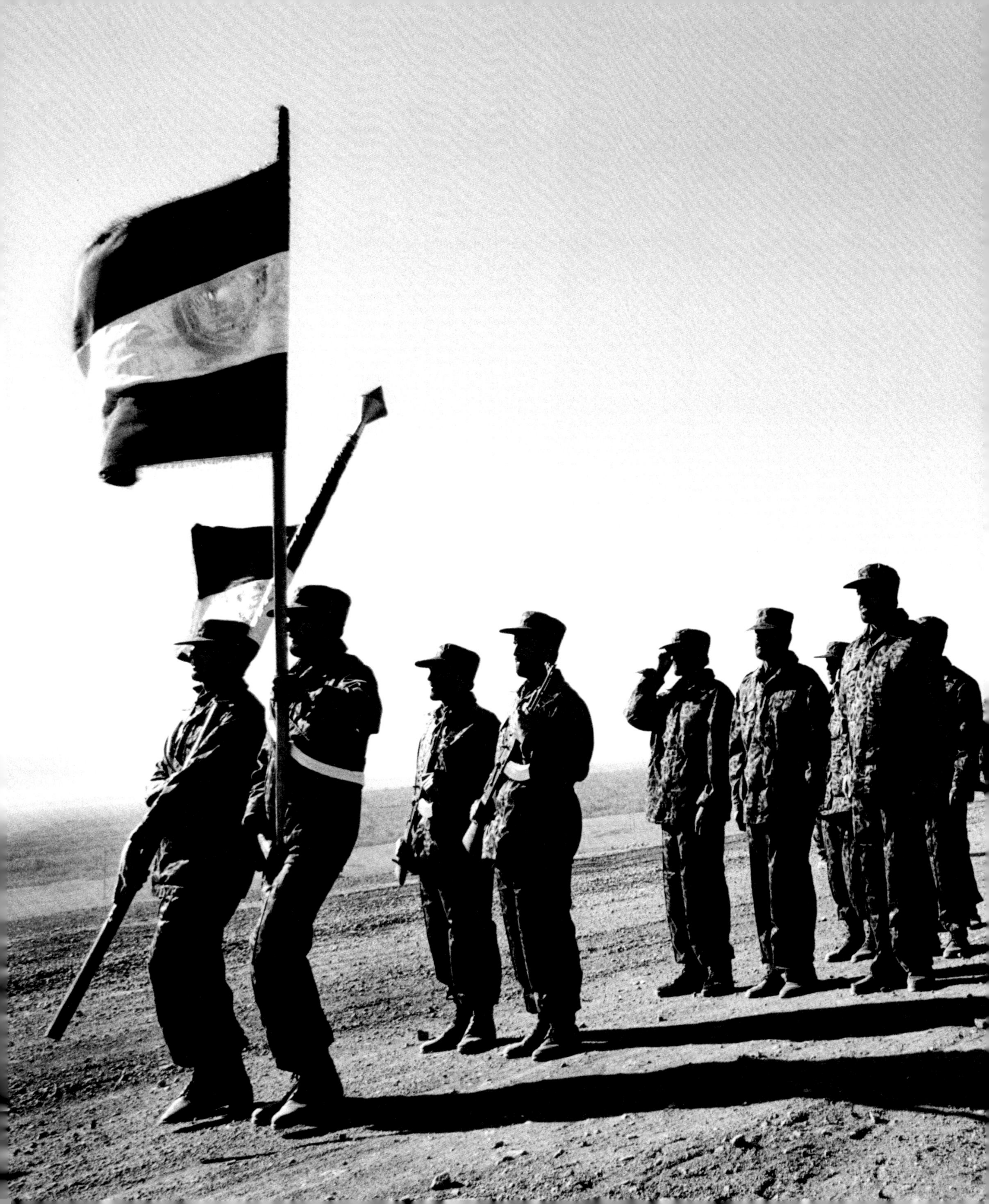

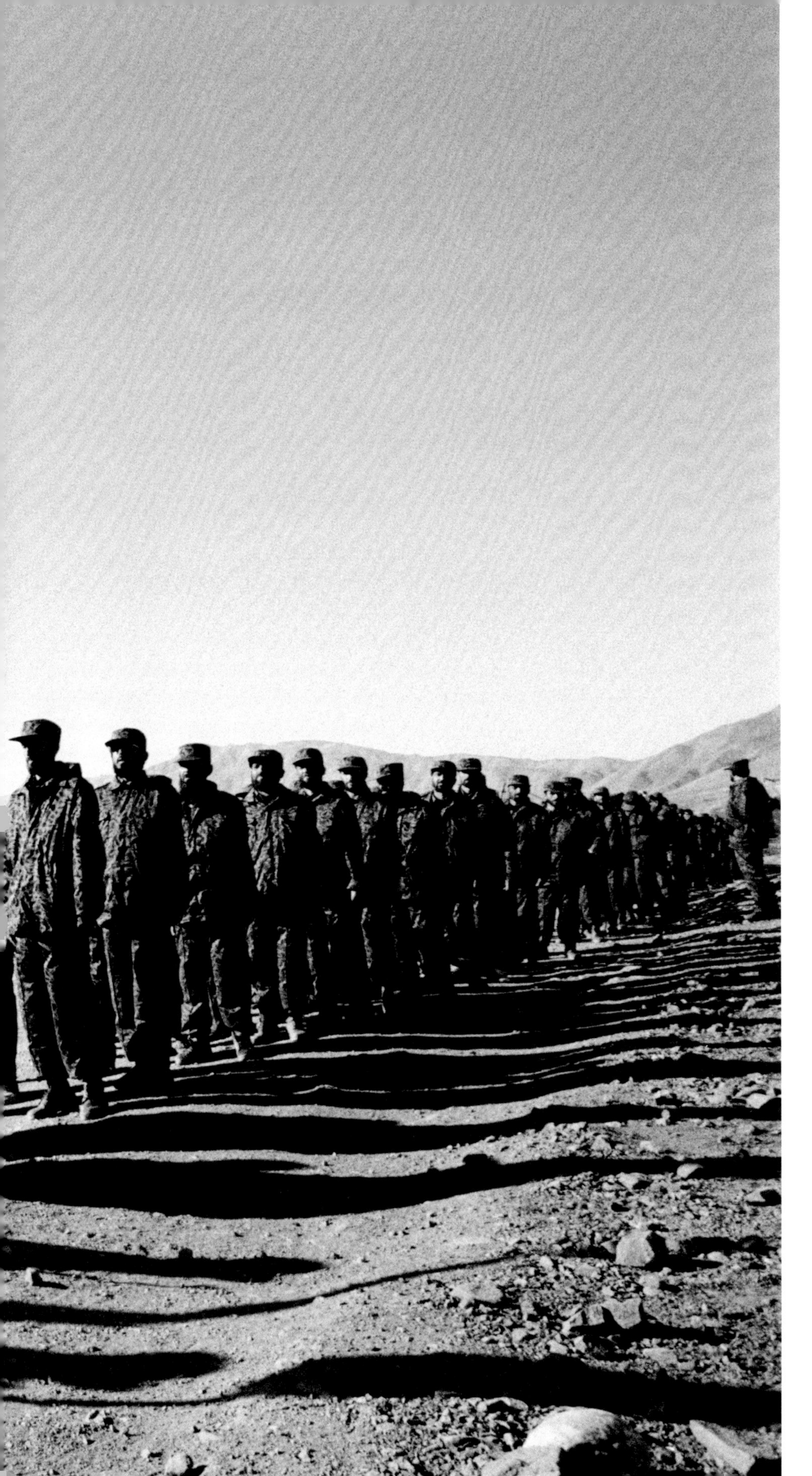

Jabul Seraj, Parwan Province: November 2001
Northern Alliance troops parade during
preparations for the major offensive to oust the
Taliban from Kabul.

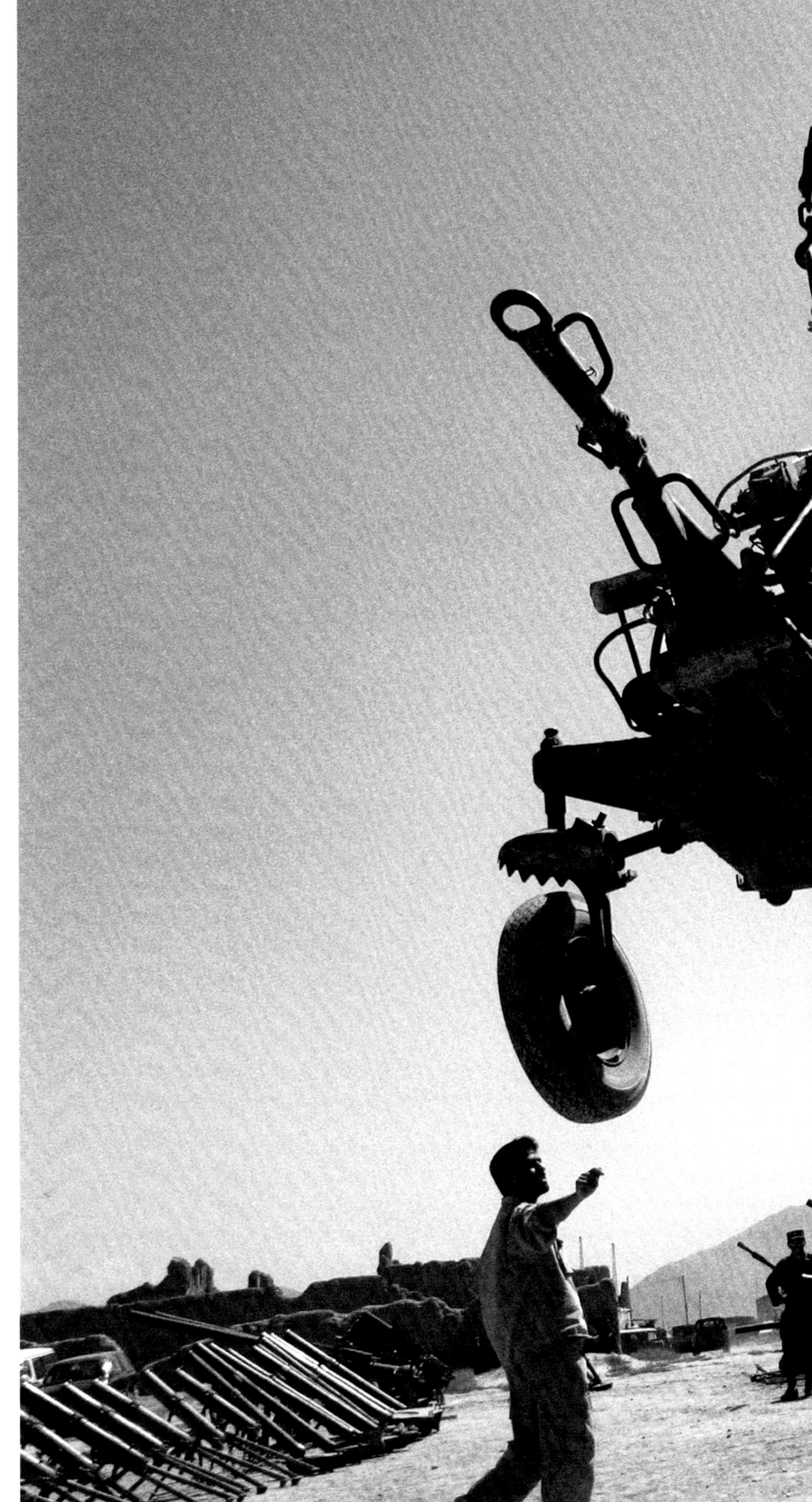

Kabul: August 2004
Decommissioning of weapons held by Northern
Alliance units.

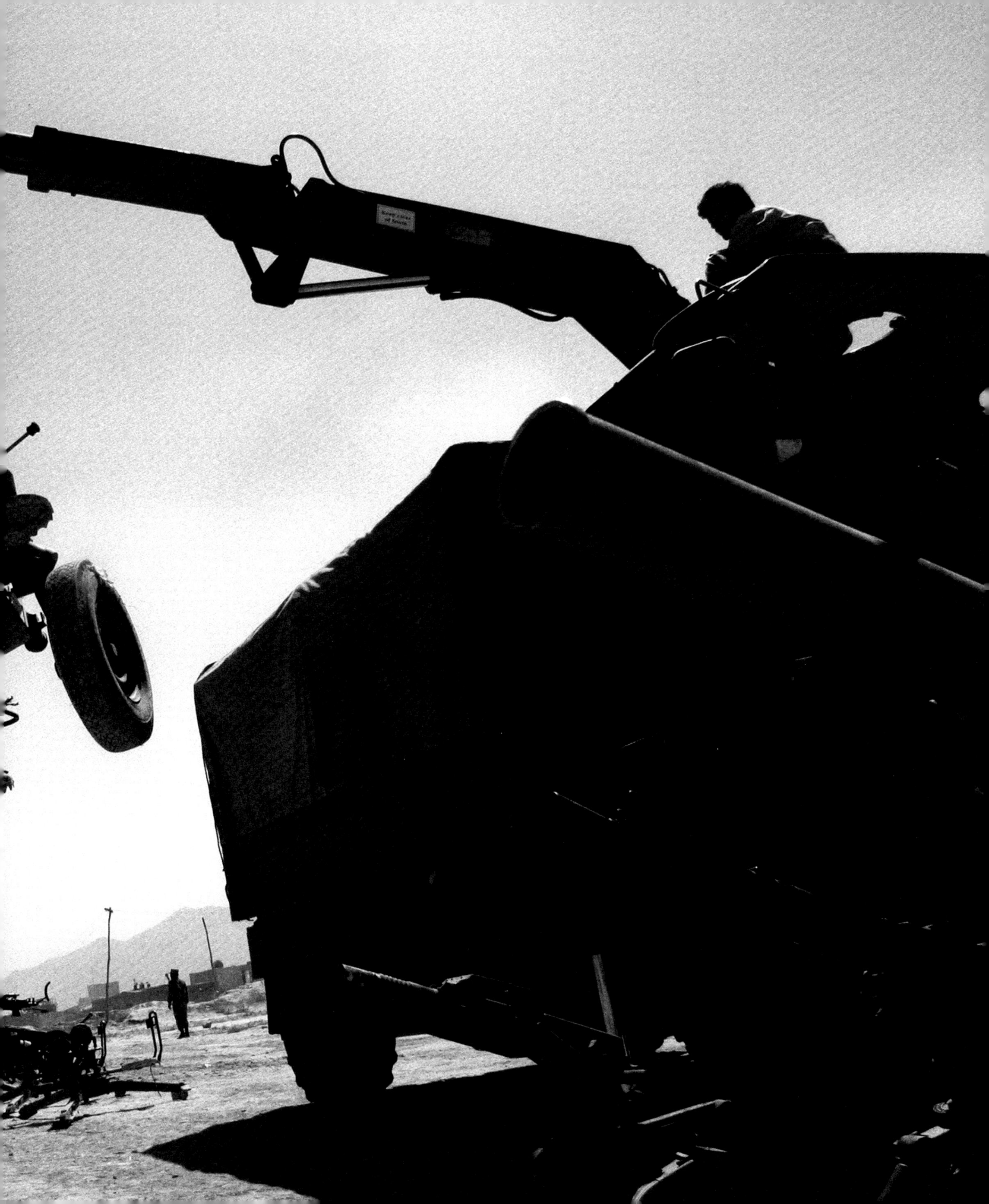

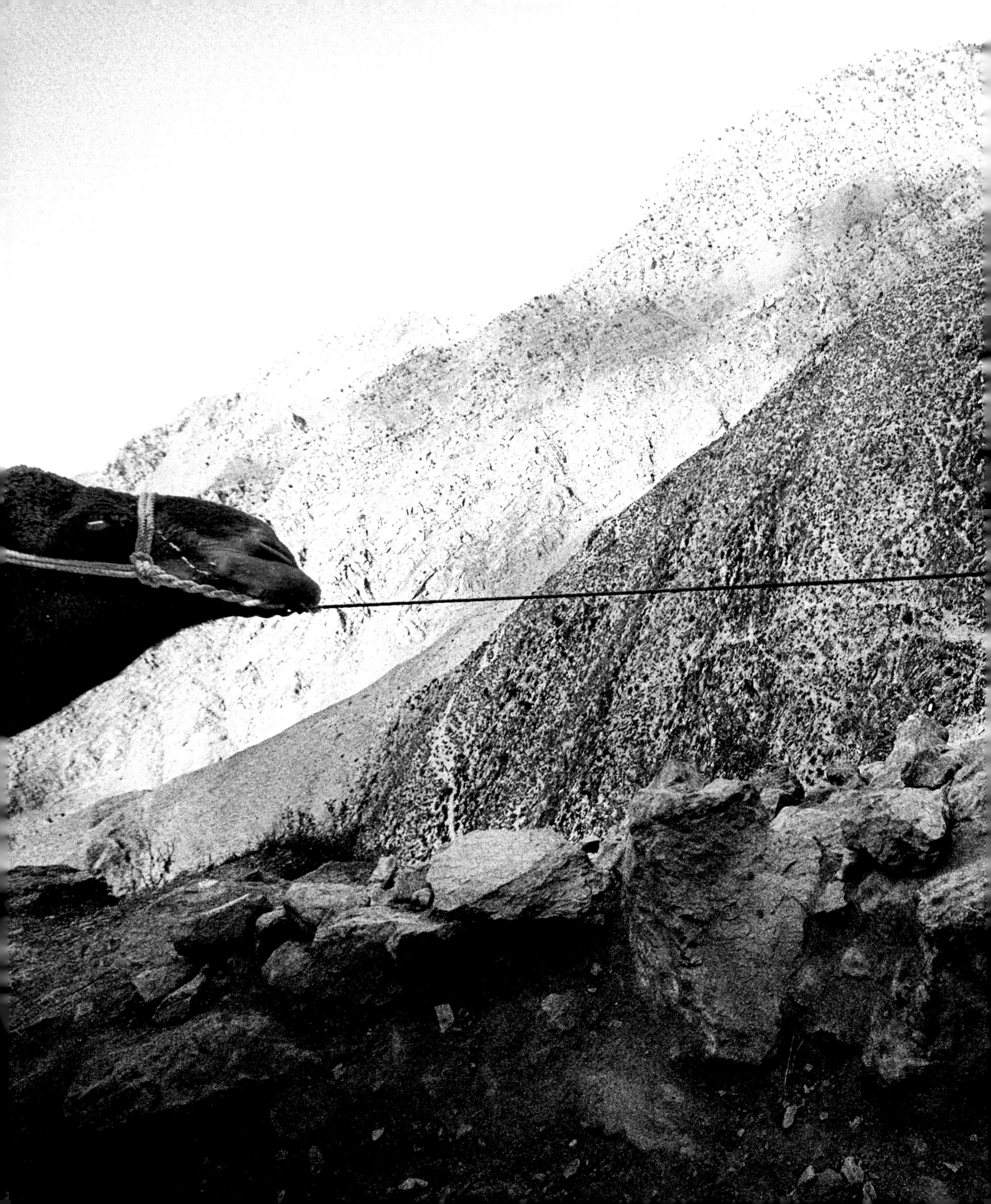

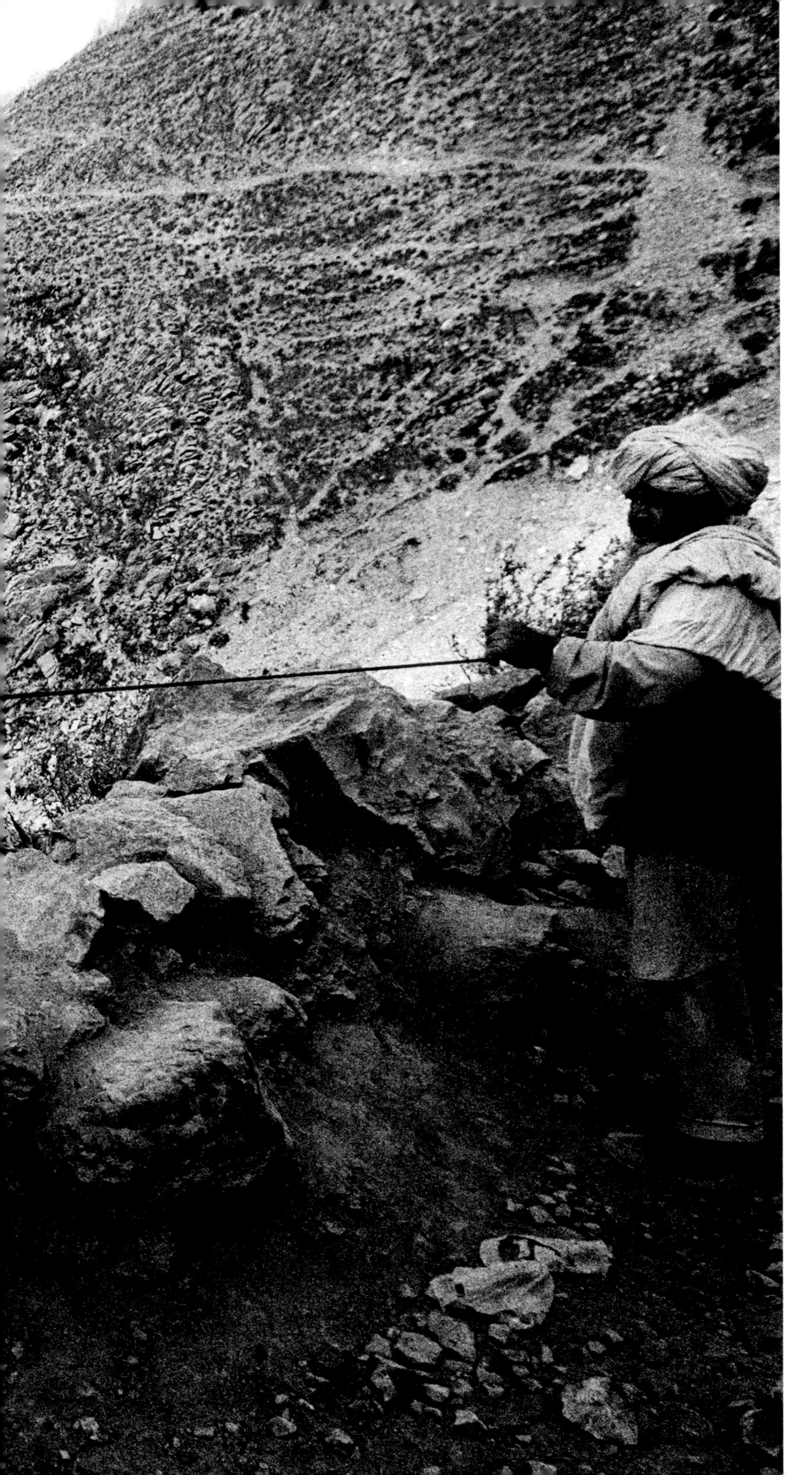

ABOVE JANGORA, NANGRAHAR PROVINCE:
APRIL 2005
The village borders the untamed tribal areas
of the North West Frontier Province. It is a
smuggling base from which drugs, weapons and
vehicle parts are carried through the mountains
using the caravan and donkey trails.

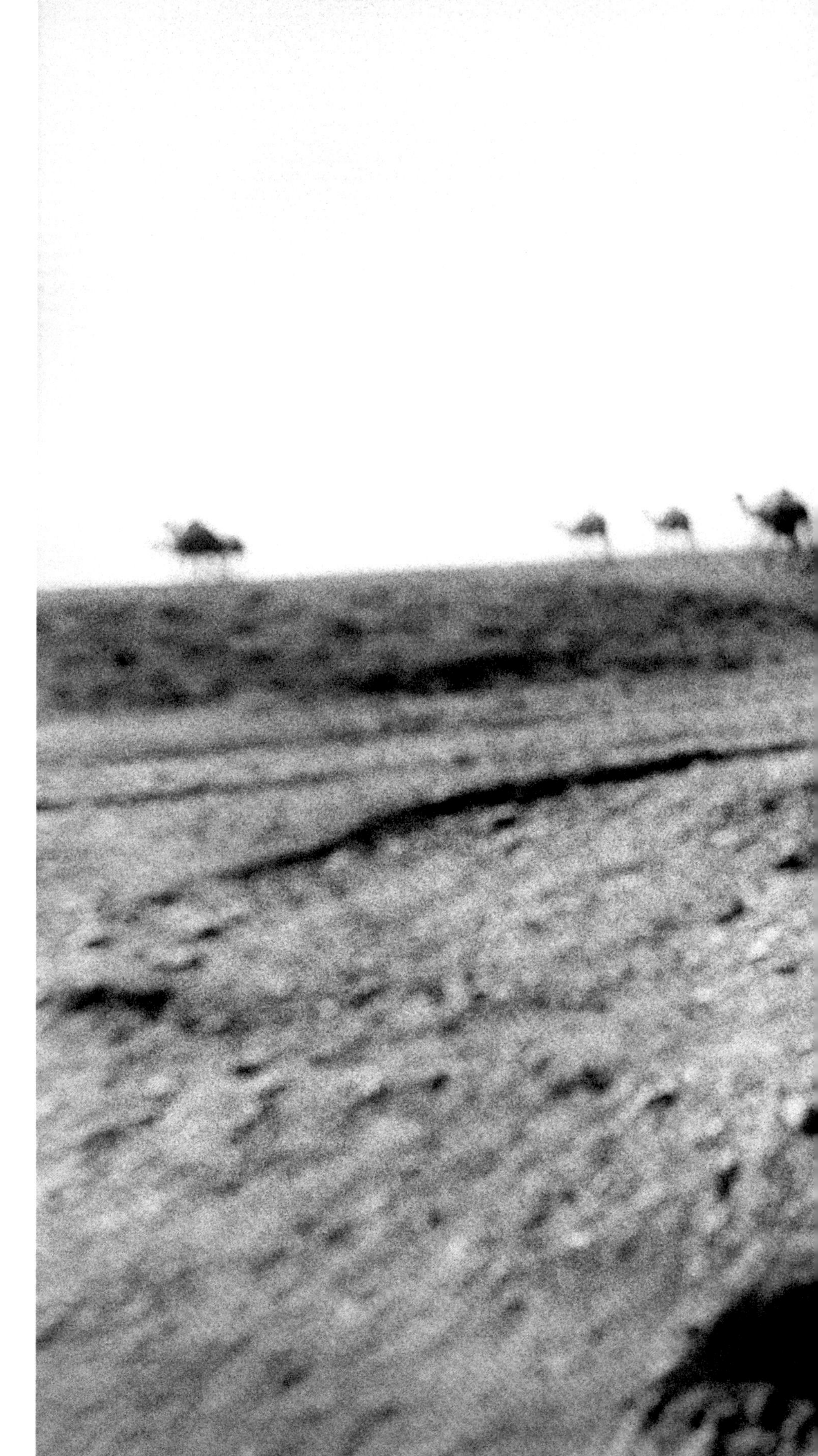

PLAINS OF HERAT, HERAT PROVINCE: JUNE 2003
Camel-herder Ajnabi Gul (Strange Flower) is
eight years old. The wind and sun on the plains
outside Herat are ferocious.

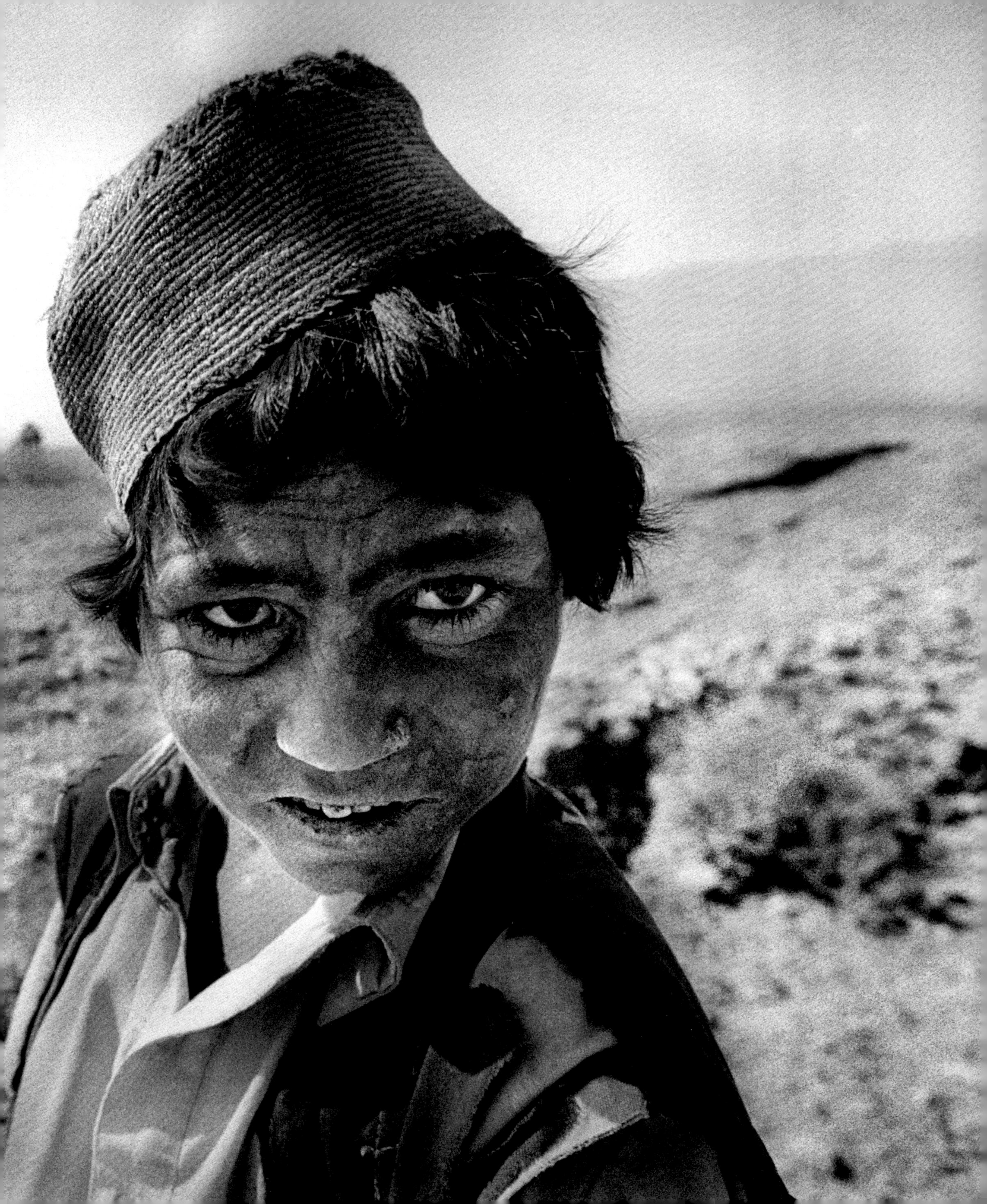

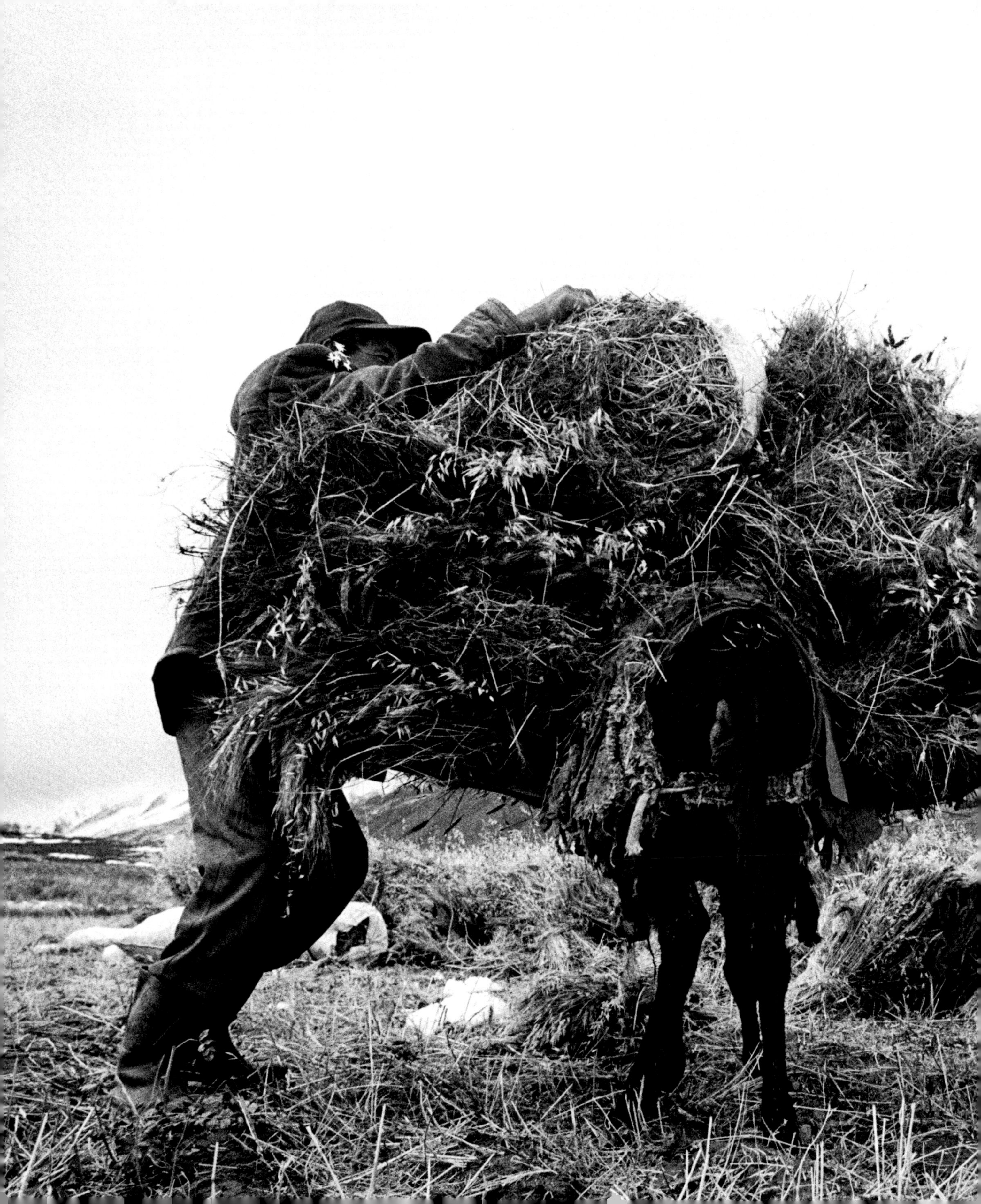

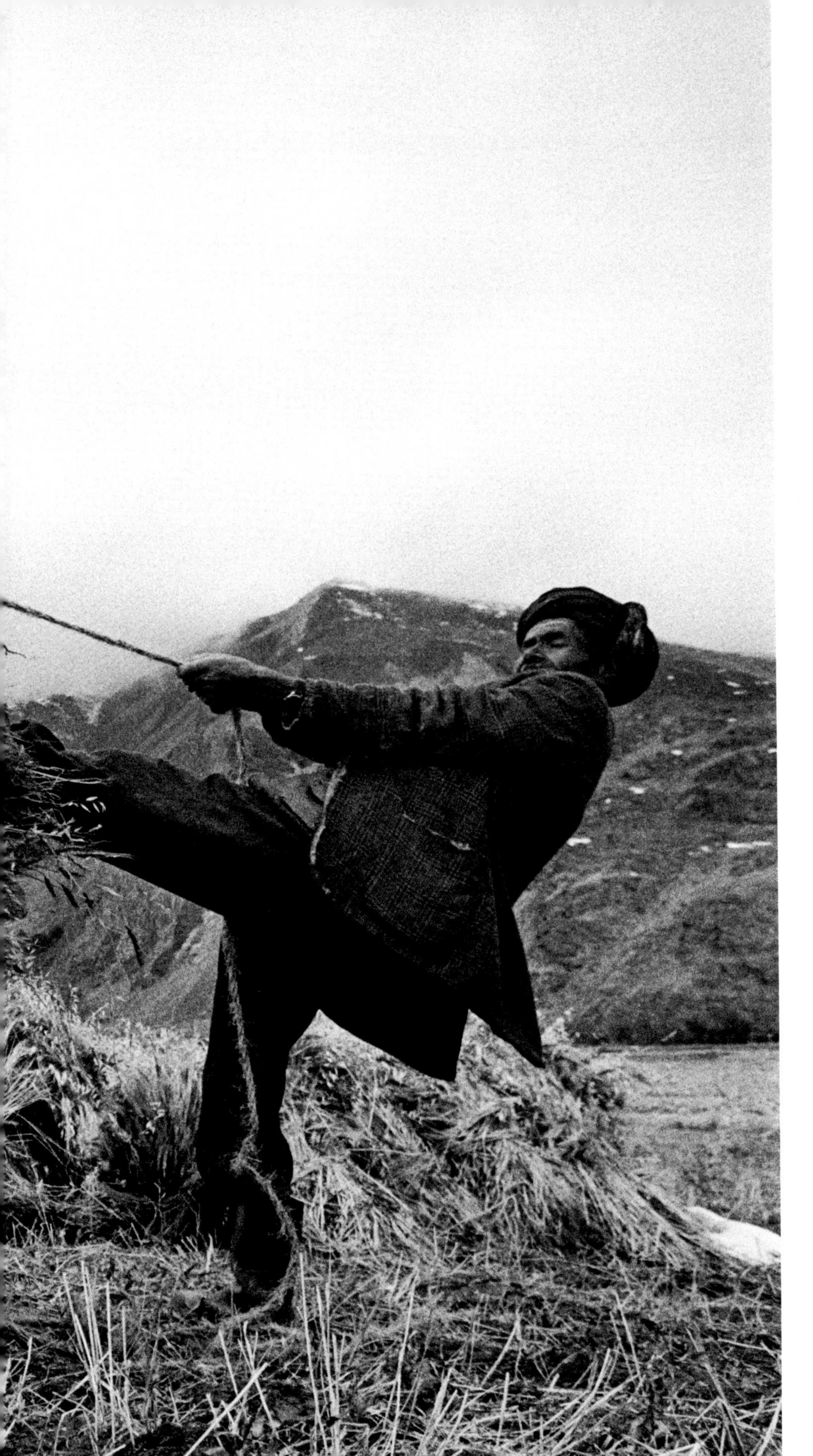

ISHKASHEM, BADAKHSHAN PROVINCE: NOVEMBER 2004
A farmer and his son loading a donkey.

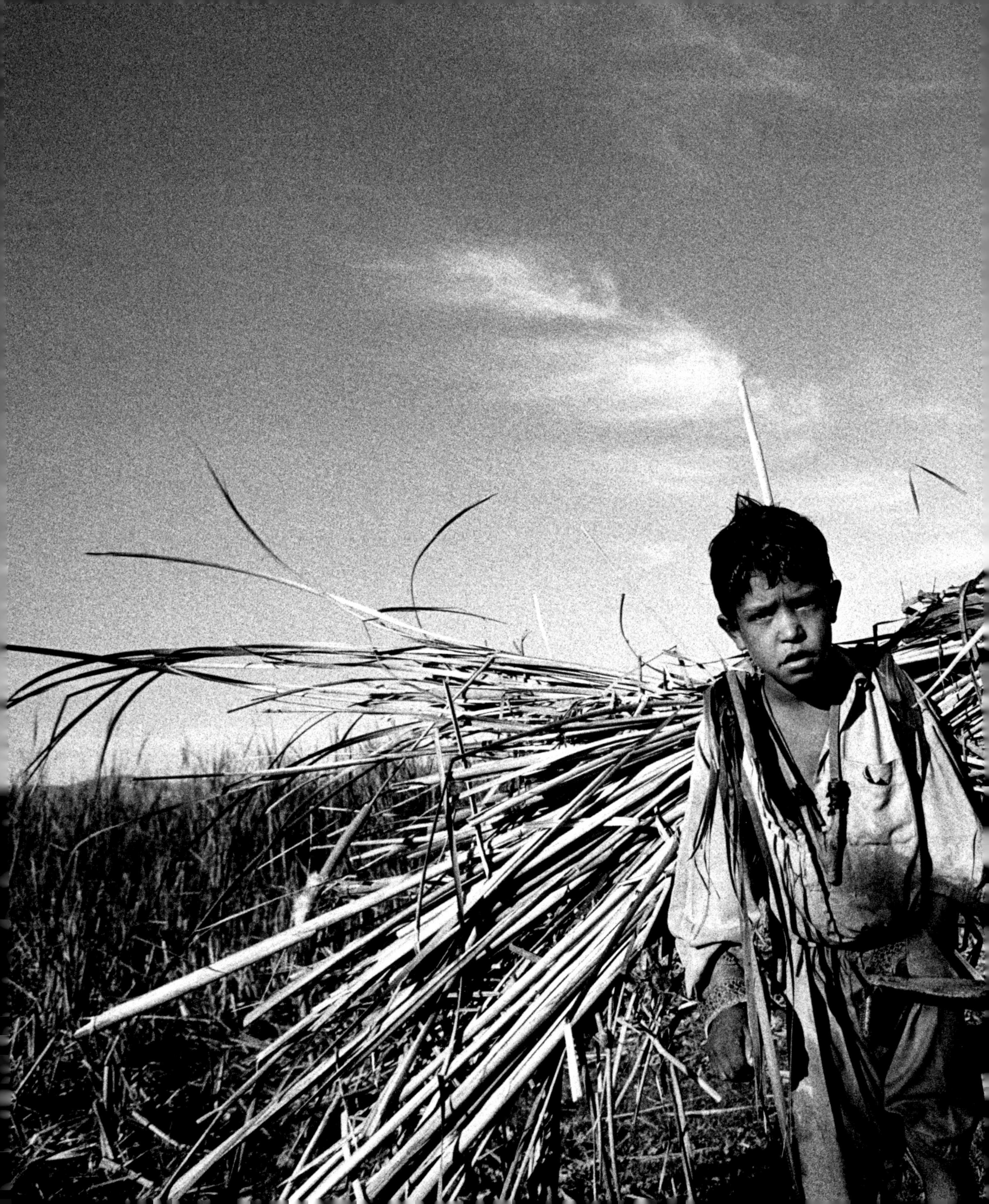

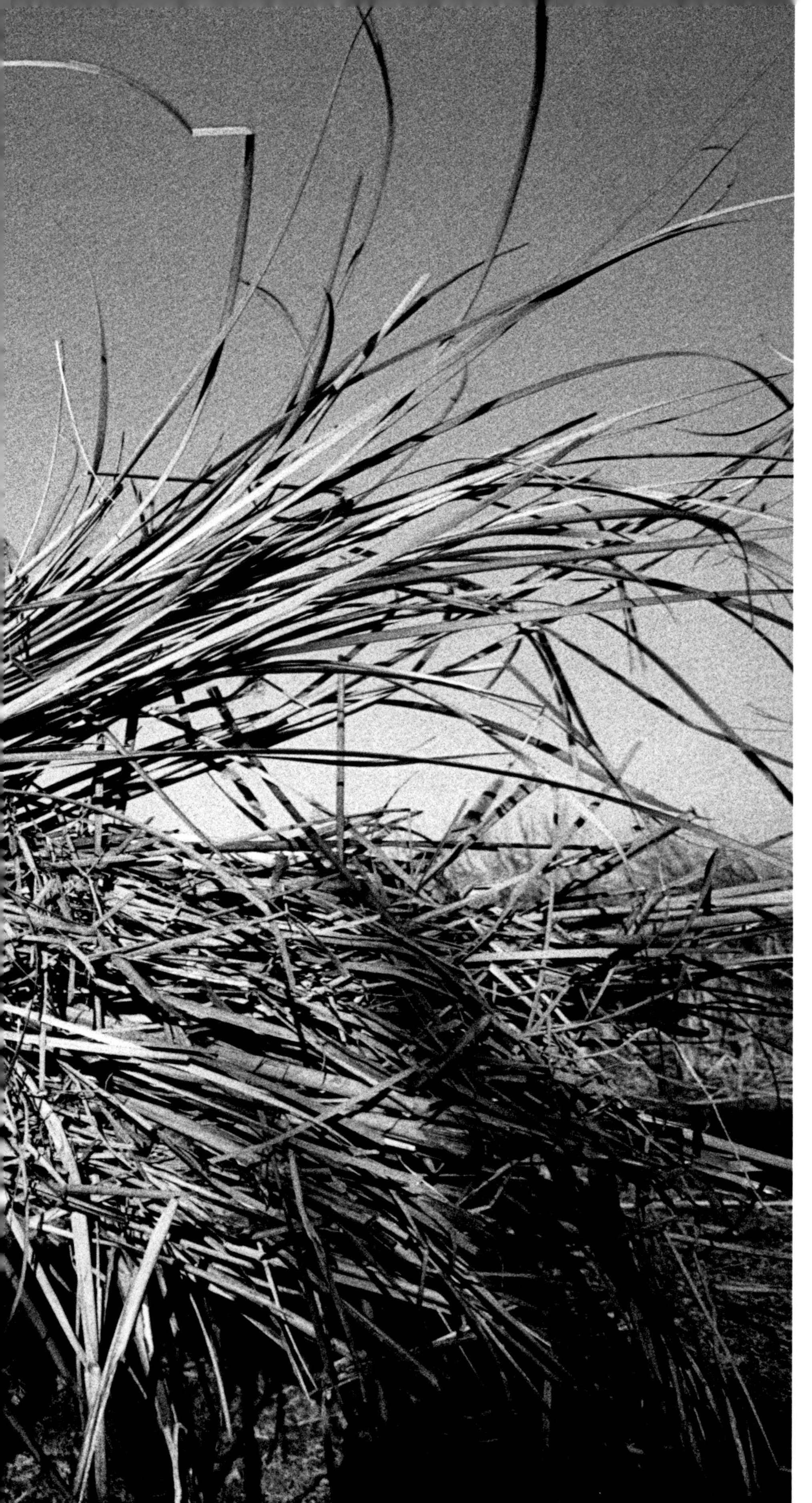

Near Jalalabad, Nangrahar Province:
October 2004
A Kuchi boy gathers rushes from the marshy
verges of the riverbank. The Kuchi are nomadic
people and in this area of Afghanistan spend
winters in the warmth of the area around
Jalalabad, and summer in the relative comfort
of the plains around Kabul.

Deh Qazi, Balkh Province: November 2004
Farm workers harvesting crops.

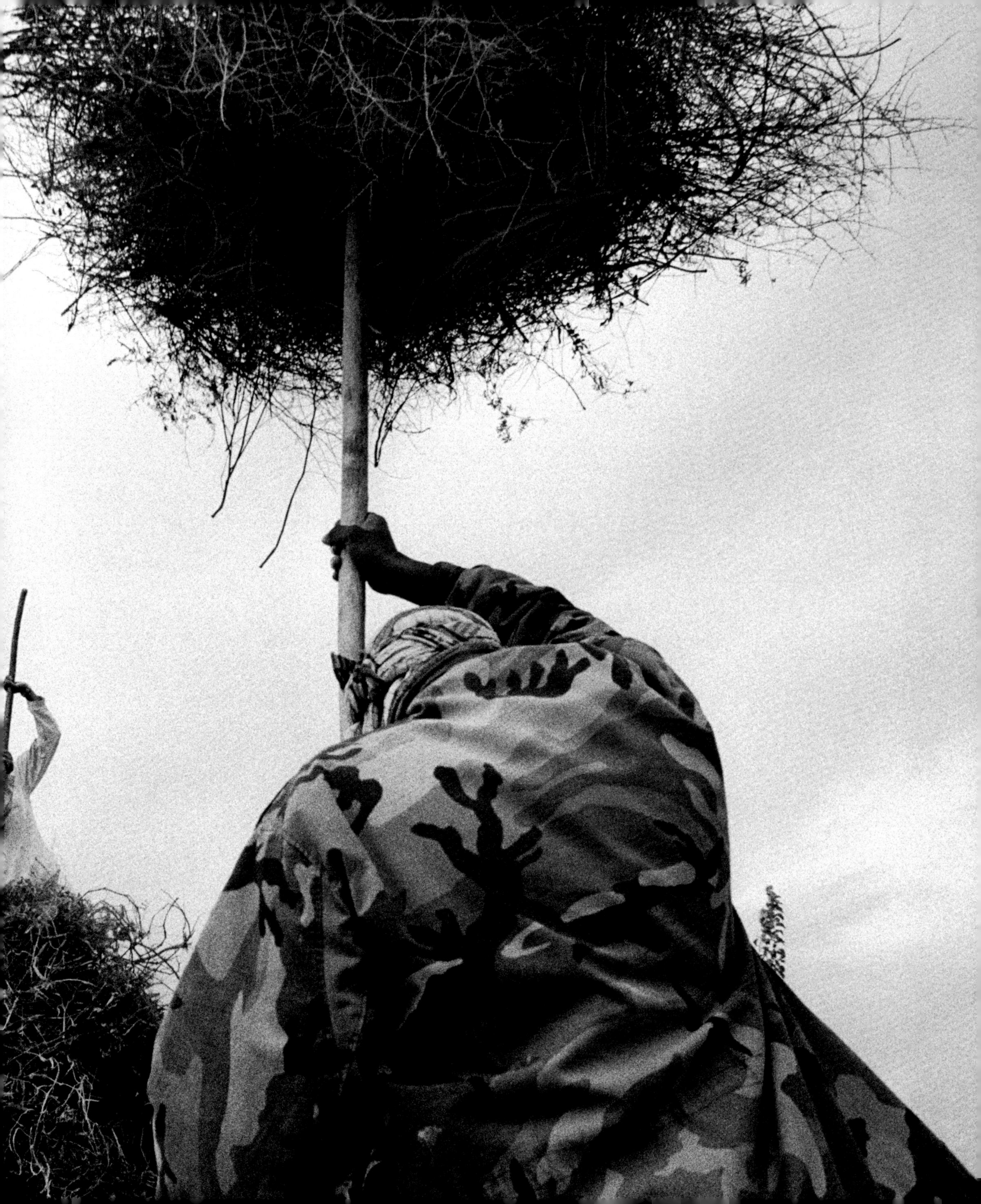

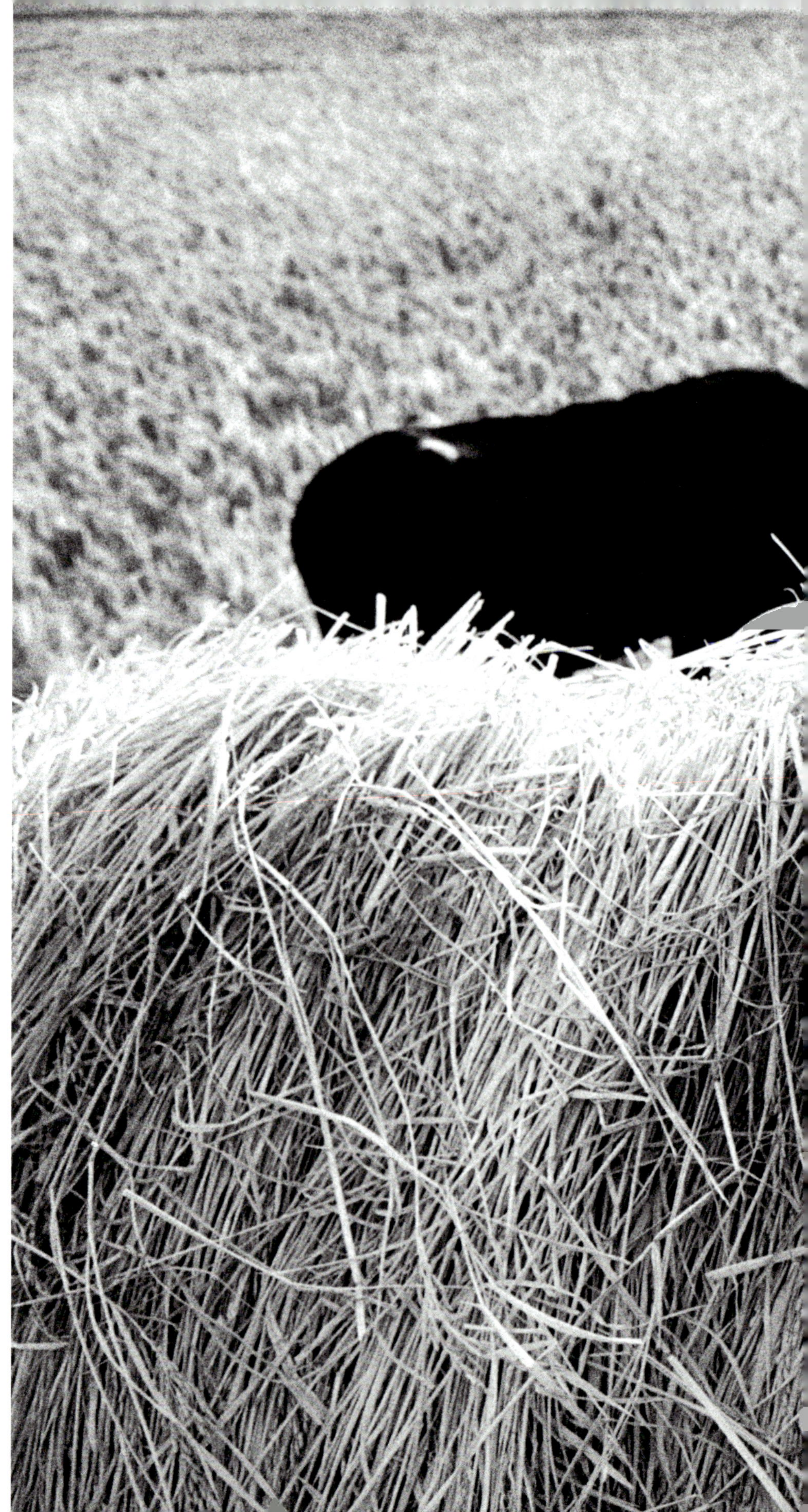

TALOQAN, TAKHAR PROVINCE: NOVEMBER 2004
An Uzbek farmer relaxes in the fields at the end
of a day's harvest.

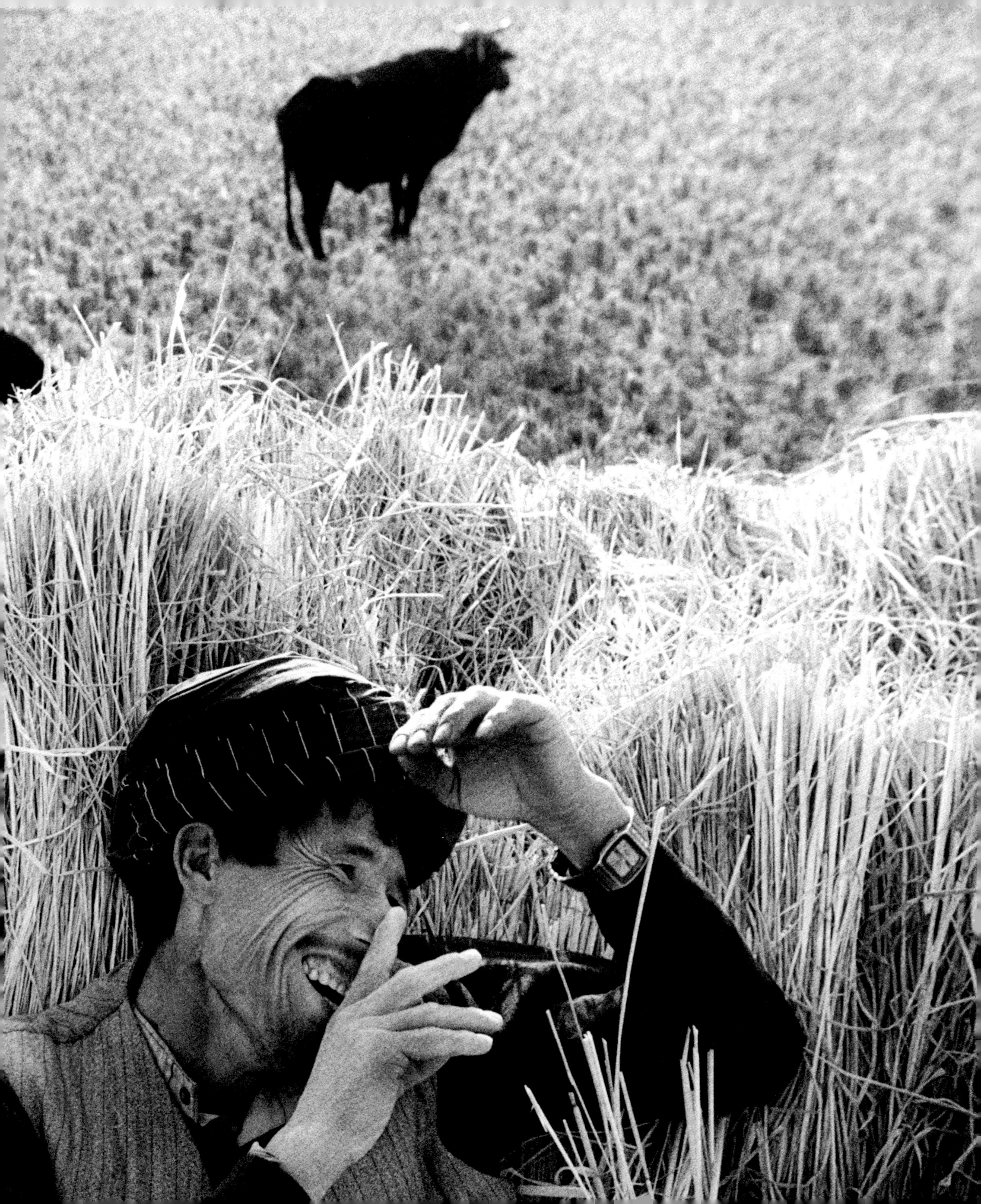

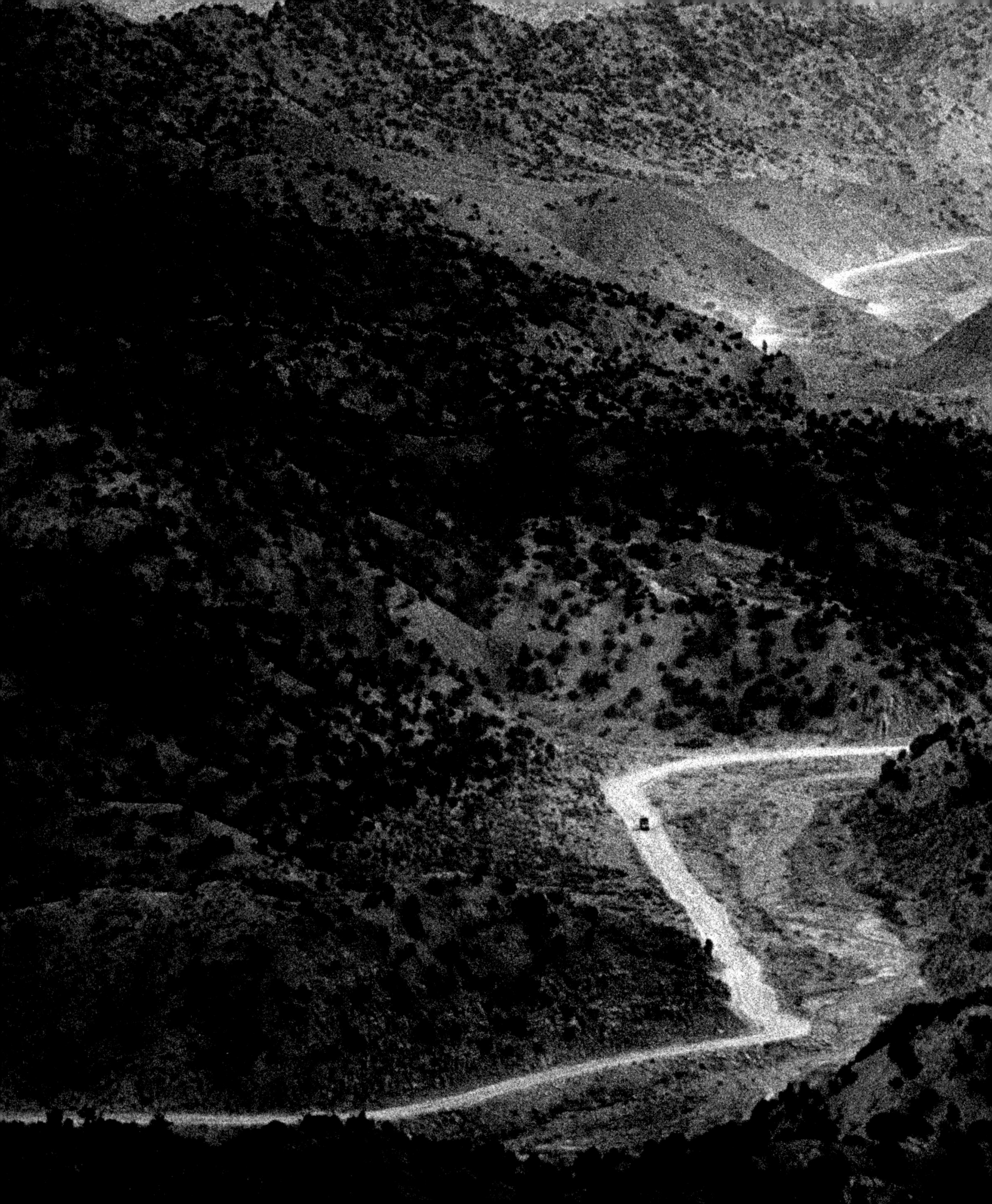

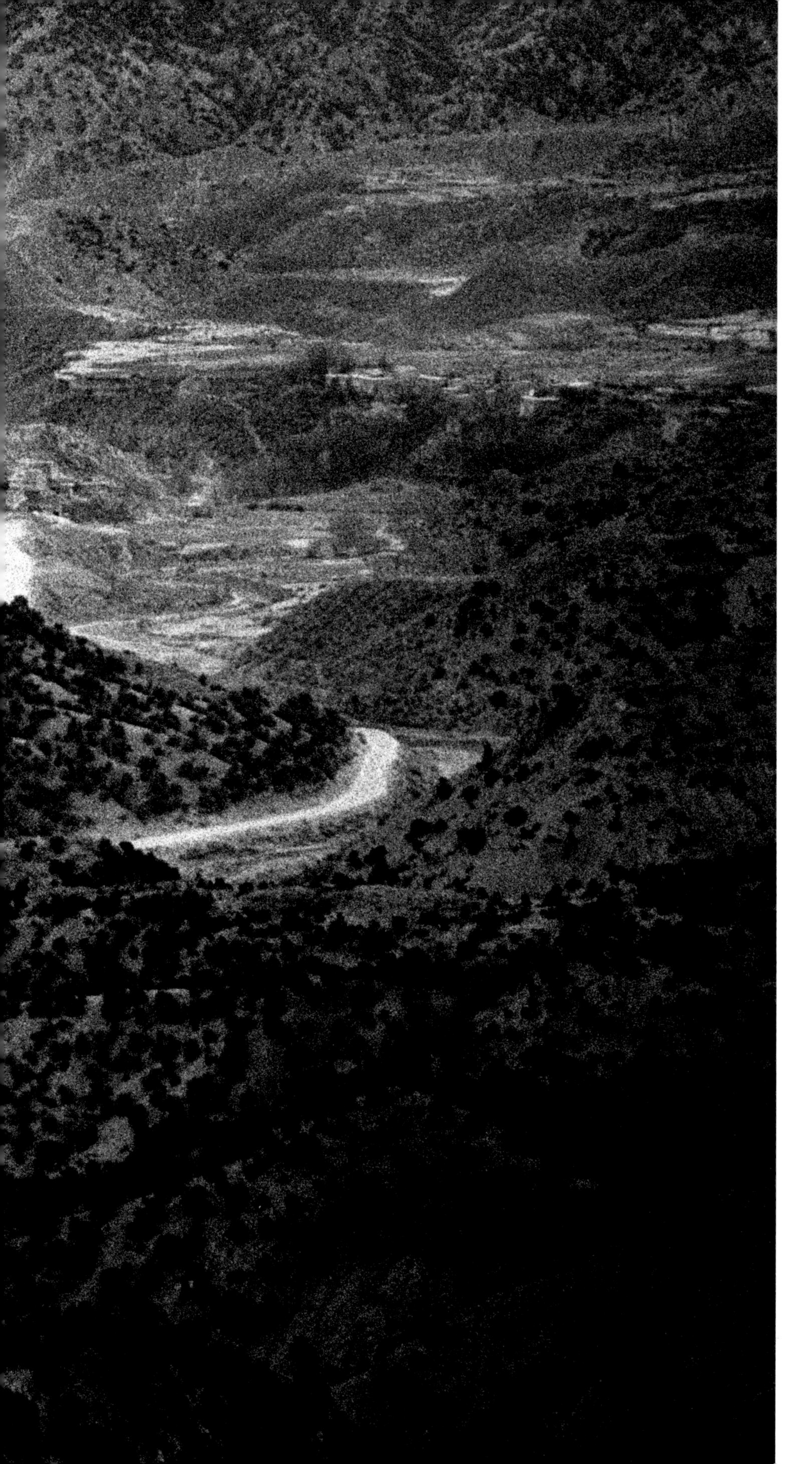

PAKTIA PROVINCE: DECEMBER 2002
The road leading to Khost and the Pakistan
border. This route – Kabul, Gardez, Khost – was
taken by the fleeing Taliban after the fall of Kabul
in November 2001.

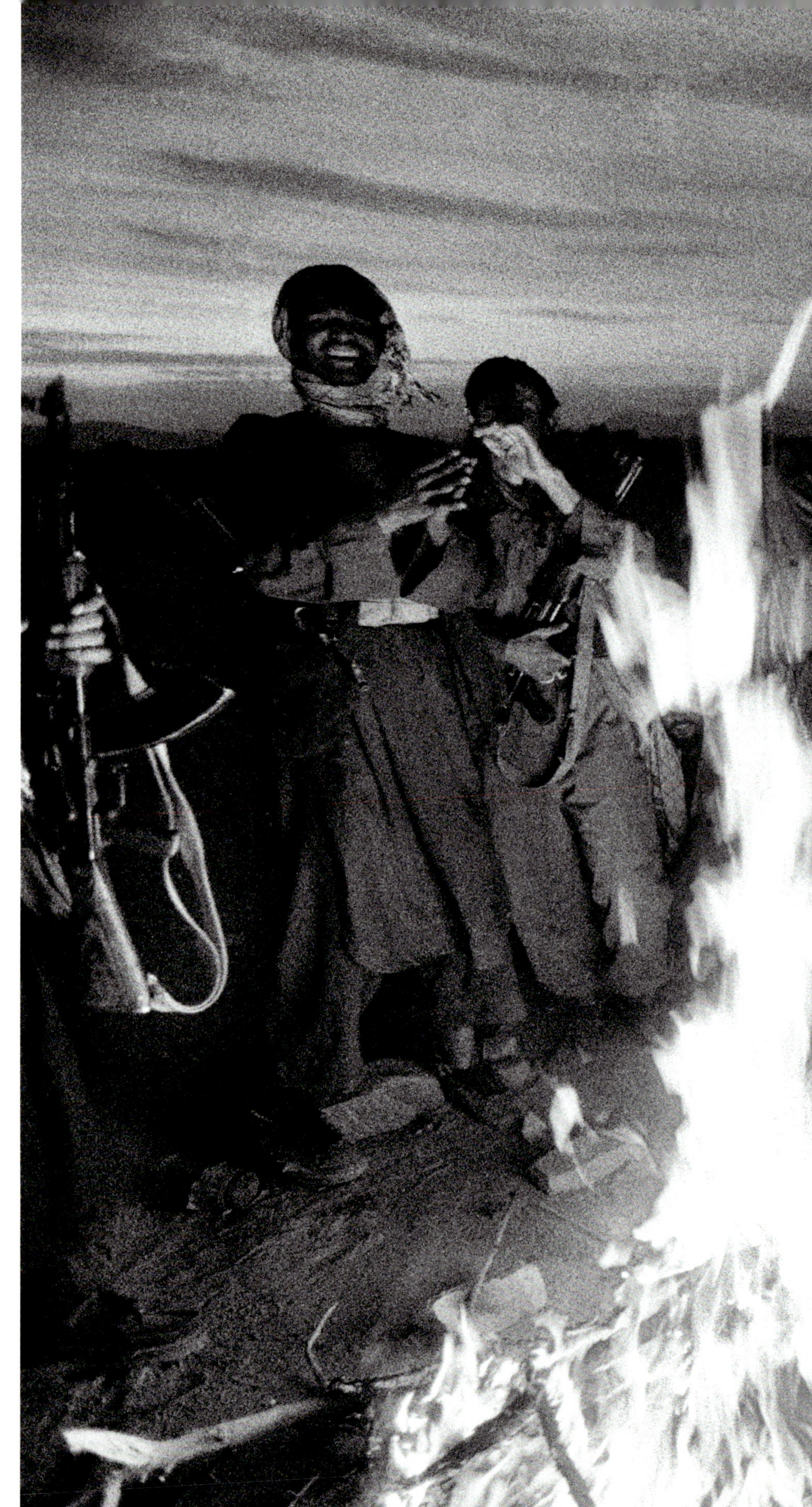

QARABAGH, KABUL: 13 NOVEMBER 2001
Soldiers tasting victory in the early hours after their successful rout of the Taliban from their final defensive lines on the Shamali Plain.

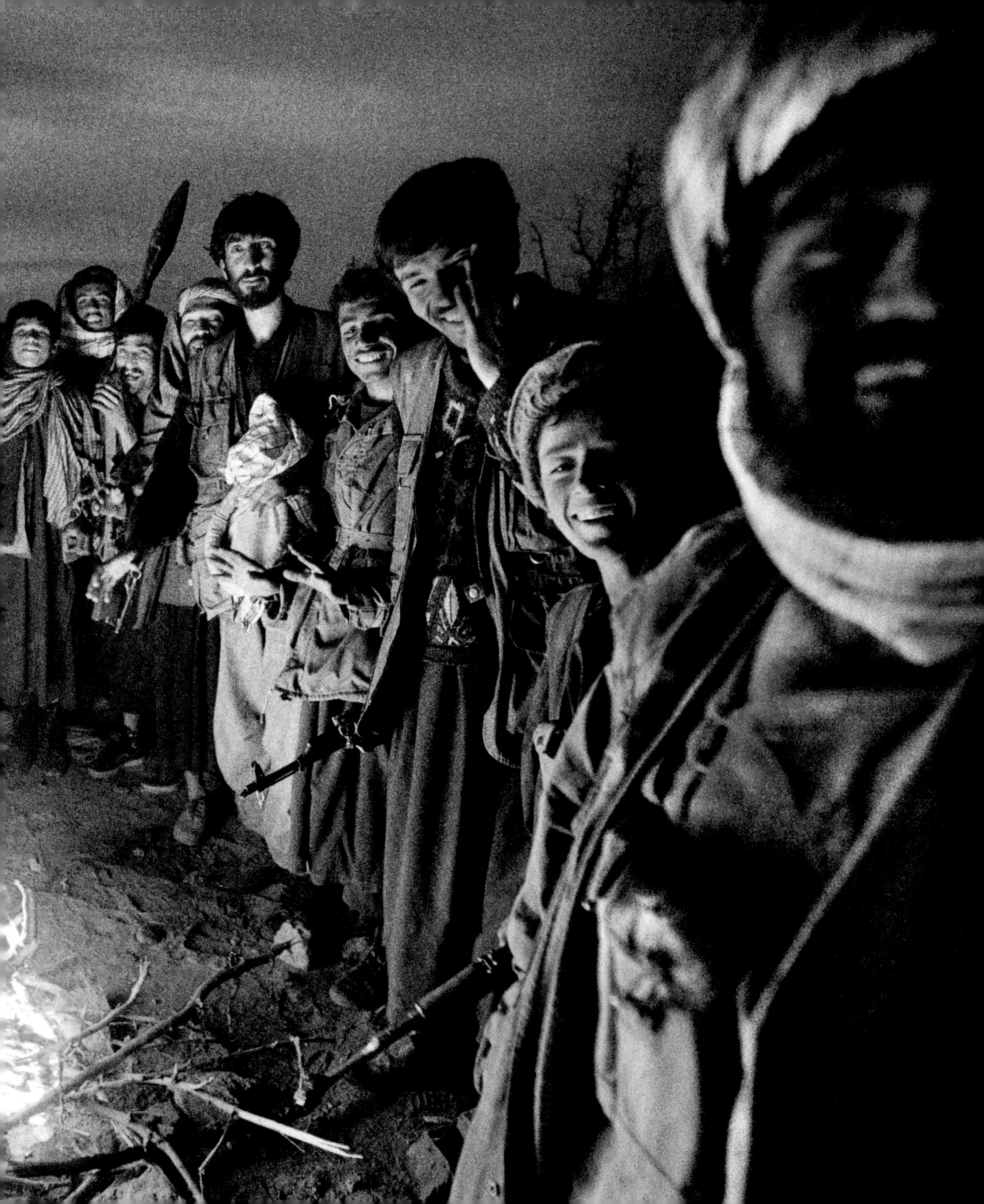

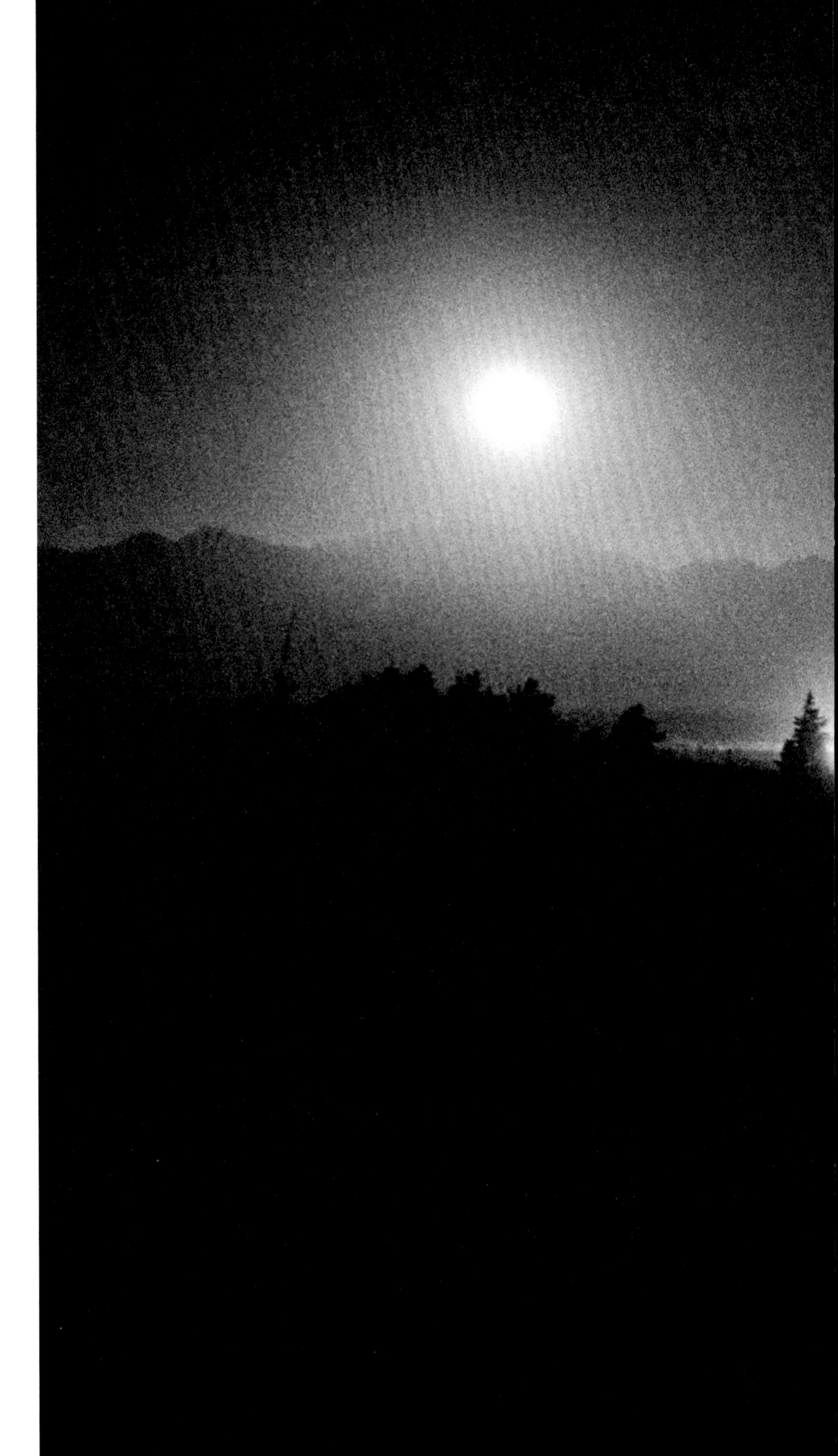

CHARIKAR, PARWAN PROVINCE: OCTOBER 2001
A Northern Alliance shell attacking a Taliban
frontline at night.

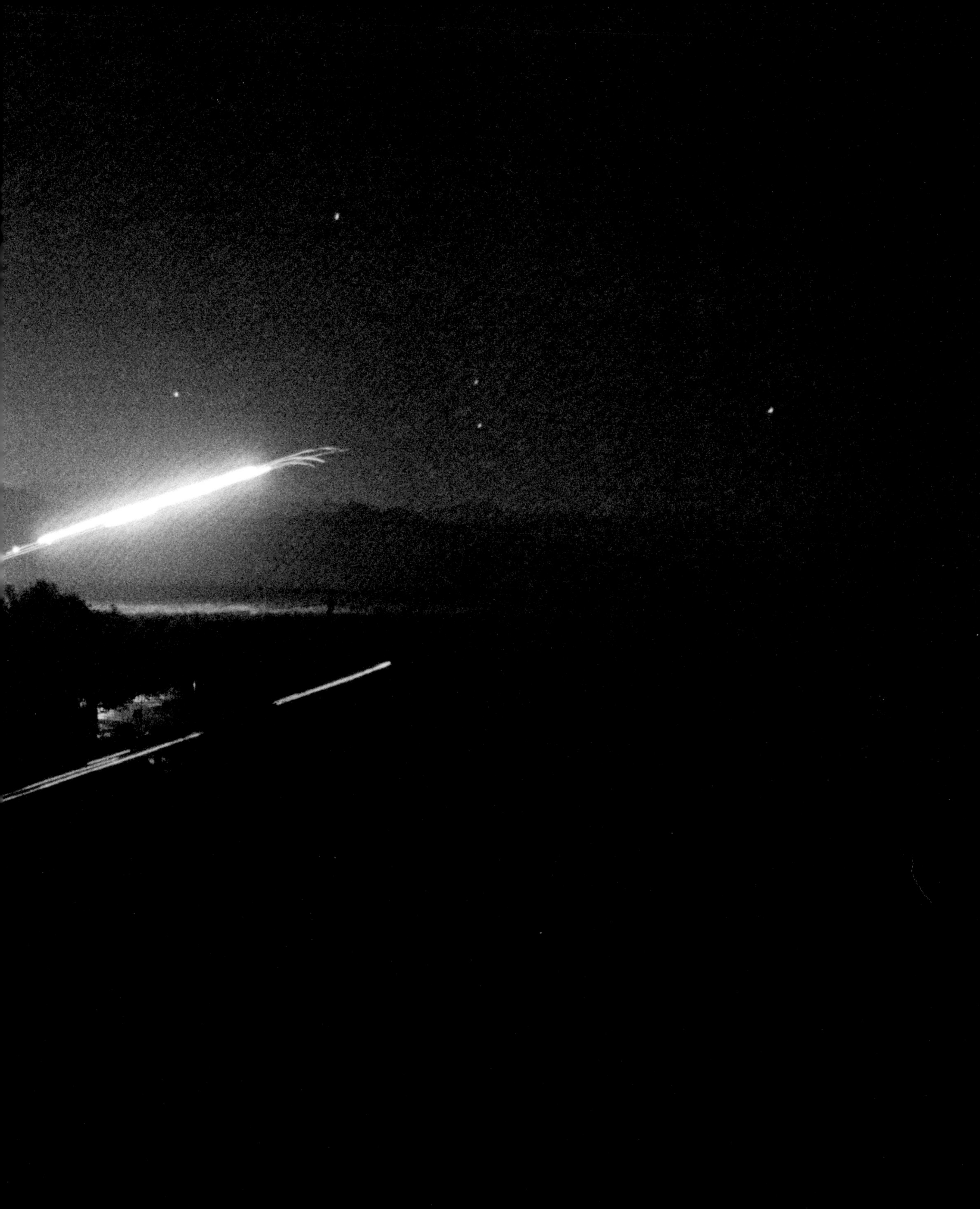

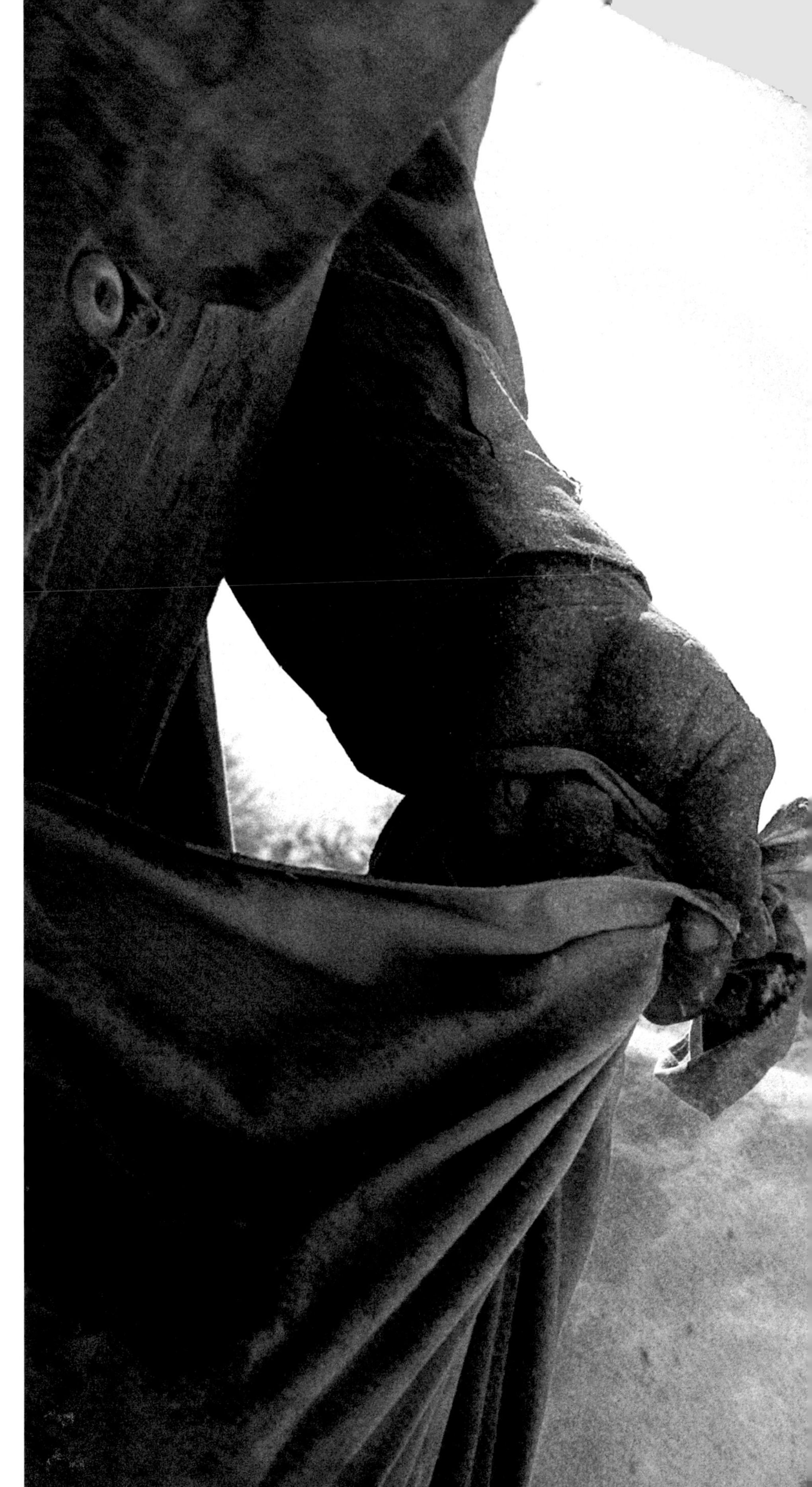

NANGRAHAR PROVINCE: AUGUST 2004
A farmer spreading poppy seed mixed
with earth.

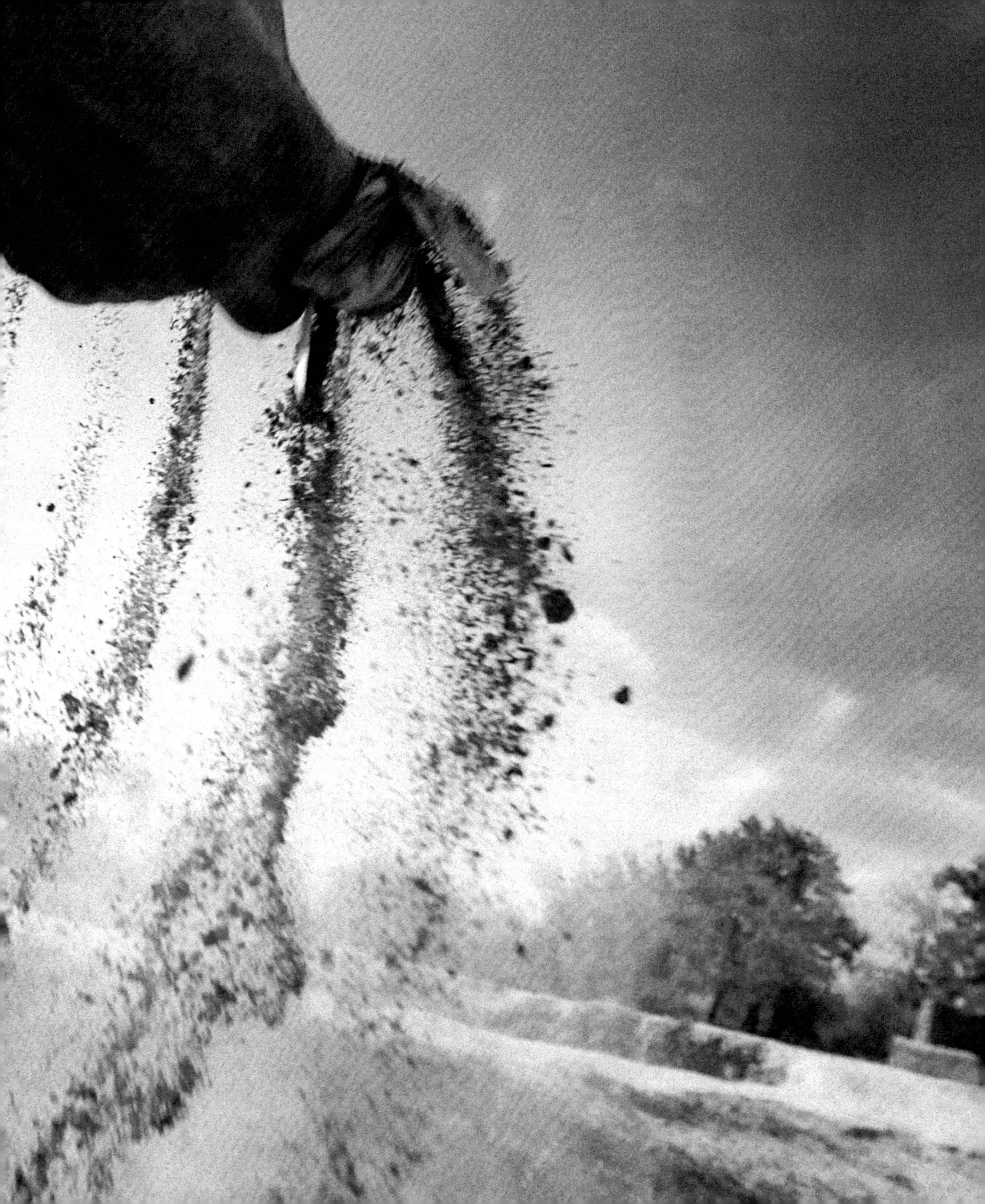

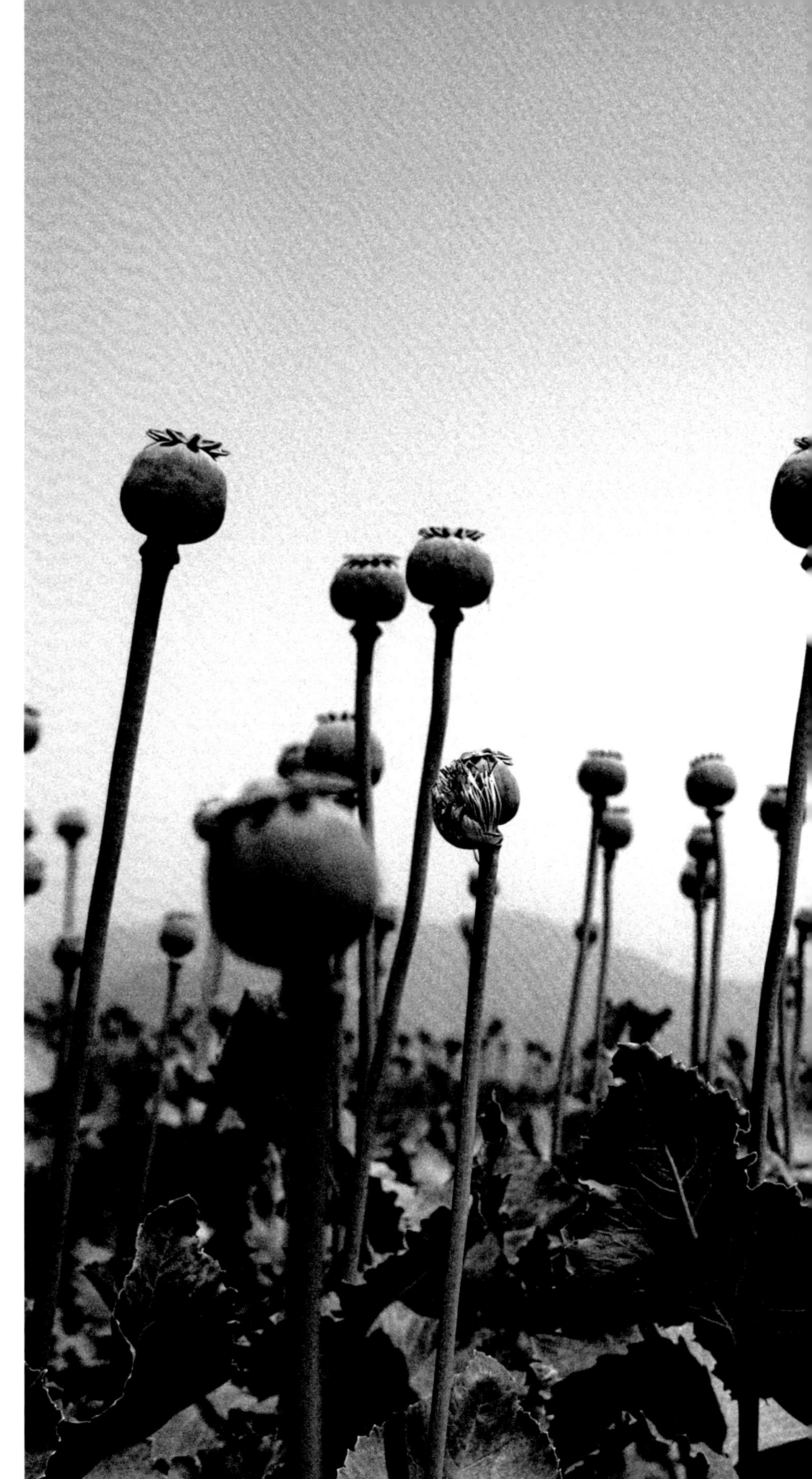

SHINWAR, NANGRAHAR PROVINCE: APRIL 2005
The poppy harvest.

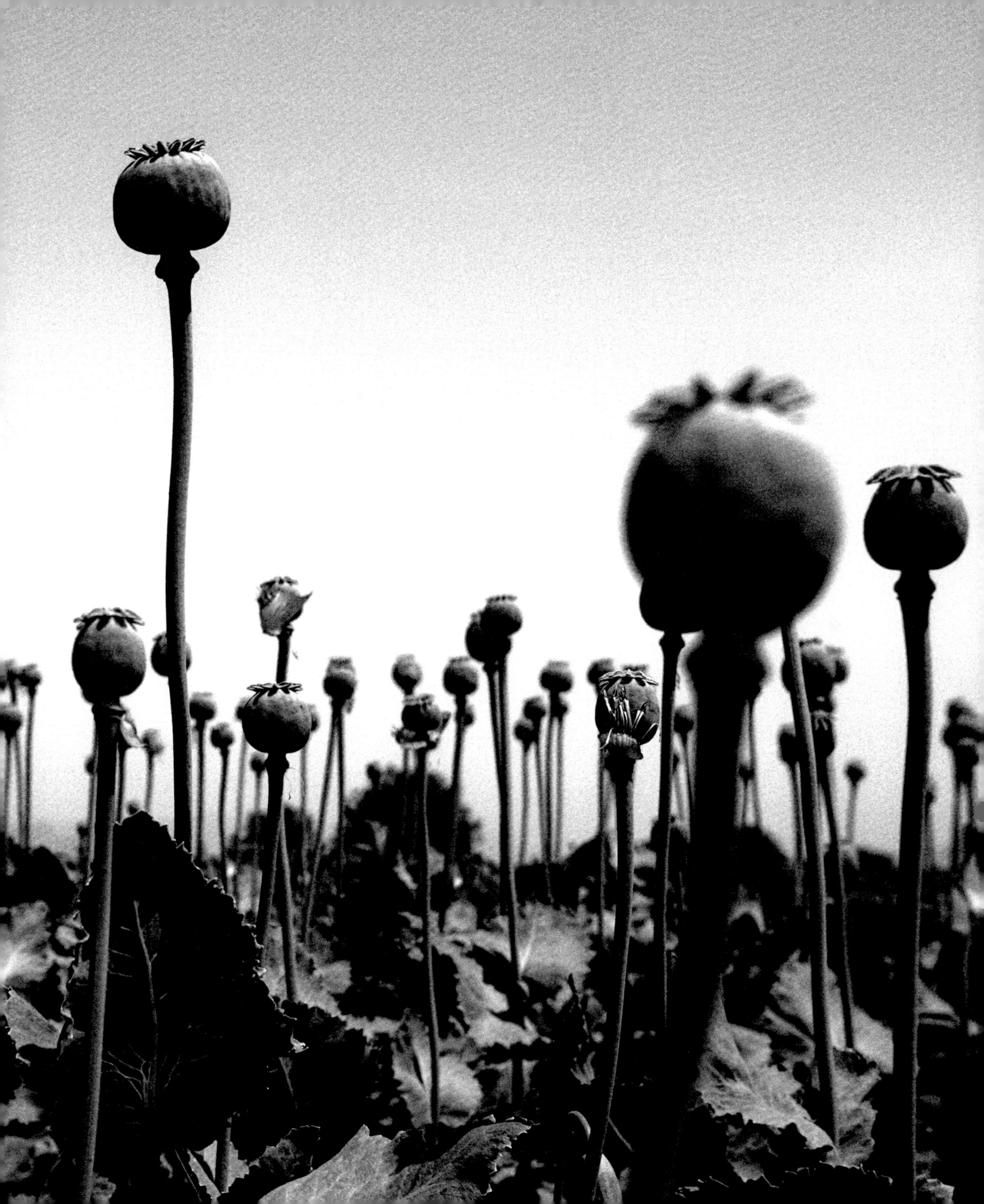

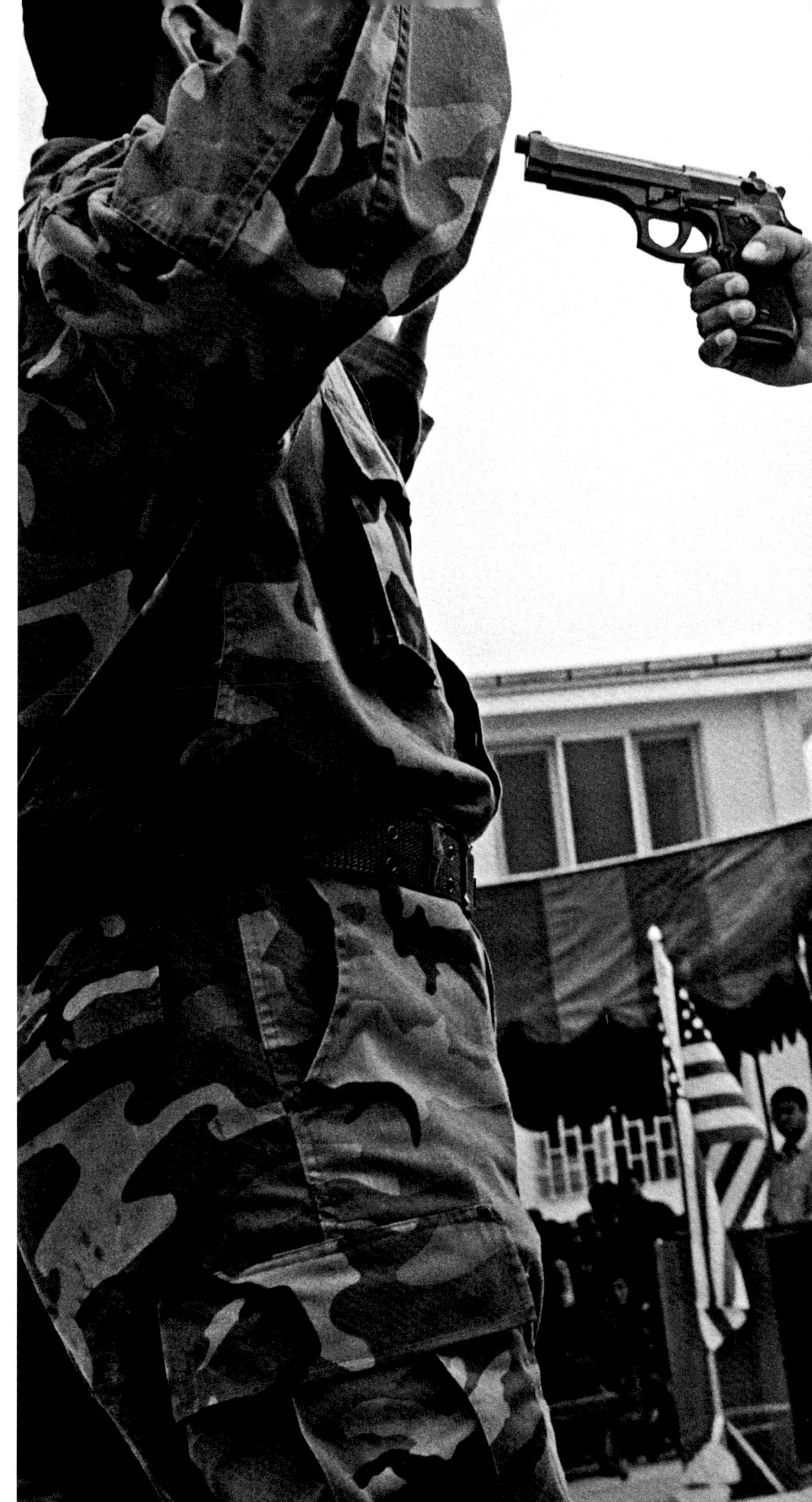

KABUL: APRIL 2005
A graduate demonstrates his skills at the
headquarters of the Counternarcotics Police of
Afghanistan (CNPA), where recruits are trained
by Blackwater, a US global security company.

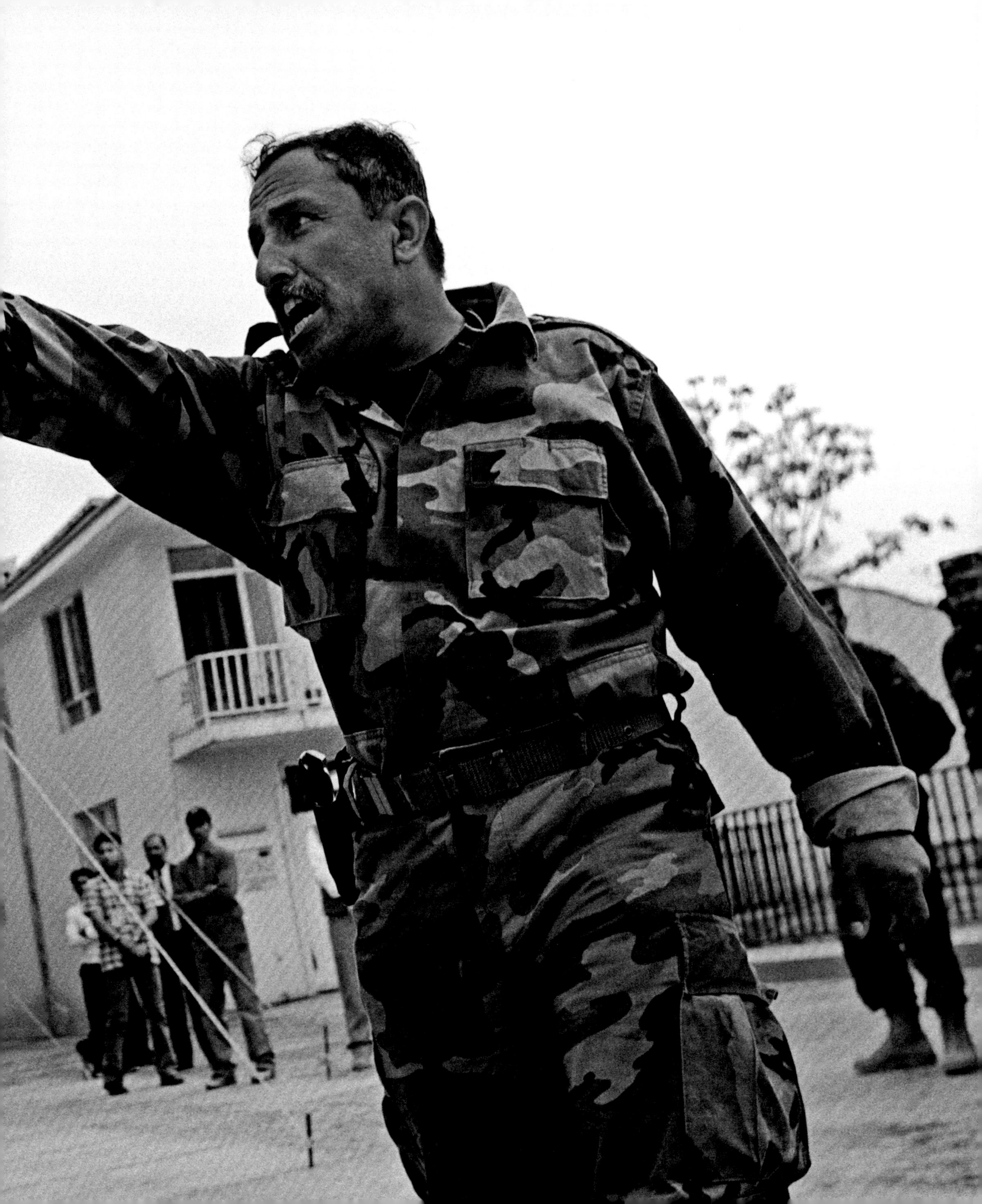

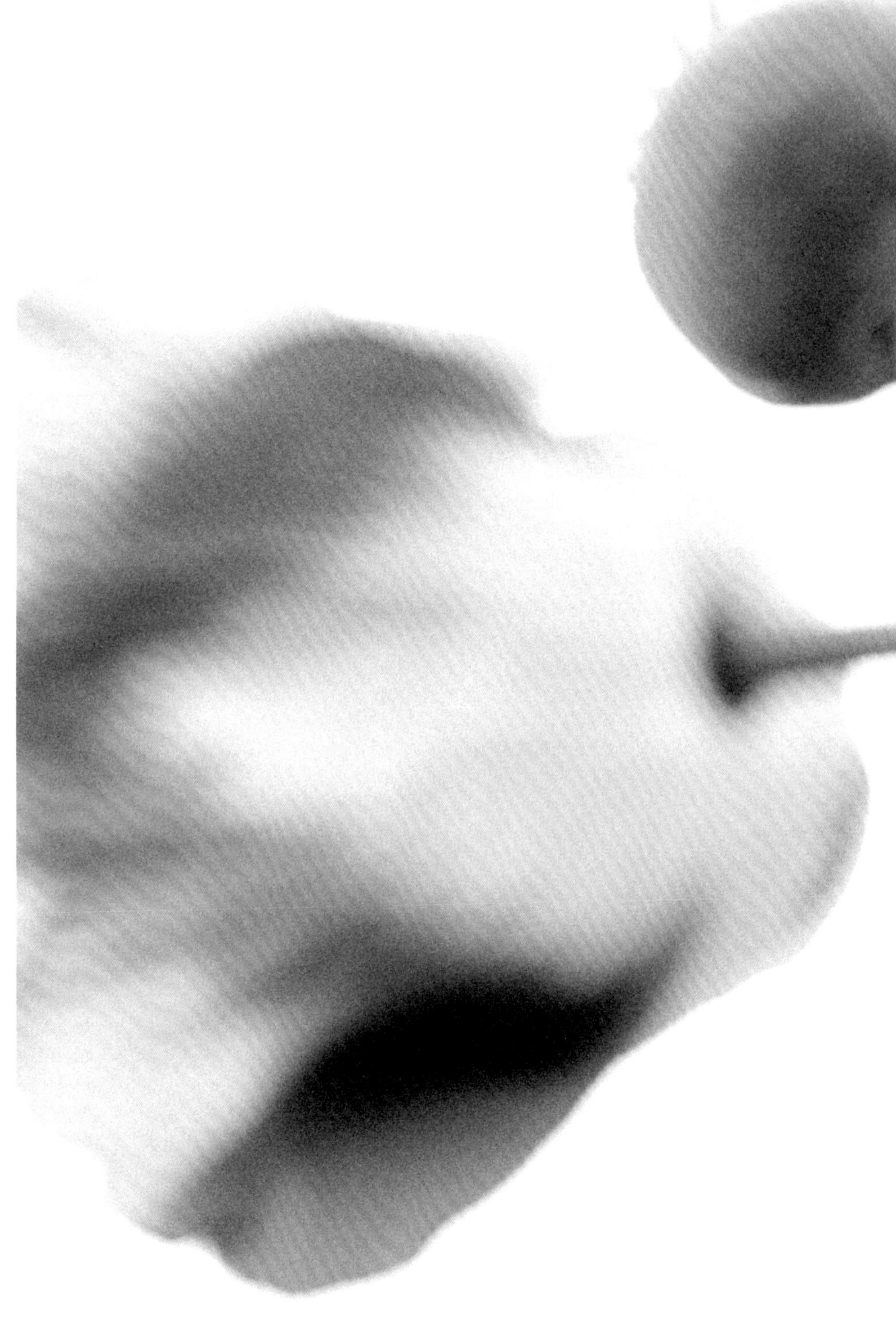

Nangrahar Province: April 2005
A young boy working in the poppy fields.

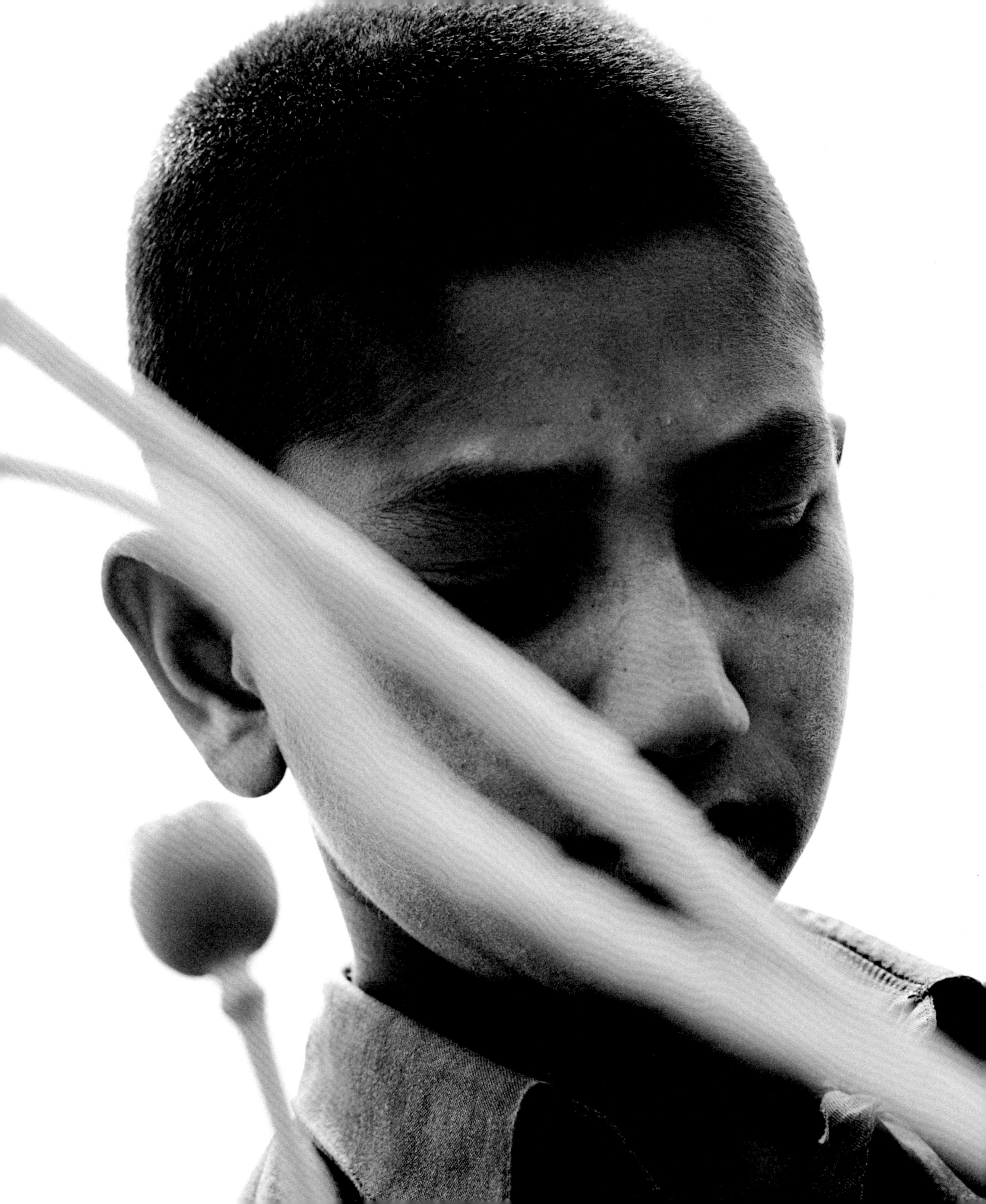

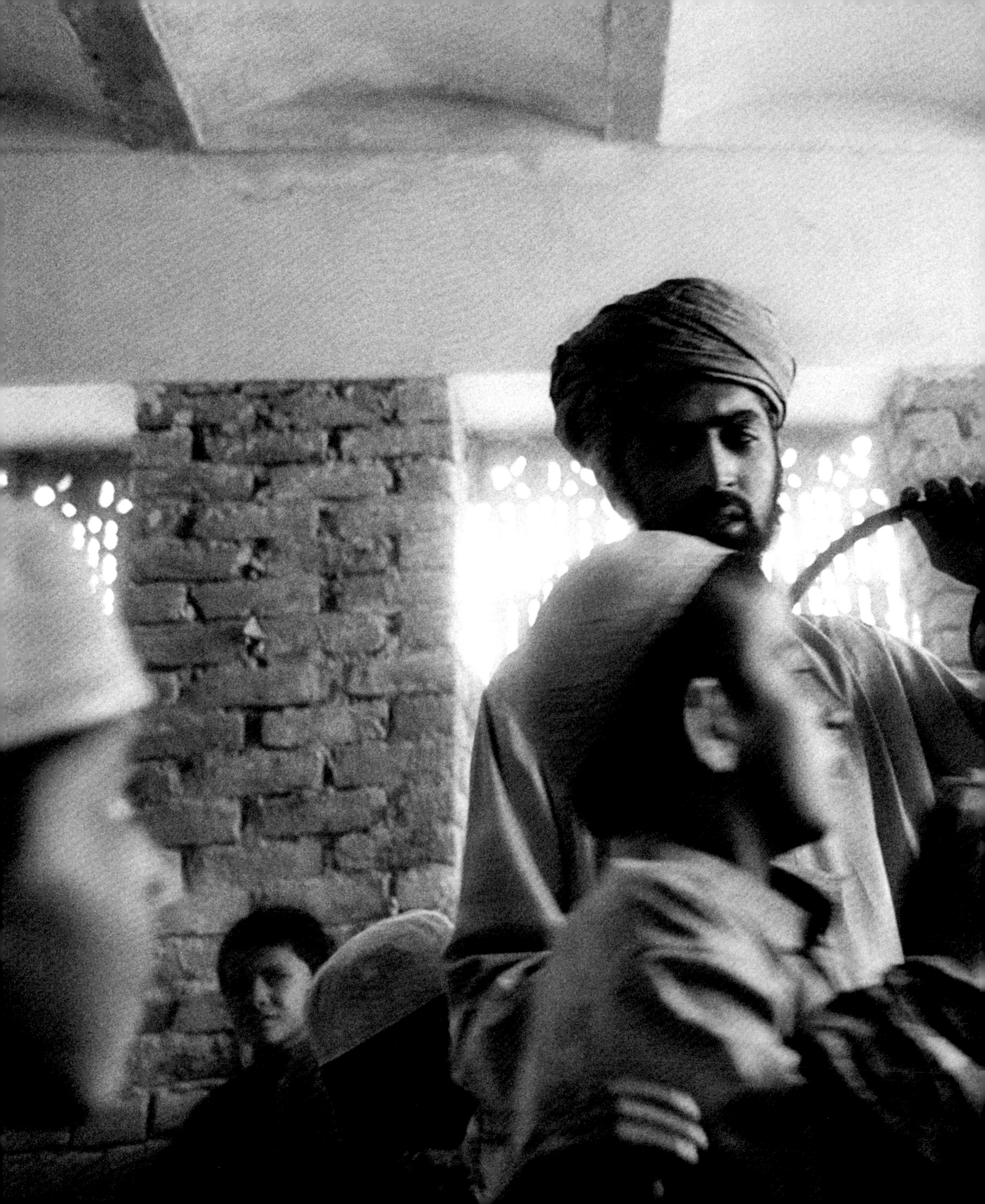

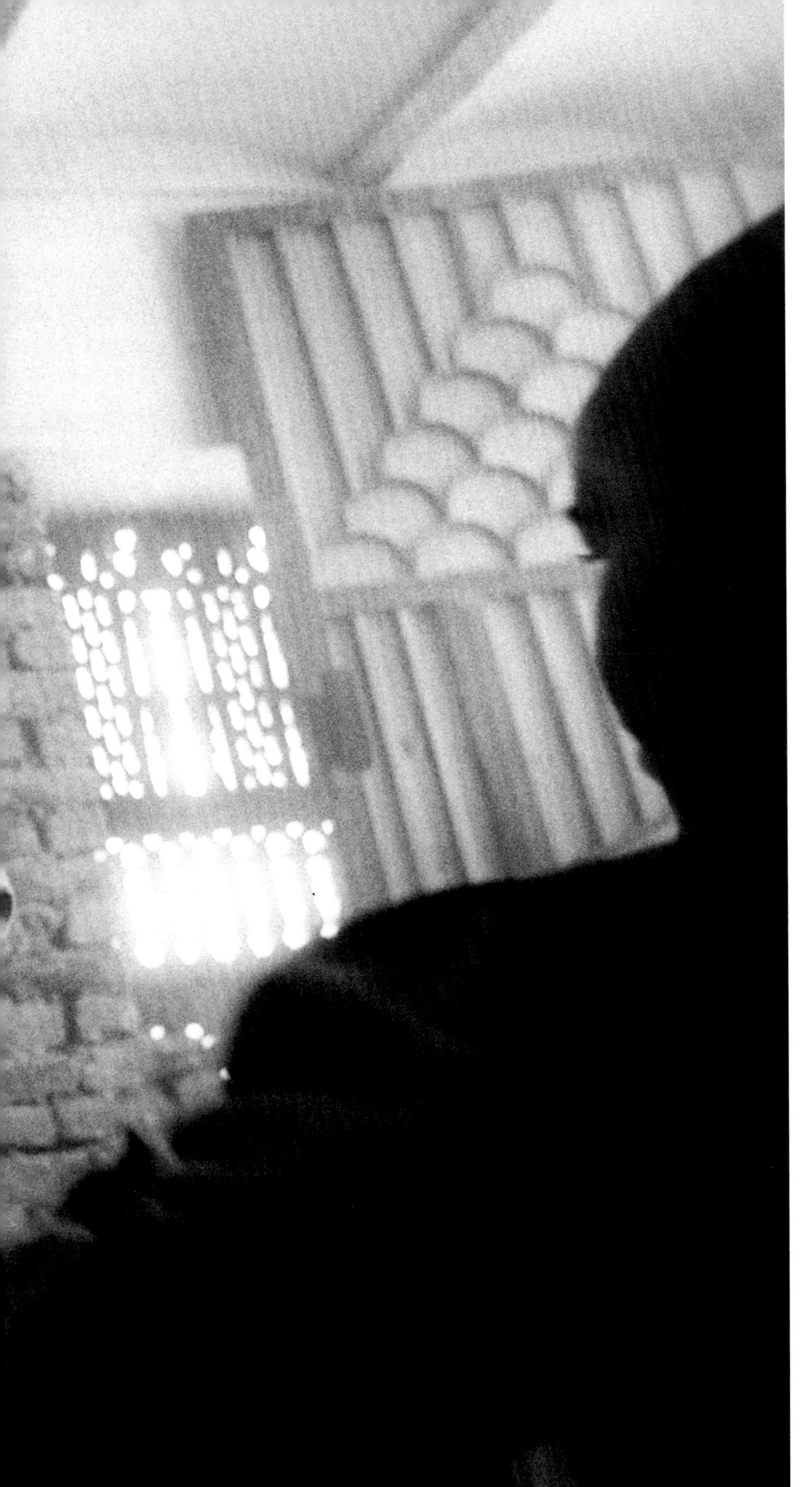

KANDAHAR, KANDAHAR PROVINCE: AUGUST 2004
A teacher wields a rubber whip to discipline boys
at a madrassa in Kandahar.

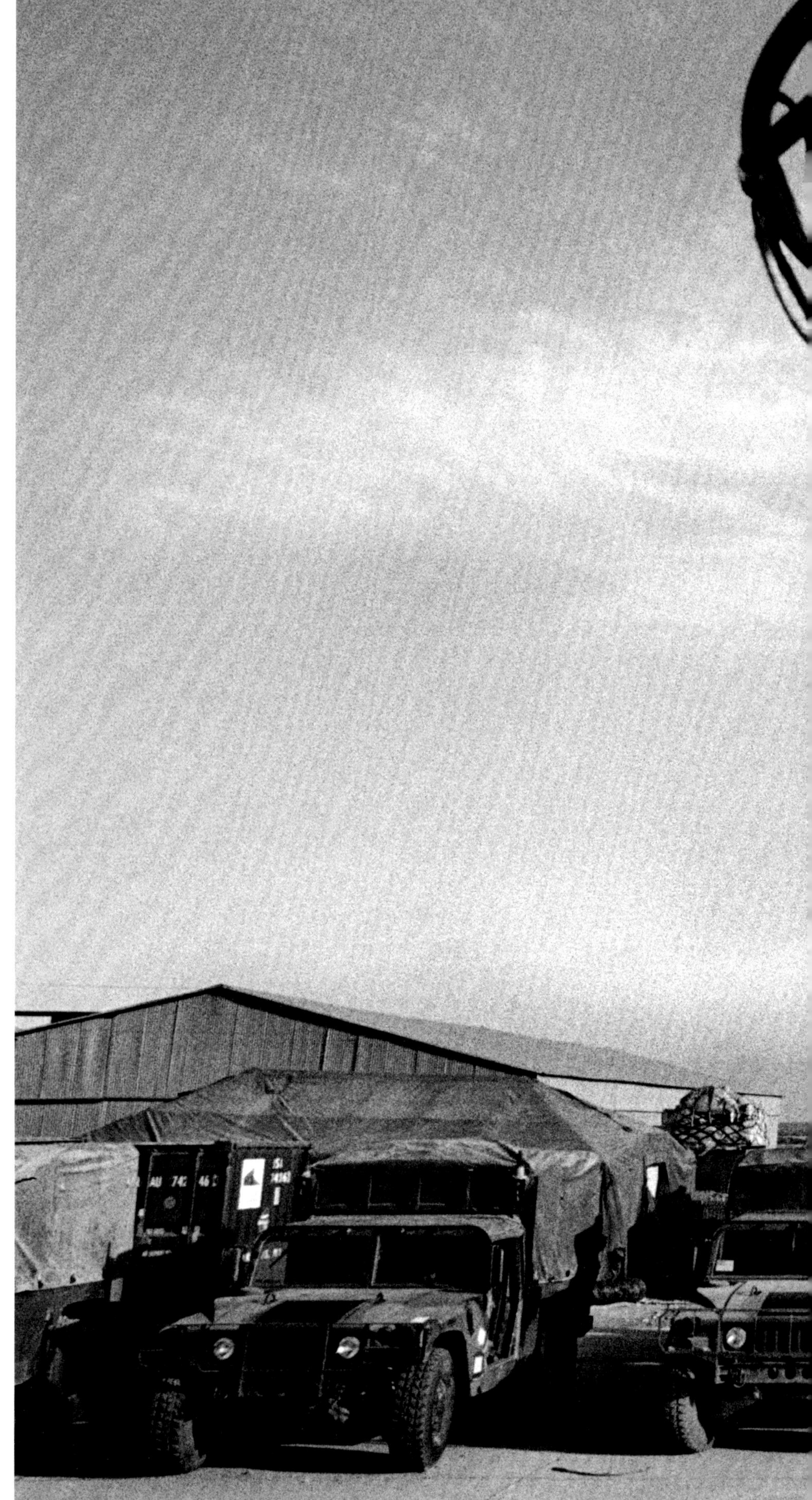

Bagram Airbase, Shamali Plain: November 2002
US military playing basketball at 'Viper City'.

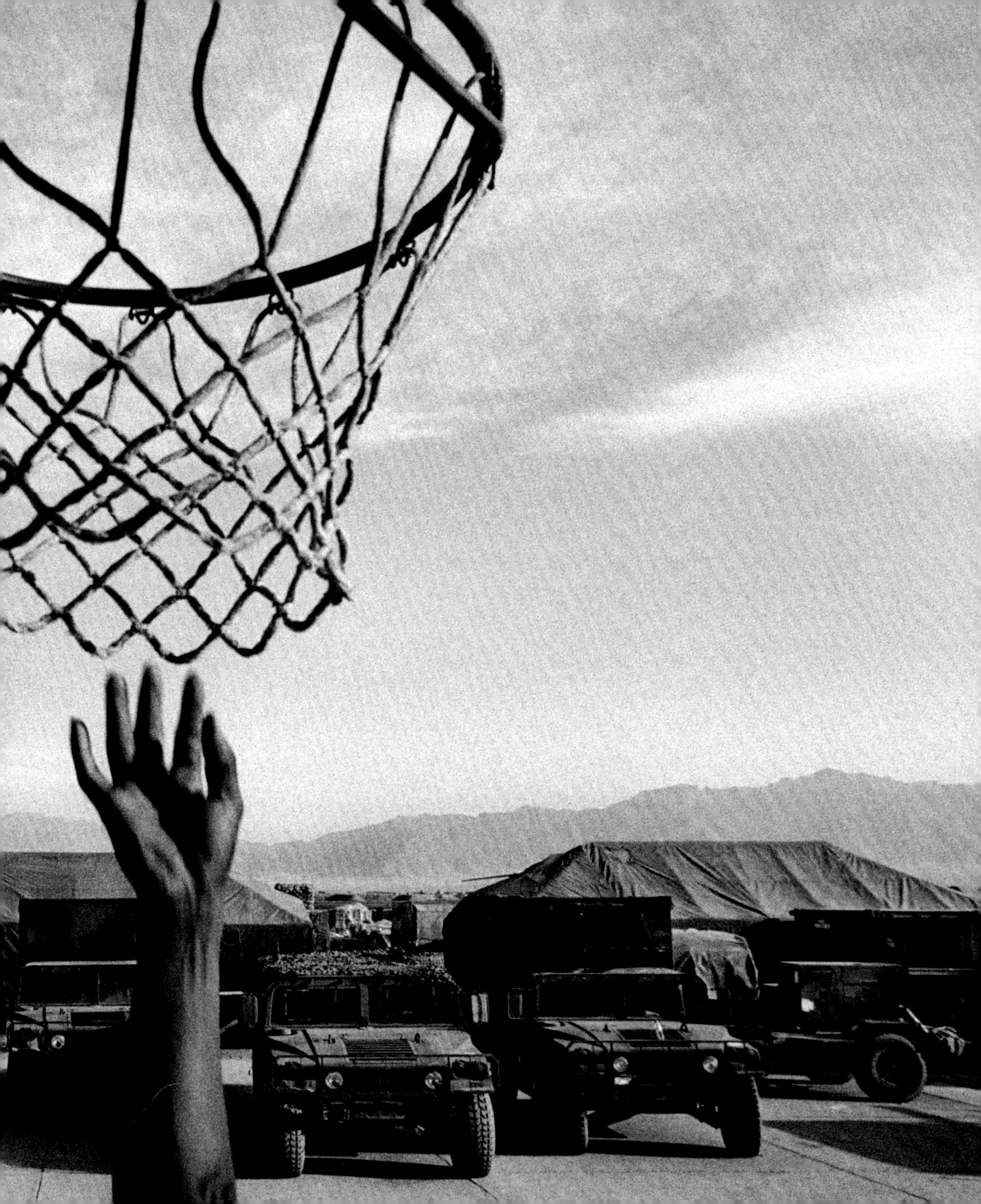

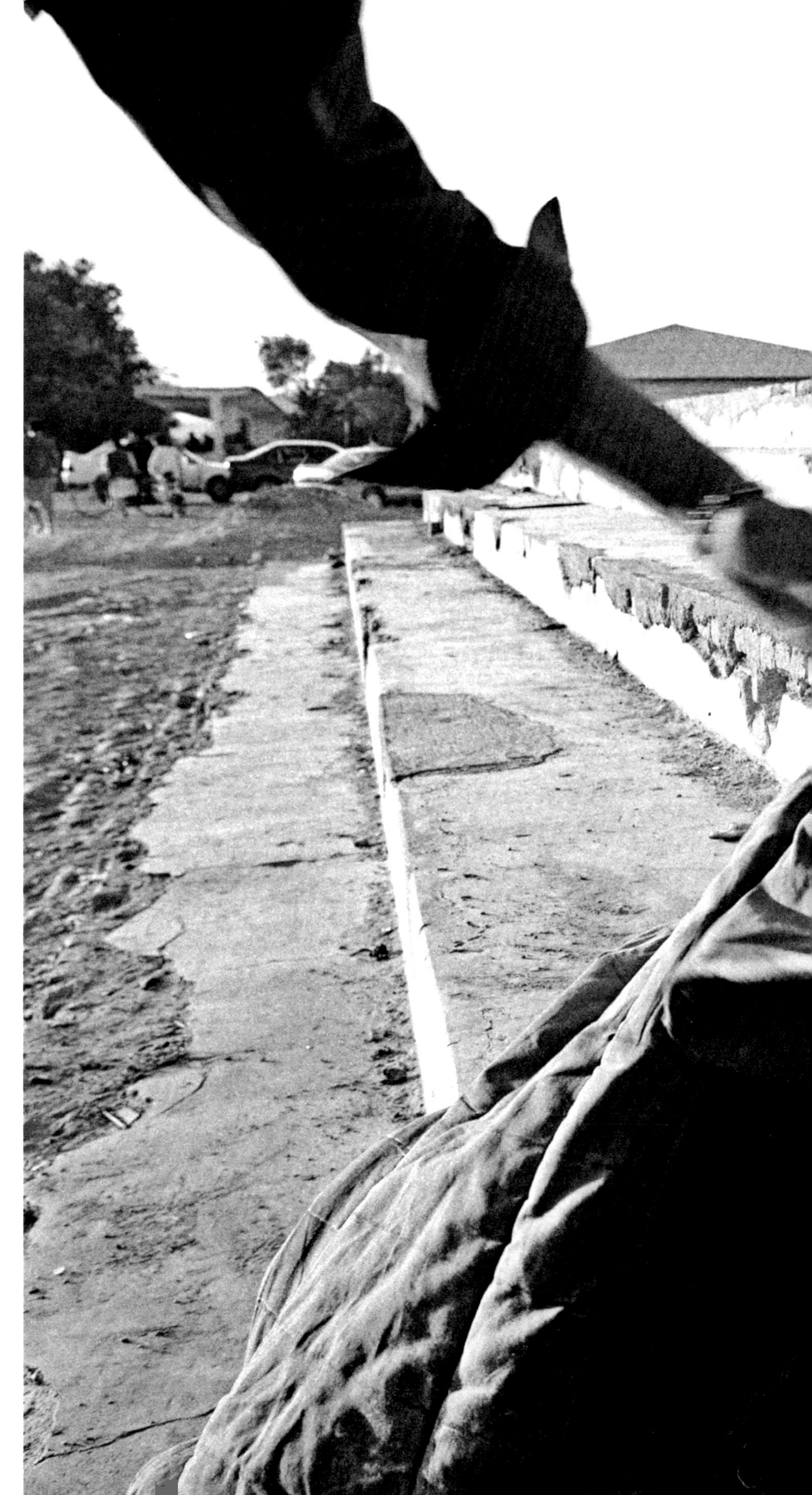

Kabul: July 2006
An opium user is beaten by a patrolling
policeman outside Ghazi Stadium.

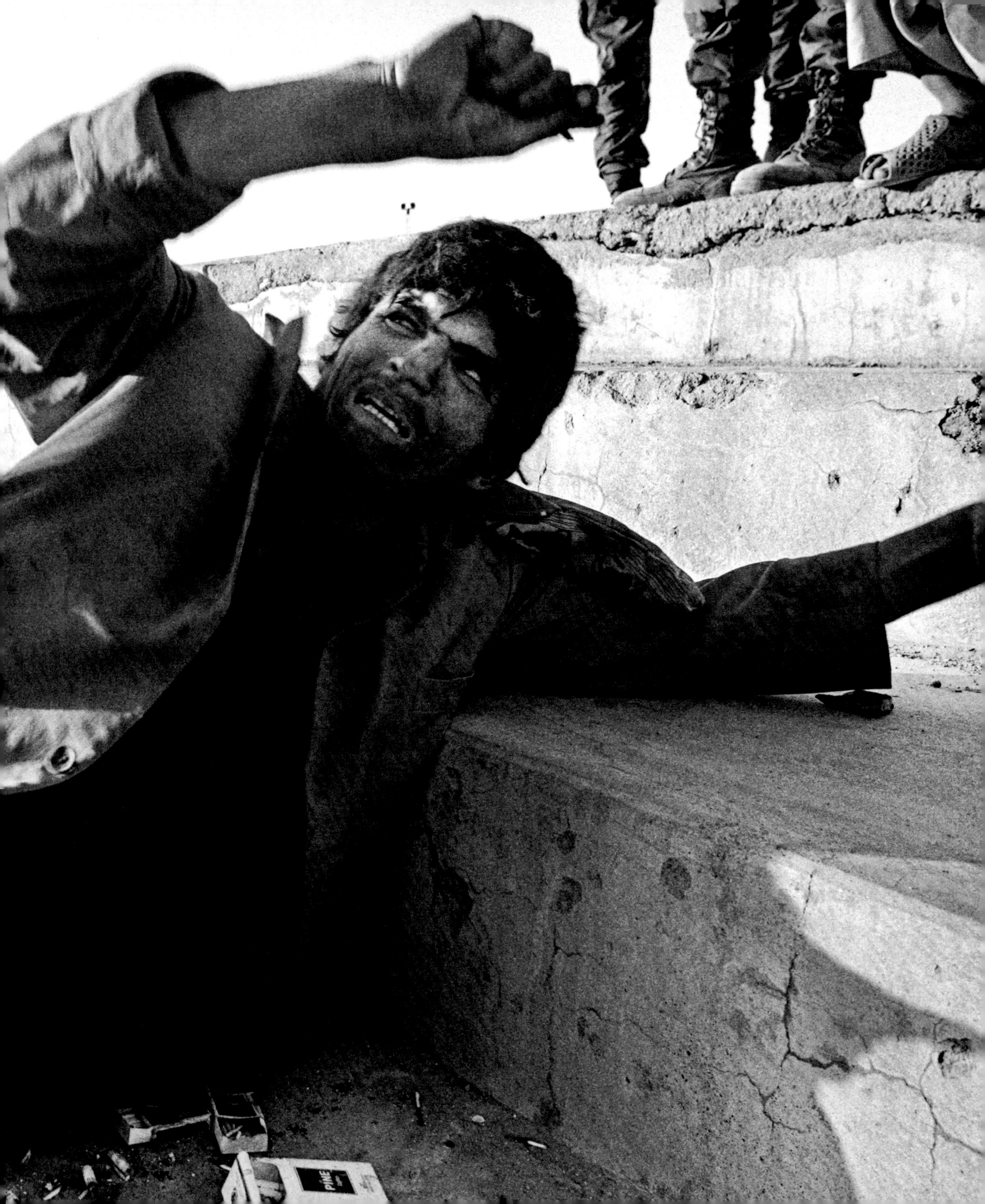

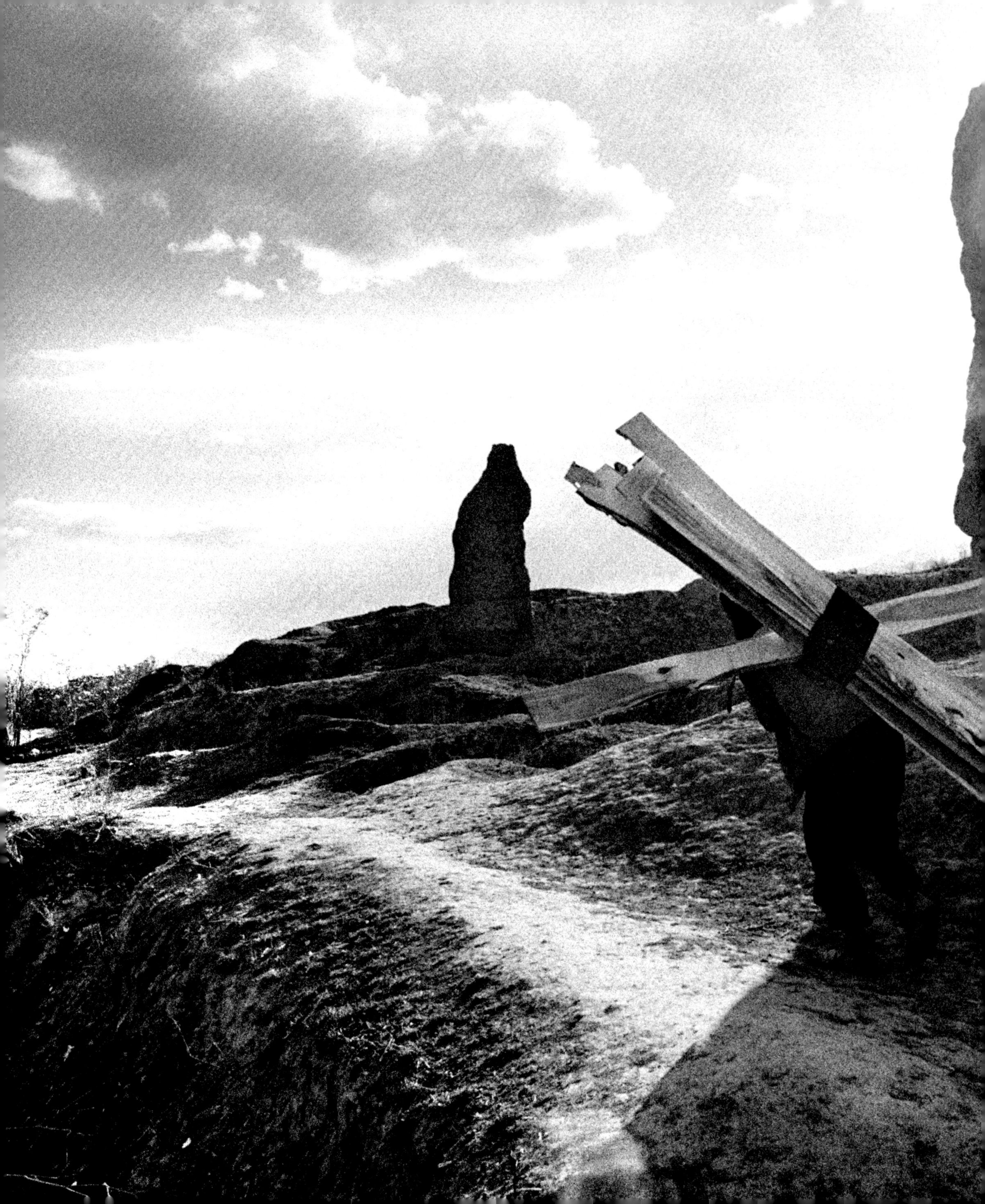

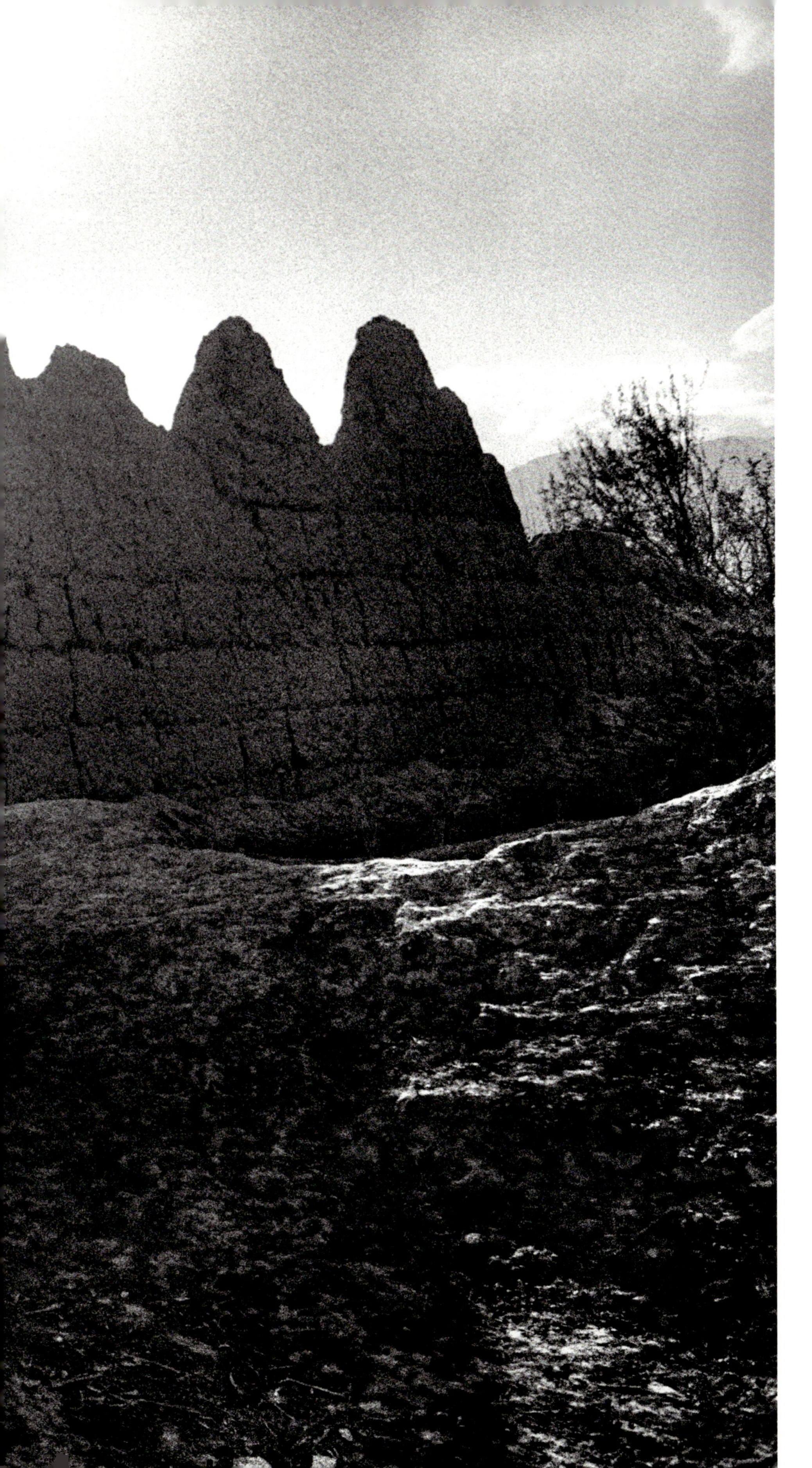

A villager returning home with timber supplied by an NGO helping in the reconstruction of housing on the Shamali Plain.

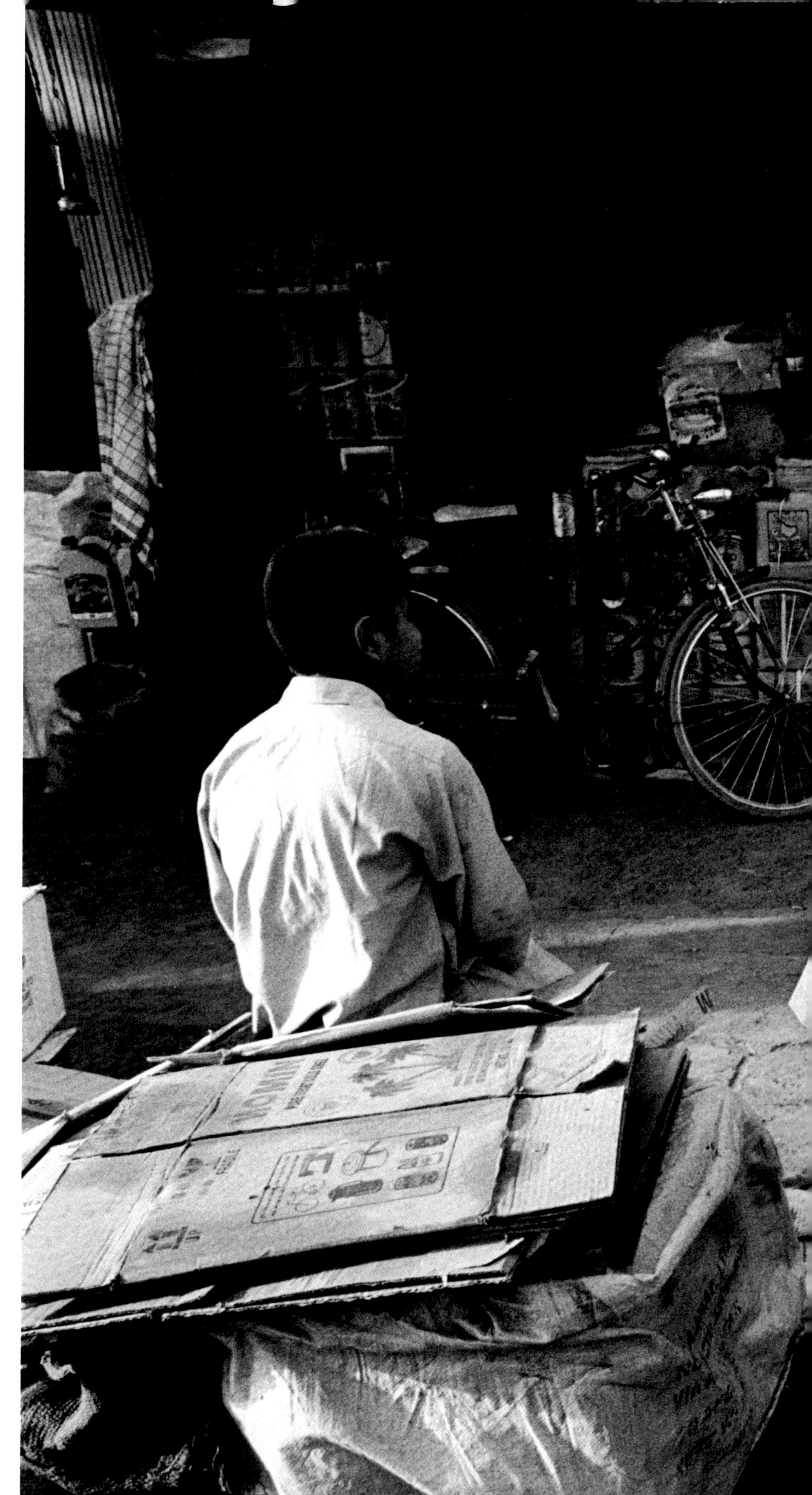

CHARIKAR, PARWAN PROVINCE: AUGUST 2004
A stallholder prepares his goods for sale.

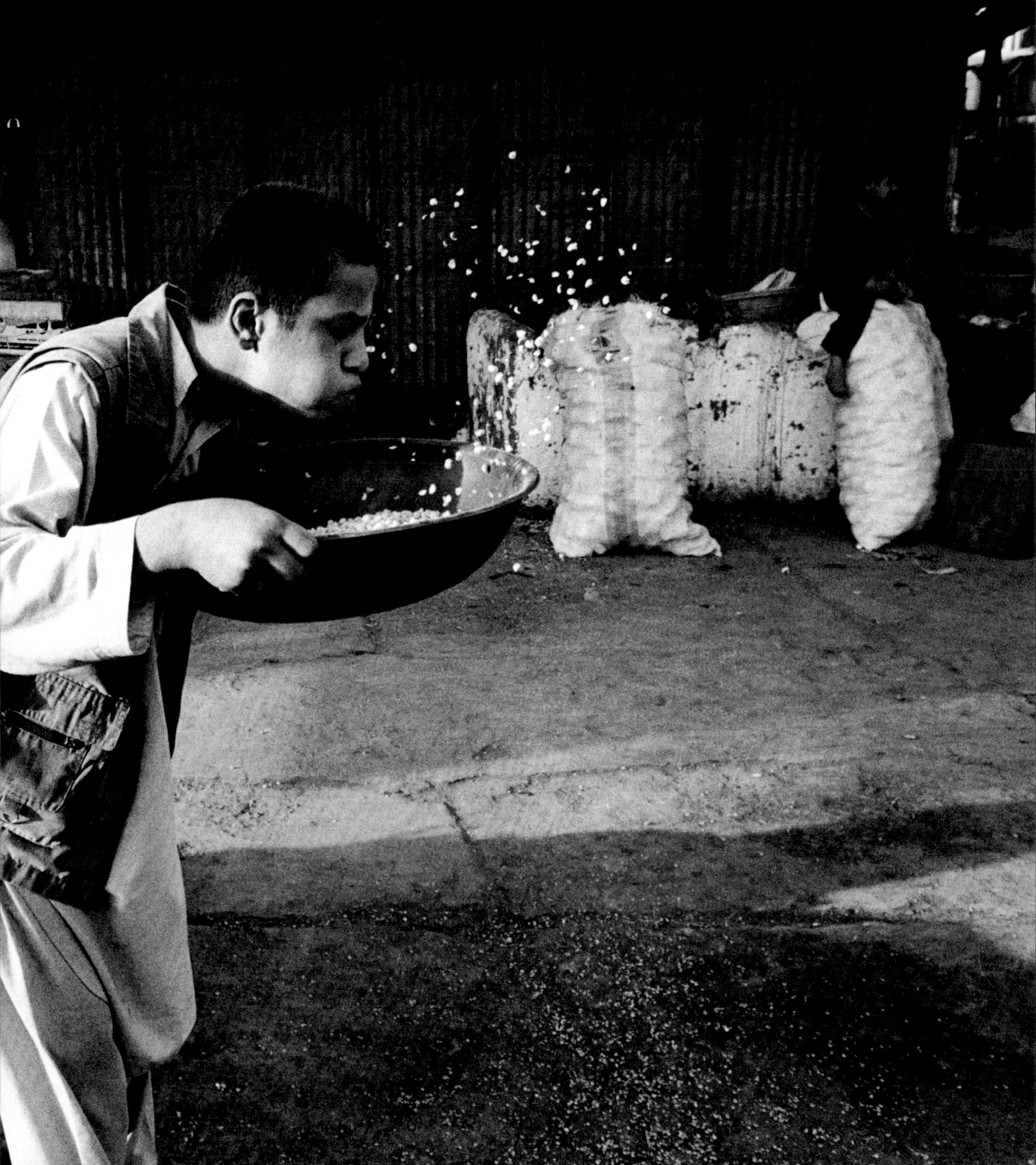

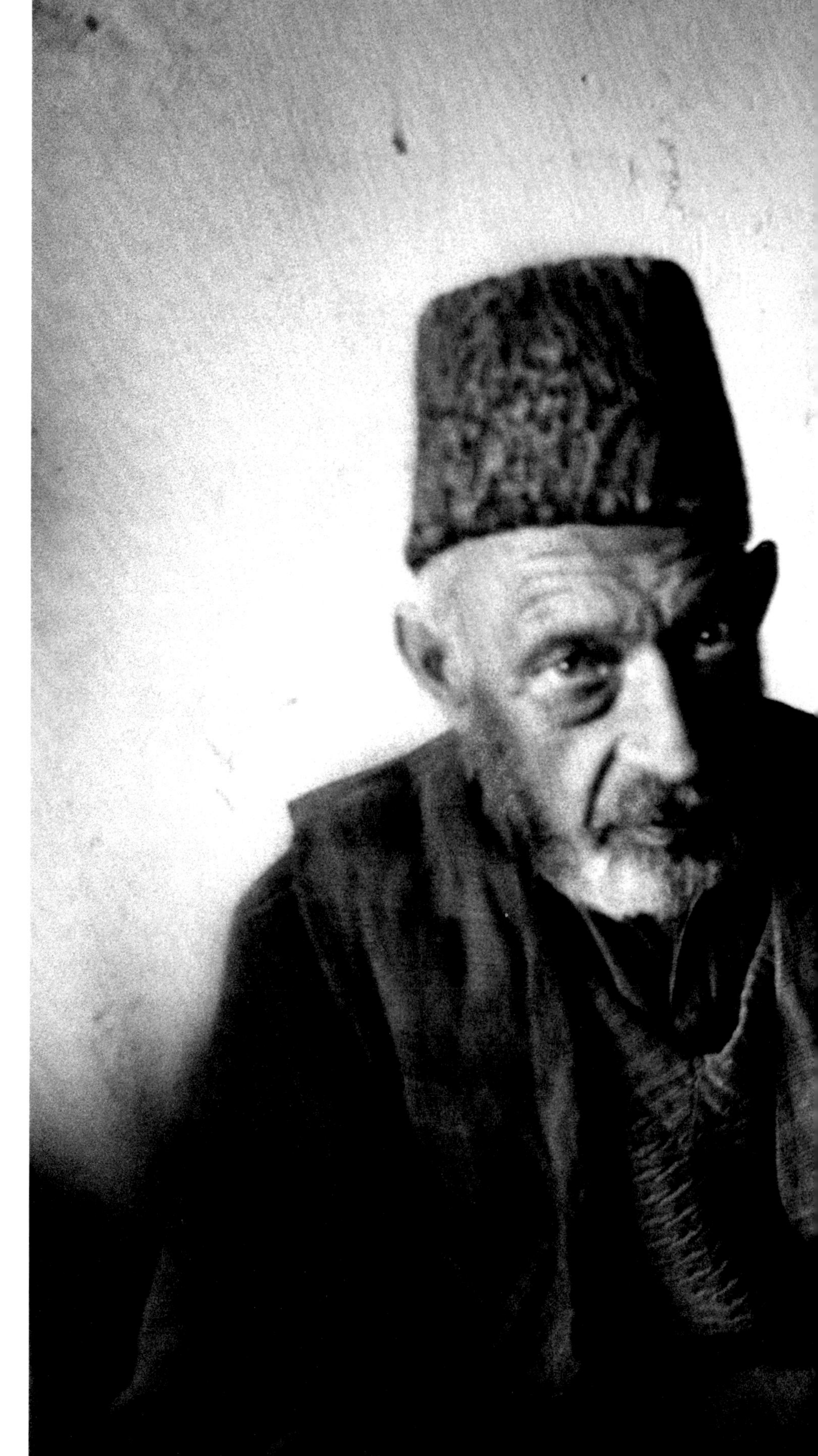

Ba Deli Family, Kabul: November 1994
The Ba Deli family live on Shor Bazaar (or Stonecutter Street) in the Old City. They are one of the few remaining in this frontline neighbourhood – most families have fled the bombing and fighting. The mother has died of illness, and the oldest son has been killed in the fighting. The fourth eldest son, Farhuddin, lost his leg in a rocket attack the previous year. The city is now a labyrinth of frontlines as the civil war escalates.

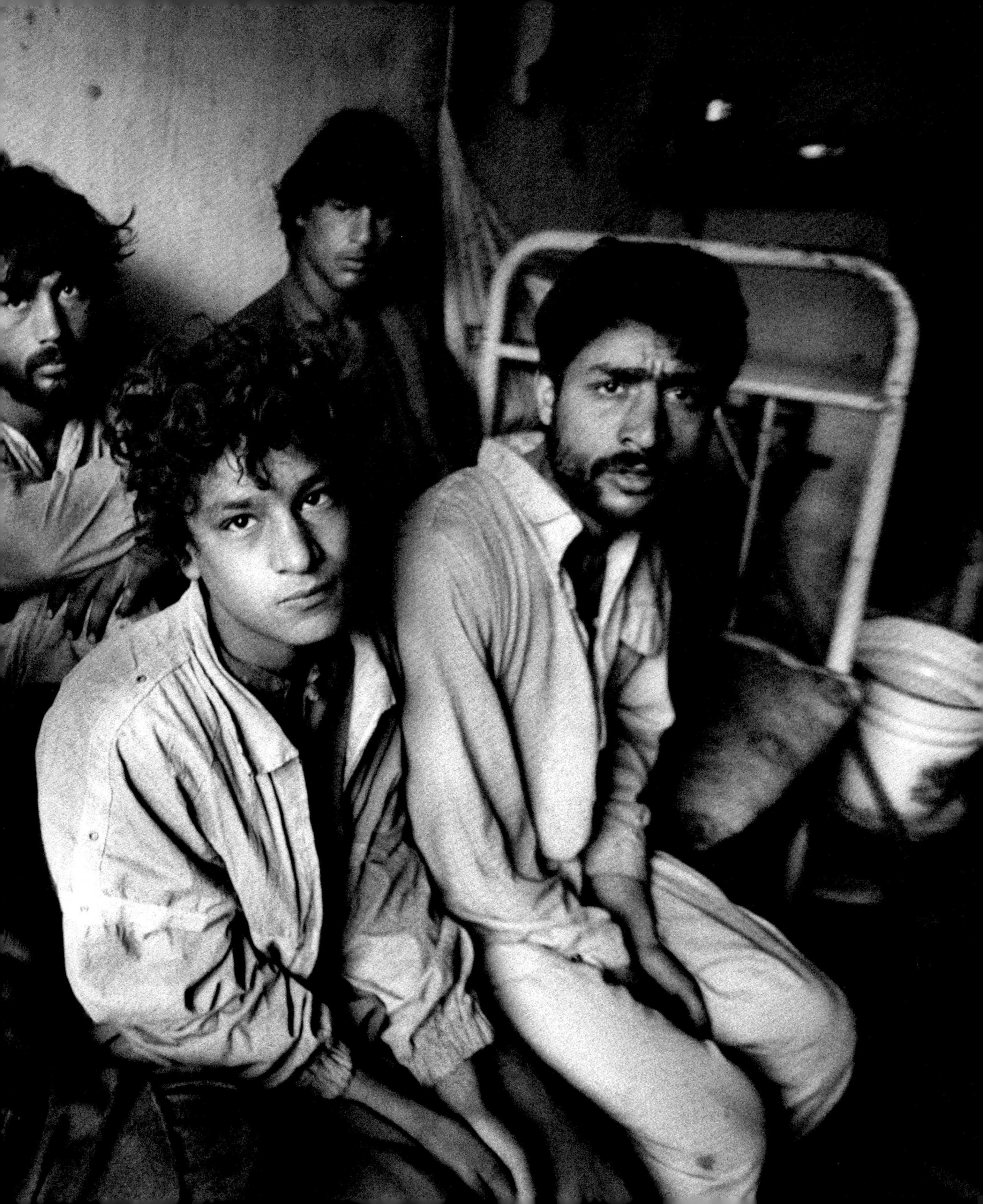

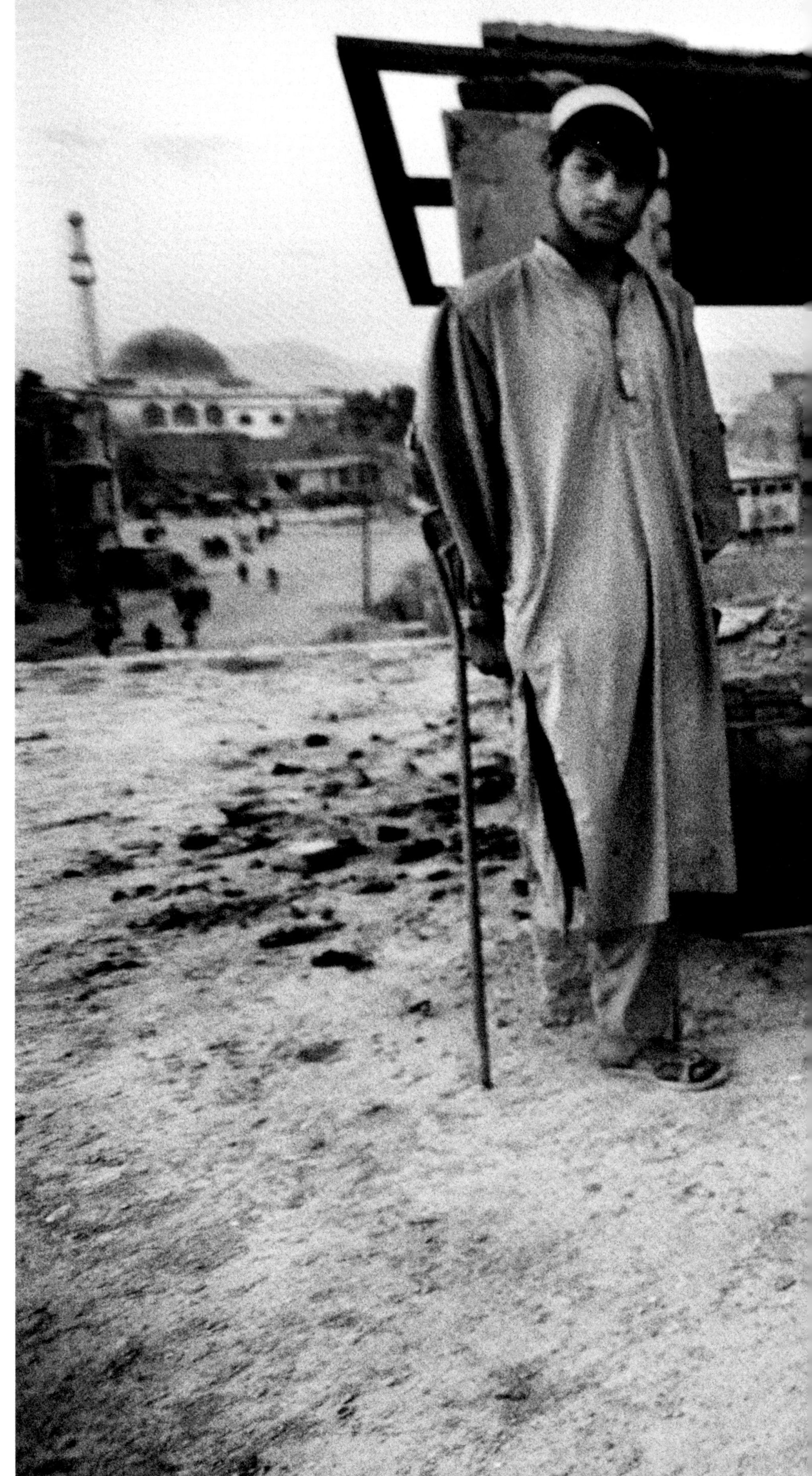

Ba Deli Family, Kabul: November 1996
On the roof of their building the remaining
sons, Farhuddin and Farhad, with their father,
Abdul Sami. Since the previous photograph,
two more sons have been killed in the fighting.
Abdul Sami is crouching, afraid of being seen by
Taliban forces roaming the streets below. The
Taliban took control of the city in September
of 1996, enforcing their strict and idiosyncratic
interpretation of Sharia law.

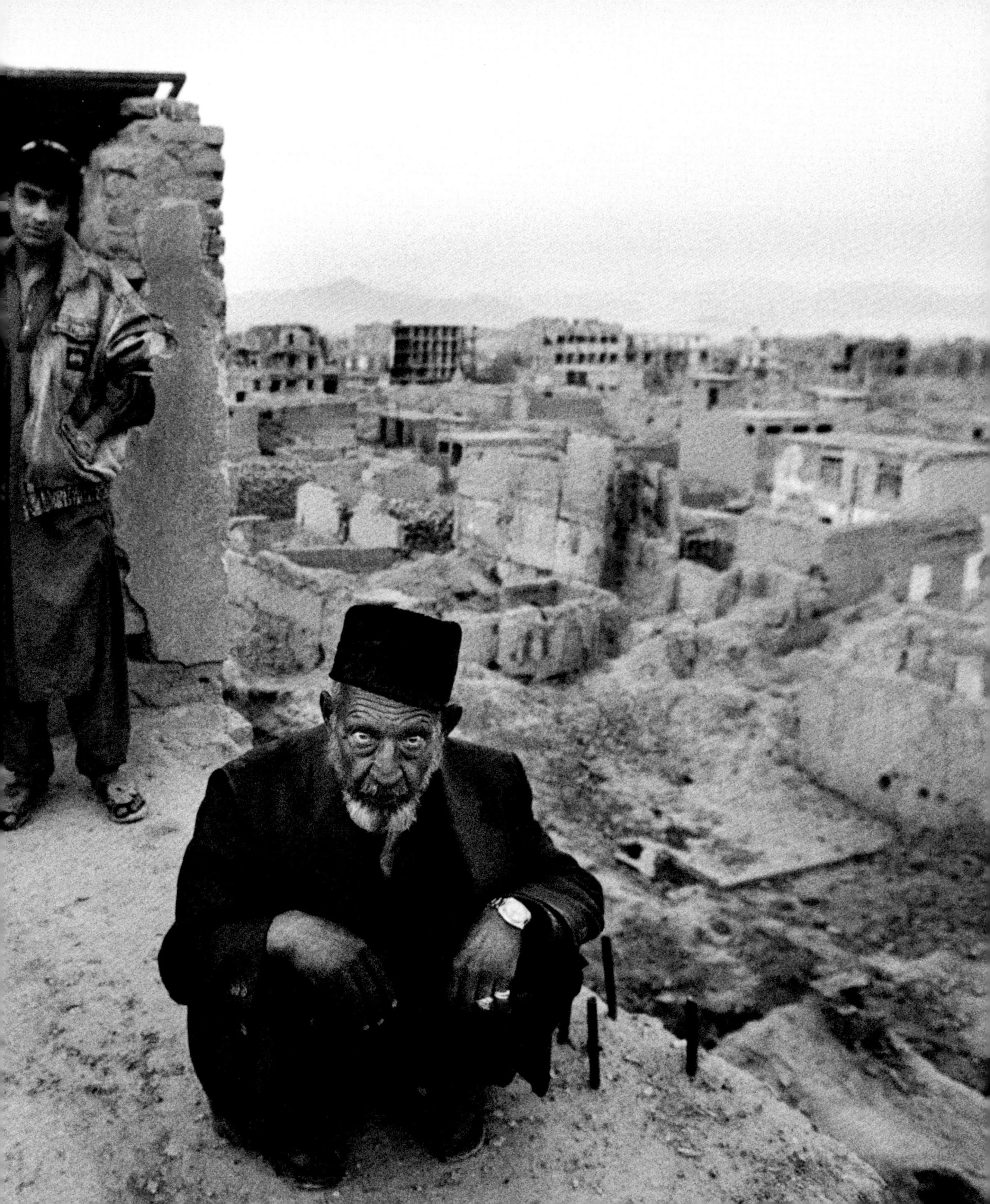

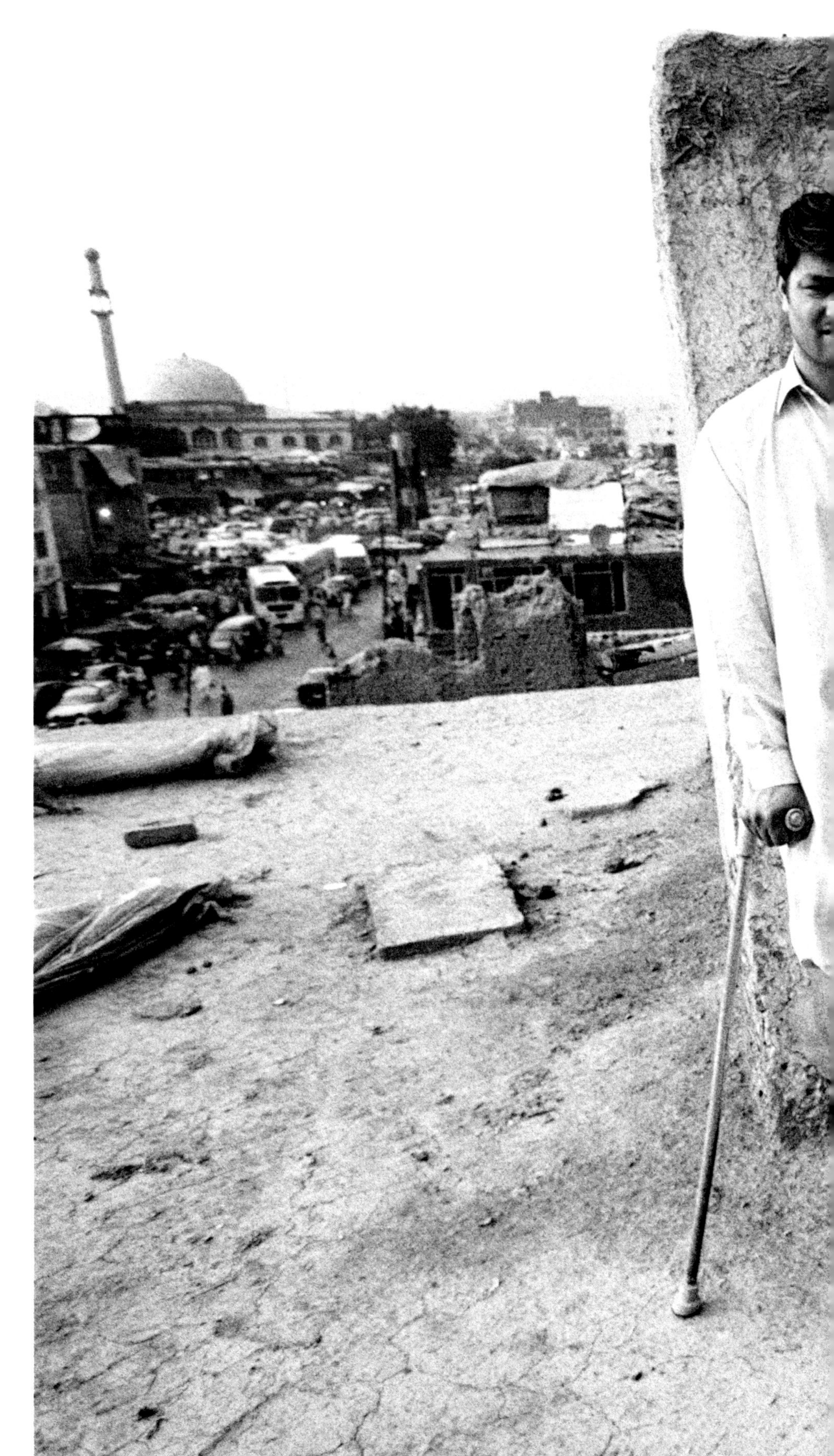

Ba Deli Family, Kabul: April 2007
Farhuddin and Farhad, now the only remaining members of the Ba Deli family. They are both married and have become fathers.

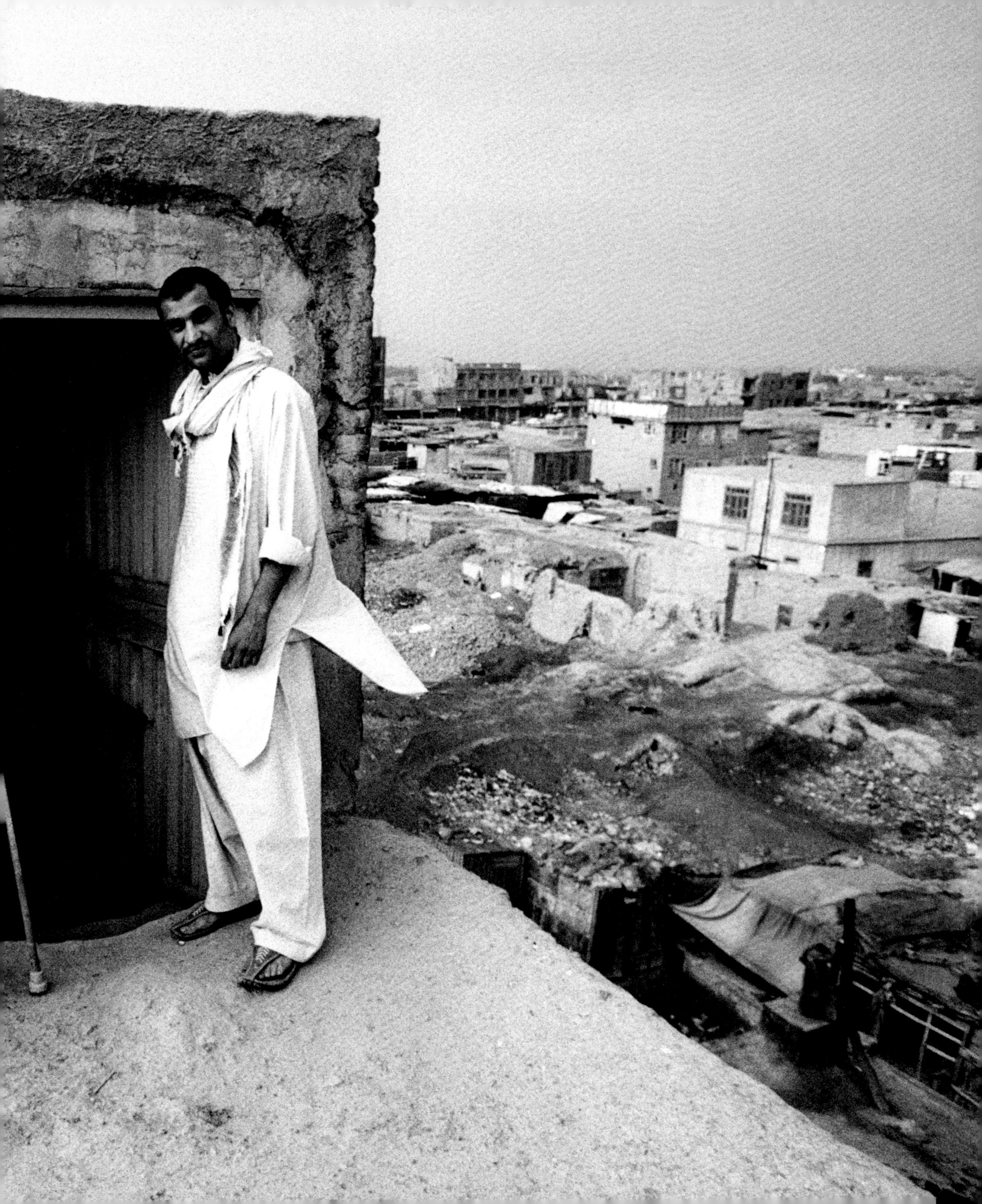

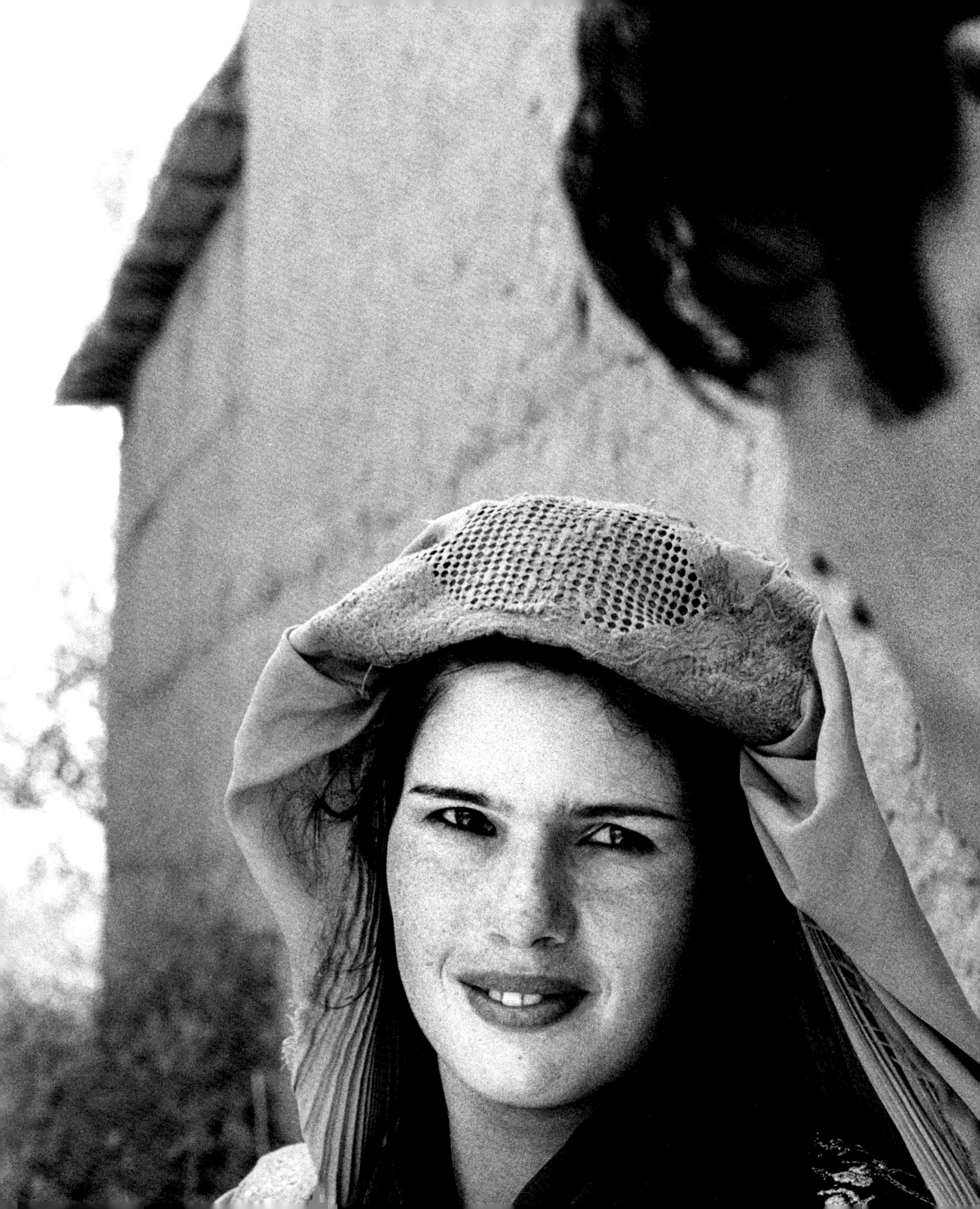

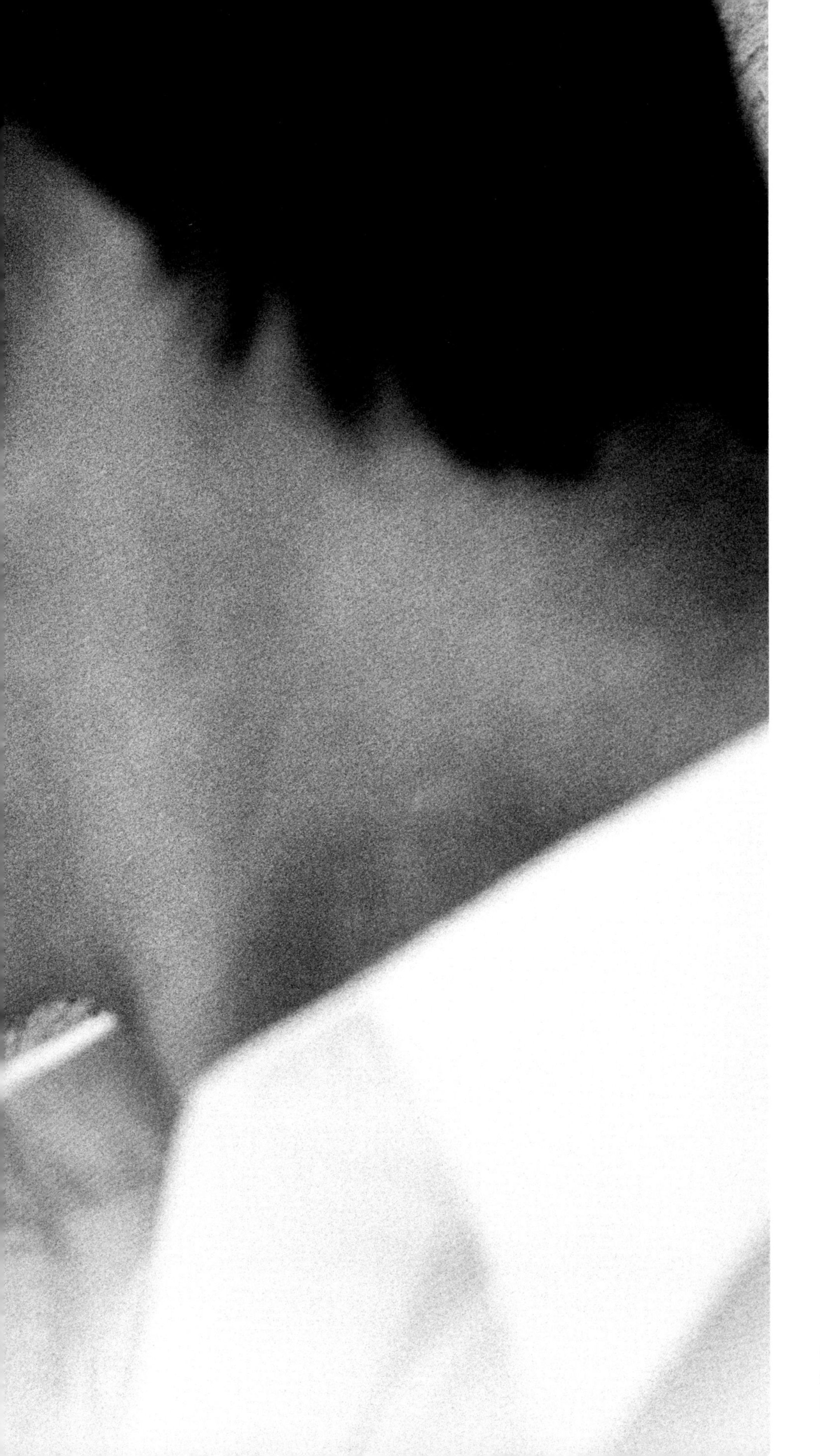

Ba Deli Family, Shamali Plain, Parwan Province:
October 2004
Farhuddin and his wife.

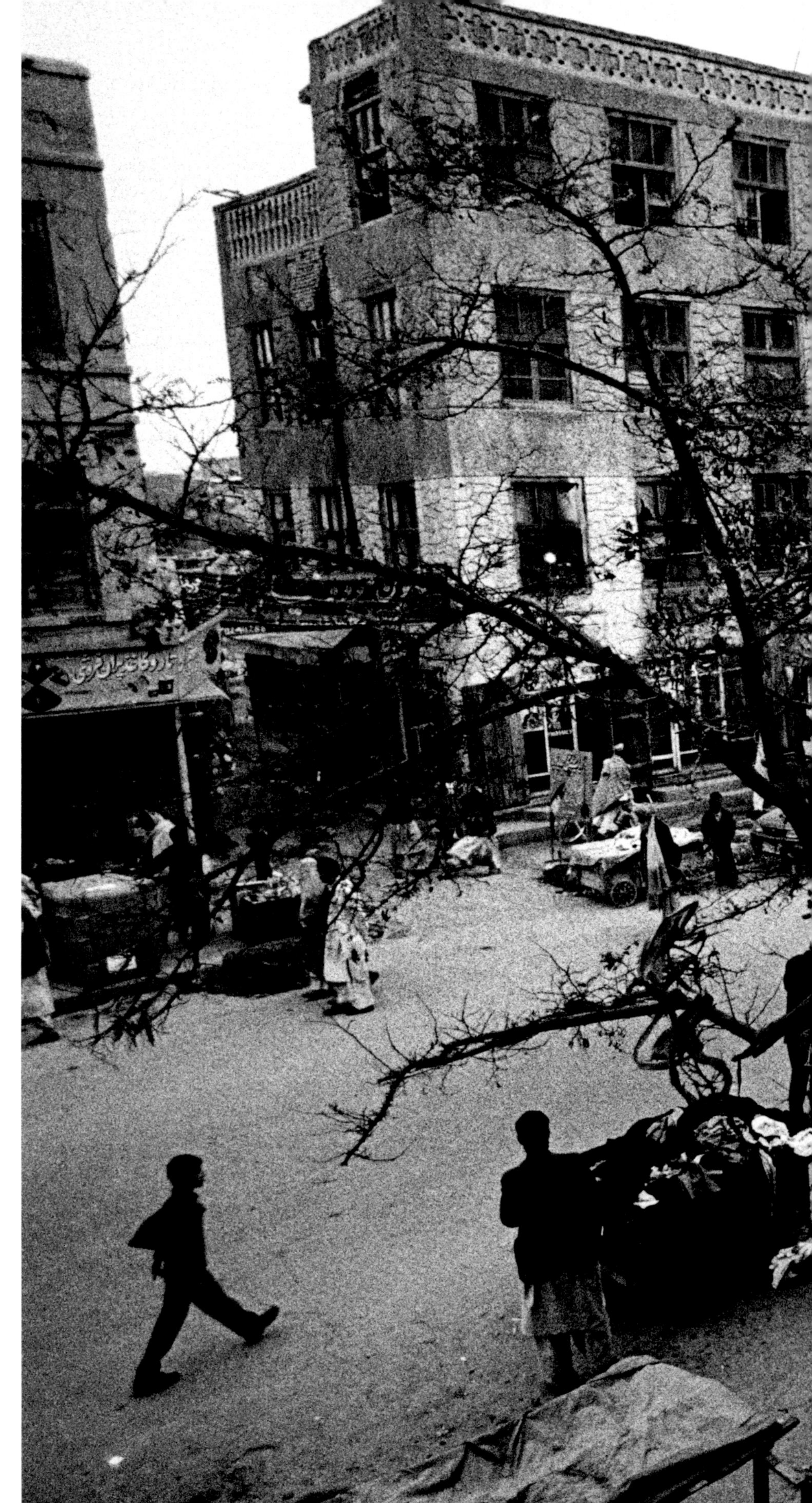

Ba Deli Family, Kabul: October 2004
Shor Bazaar seen from the apartment where the
Ba Deli family lived in 1994.

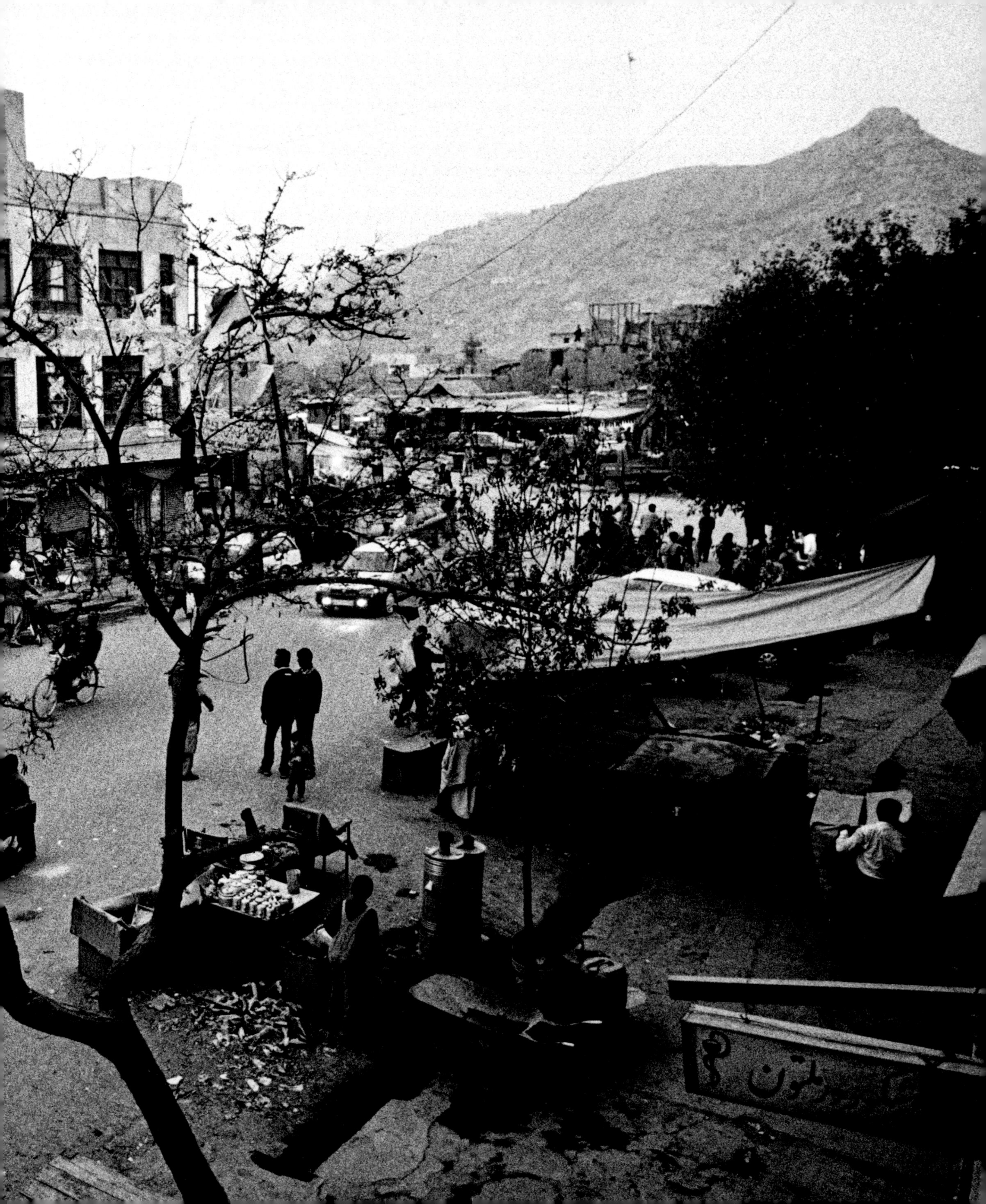

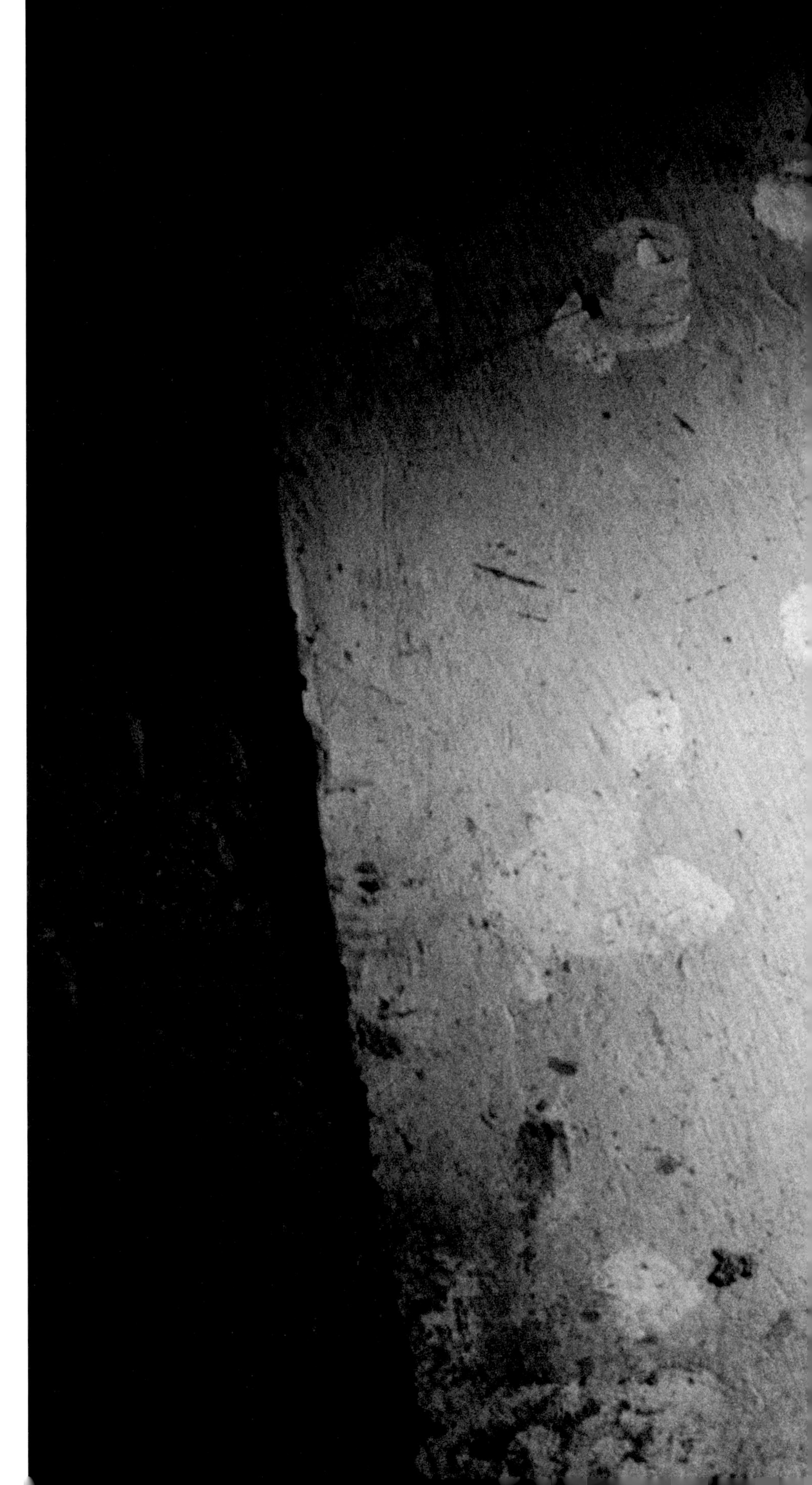

BA DELI FAMILY, KABUL: APRIL 2007
Farhad with Samiullah, his one-month-old son.

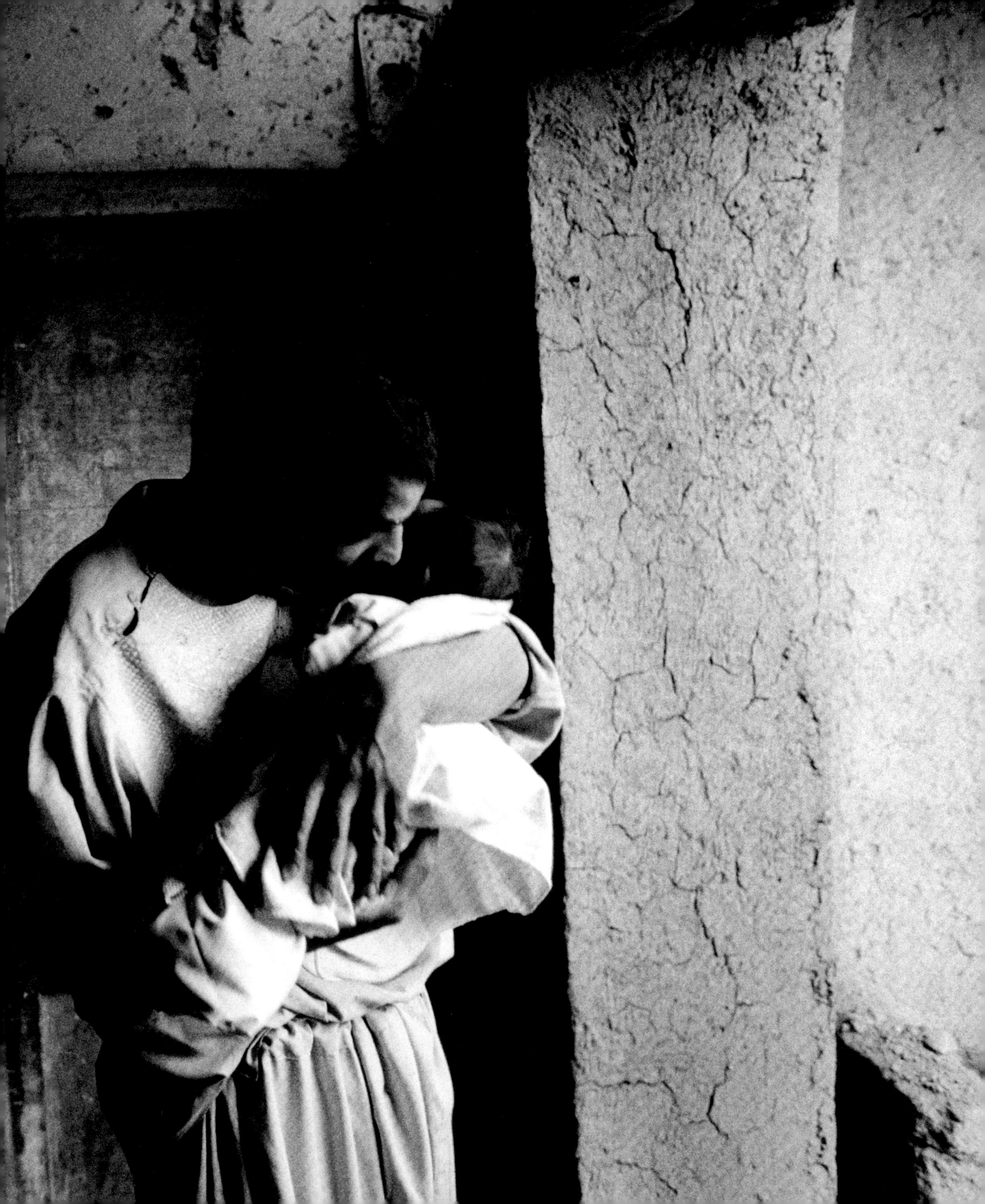

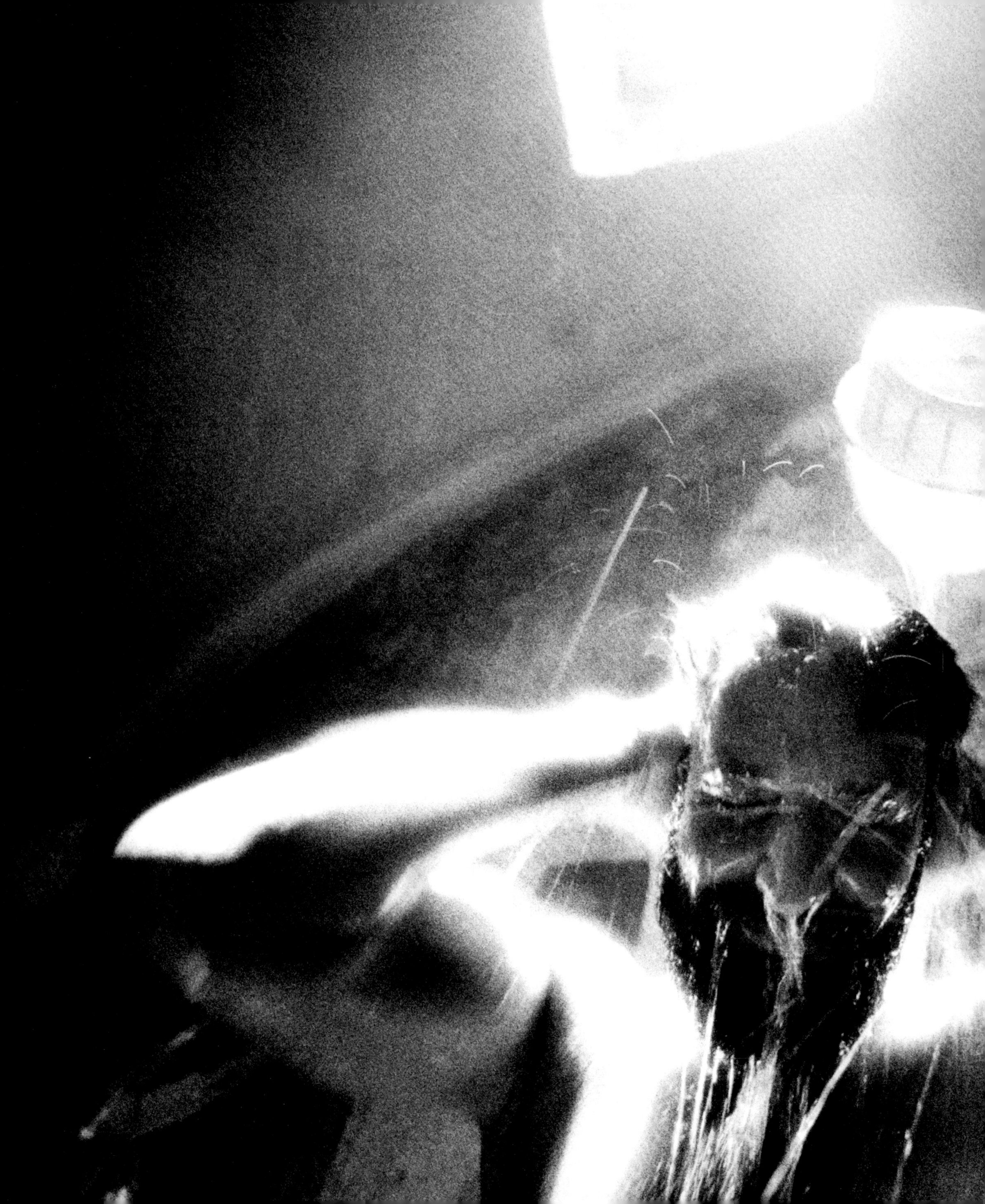

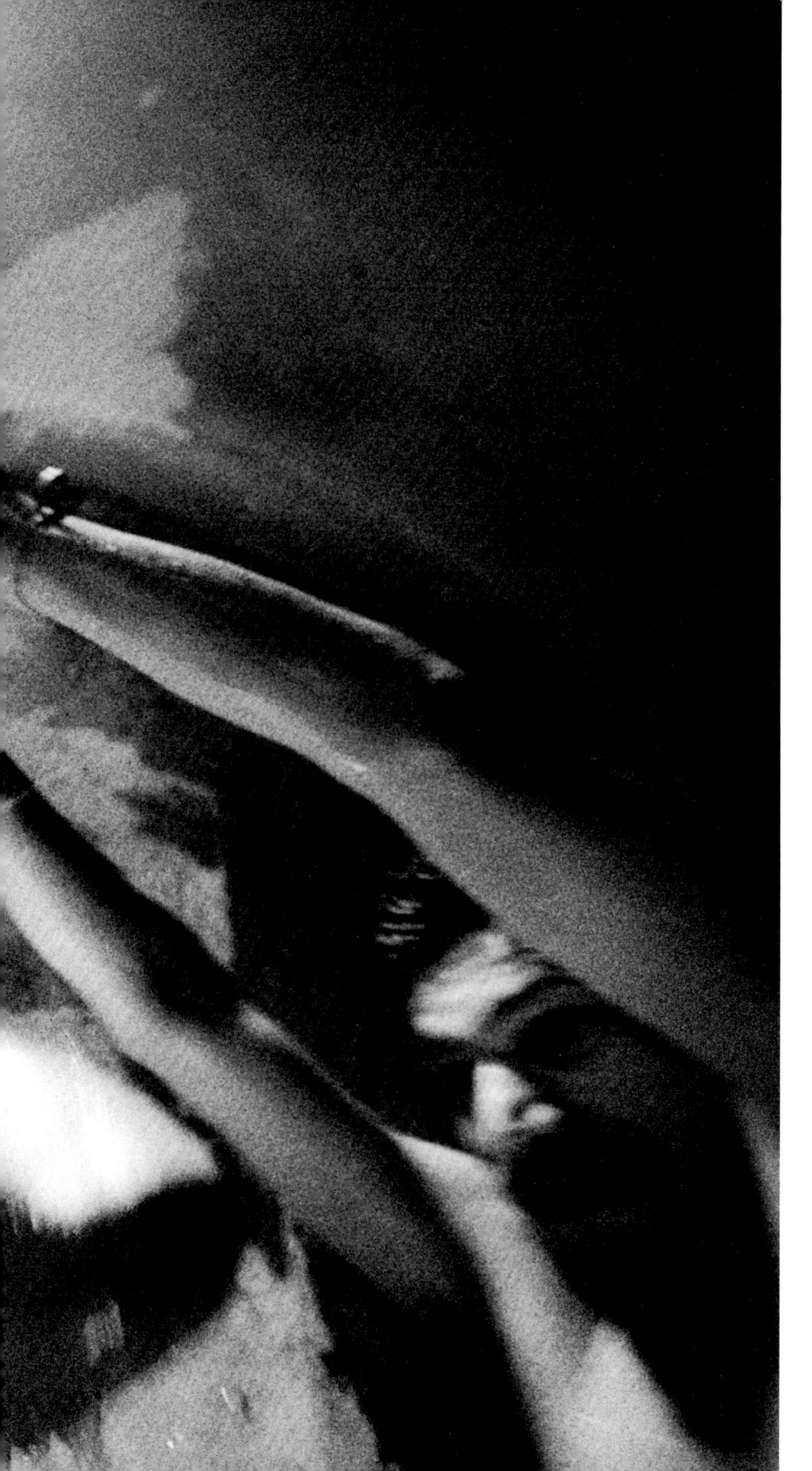

HERAT, HERAT PROVINCE: JUNE 2003
Bathhouse in the Jadai Masegara Massoudi Hamam.

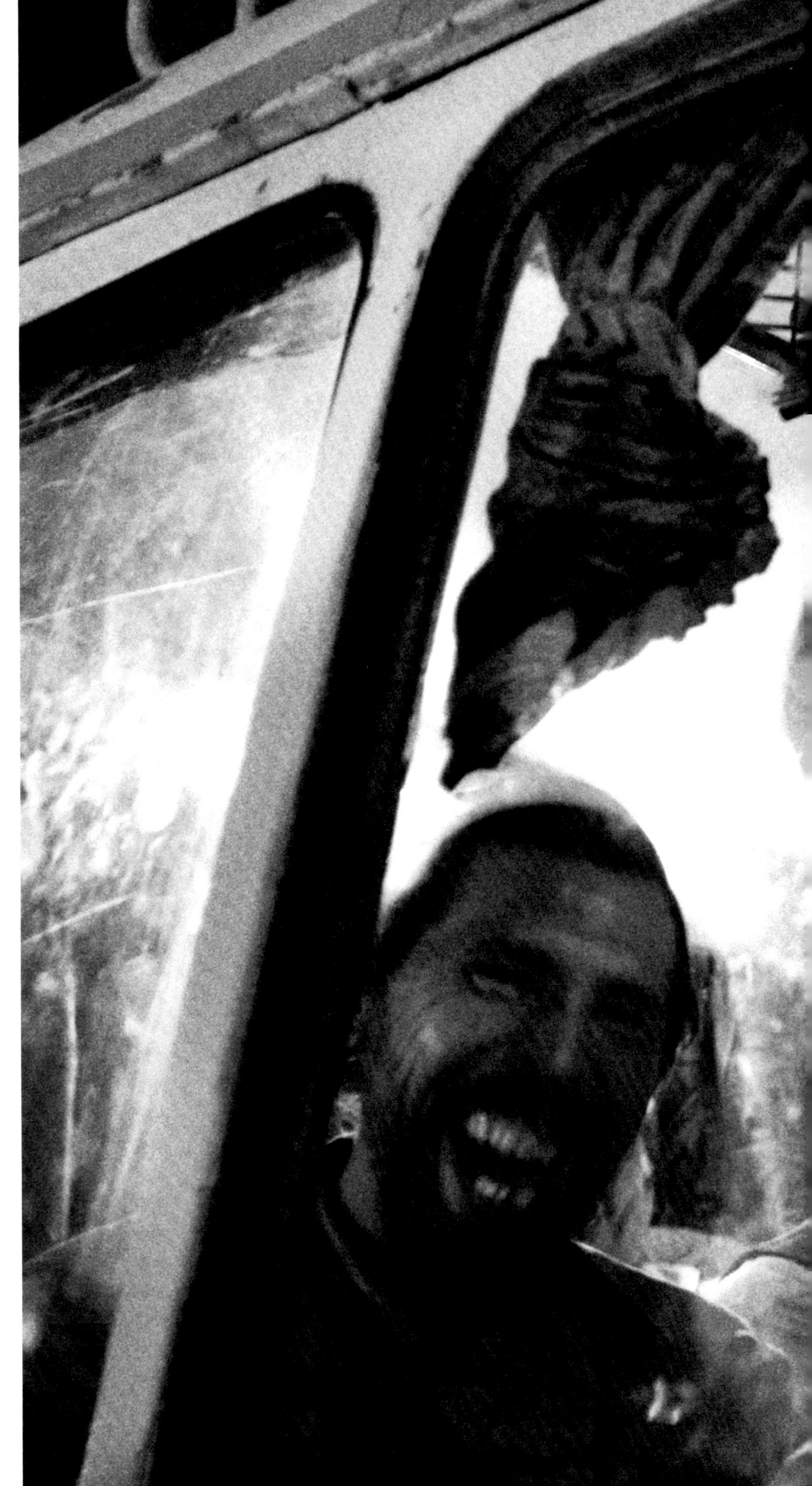

KABUL: JULY 2006
Evening bus passengers.

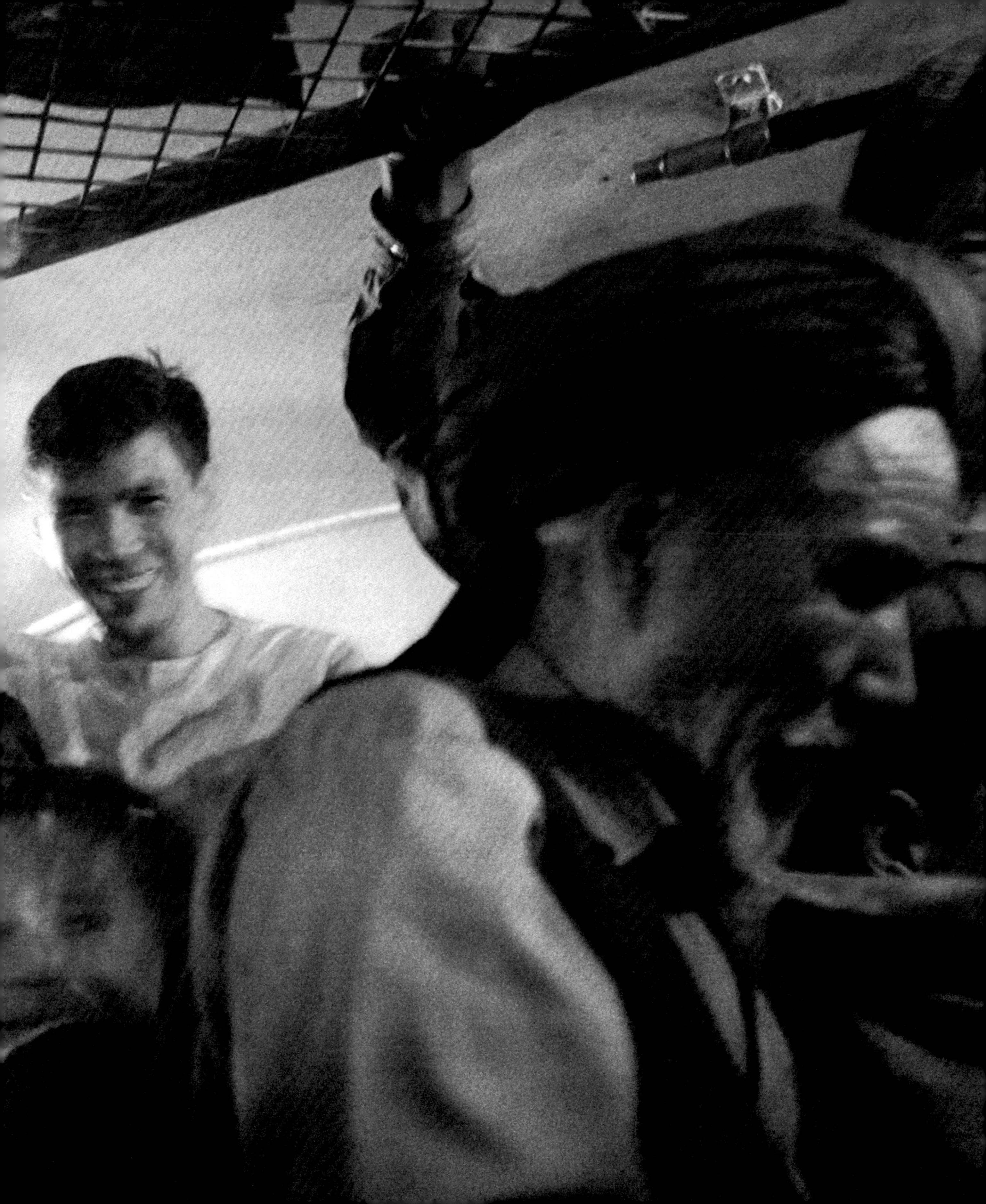

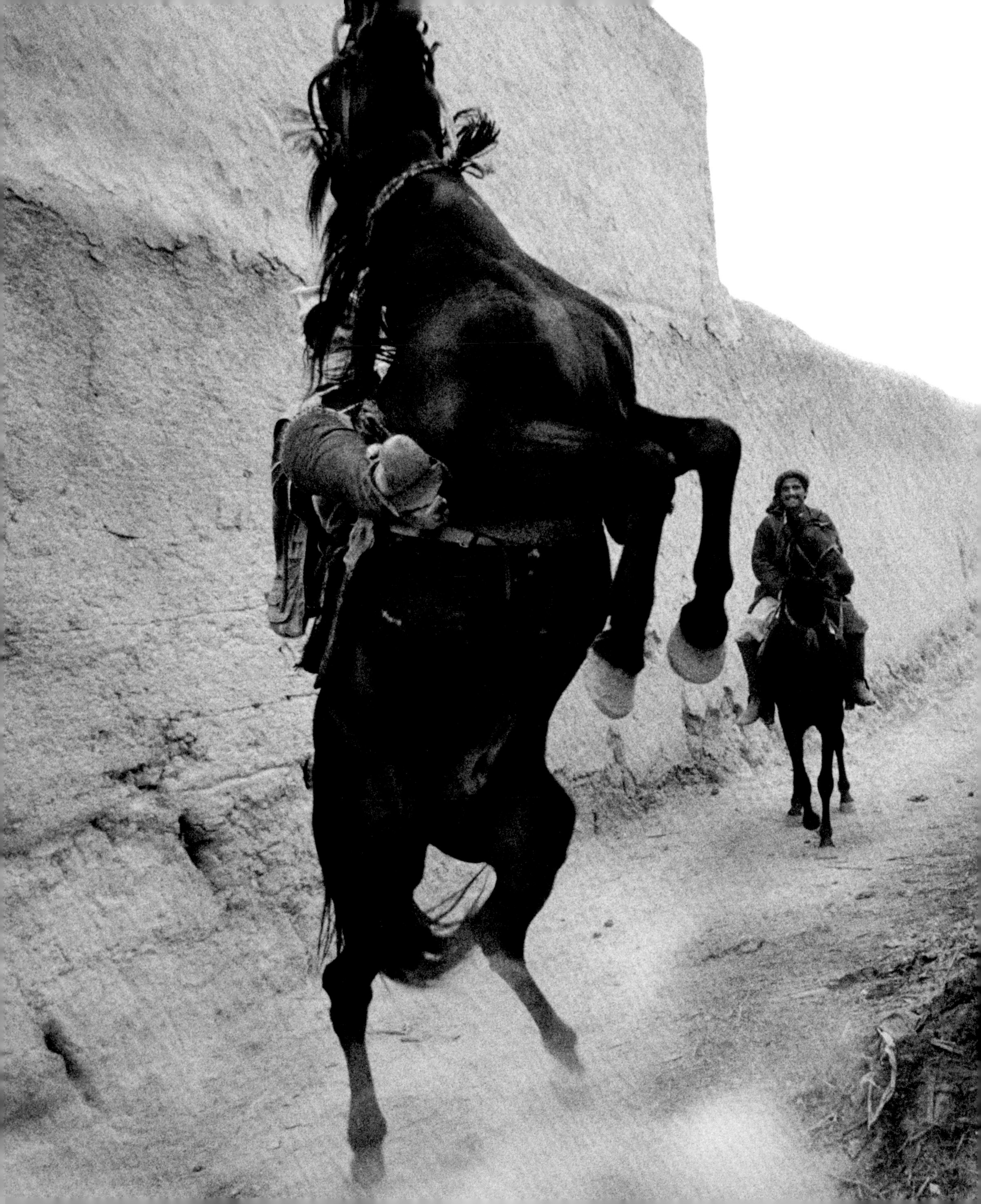

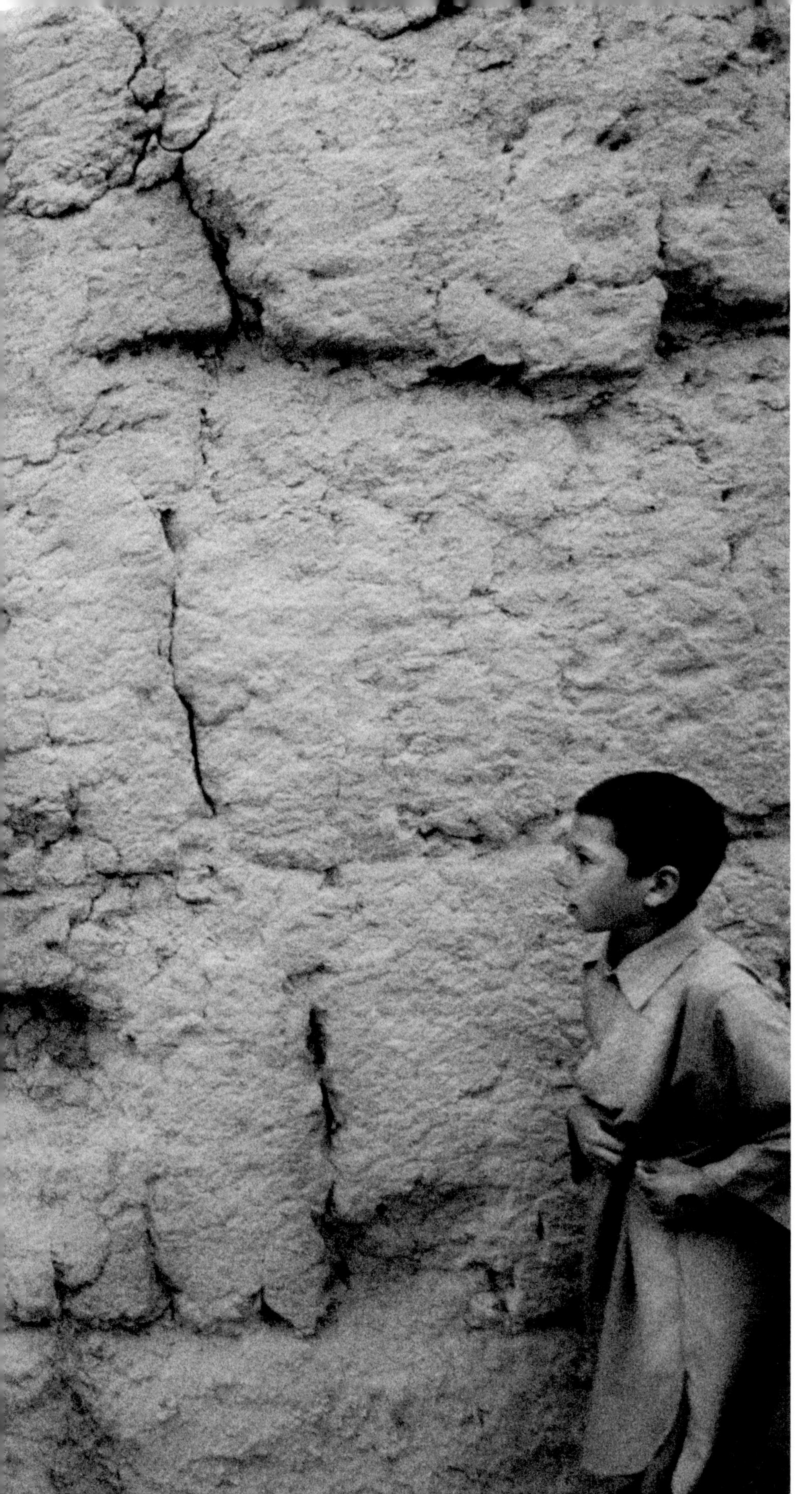

Hisarak, Balkh Province: November 2004
Horsemen of the village.

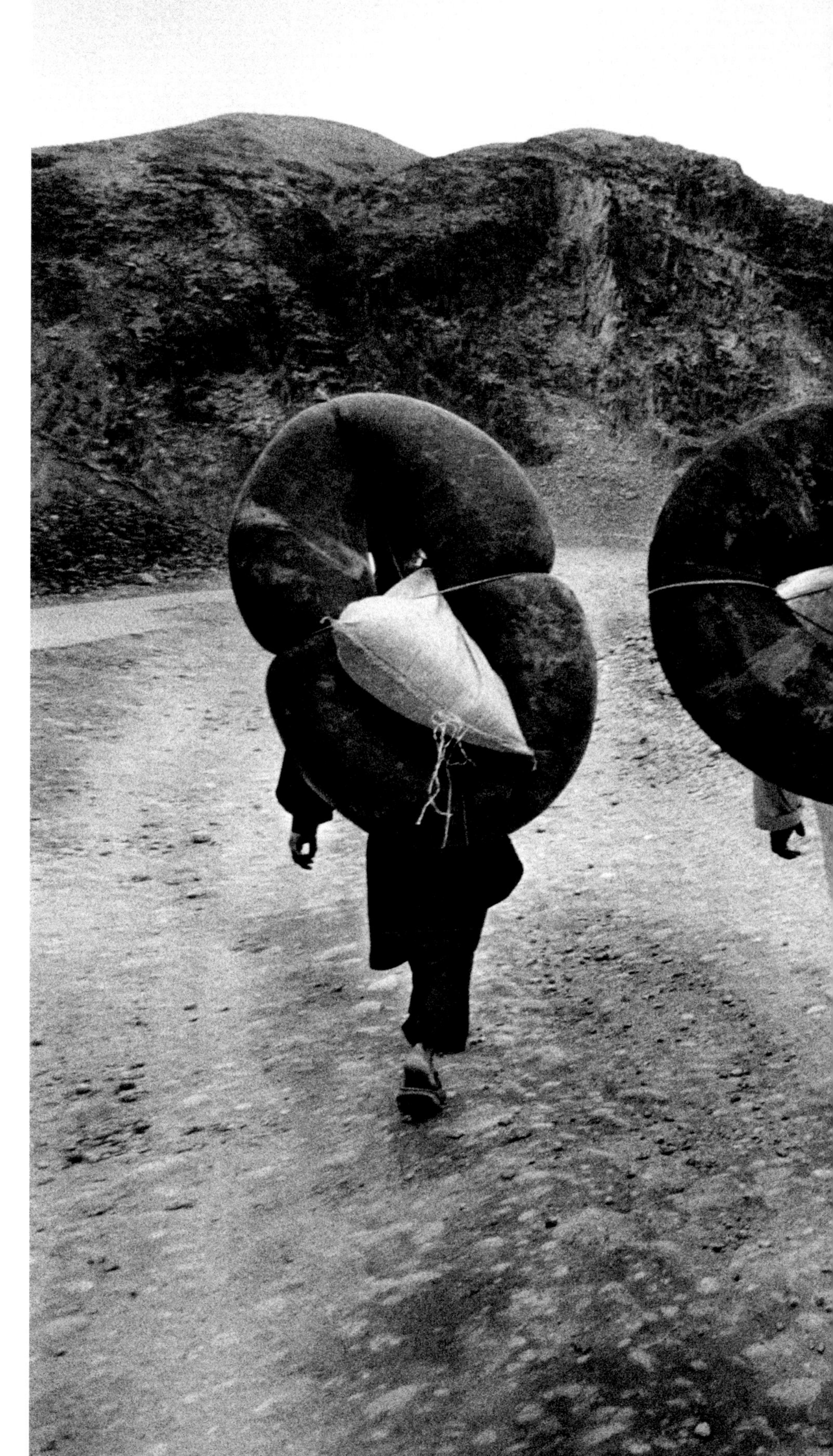

NEAR JALALABAD, NANGRAHAR PROVINCE:
NOVEMBER 2002
Fishermen walking home with the rubber tubes
they use as craft to fish on the river.

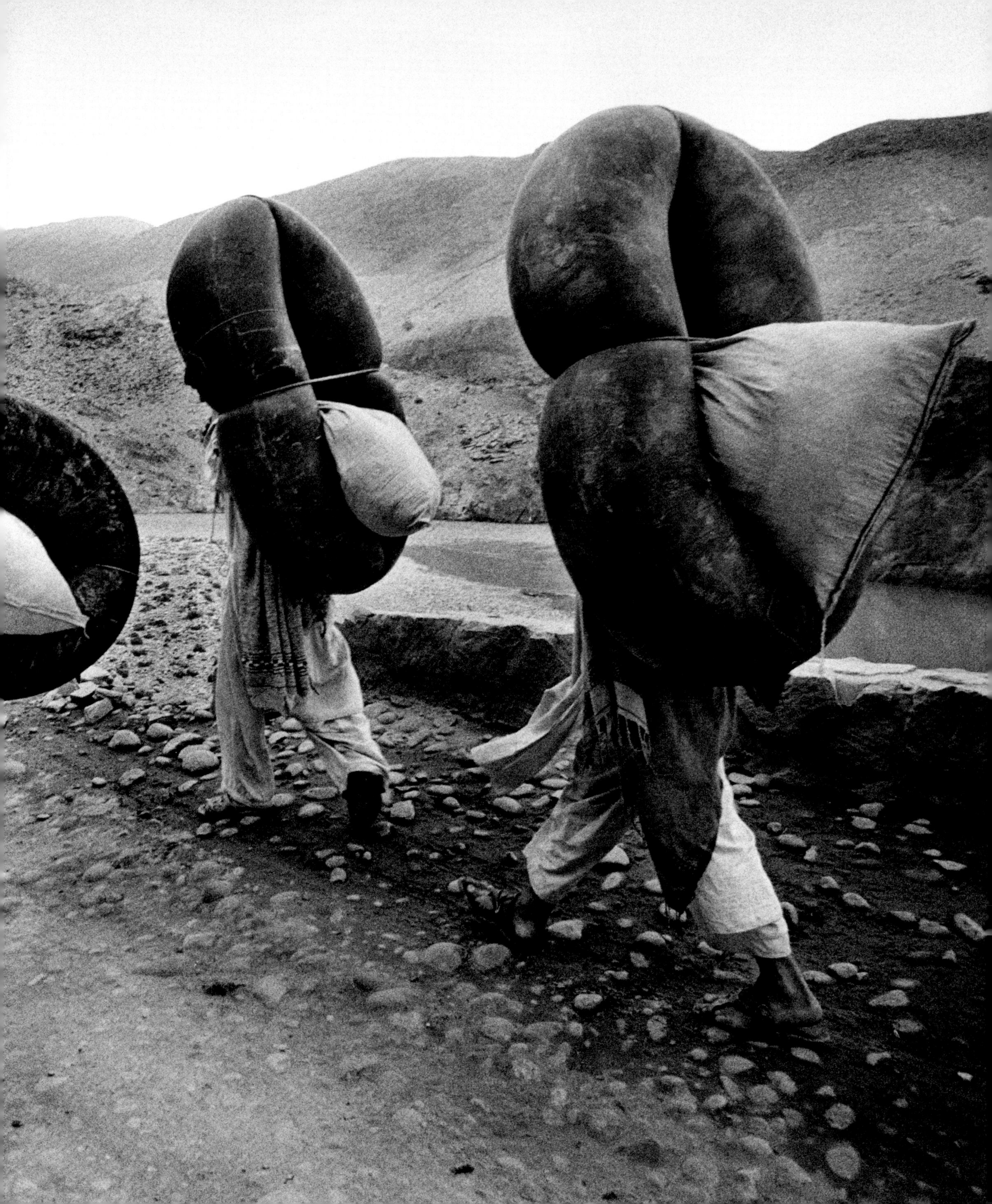

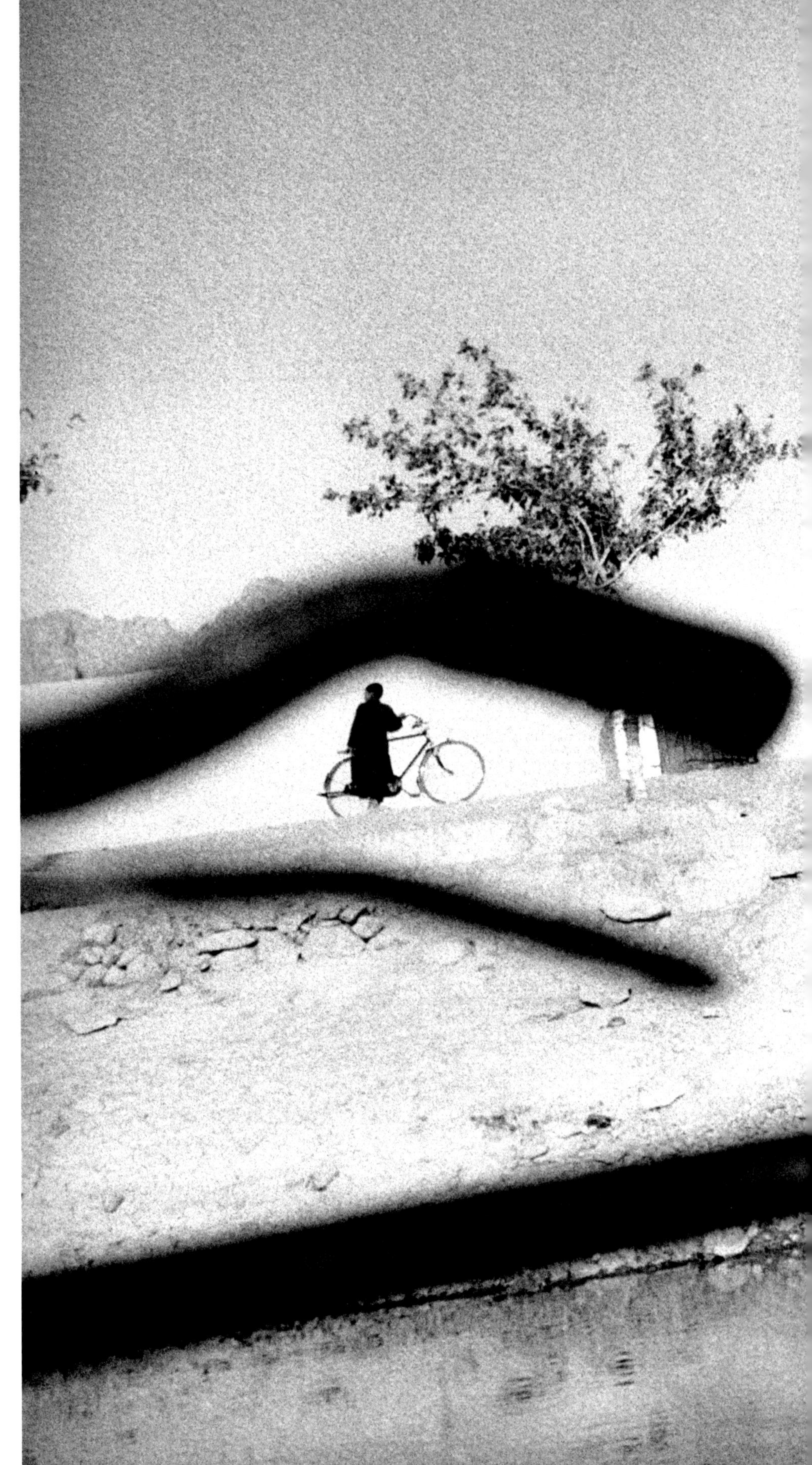

KANDAHAR, KANDAHAR PROVINCE: AUGUST 2004
Summer respite.

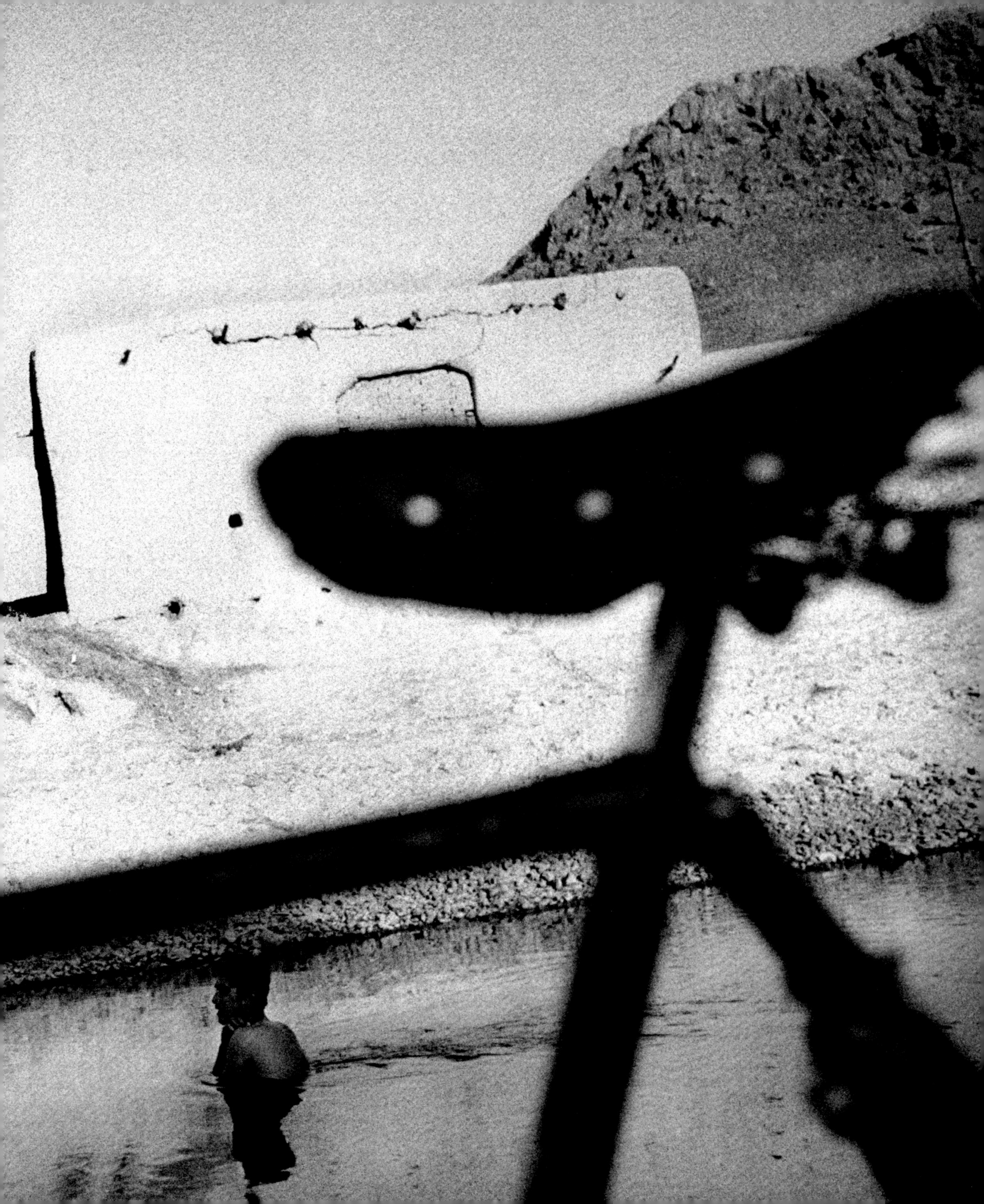

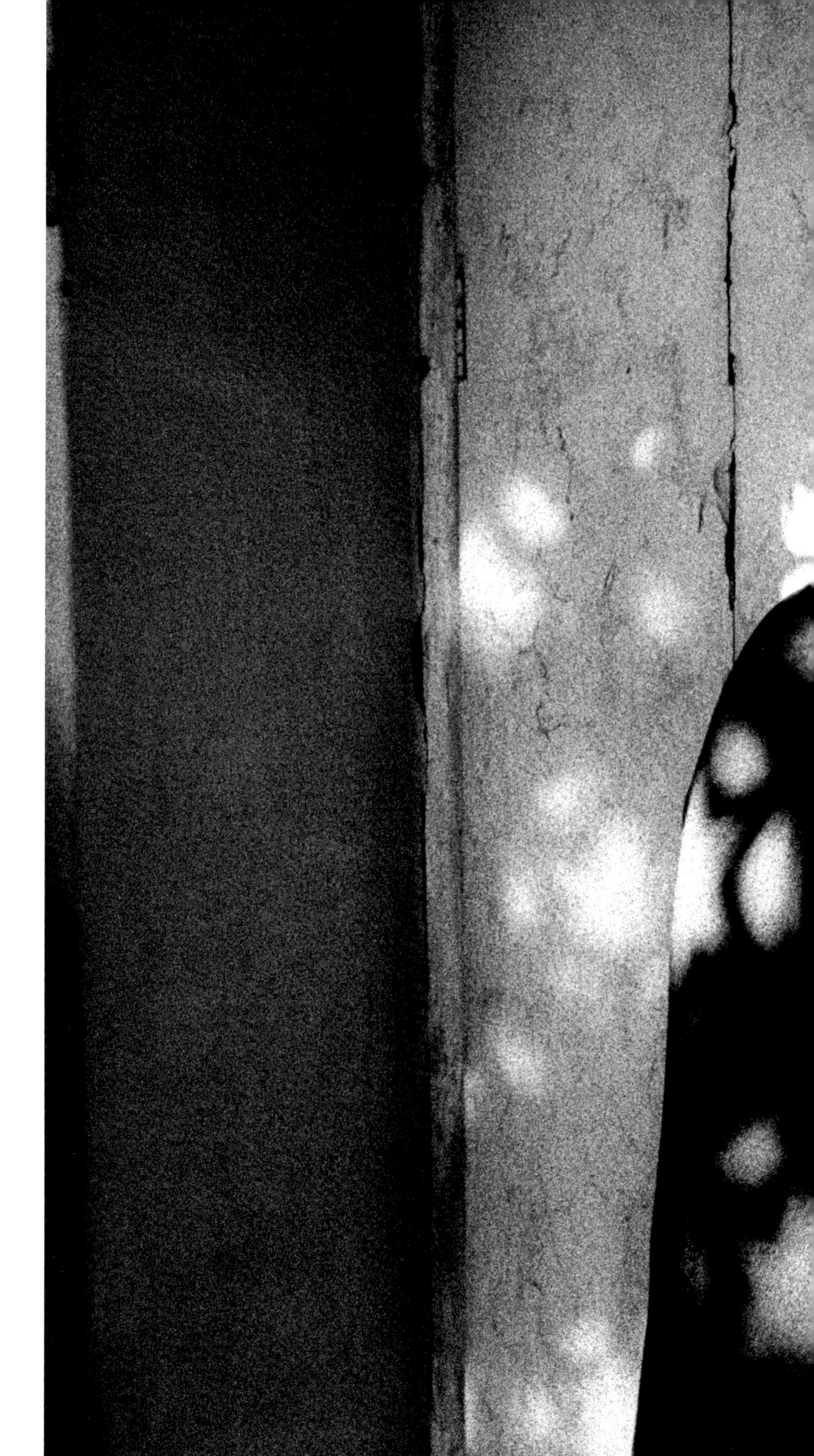

Isaac Levi locks the door of the synagogue on
Flower Street. Along with Zavolan Simantov, they
are the last Jews of Kabul. Both are tenants in the
building and have maintained a feud for years,
refusing to speak to one another. They stayed
here throughout the reign of the Taliban, at times
informing on each other and as a result being
imprisoned at different times.

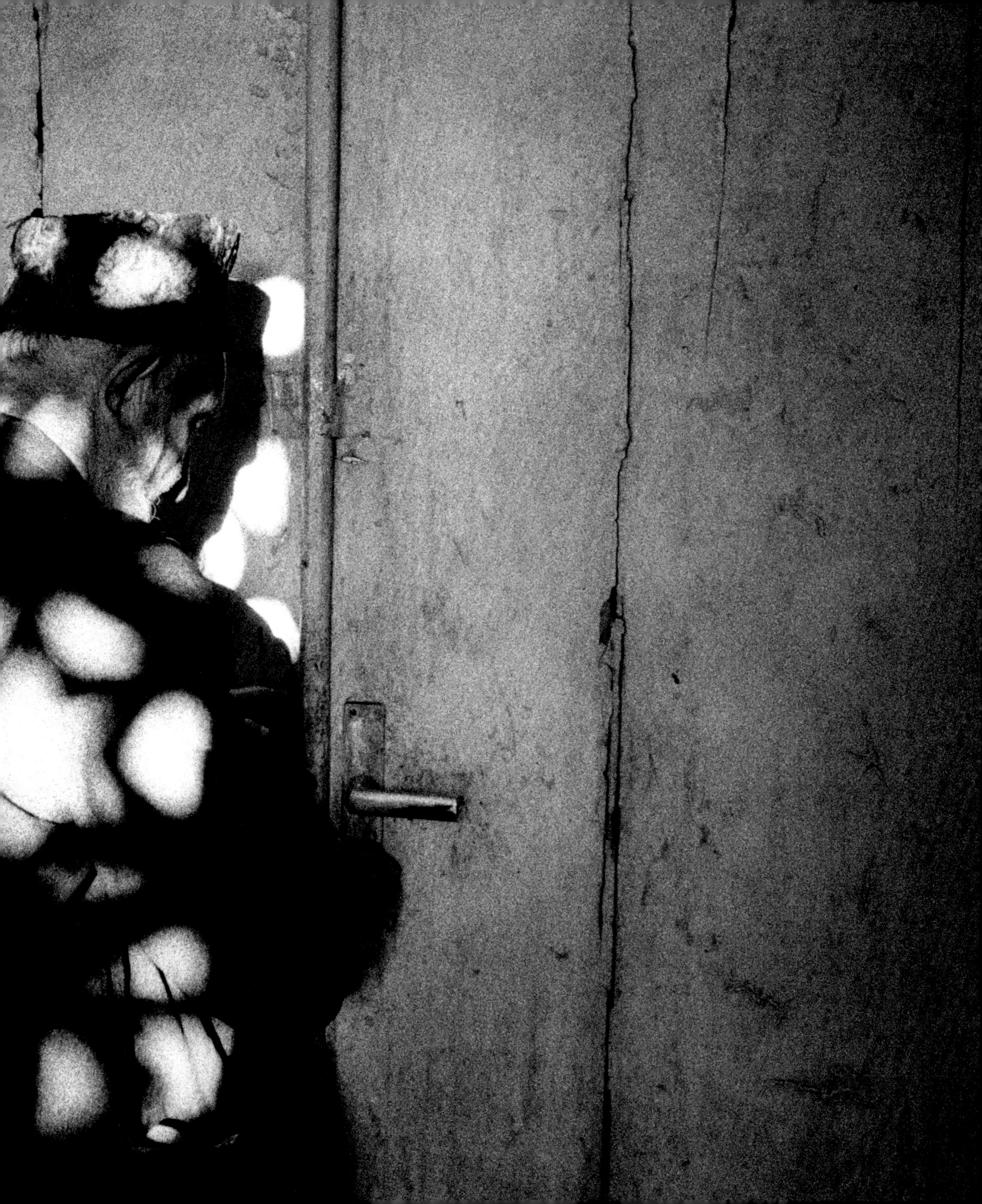

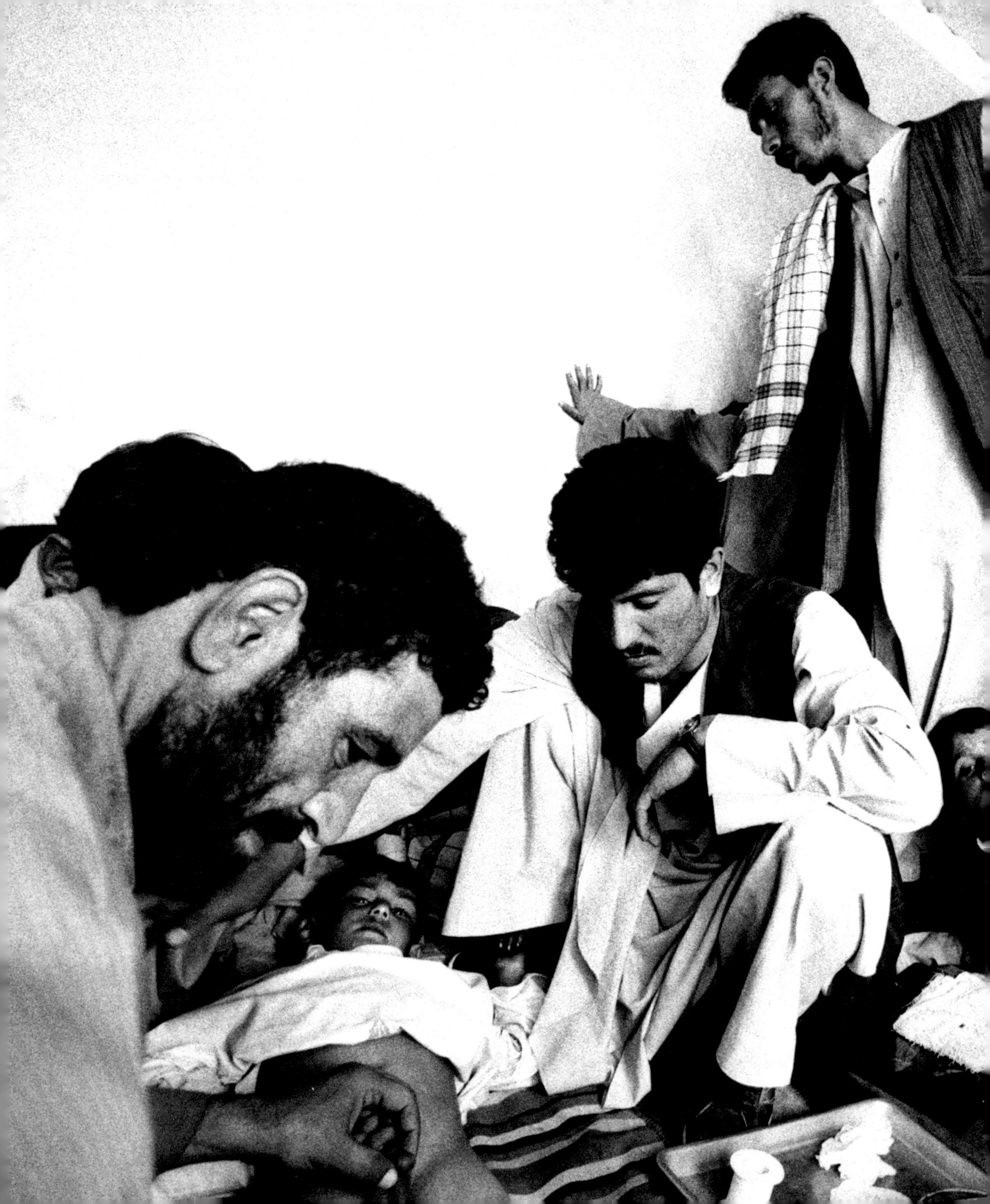

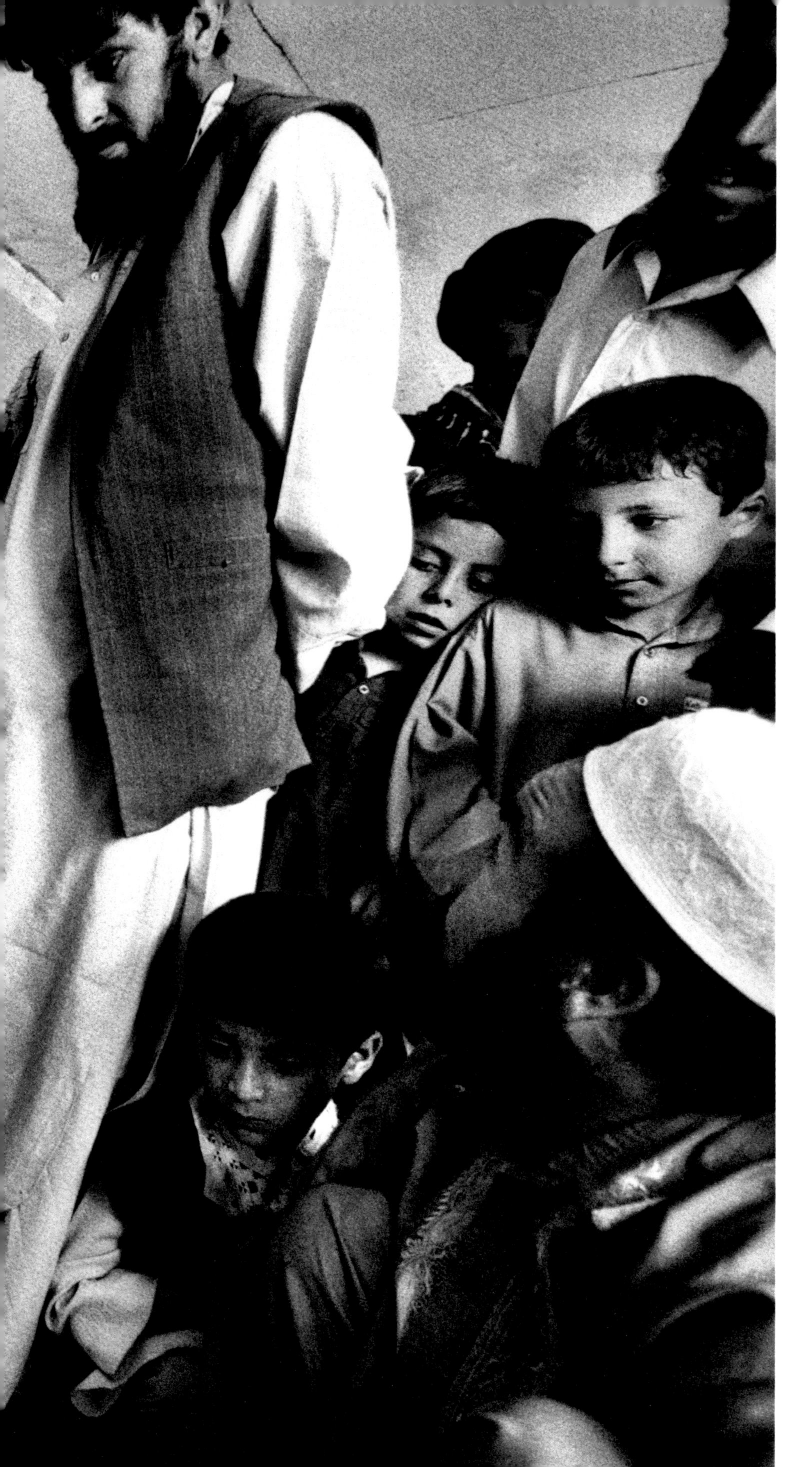

GHULAM ALI, PARWAN PROVINCE: OCTOBER 2001
A young boy being circumcised in his village on
the Shamali Plain.

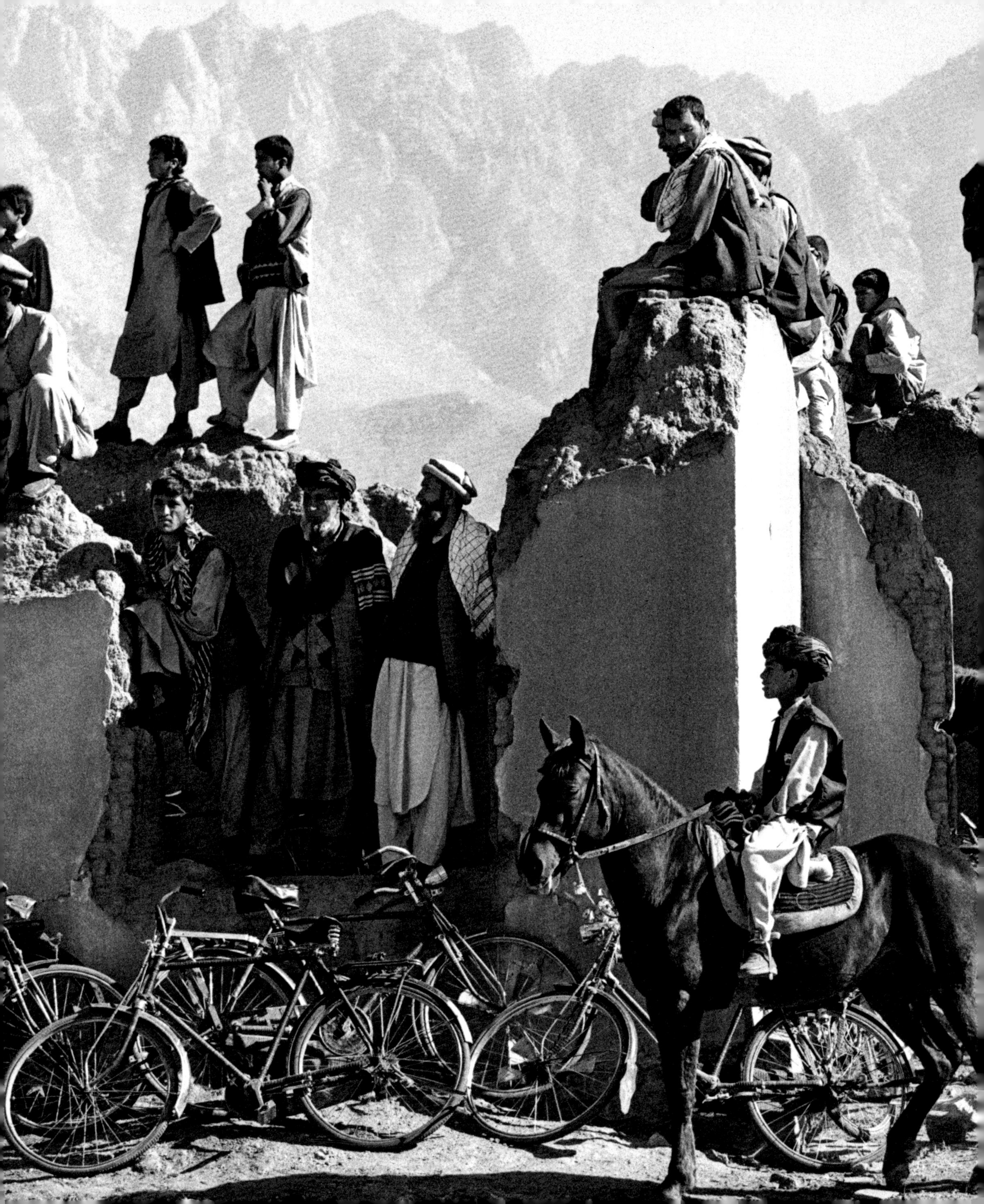

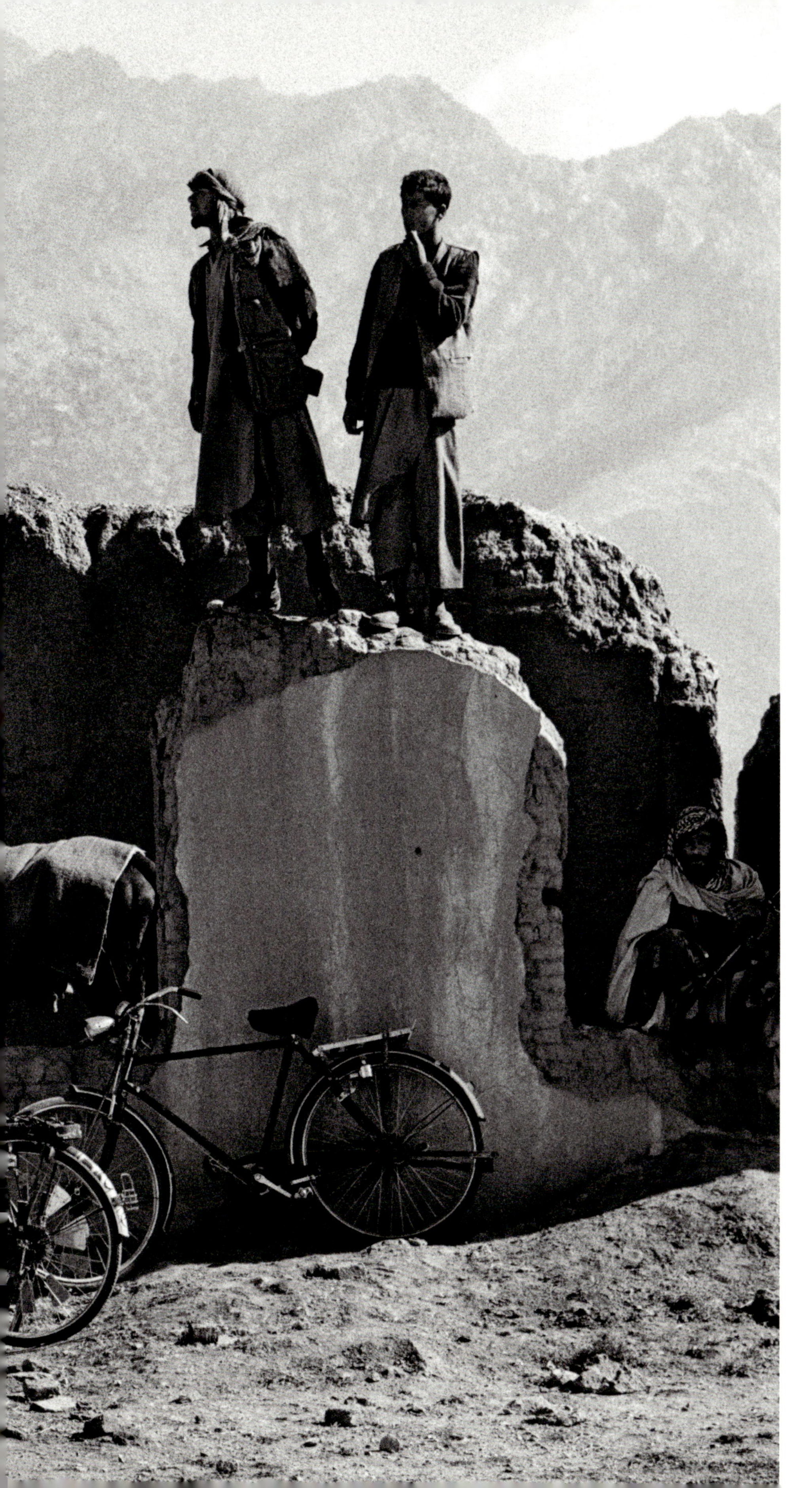

Immediately before the military offensive on Kabul and in anticipation of victory, the Northern Alliance has organised a game of Buzkashi , a wild sport that involves competing on horseback over a headless goat. It was banned under the Taliban.

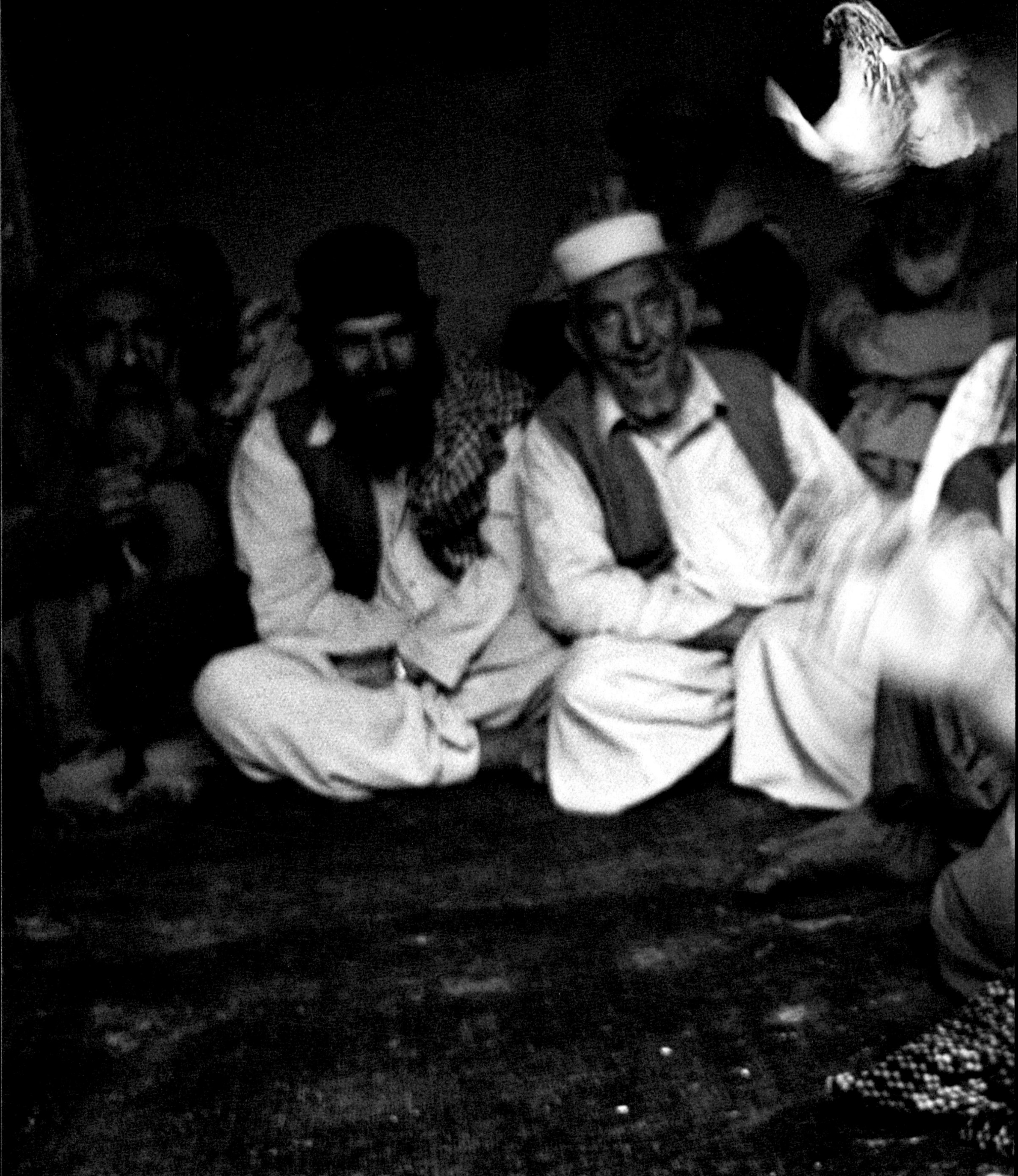

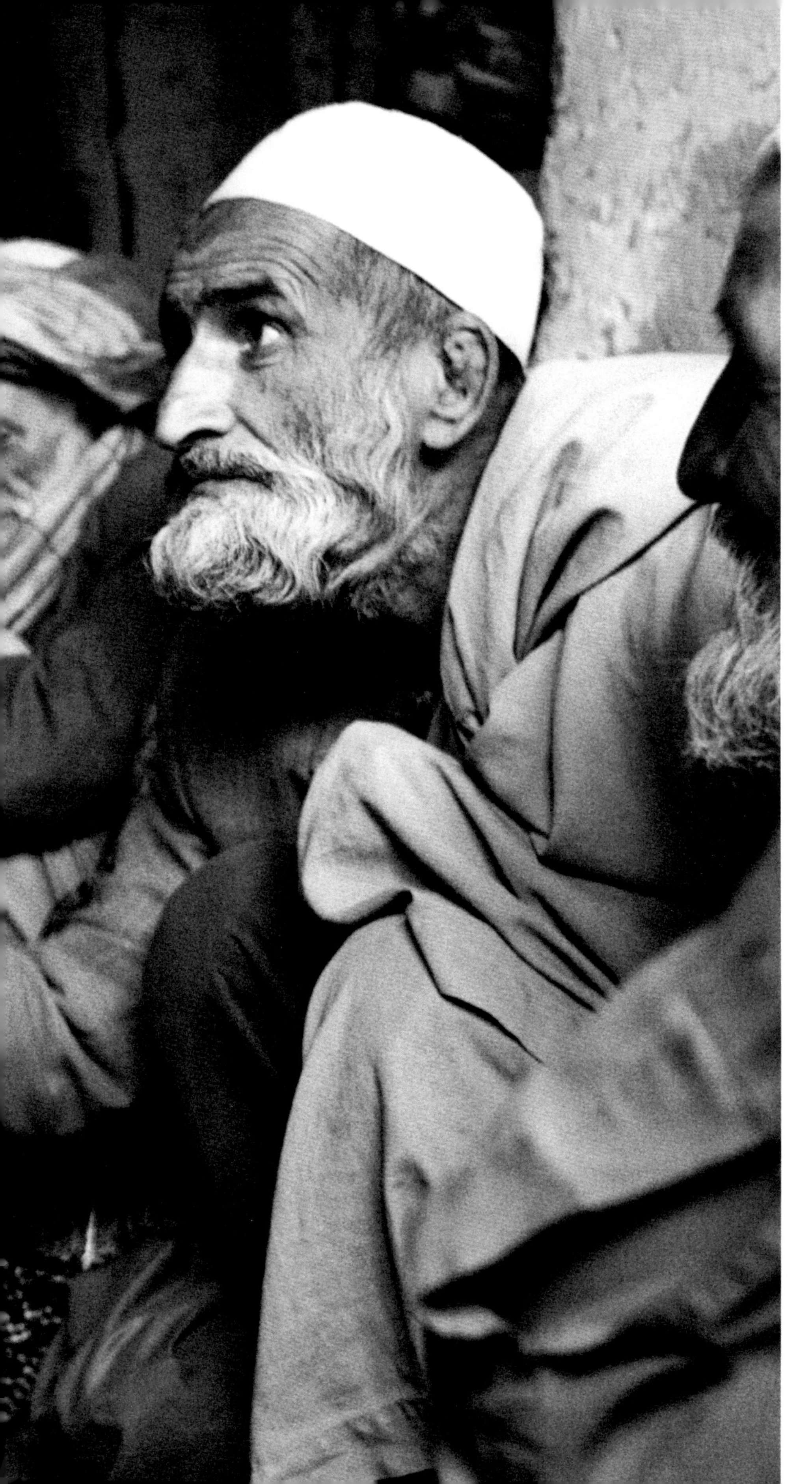

Kabul: November 2004
A bodahna bird owner tosses his bird in the air
prior to the fight.

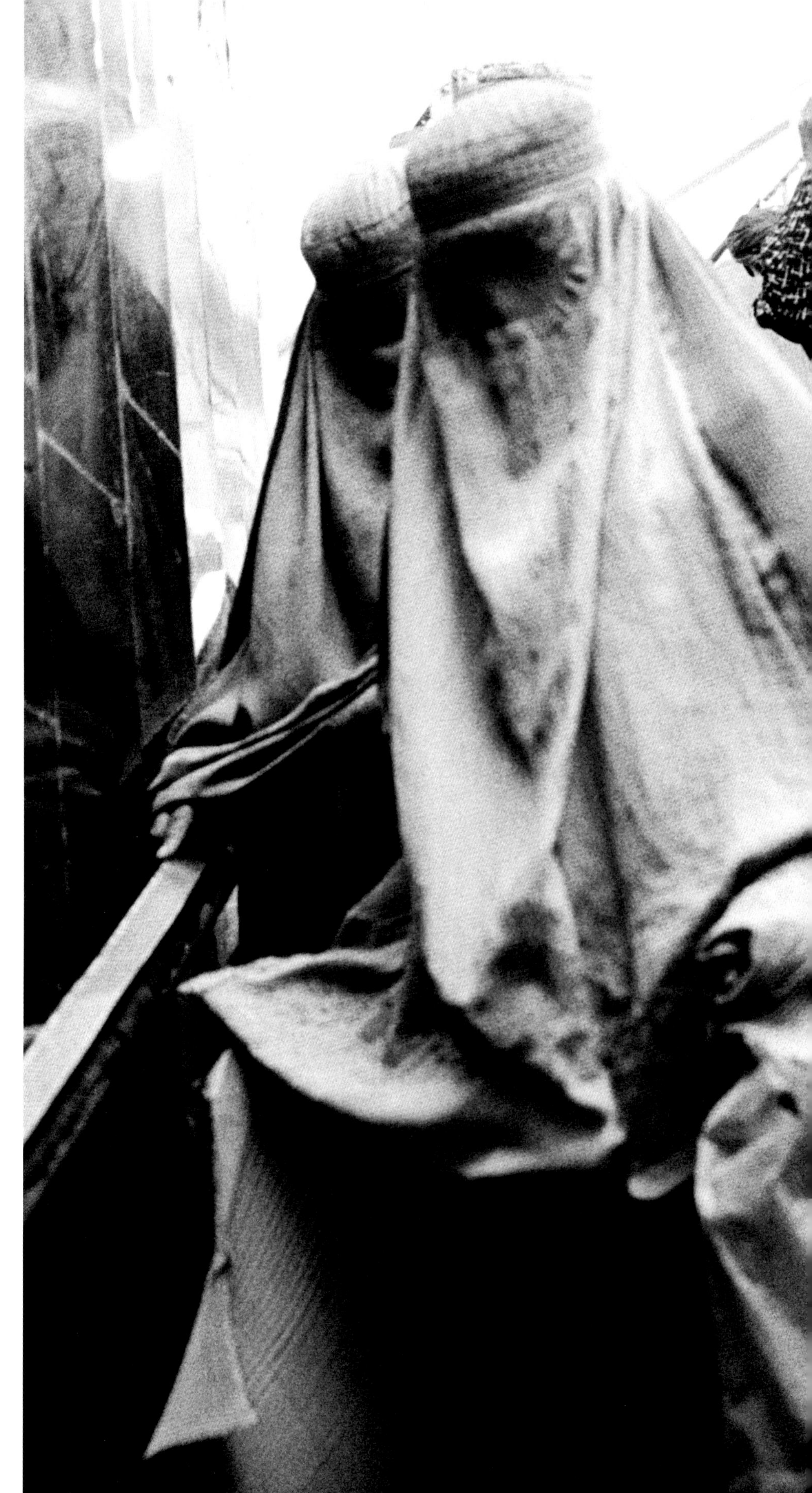

KABUL: AUGUST 2004
After 25 years of war, Afghanistan has a reputed
two million war widows.

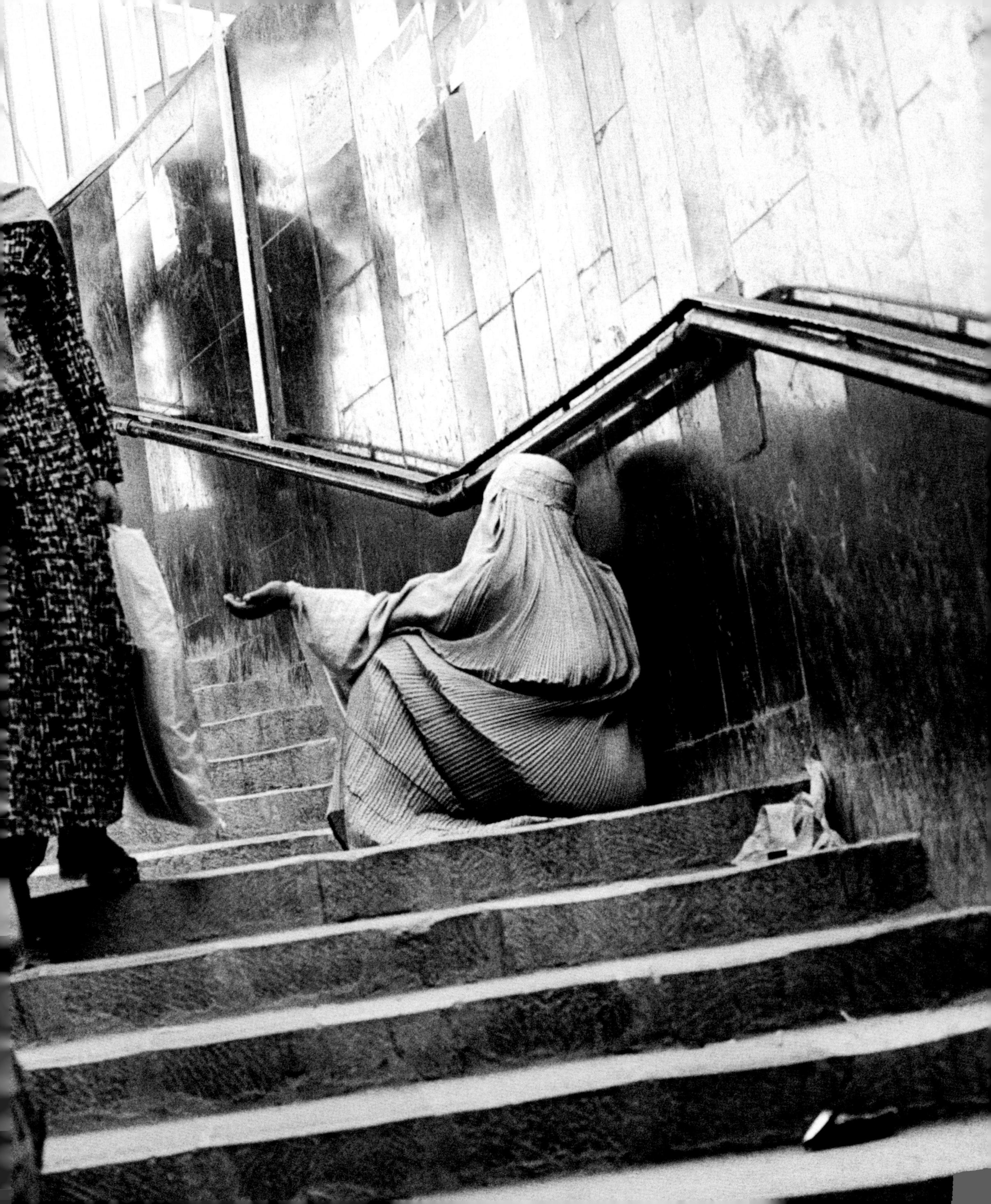

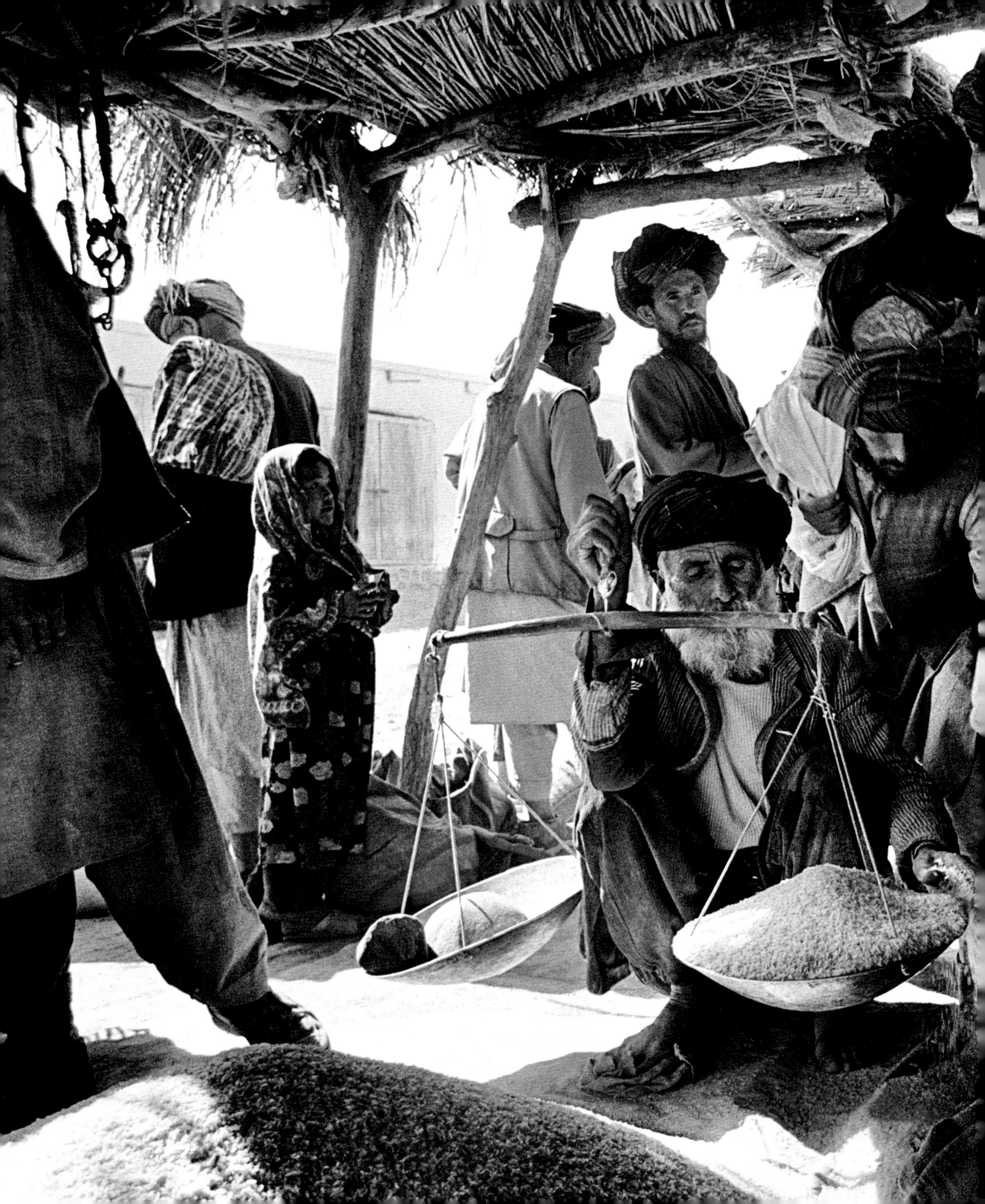

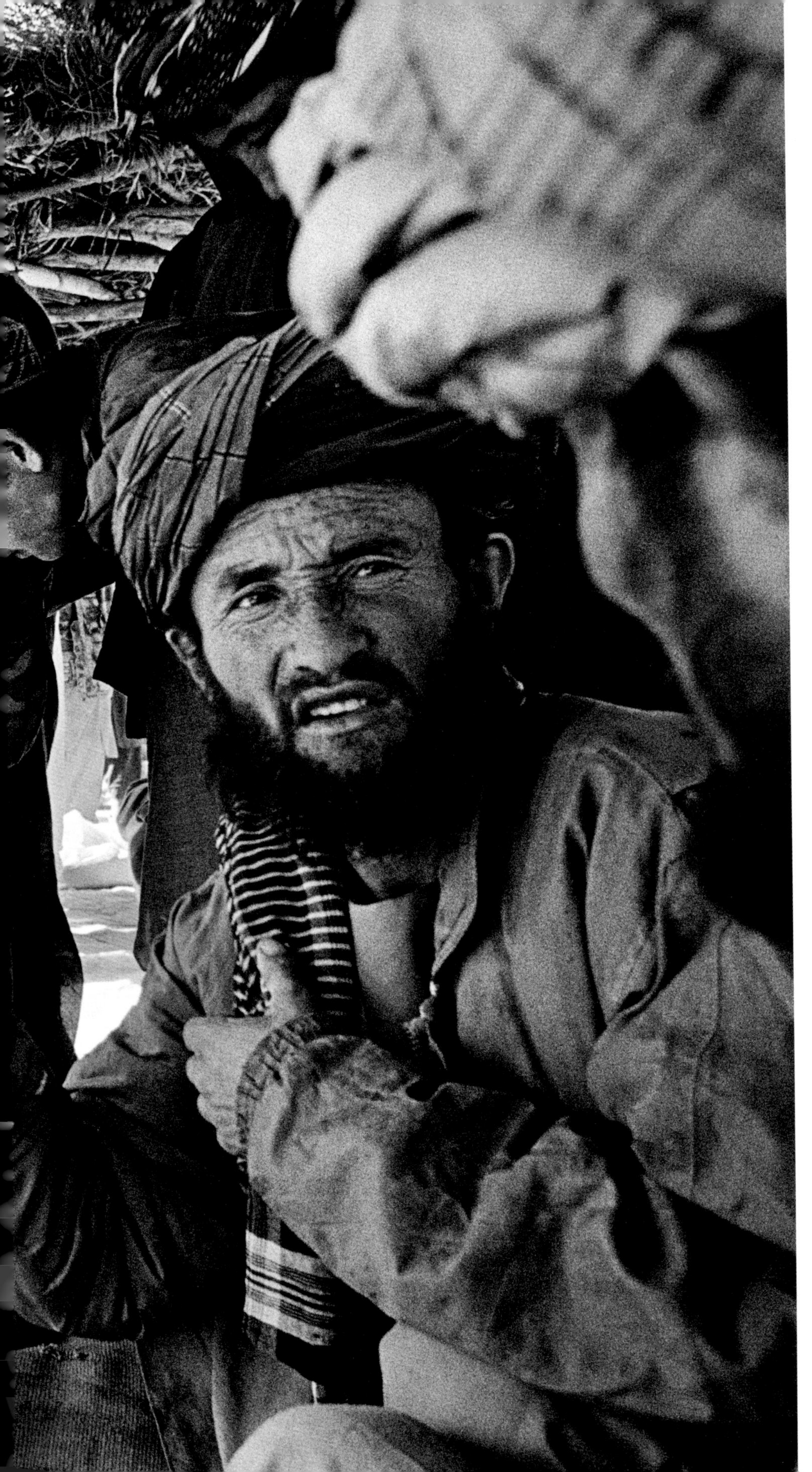

KHWAJA BAHAUDDIN, TAKHAR PROVINCE:
OCTOBER 2001
Bazaar in the centre of town.

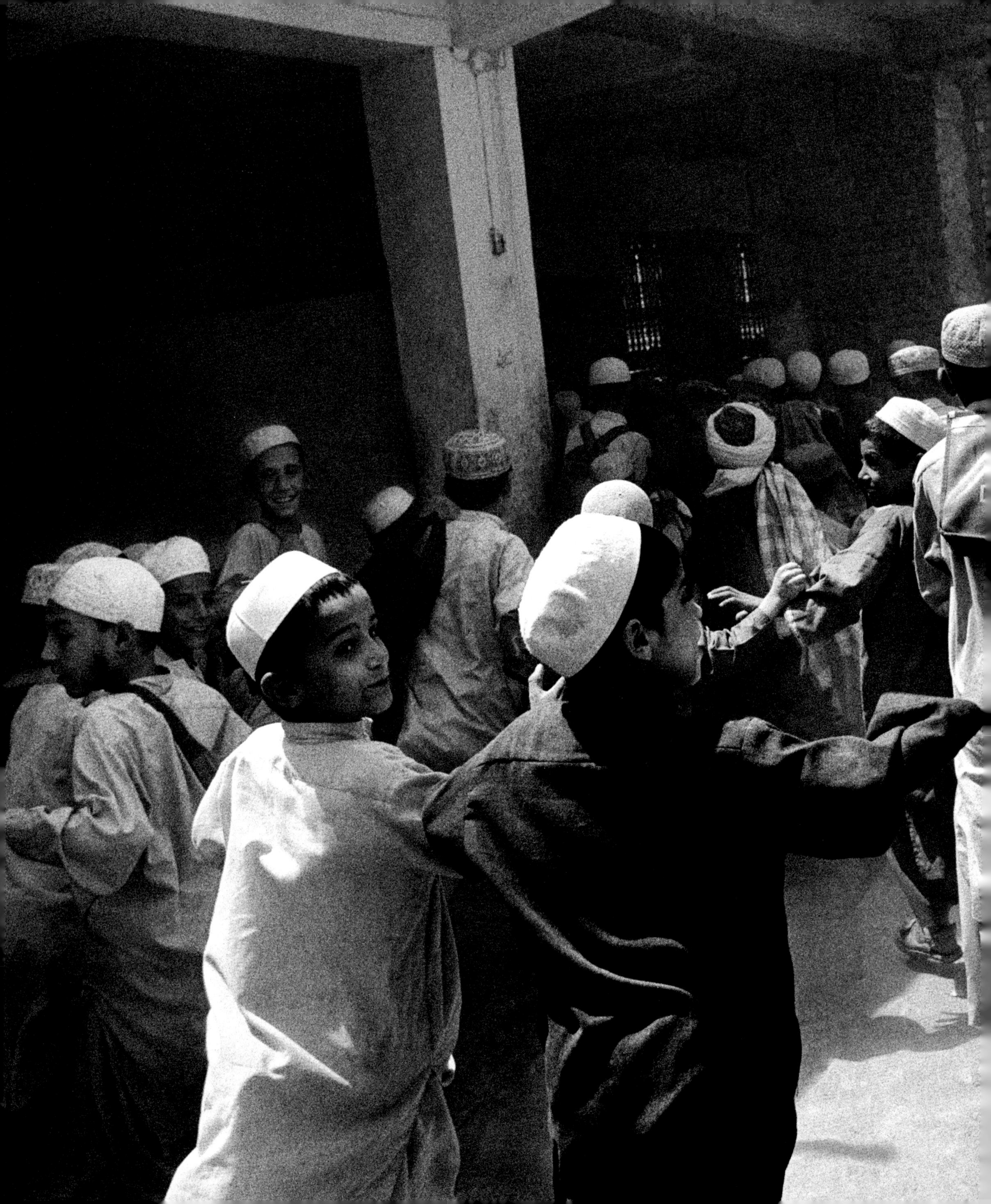

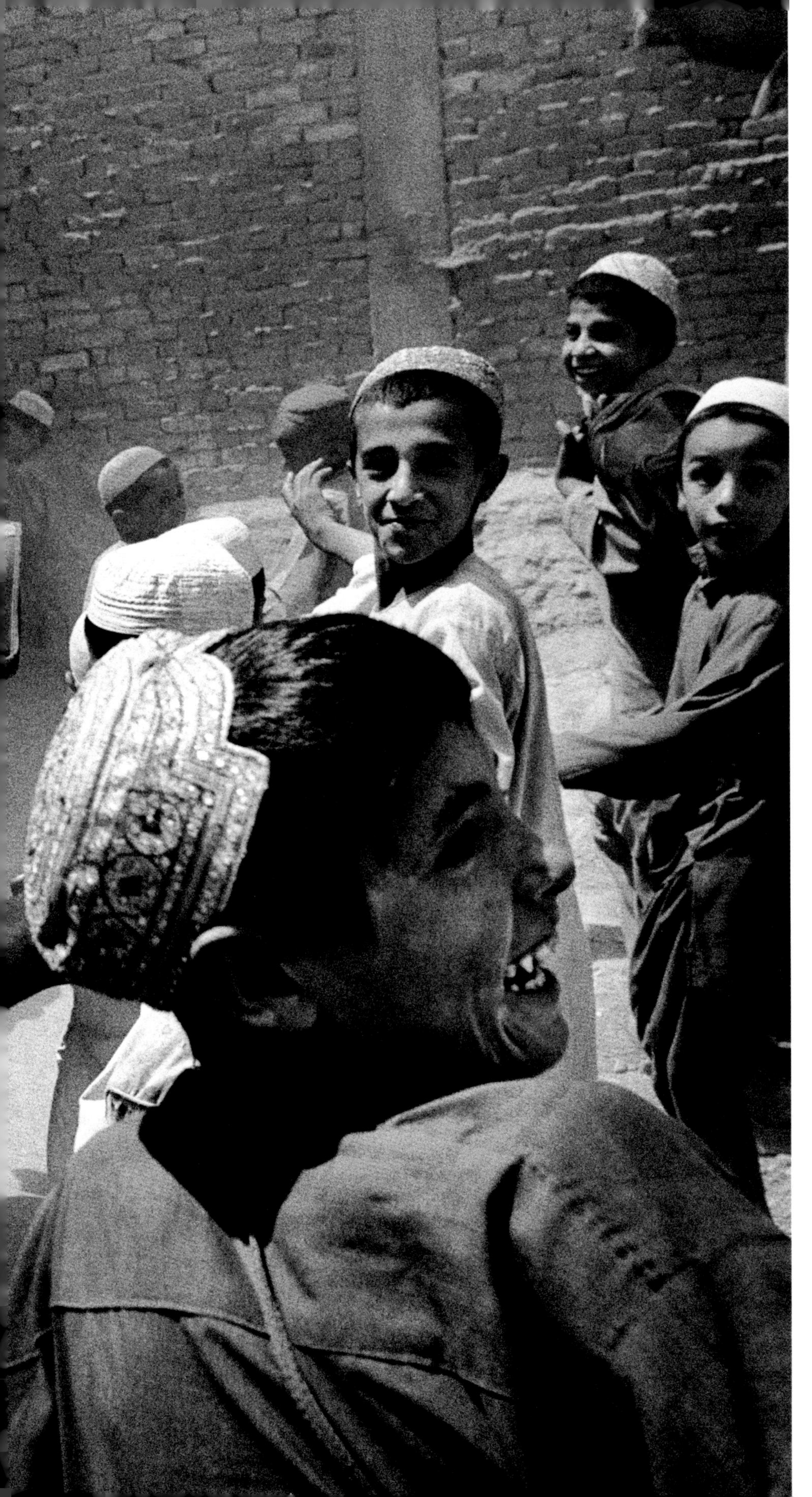

KANDAHAR, KANDAHAR PROVINCE: AUGUST 2004
The end of classes at a madrassa.

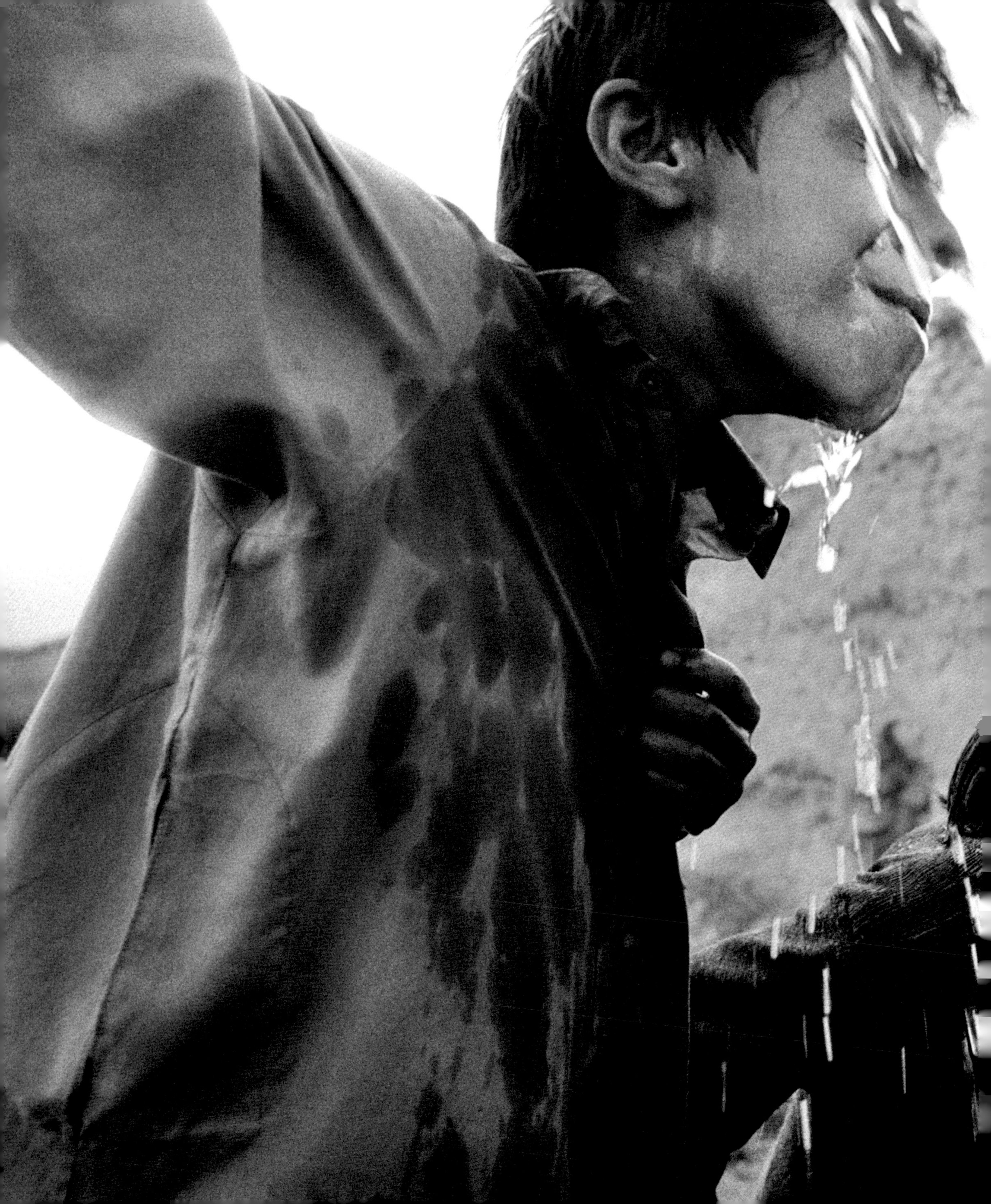

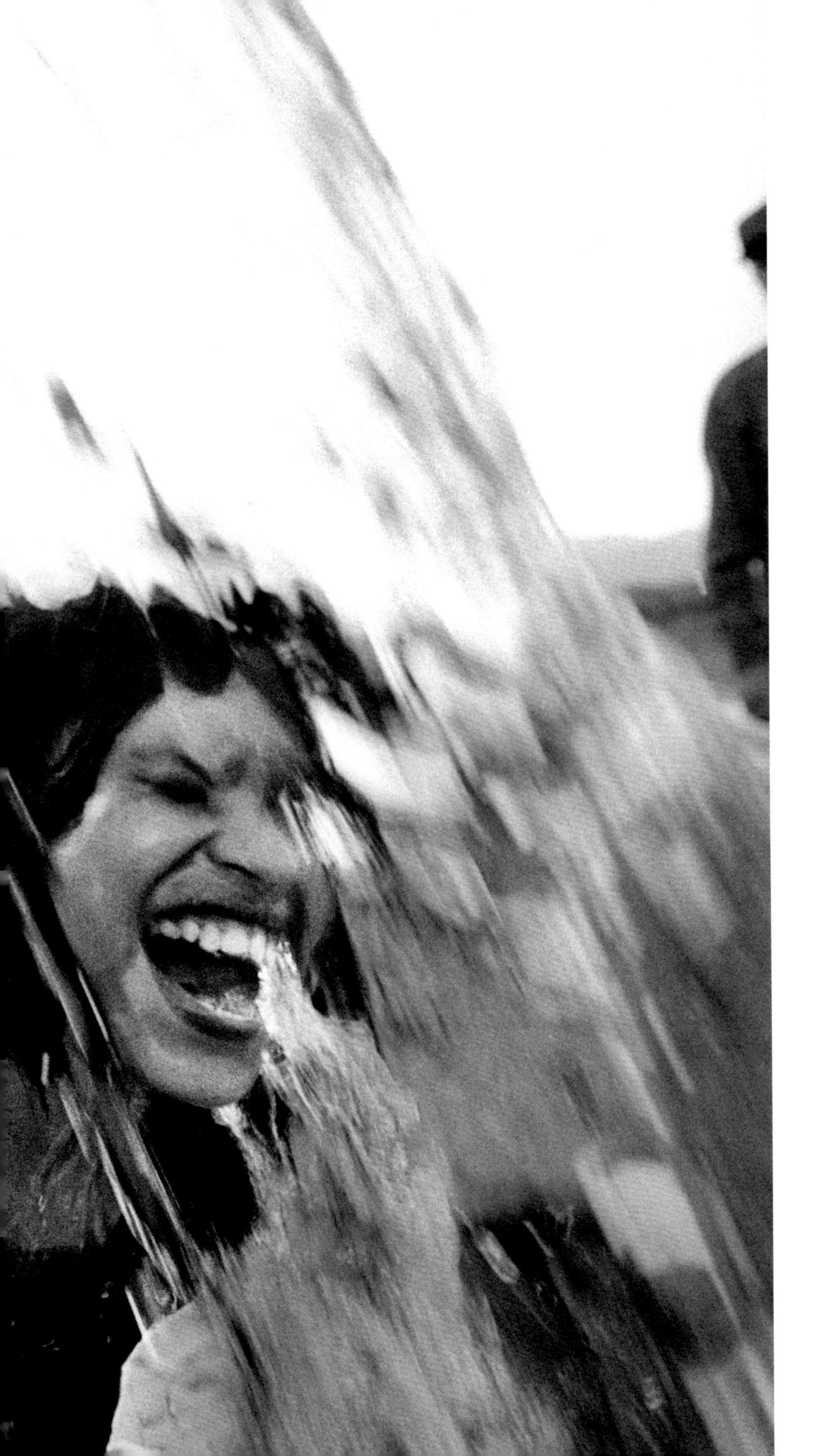

SHAMALI PLAIN, PARWAN PROVINCE: AUGUST 2004
Children cooling down after a day's work in the
fields. The Shamali Plain traditionally supported a
multitude of vines and crops. It was the site
of many battles for the capital, and suffered
immeasurably over the years.

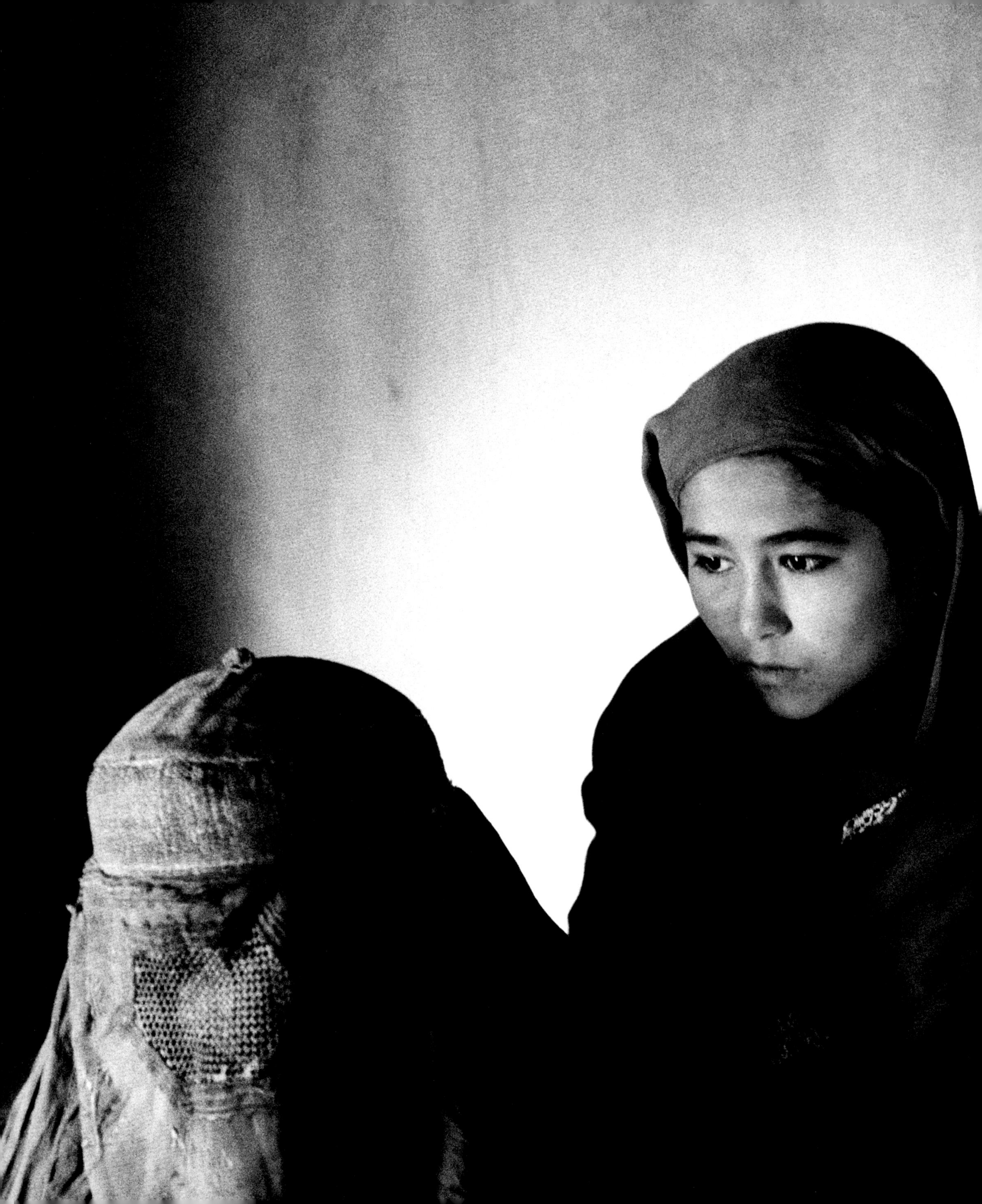

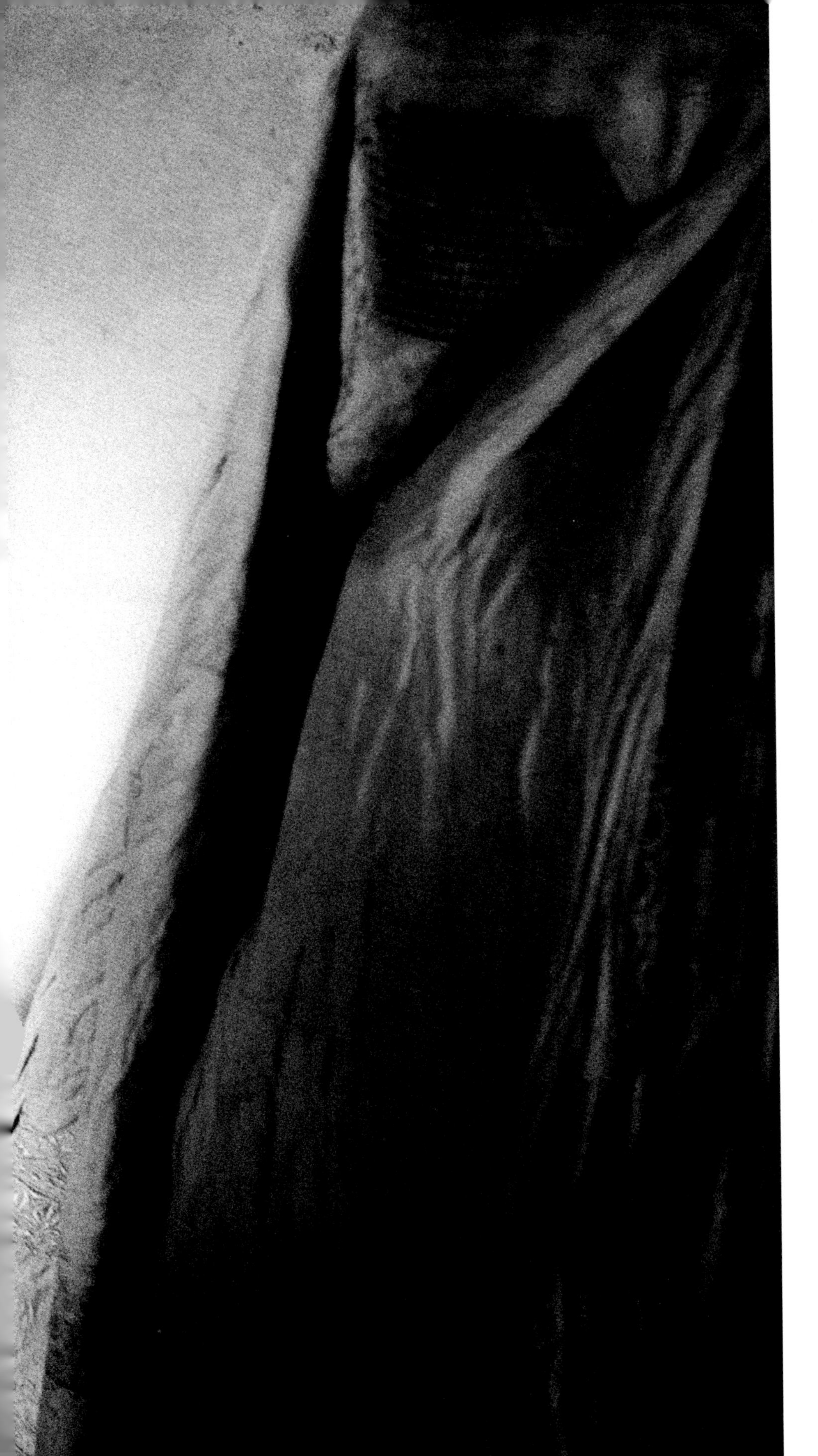

DASHT-E-QALA, TAKHAR PROVINCE: NOVEMBER 2000
Having fled the fighting in their home village
of Dashti Archi, Sabzag Gul, 13, and her family
became internally displaced persons (IDPs).
Despite efforts by Massoud's Northern Alliance
forces, the Taliban are on the advance.

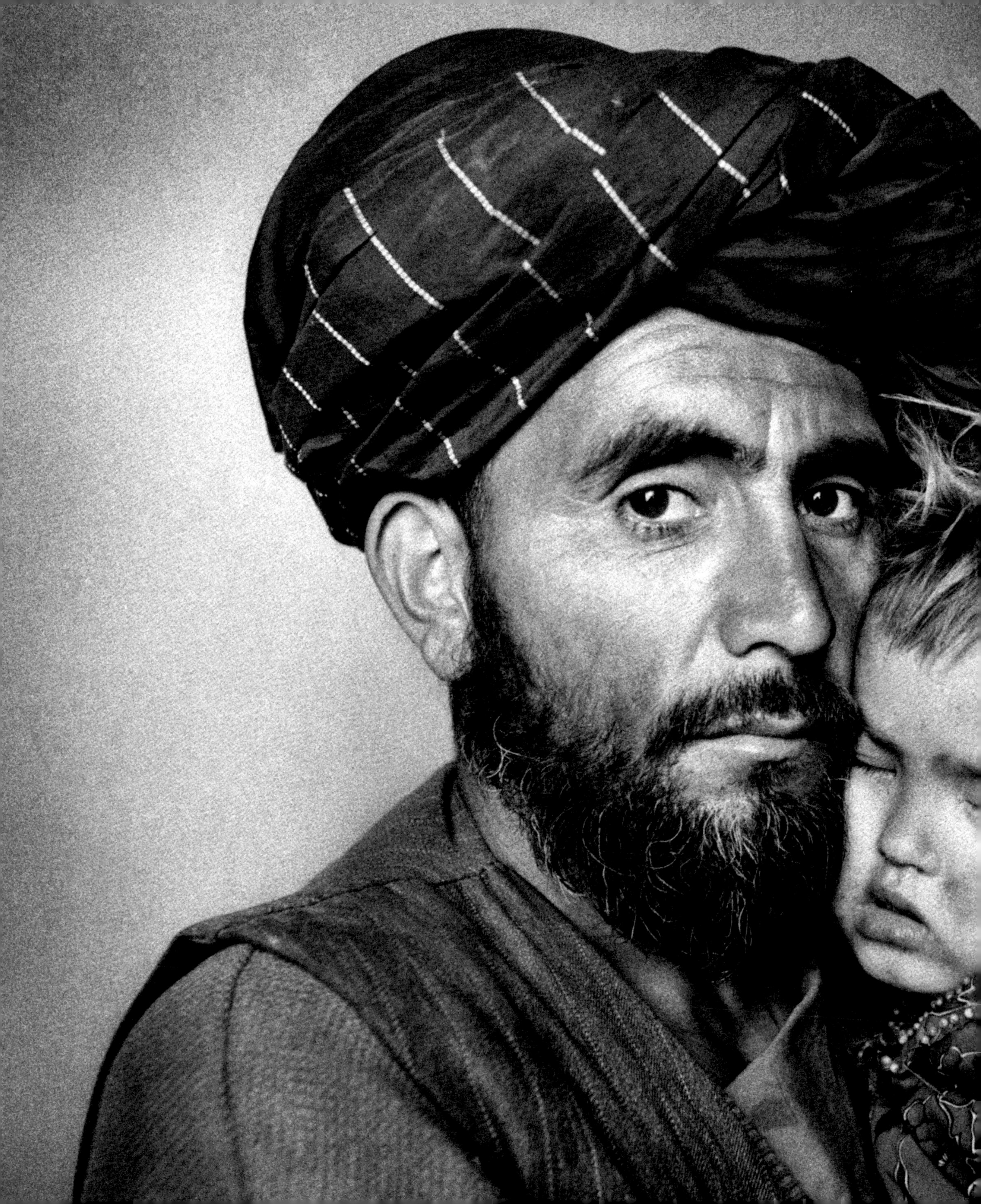

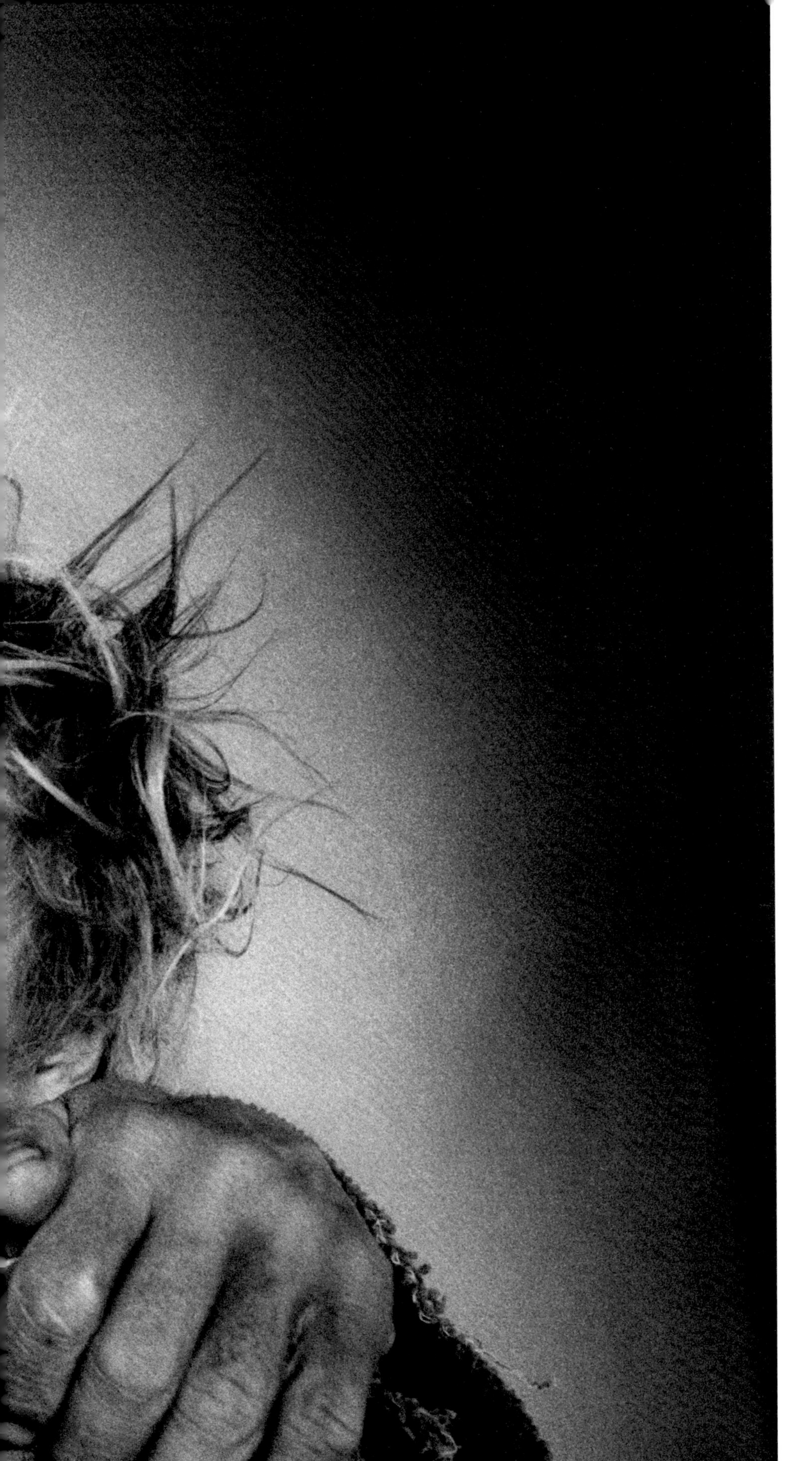

DASHT-E-QALA, TAKHAR PROVINCE: NOVEMBER 2000
A father with his daughter, ill with malaria, waits
for treatment at a Swedish Committee clinic.

MINAR-E-JAM, GHOR PROVINCE: JUNE 2003
Inside the Minaret.

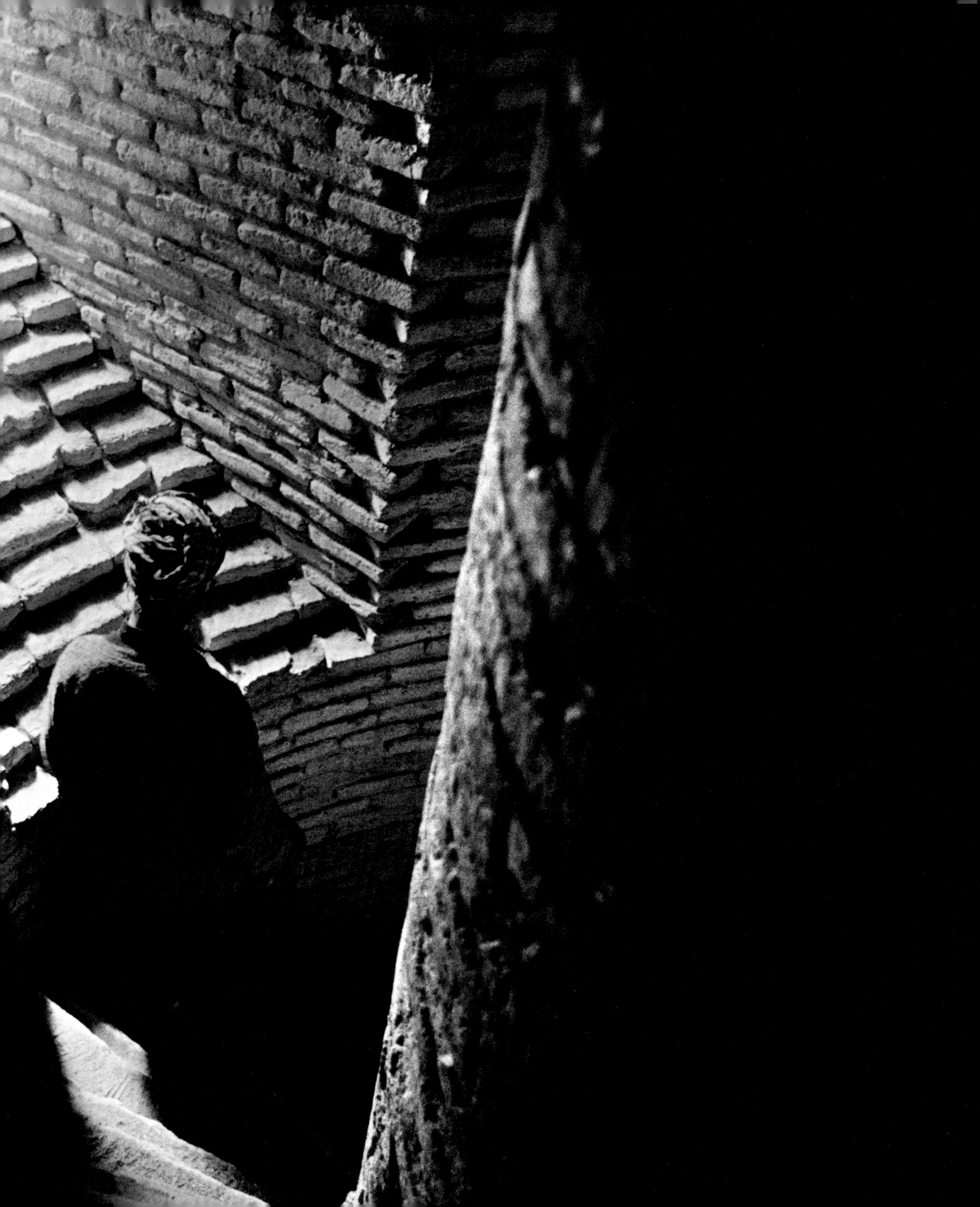

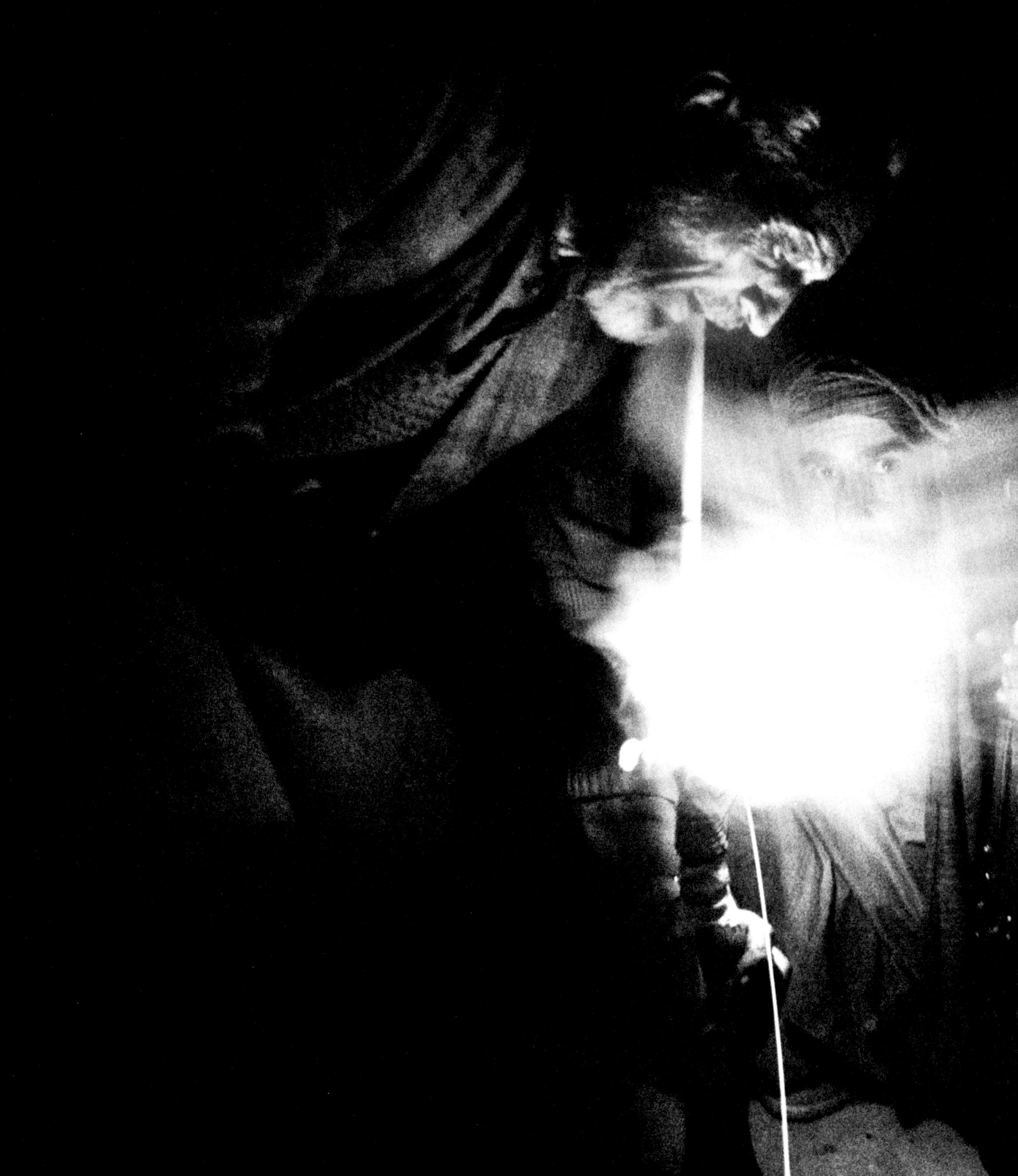

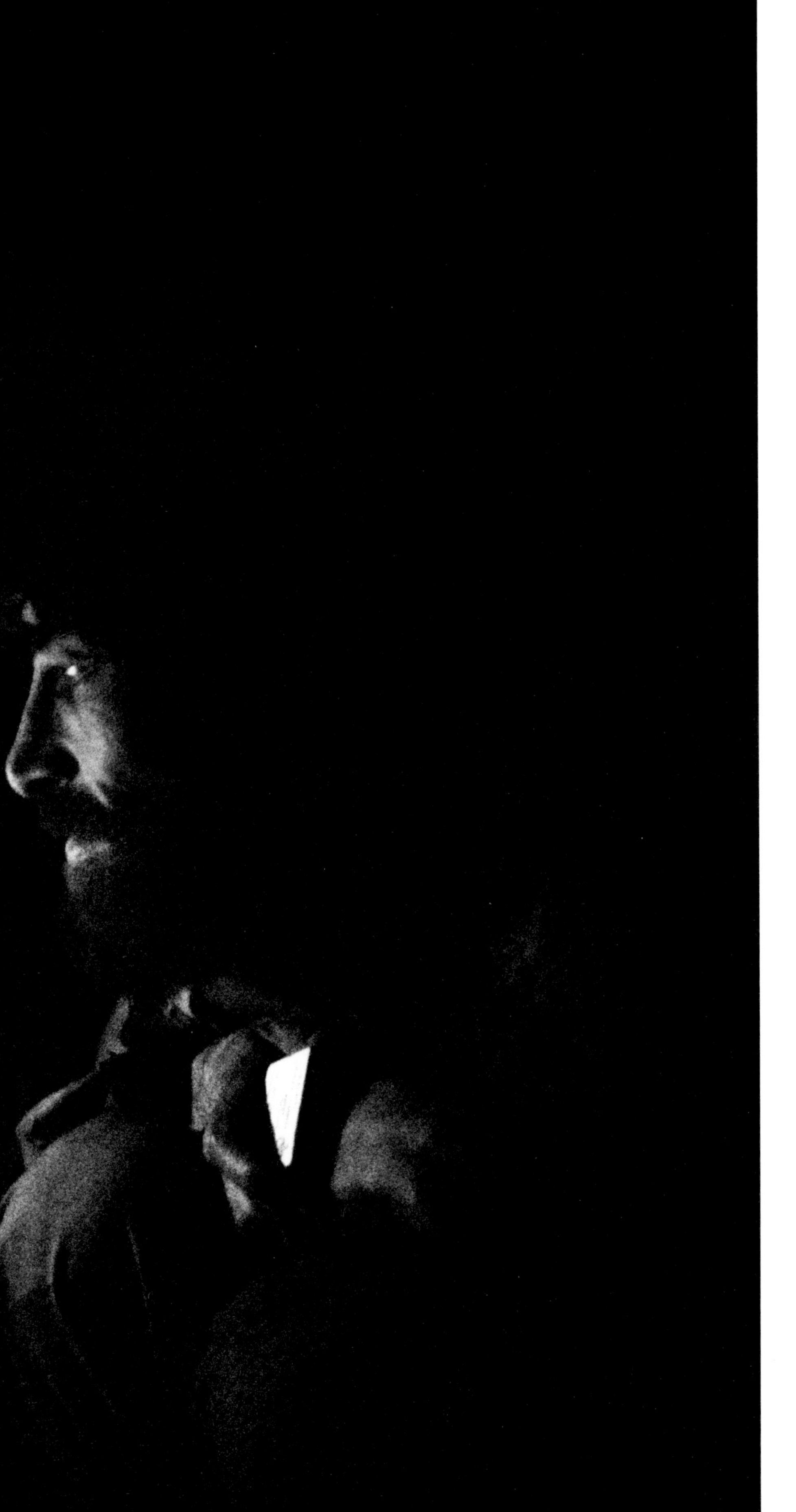

Kabul: November 1994
Mujahideen fighters smoking hashish in the
Old City.

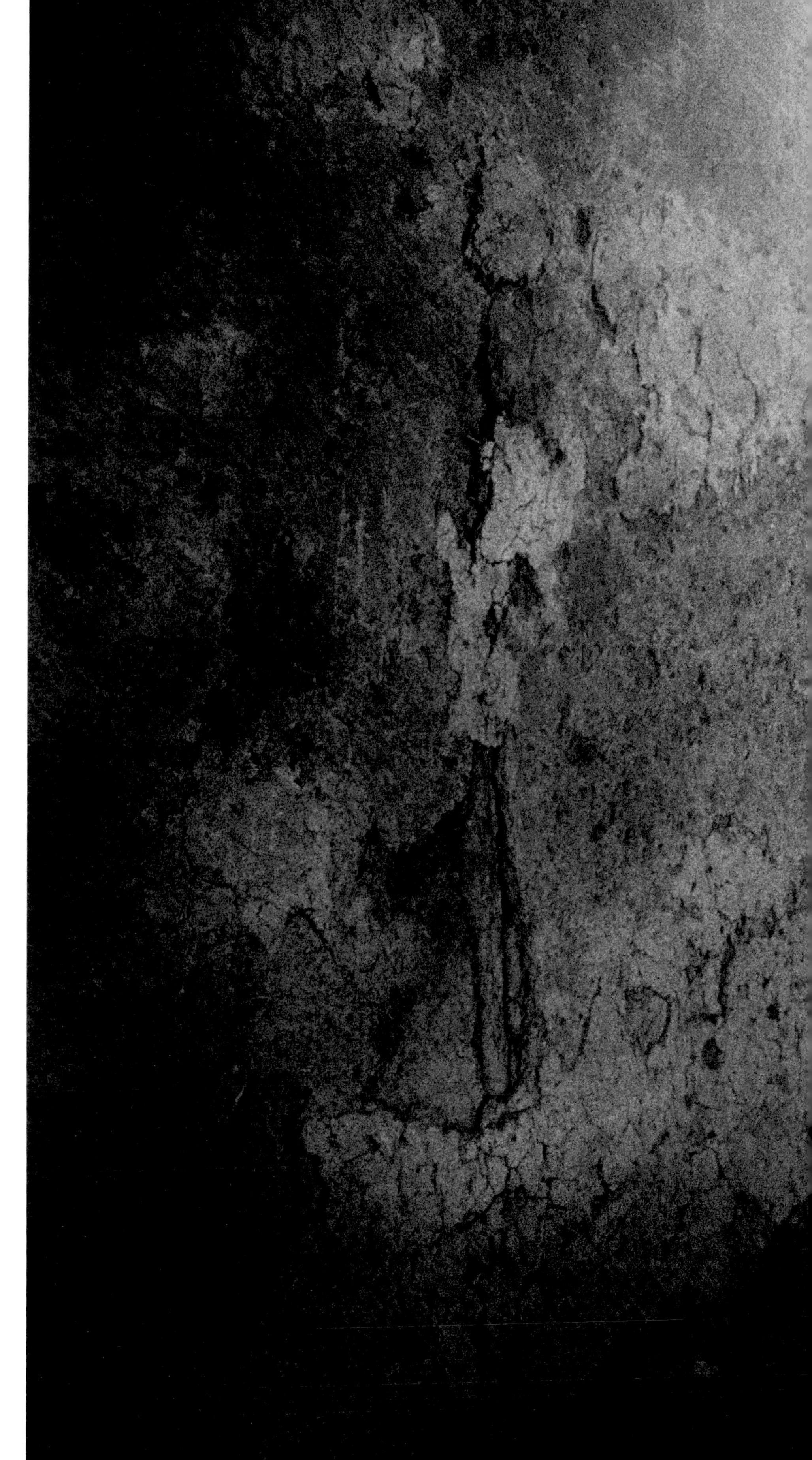

Old City, Kabul: November 1994
Fighters loyal to Ahmad Shah Massoud.

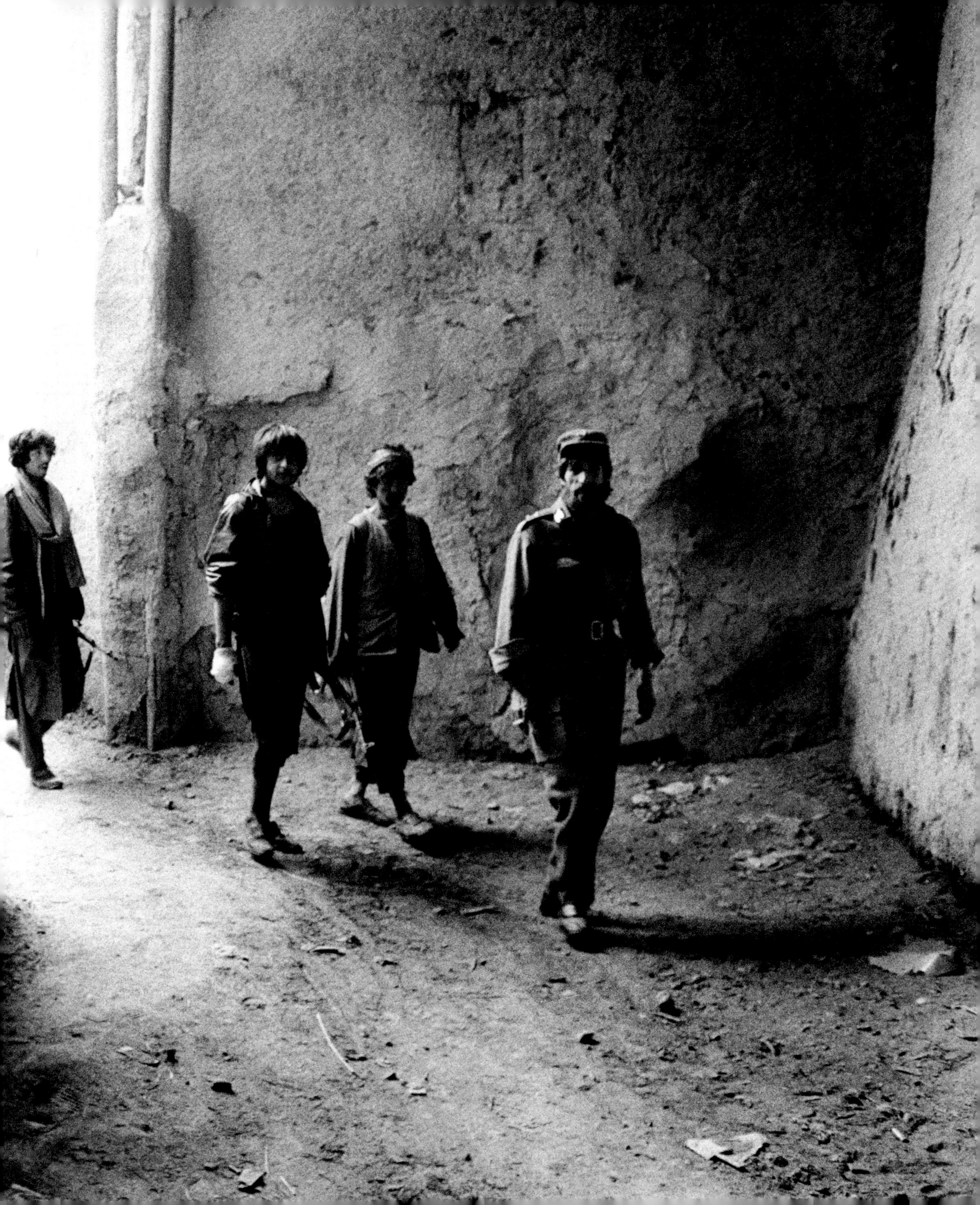

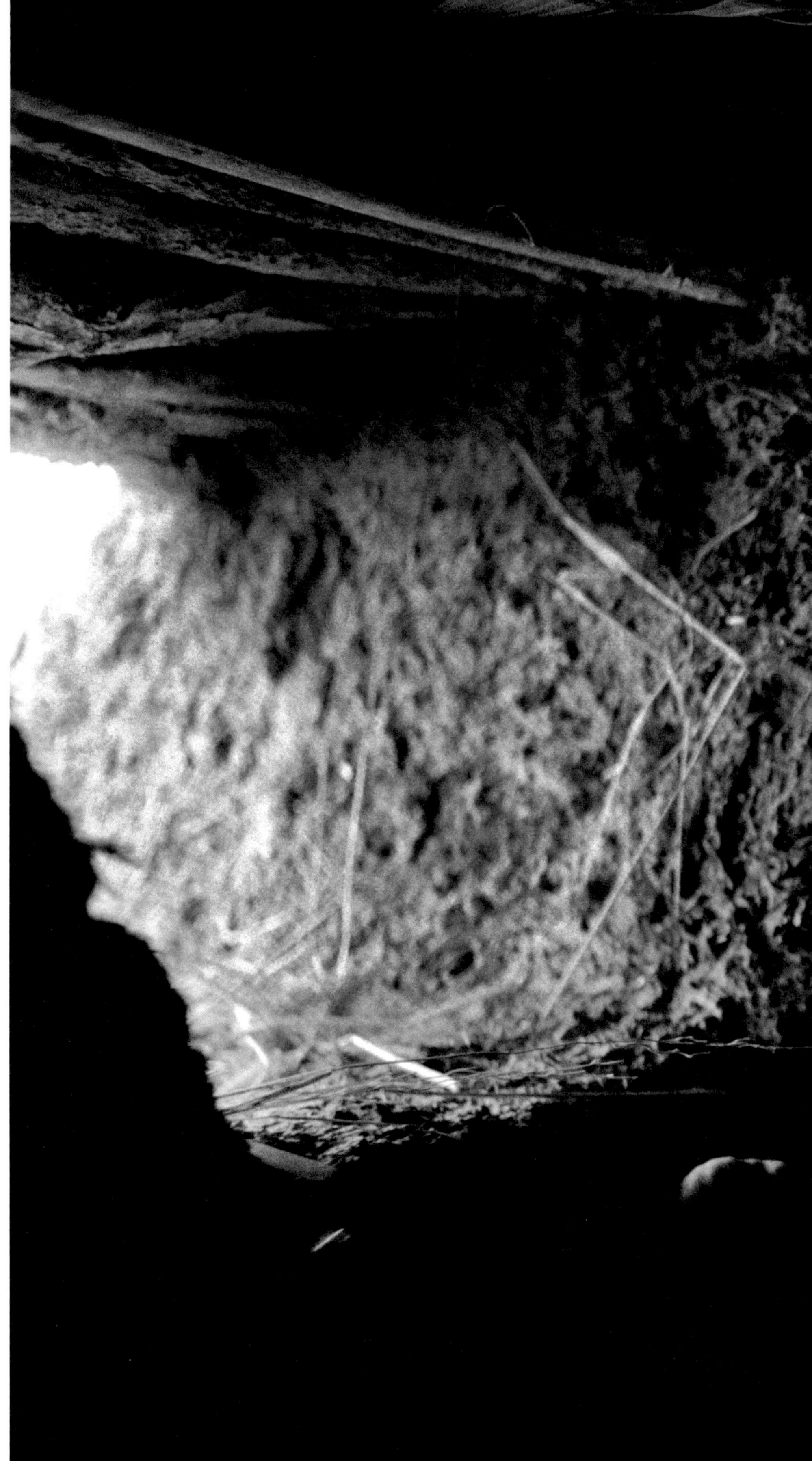

Dasht-e-Qala, Takhar Province: November 2000
Ahmad Shah Massoud, Afghanistan's tragic
resistance hero. A brilliant tactician, as a young
mujahideen commander Massoud outwitted nine
Soviet offensives designed to destroy his Panjshir
Valley bases. Described as "unbeatable" by one
Russian general, in 1992 he led his forces into
Kabul to overthrow the communist regime of
President Najibullah, and was appointed Minister
of Defence in the new government. Yet victory
was shortlived and civil war quickly ensued. In
1996 Massoud and his men were driven from
Kabul by the Taliban. He fought on, occupying a
shrinking piece of territory in the north of the
country until his assassination by suicide bombers
on September 9th, 2001. Two months later his
mujahideen again entered Kabul.

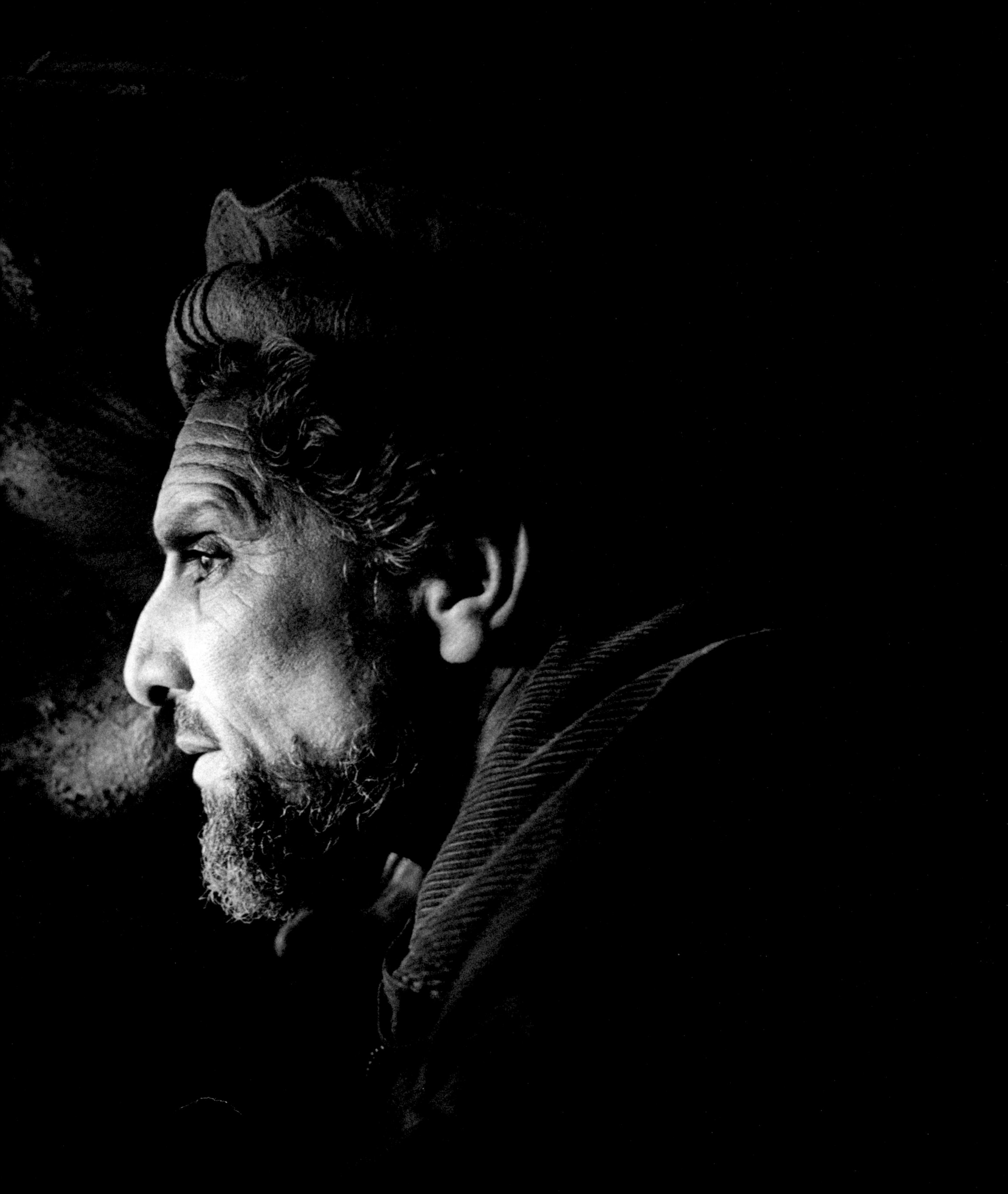

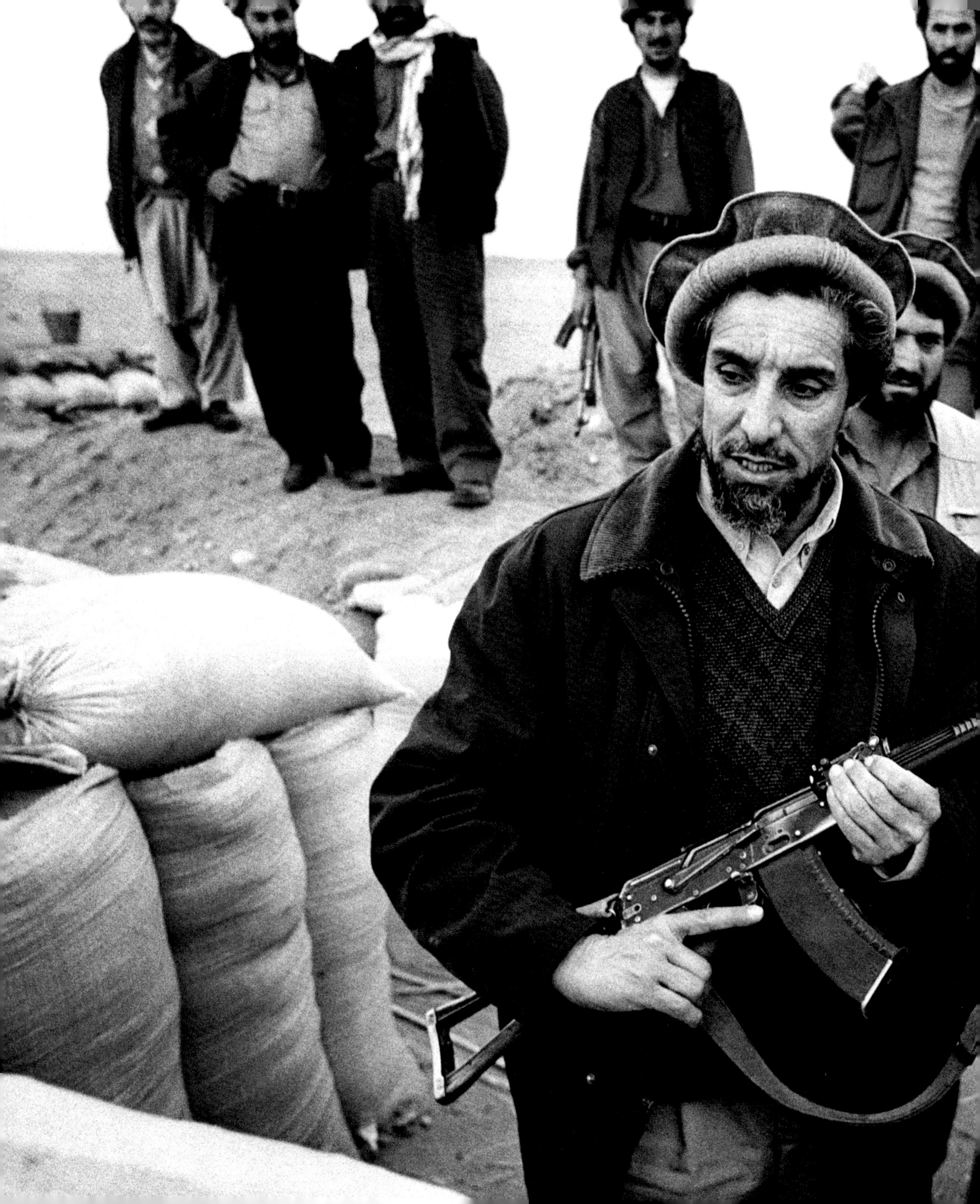

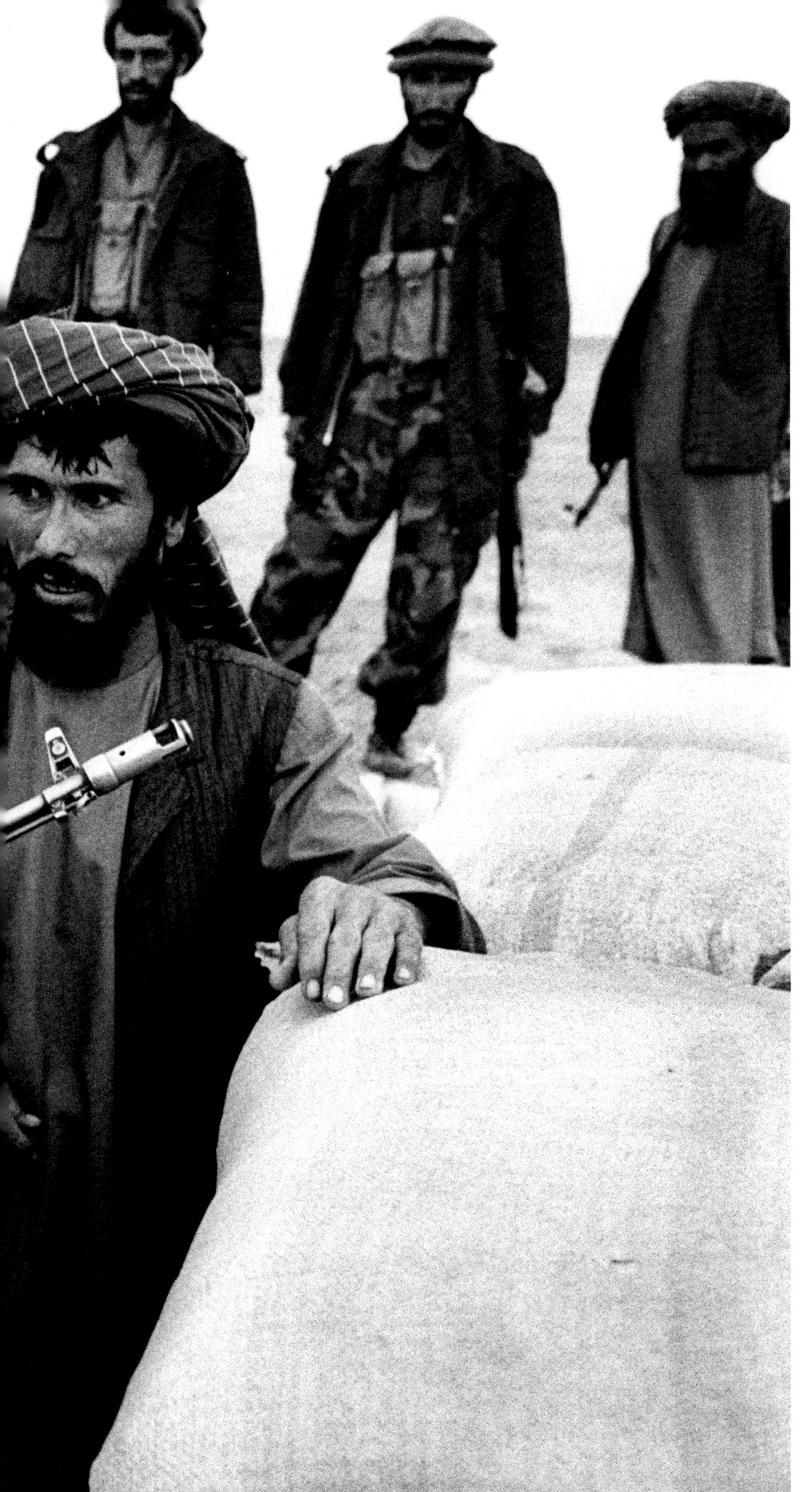

DASHT-E-QALA, TAKHAR PROVINCE: NOVEMBER 2000
Ahmad Shah Massoud instructing his troops on a
visit to frontline positions.

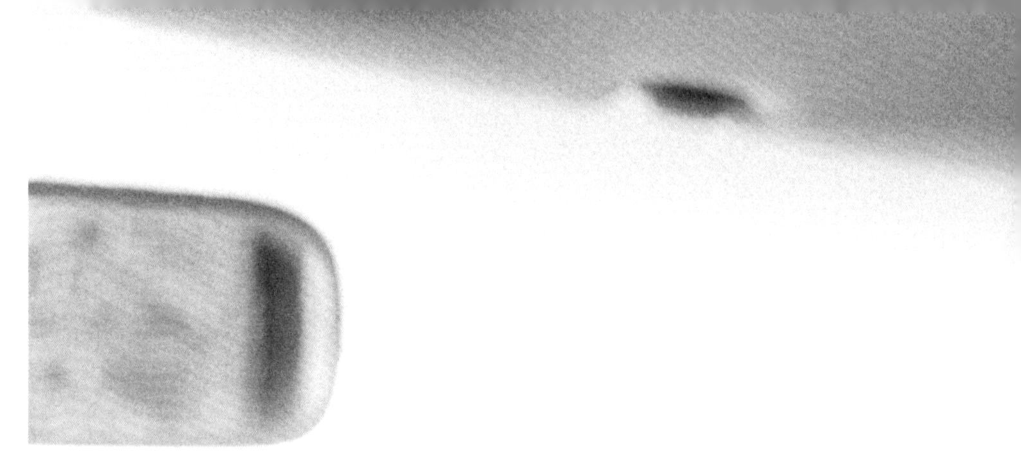

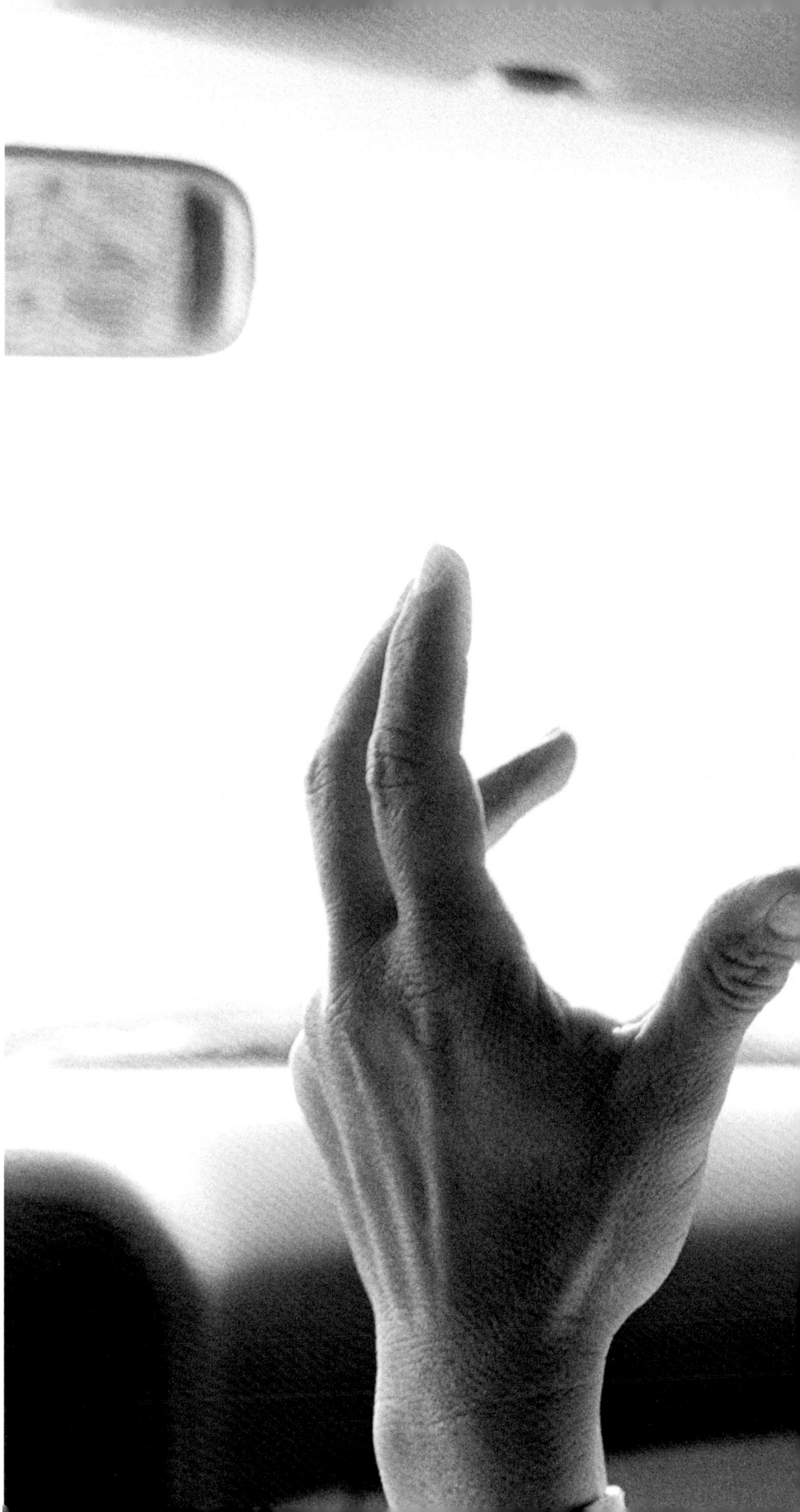

Dasht-e-Qala, Takhar Province: November 2000
Ahmad Shah Massoud en route to his forces at
the front.

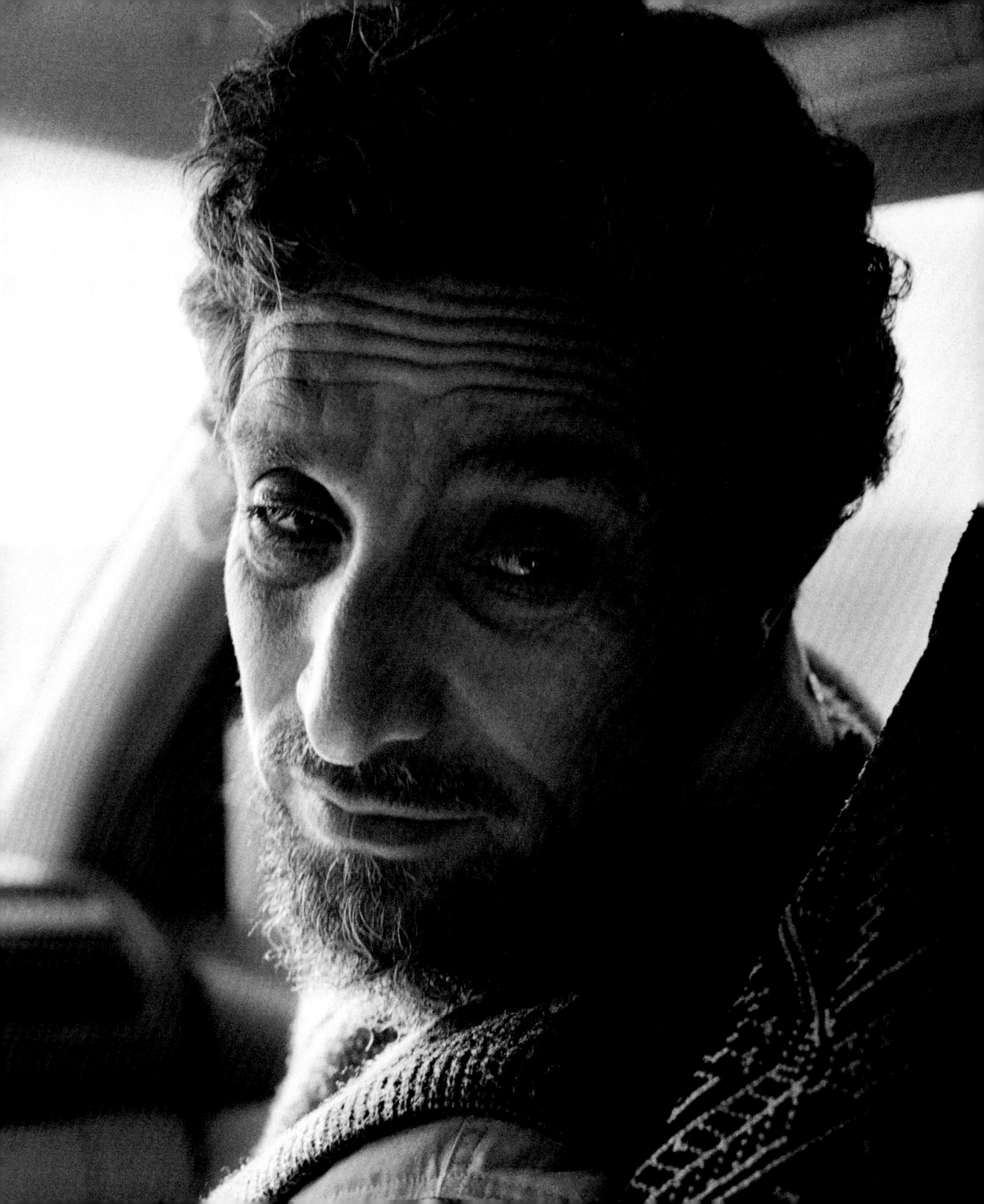

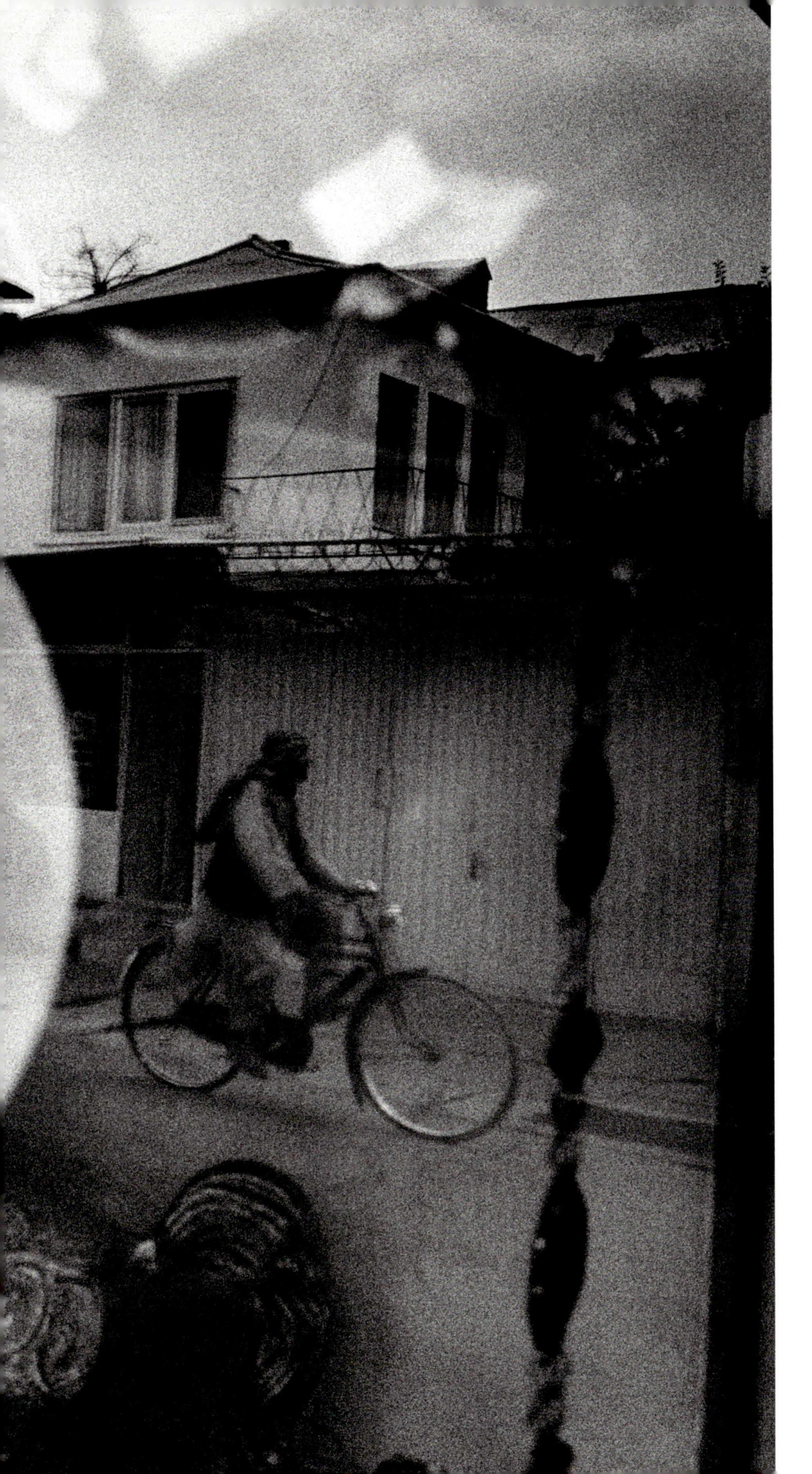

KABUL: JULY 2003
Image of Afghanistan's last king, Mohammad Zahir Shah, in a window on Chicken Street.

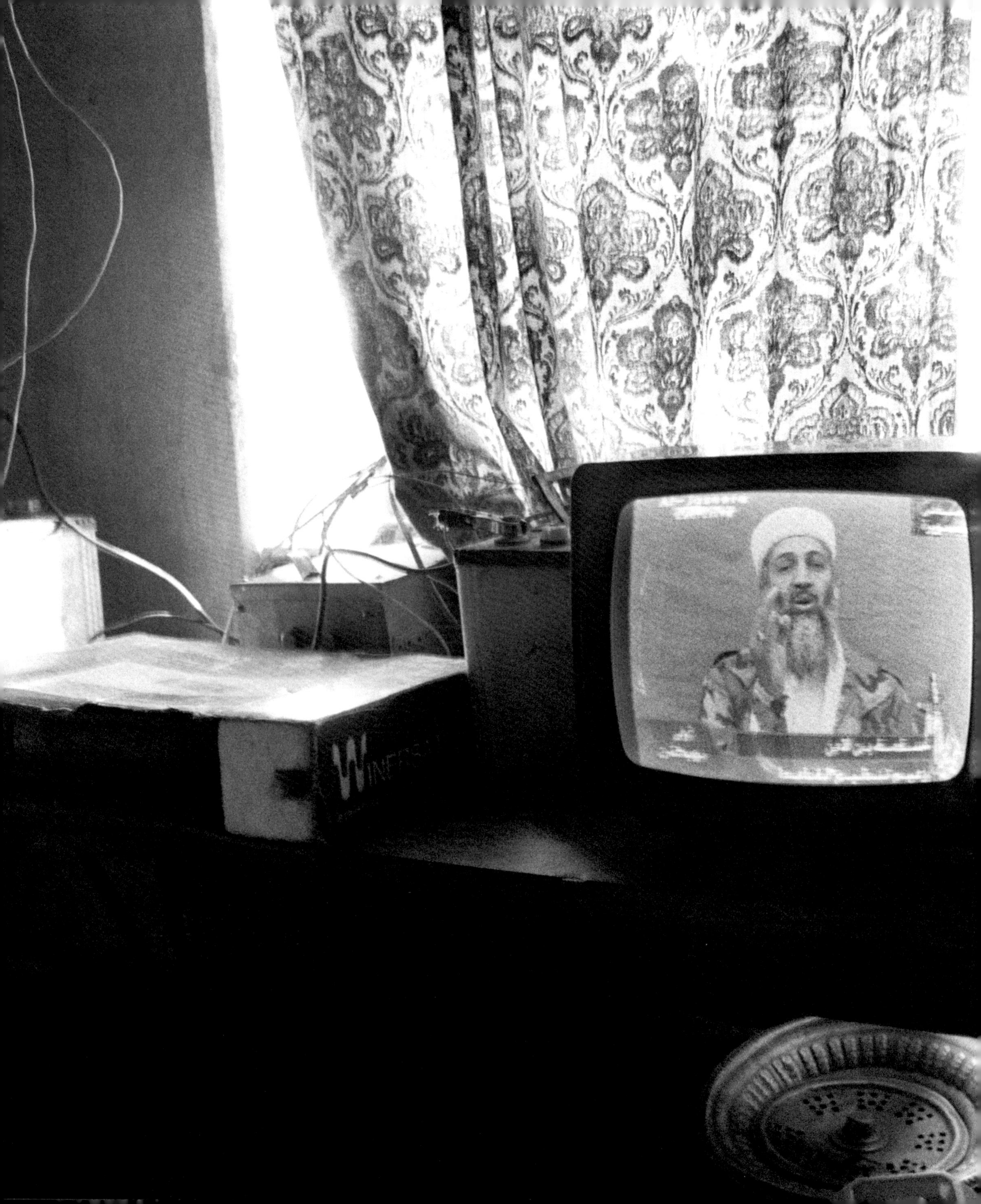

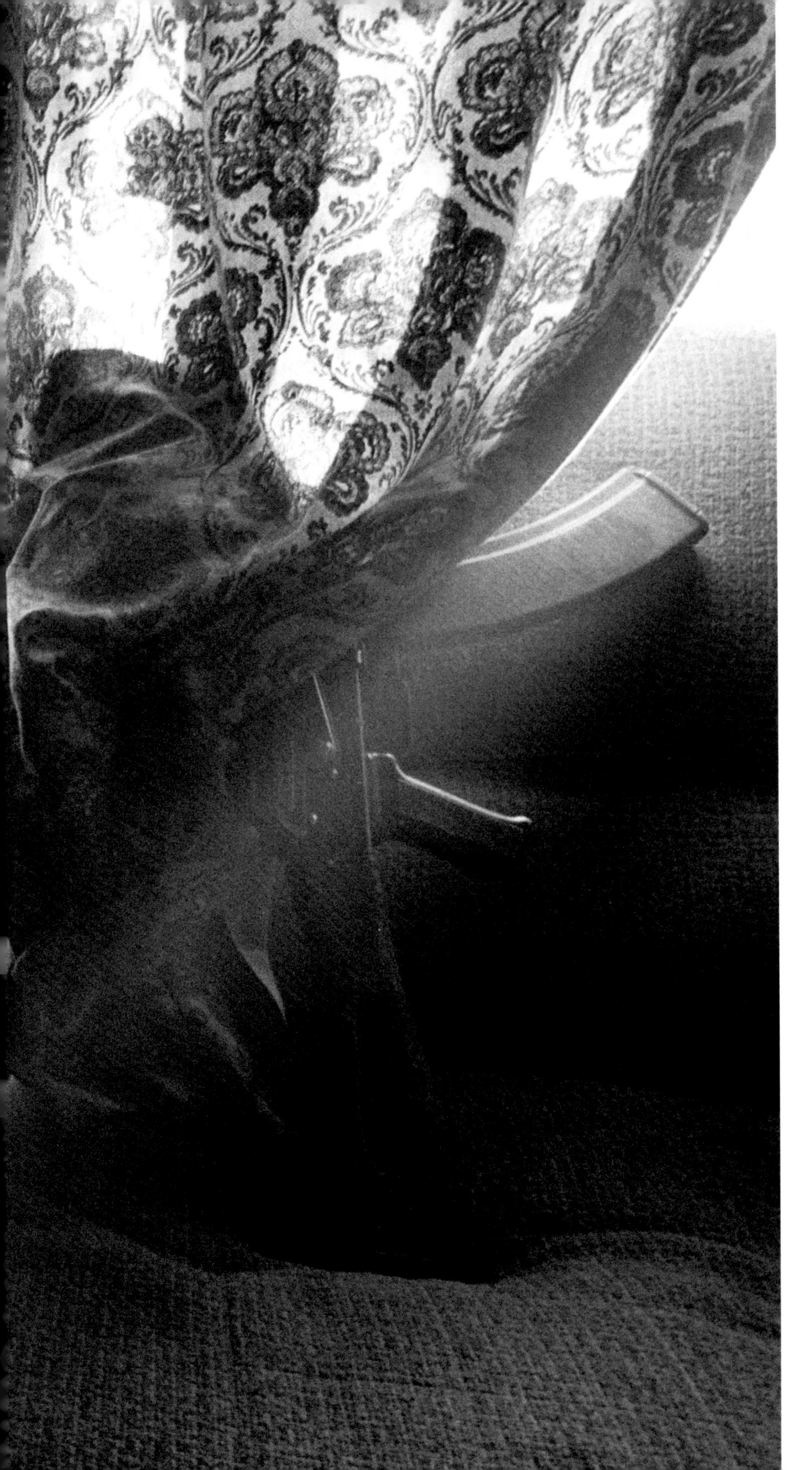

Ghulam Ali, Parwan Province: November 2001
Osama bin Laden on television before the fall
of Kabul. The broadcasting of tapes claiming the
survival of bin Laden emphasised the Coalition's
failure to capture him. Ironically the message was
delivered via a medium outlawed by the Taliban.

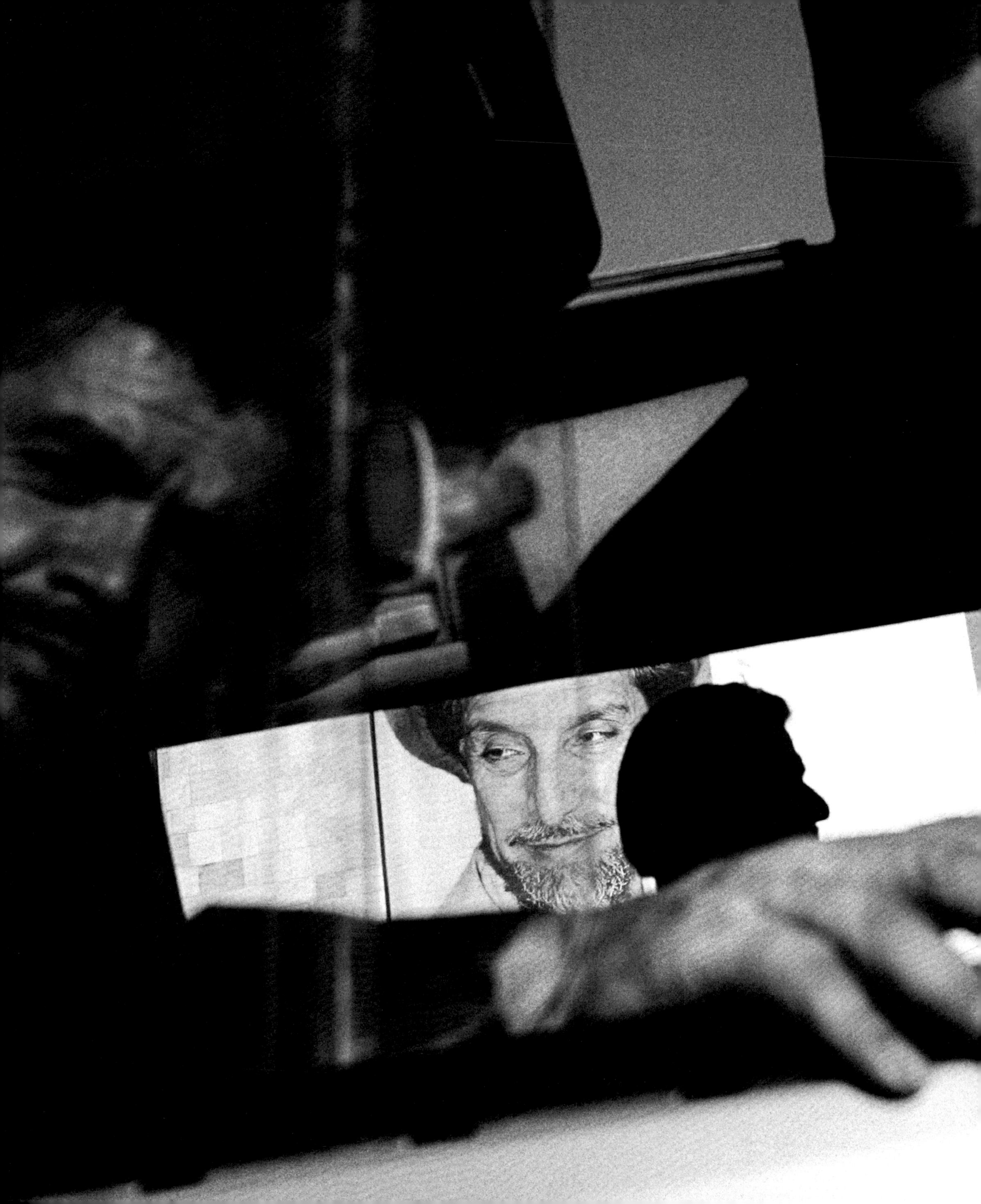

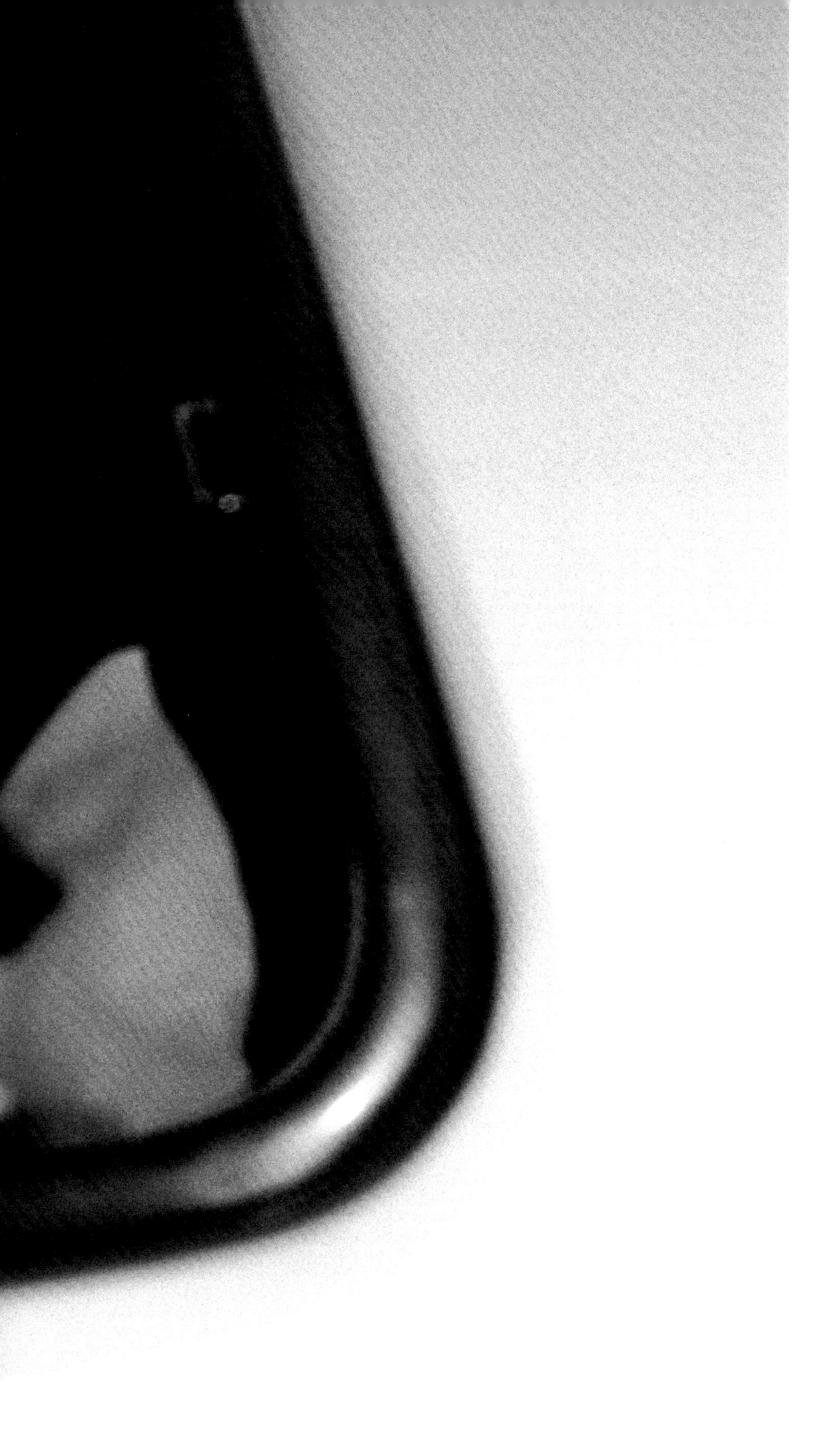

KABUL: AUGUST 2004
Poster of the late Ahmad Shah Massoud.

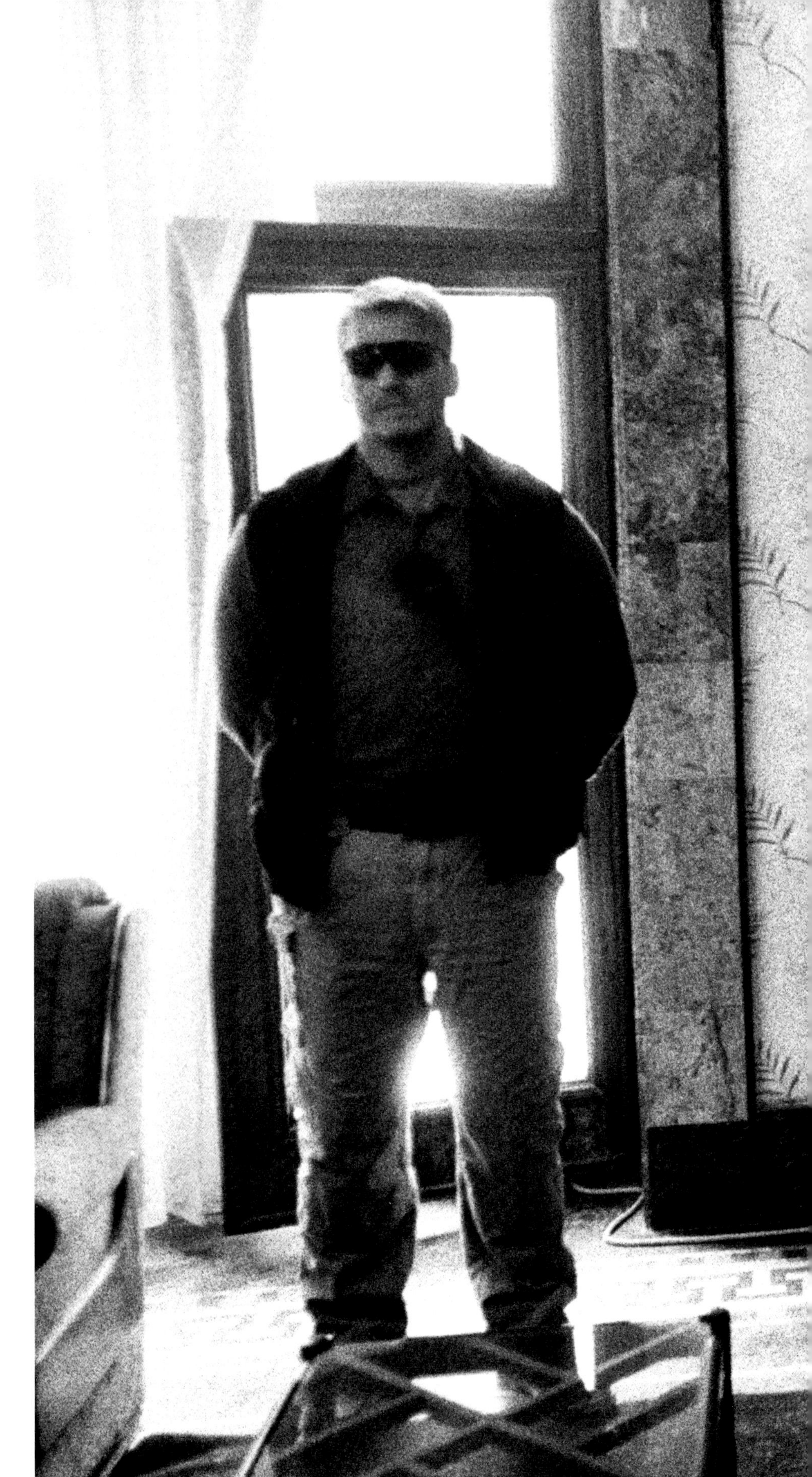

ARG PALACE, KABUL: NOVEMBER 2002
President Hamid Karzai in his office, protected by
an American bodyguard.

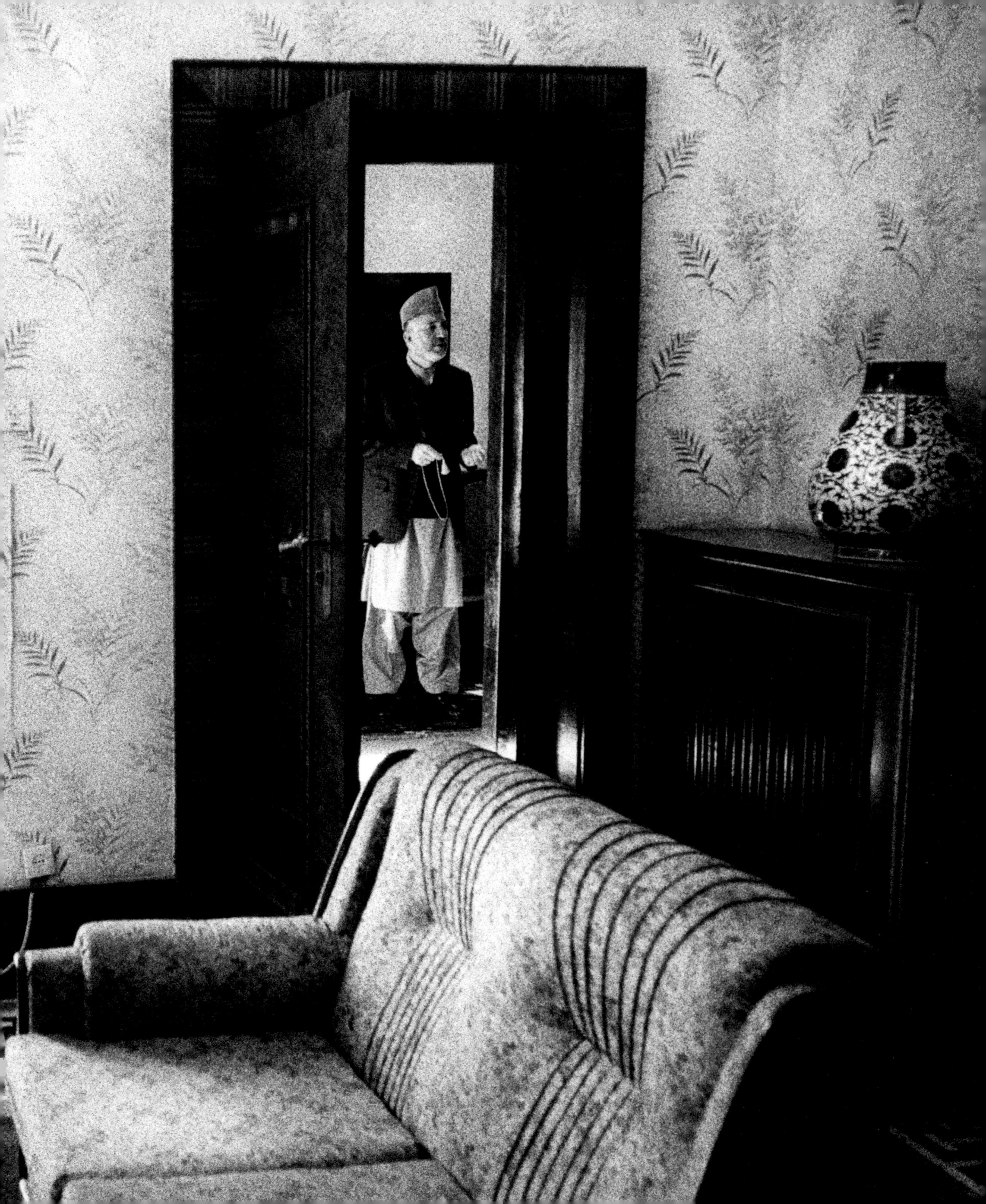

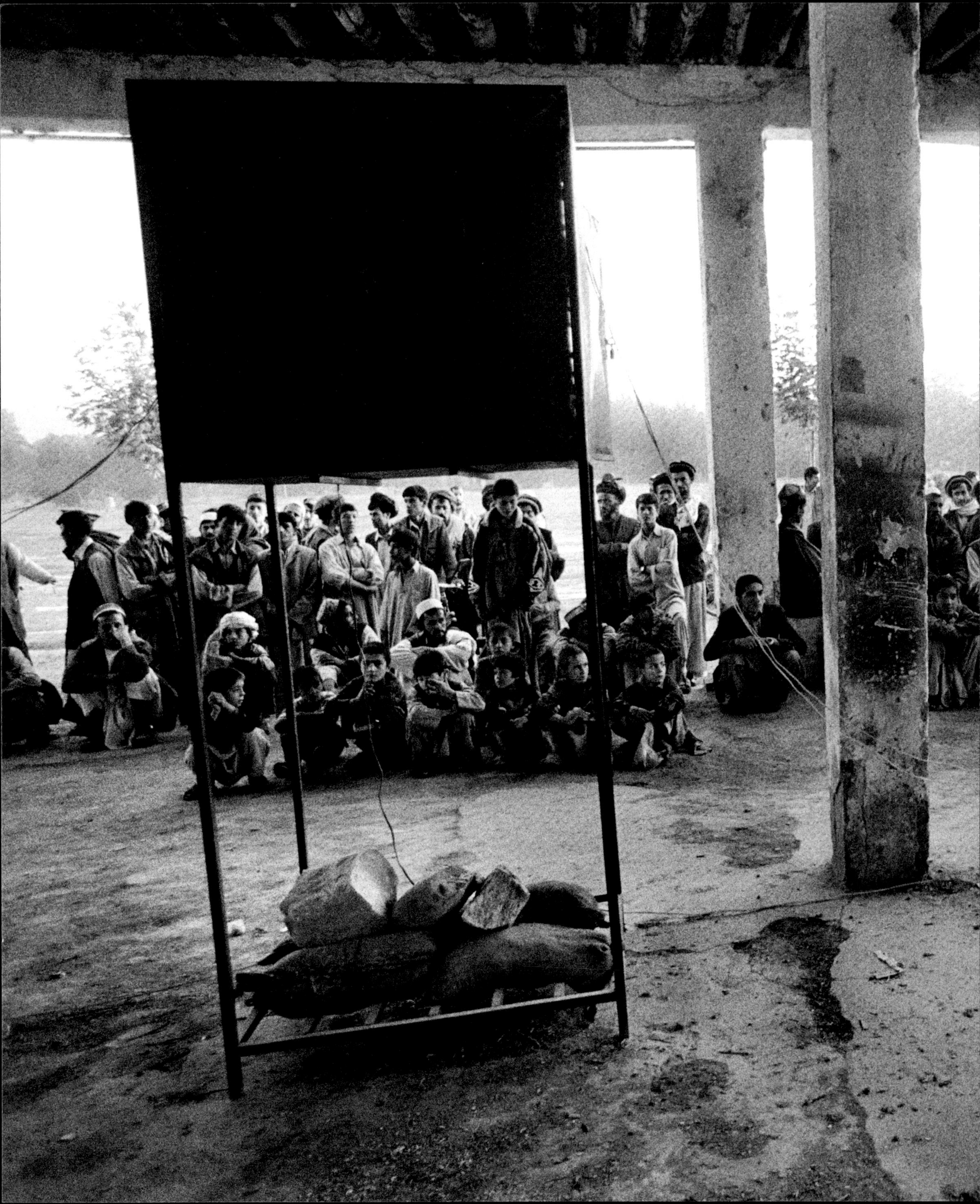

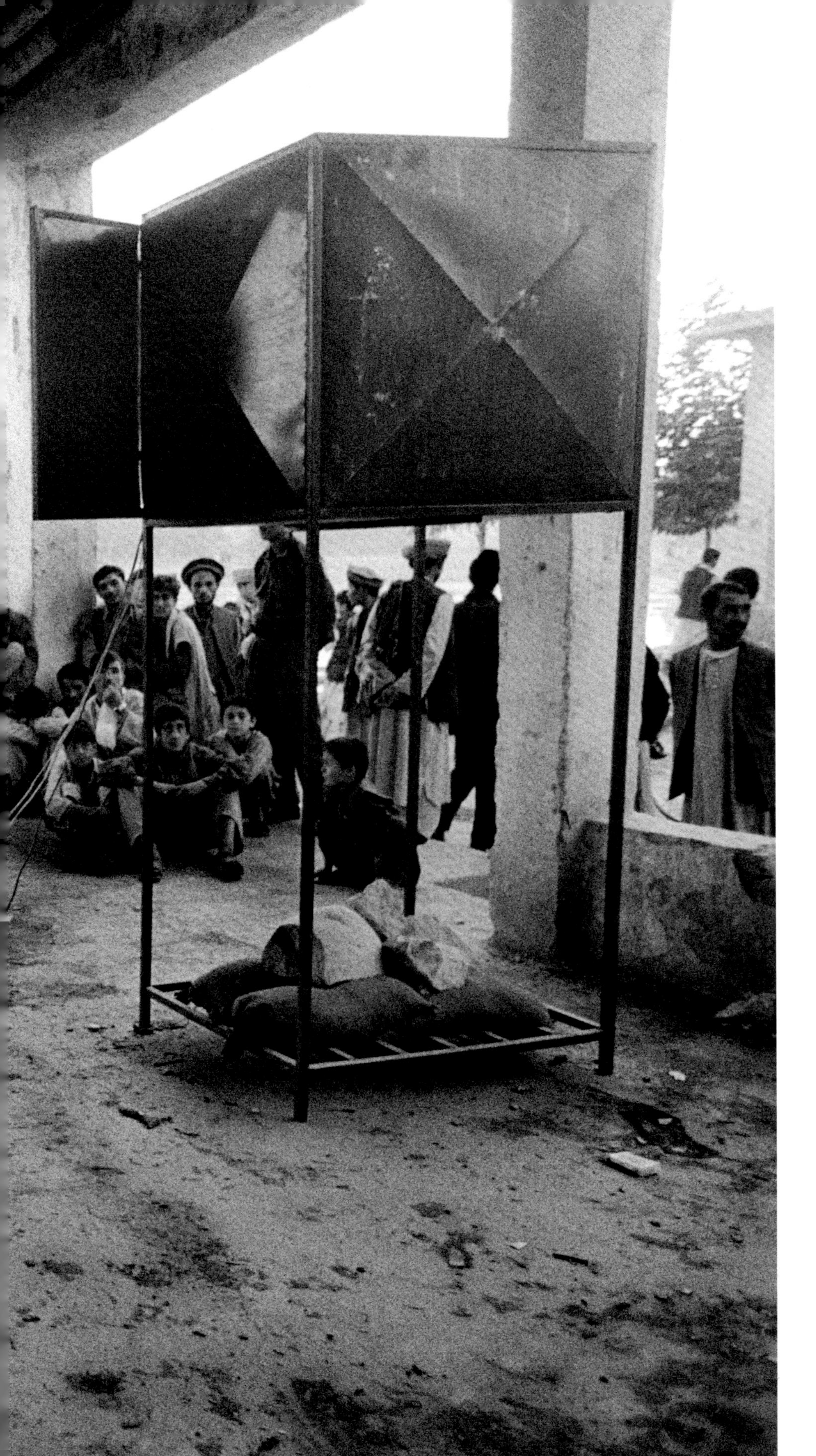

TALOQAN, TAKHAR PROVINCE: OCTOBER 2004
People watching votes being counted during
Afghanistan's presidential elections. TV sets were
installed in towns across Afghanistan to reassure
people of the legitimacy of the process.

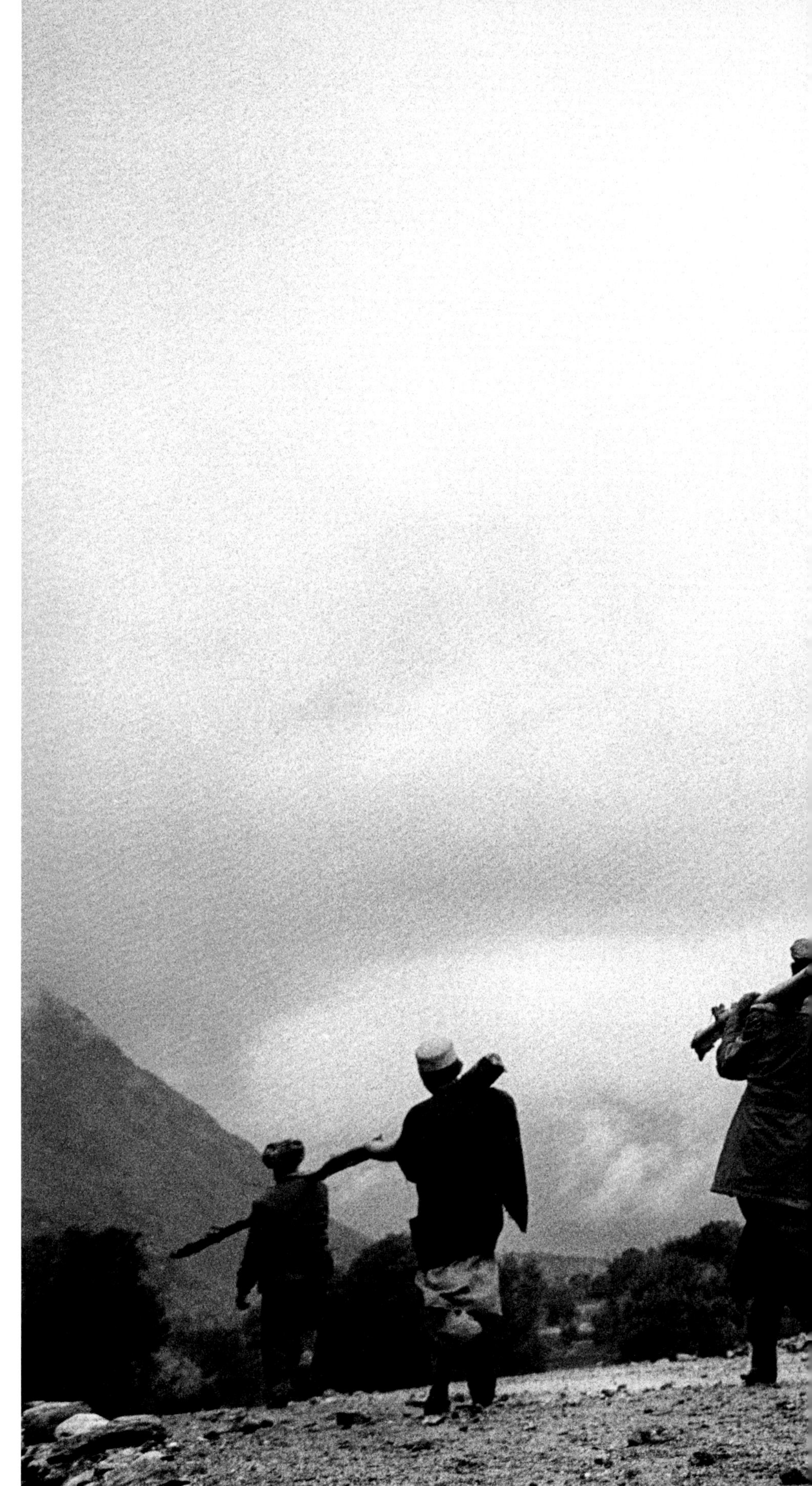

BAHARAK, BADAKHSHAN PROVINCE: NOVEMBER 2004
Farmers carrying timber in a remote mountainous
area in the north-east of the country.

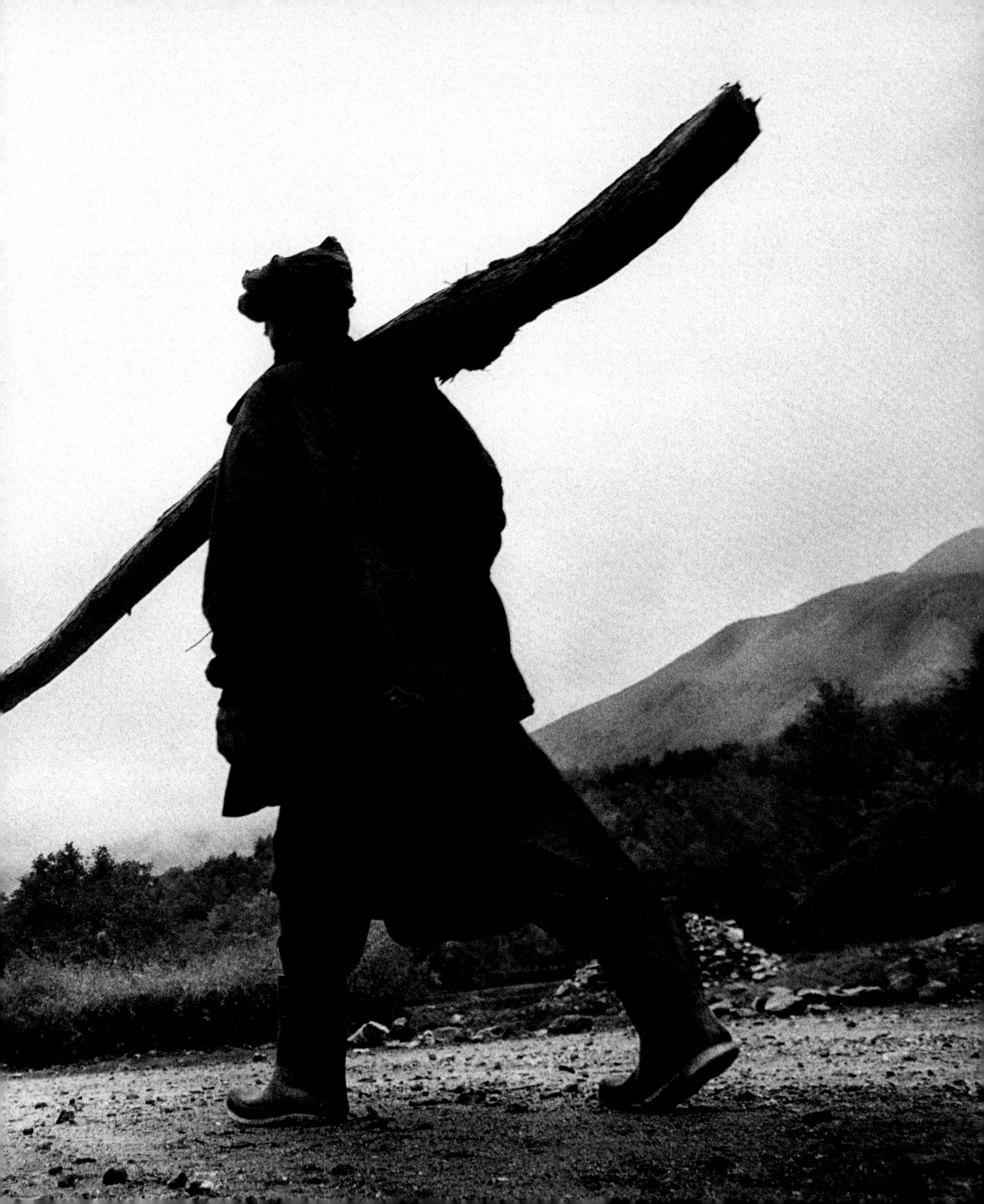

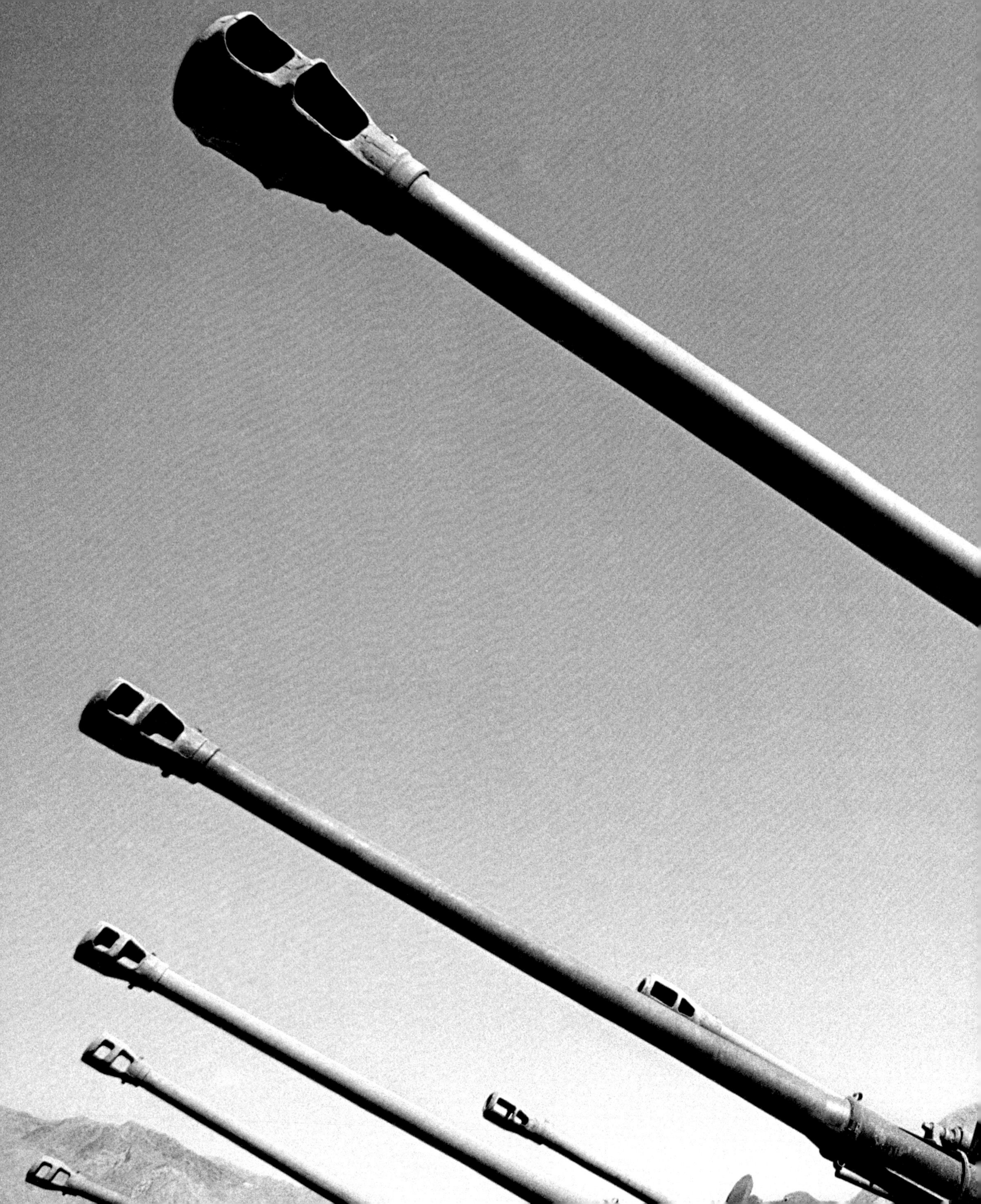

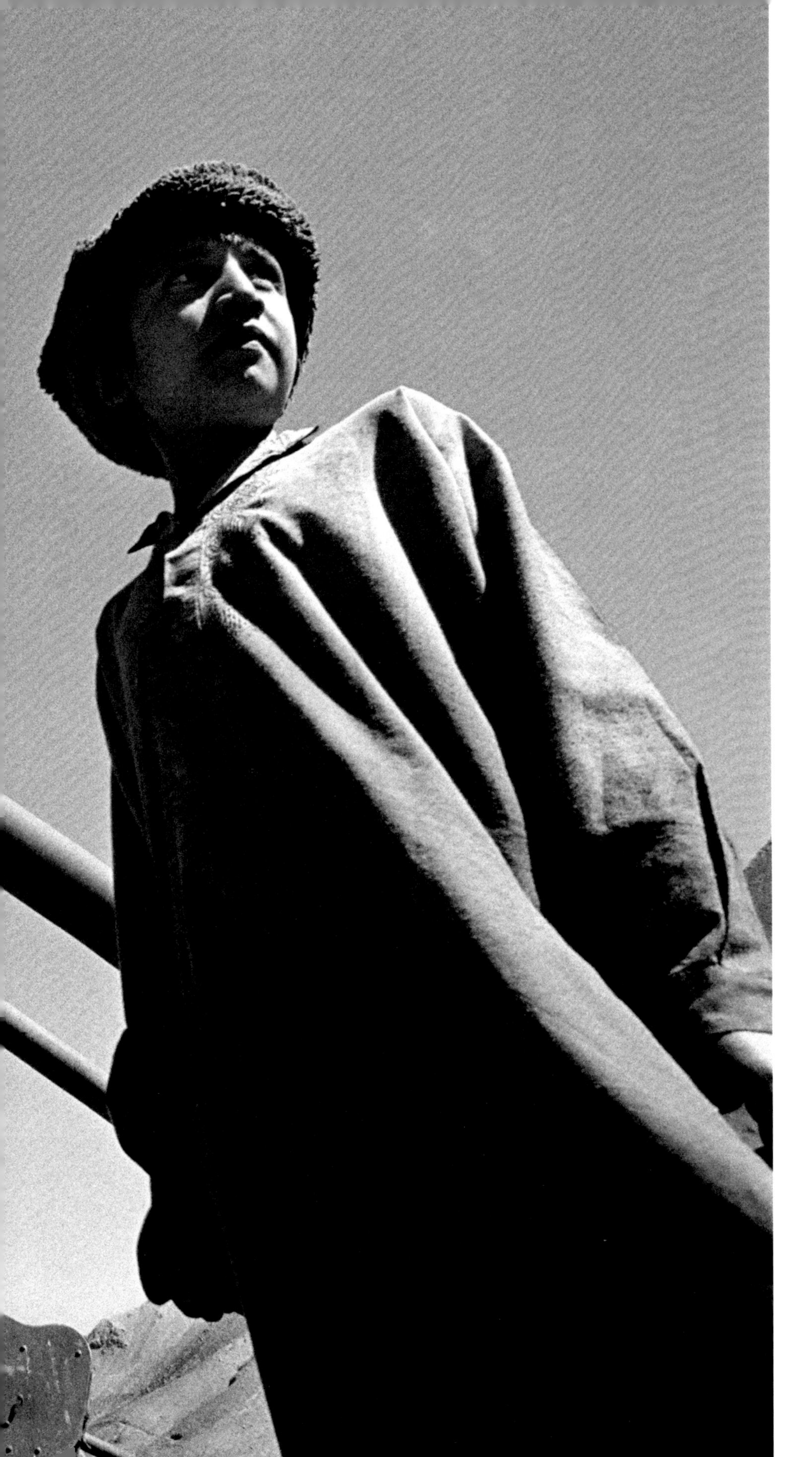

Parakh, Panjshir Valley: October 2001
A line of howitzers outside an armaments
workshop. Old Soviet arms and equipment were
redesigned or renovated by mujahideen field
engineers in order to equip their forces for the
battle to win Kabul.

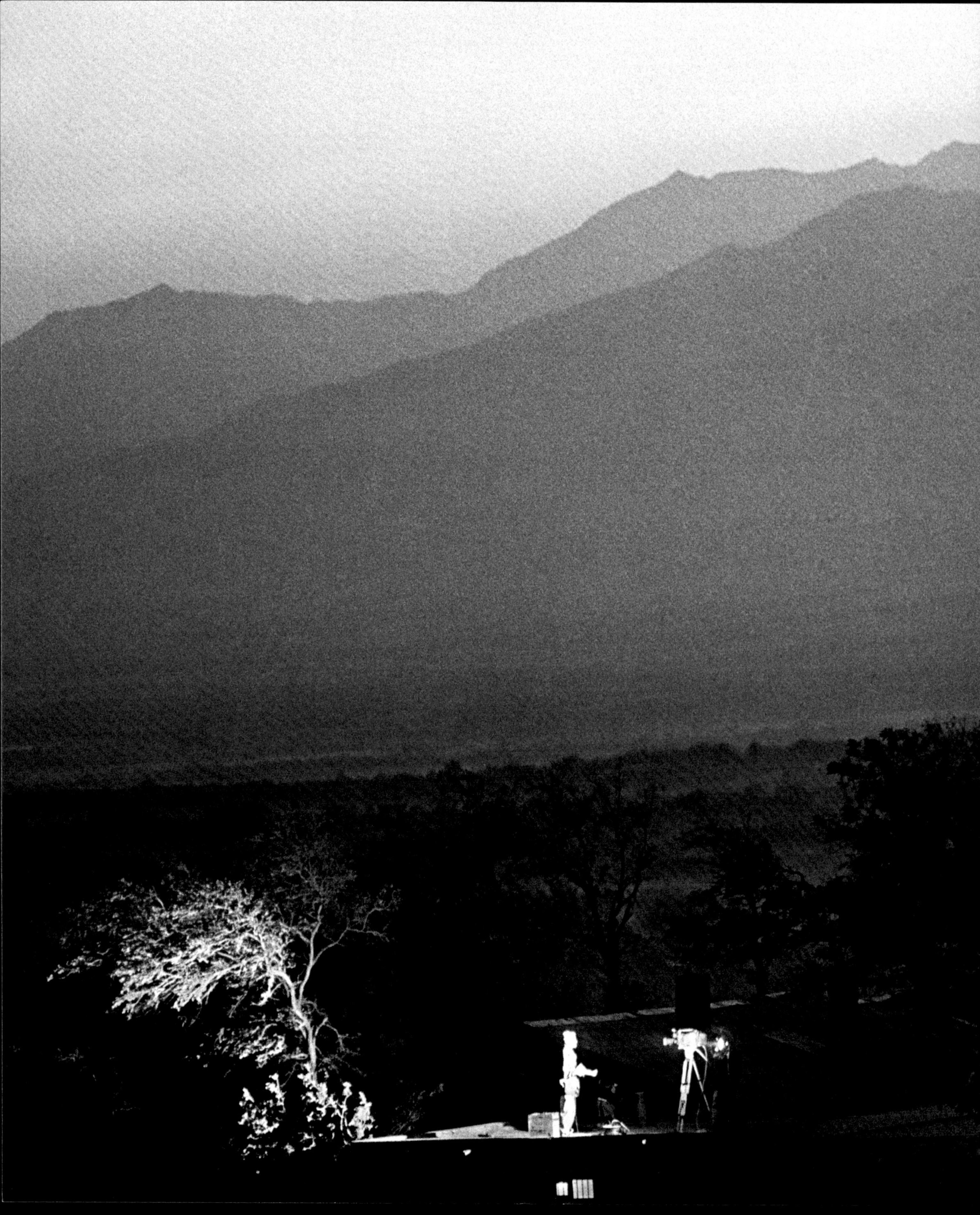

JABUL SERAJ, PARWAN PROVINCE: OCTOBER 2001
A US television news crew broadcasts a live
report during the build-up to US bombing.

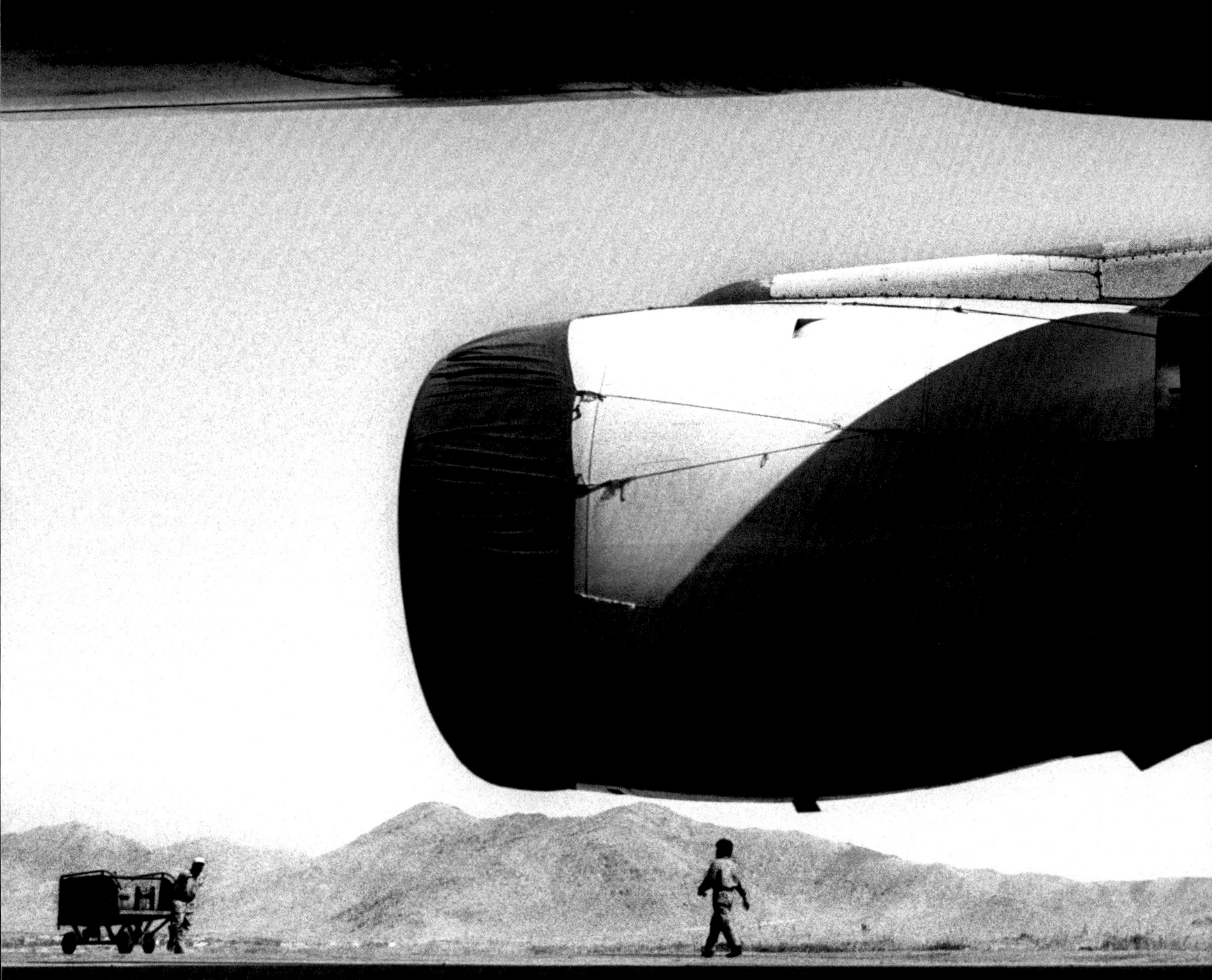

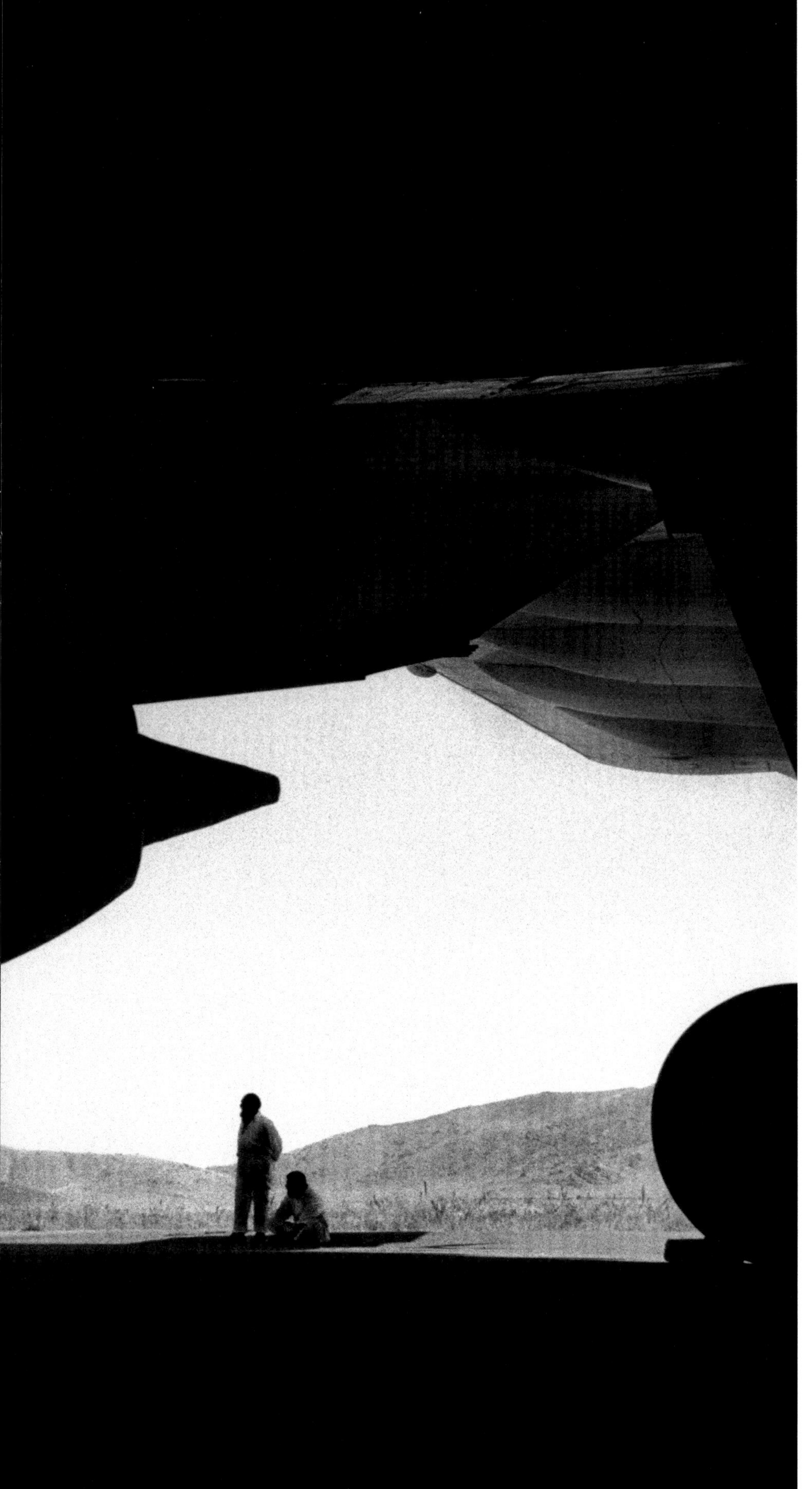

KABUL INTERNATIONAL AIRPORT: JUNE 2003
Preparing an Ariana Airlines aircraft.

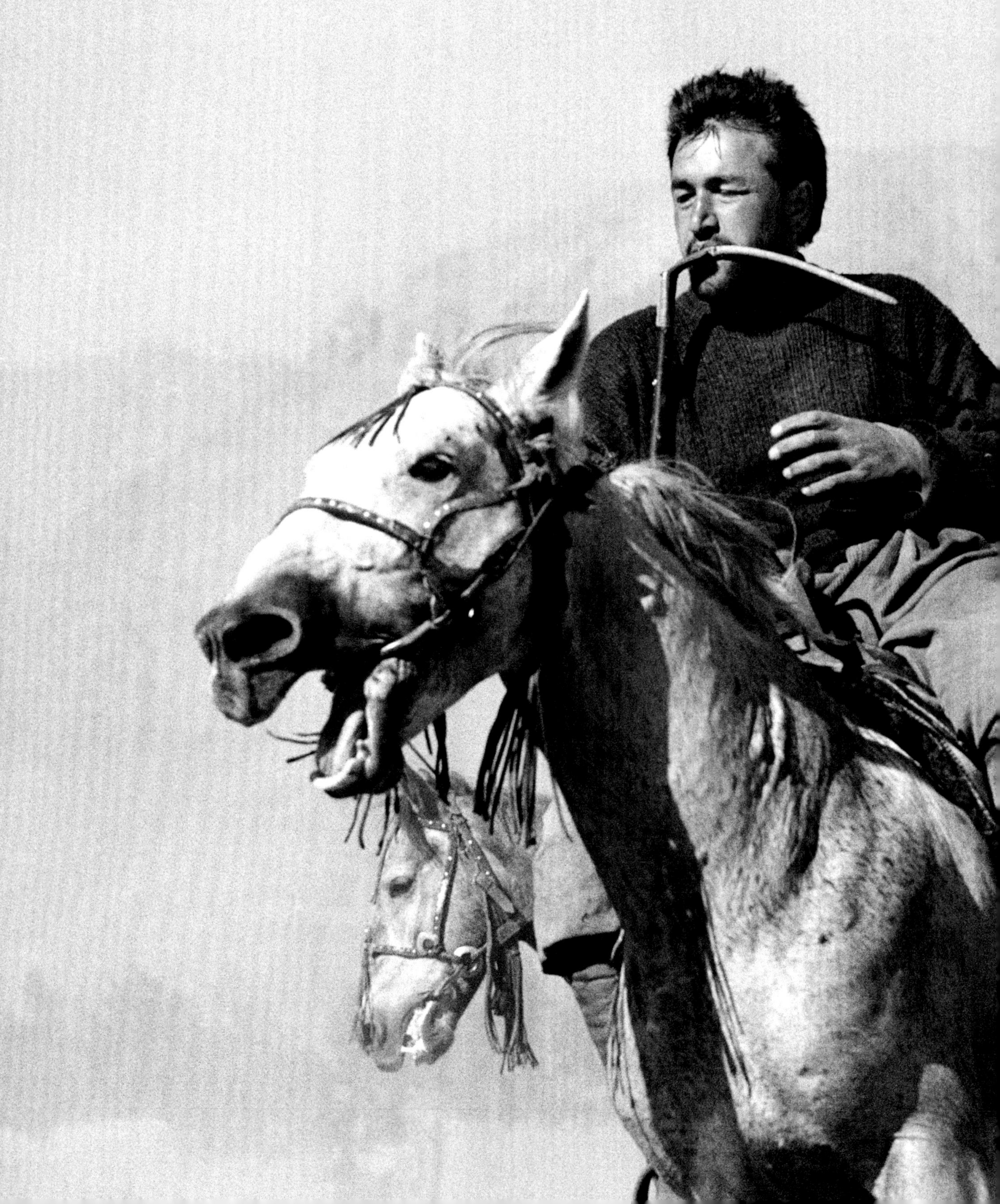

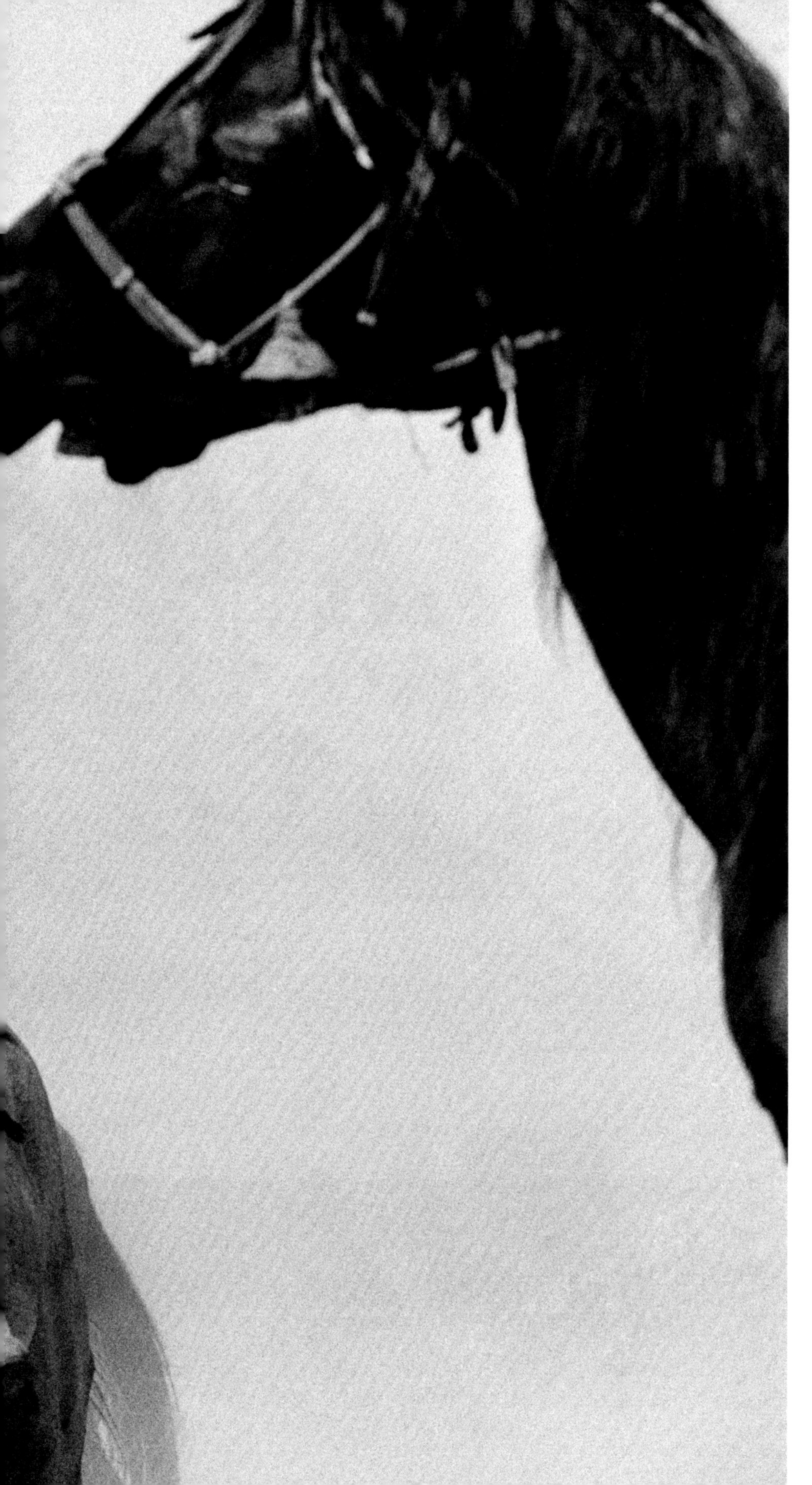

GULBAHAR, KAPISA PROVINCE: NOVEMBER 2001
A horseman competing at Buzkashi.

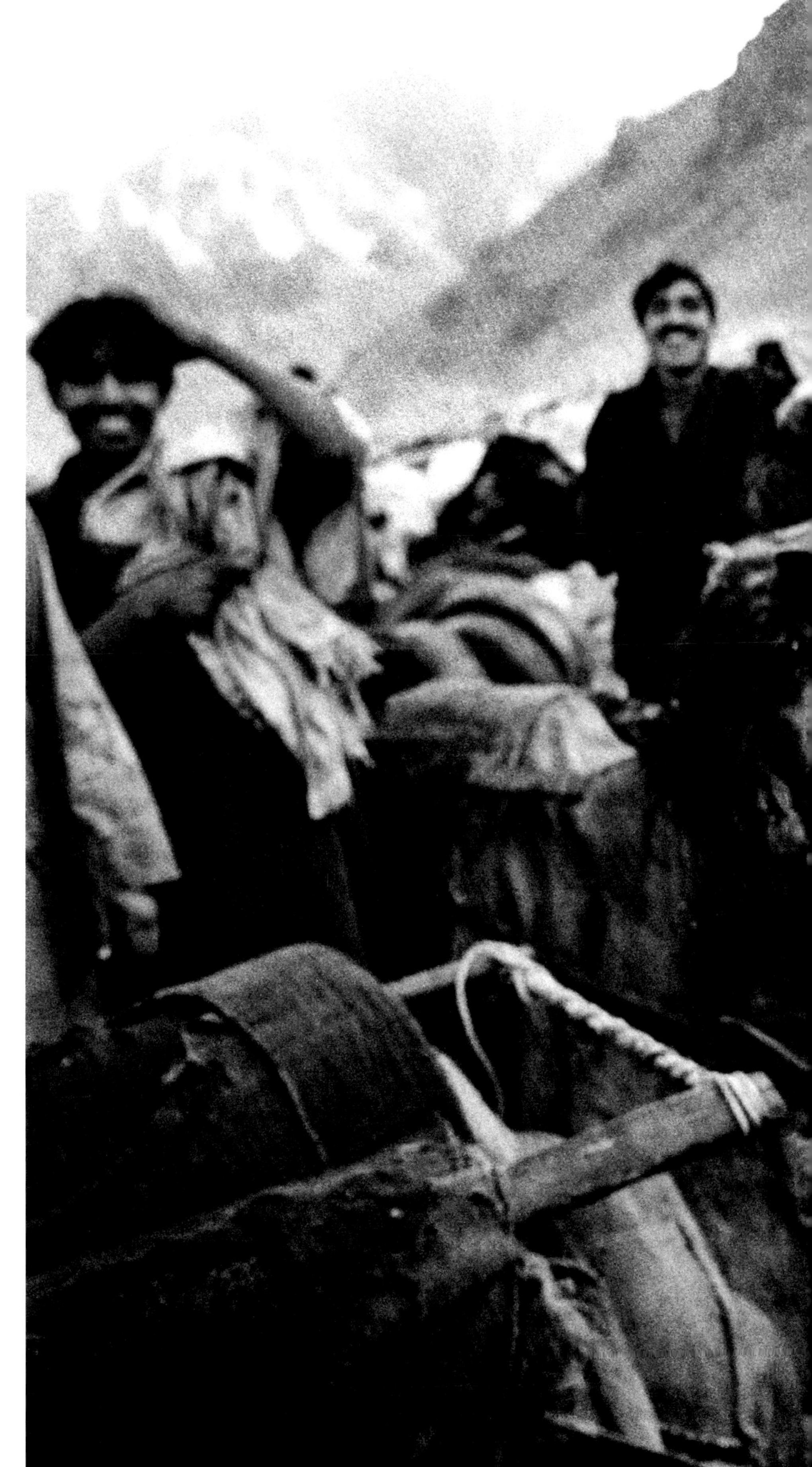

JANGORA, NANGRAHAR PROVINCE: APRIL 2005
A young smuggler is teased by his friends at their
tented village in Jangora, bordering the tribal
areas of North West Frontier Province. Drugs,
weapons and vehicle parts are carried by
camel over the mountains into the tribal areas
and Pakistan.

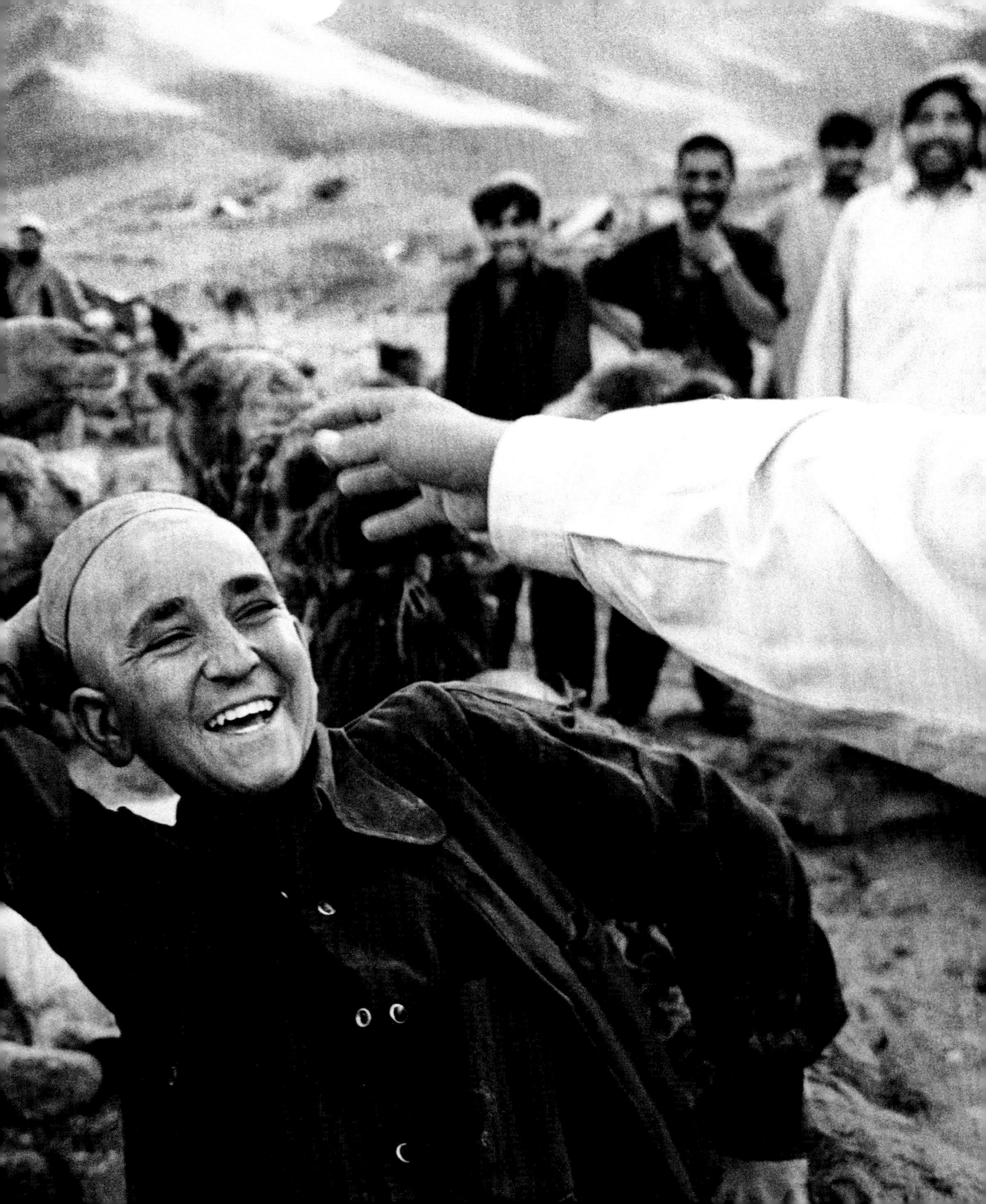

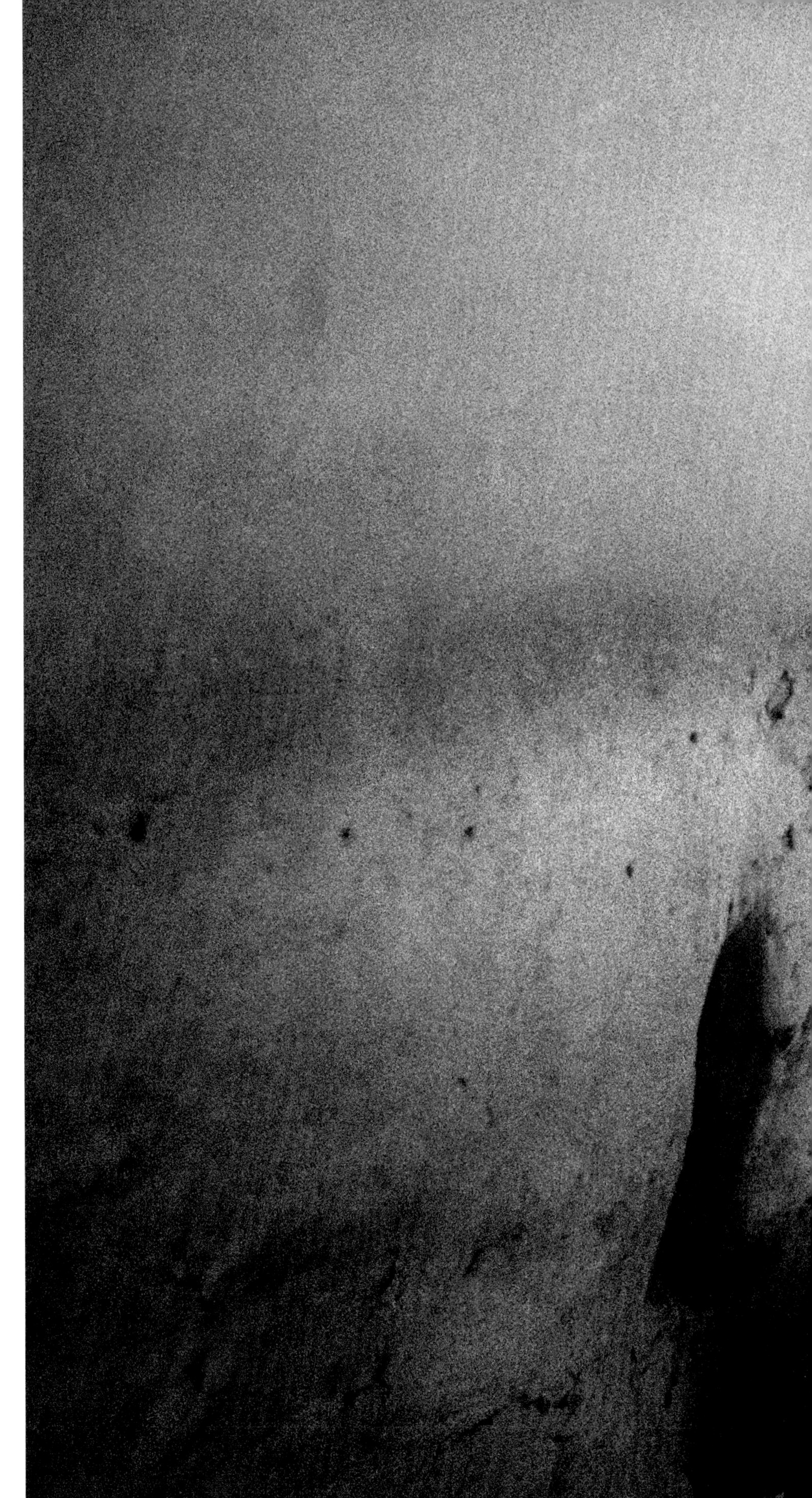

BAMIYAN, BAMIYAN PROVINCE: NOVEMBER 2002
A displaced family living in a cave on the site of
the destroyed Buddhas.

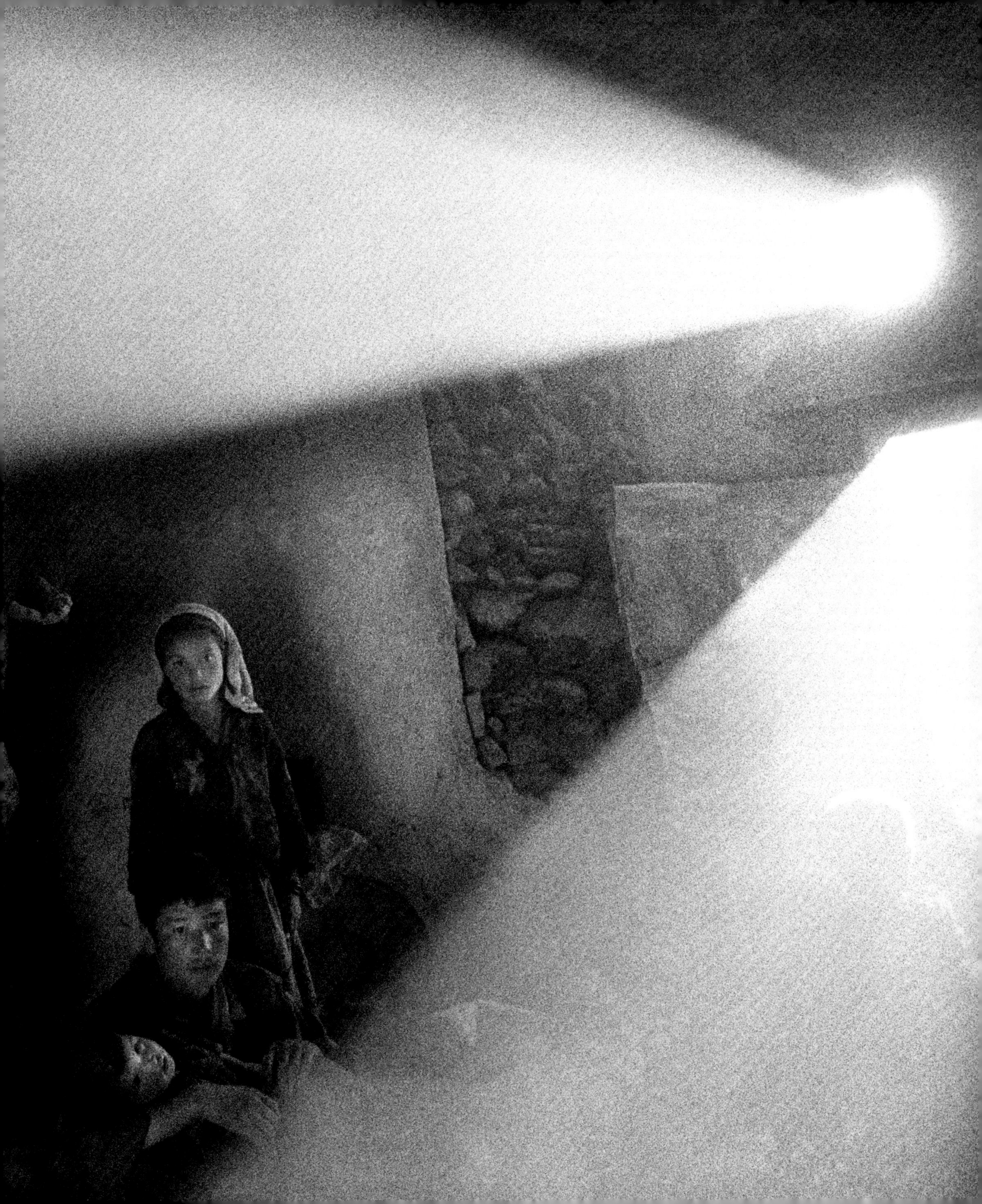

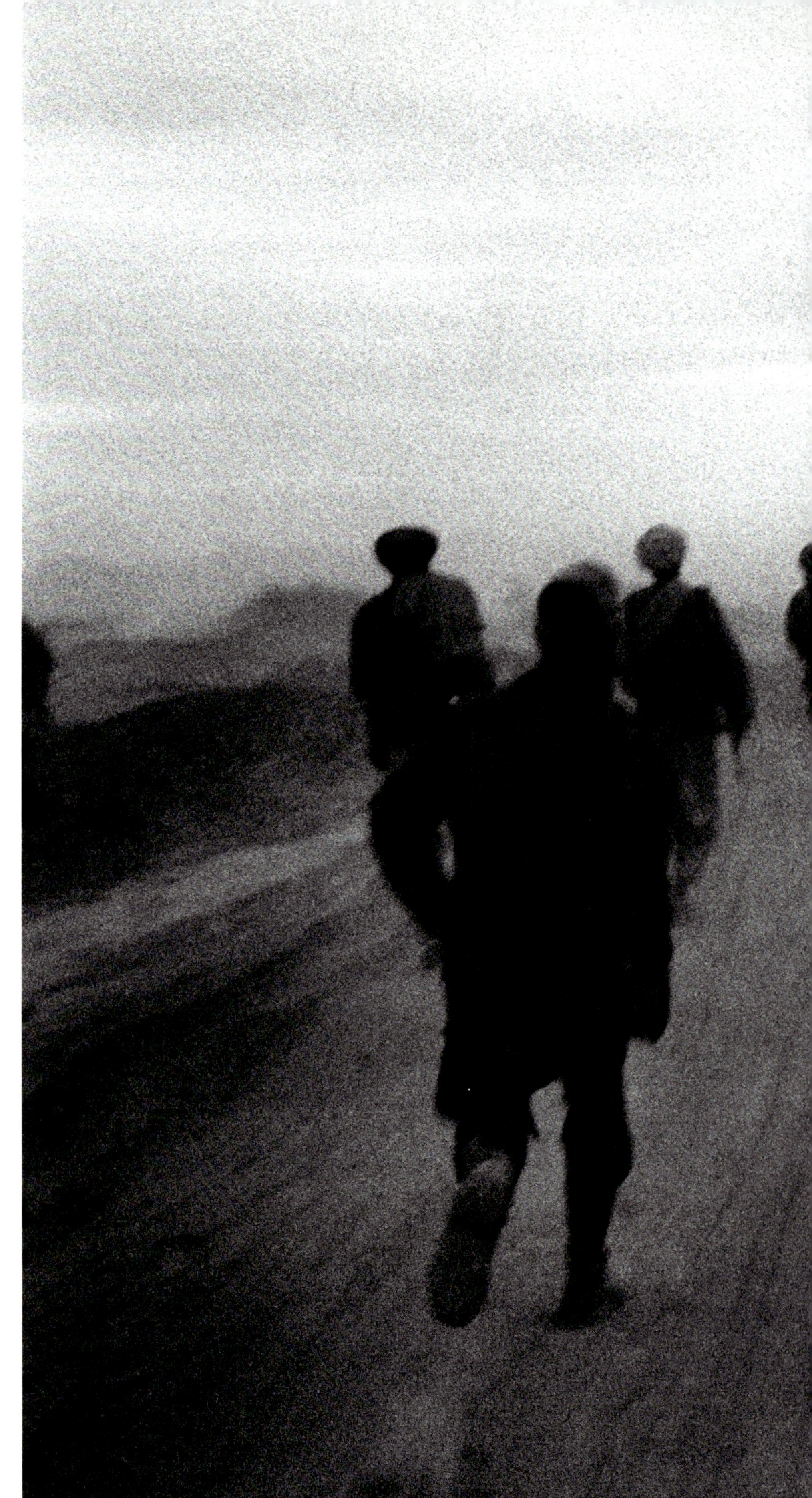

SHAMALI PLAIN, KABUL: 12 NOVEMBER 2001
Northern Alliance fighters on the offensive,
having breached the last front before Kabul.

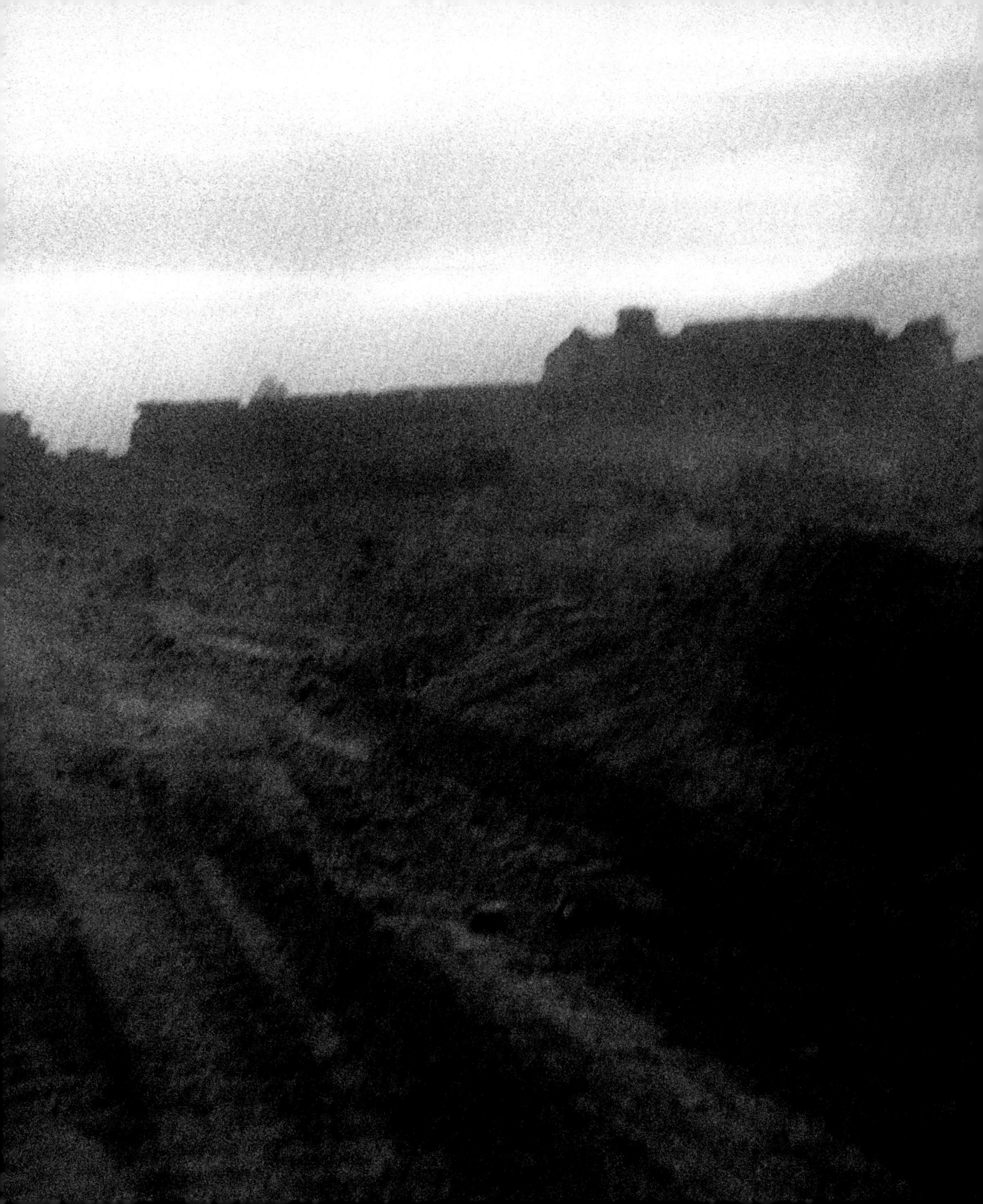

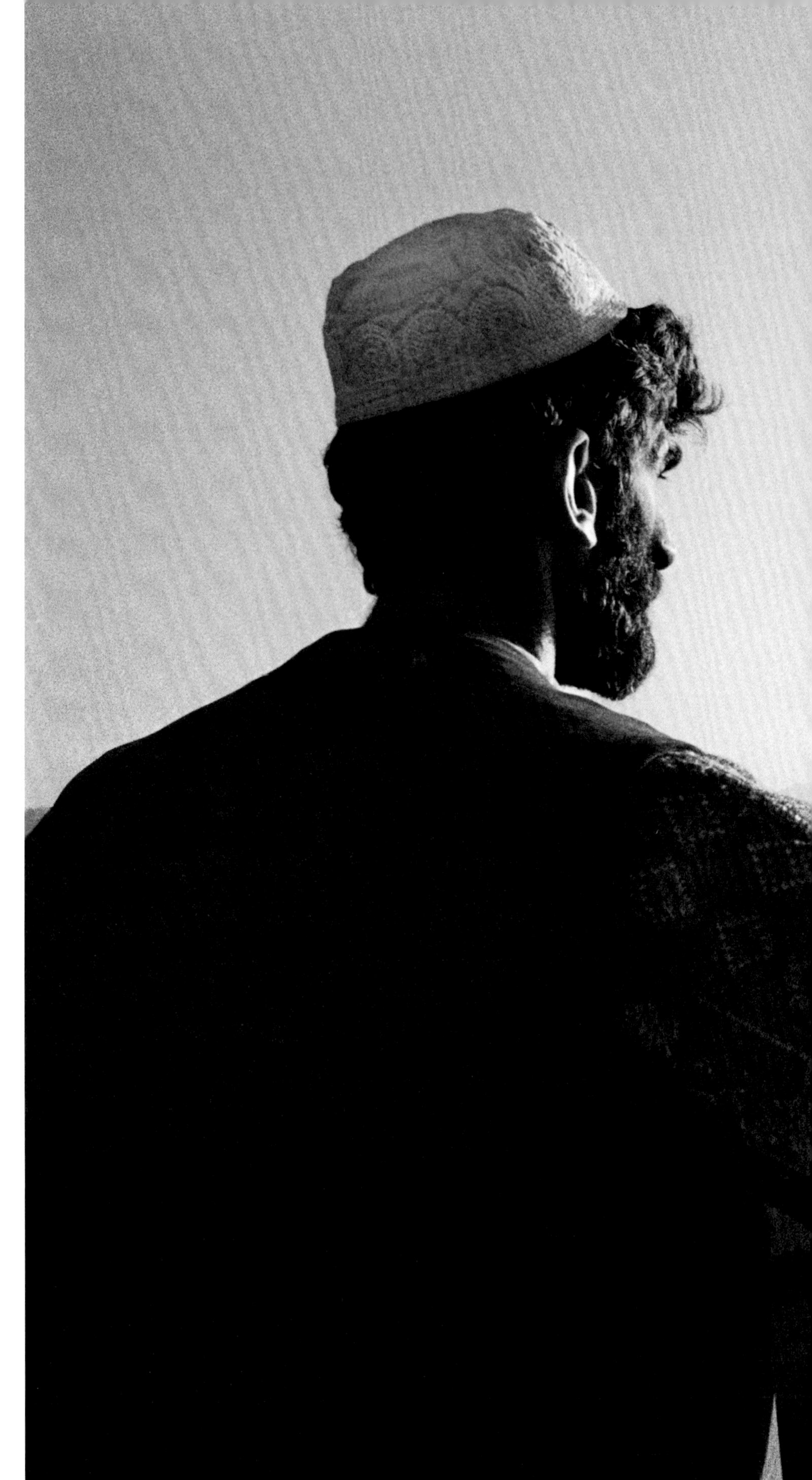

CHARIKAR, PARWAN PROVINCE: NOVEMBER 2001
Agha Reza releases his pigeons for Kaftar Bazi.

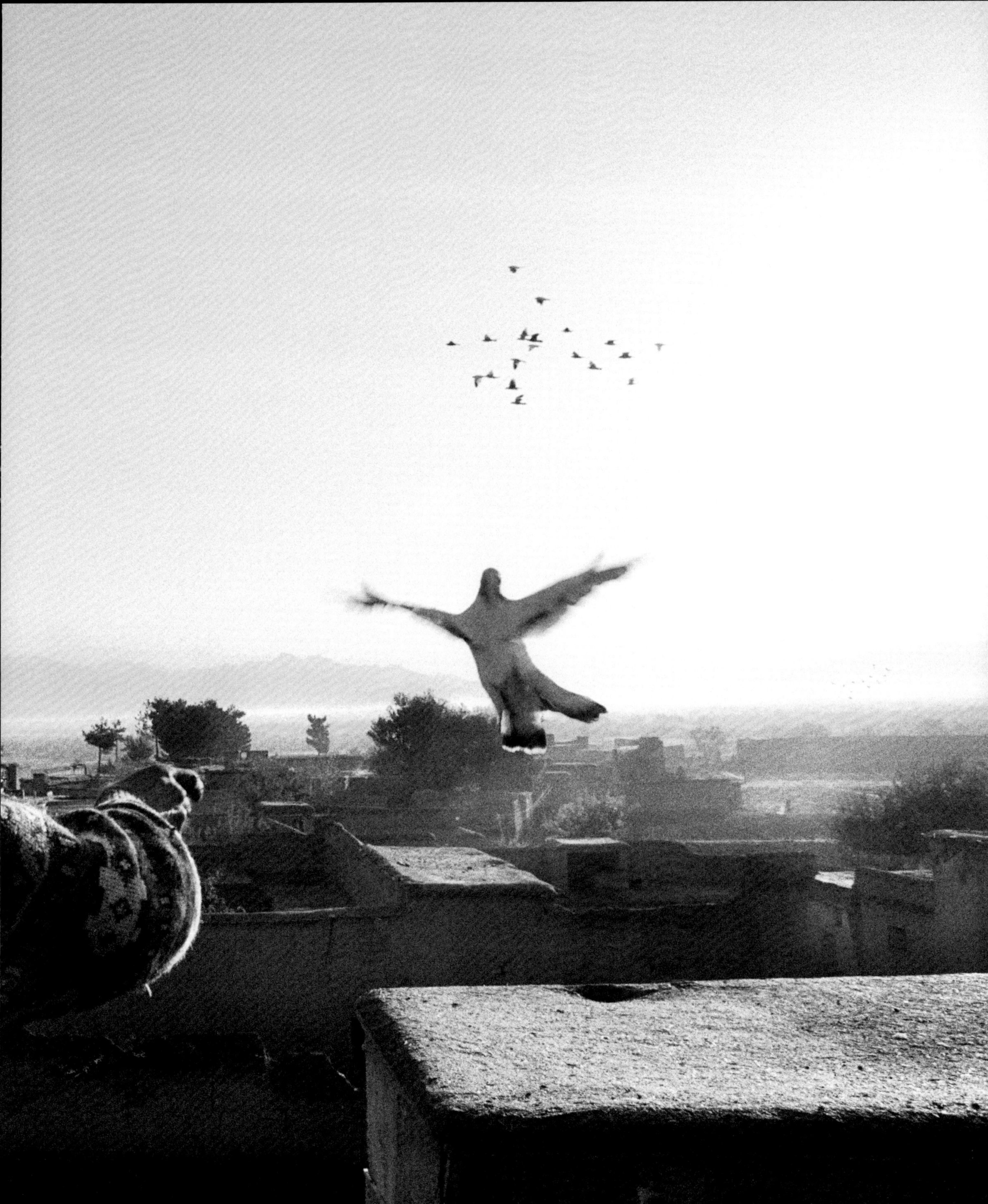

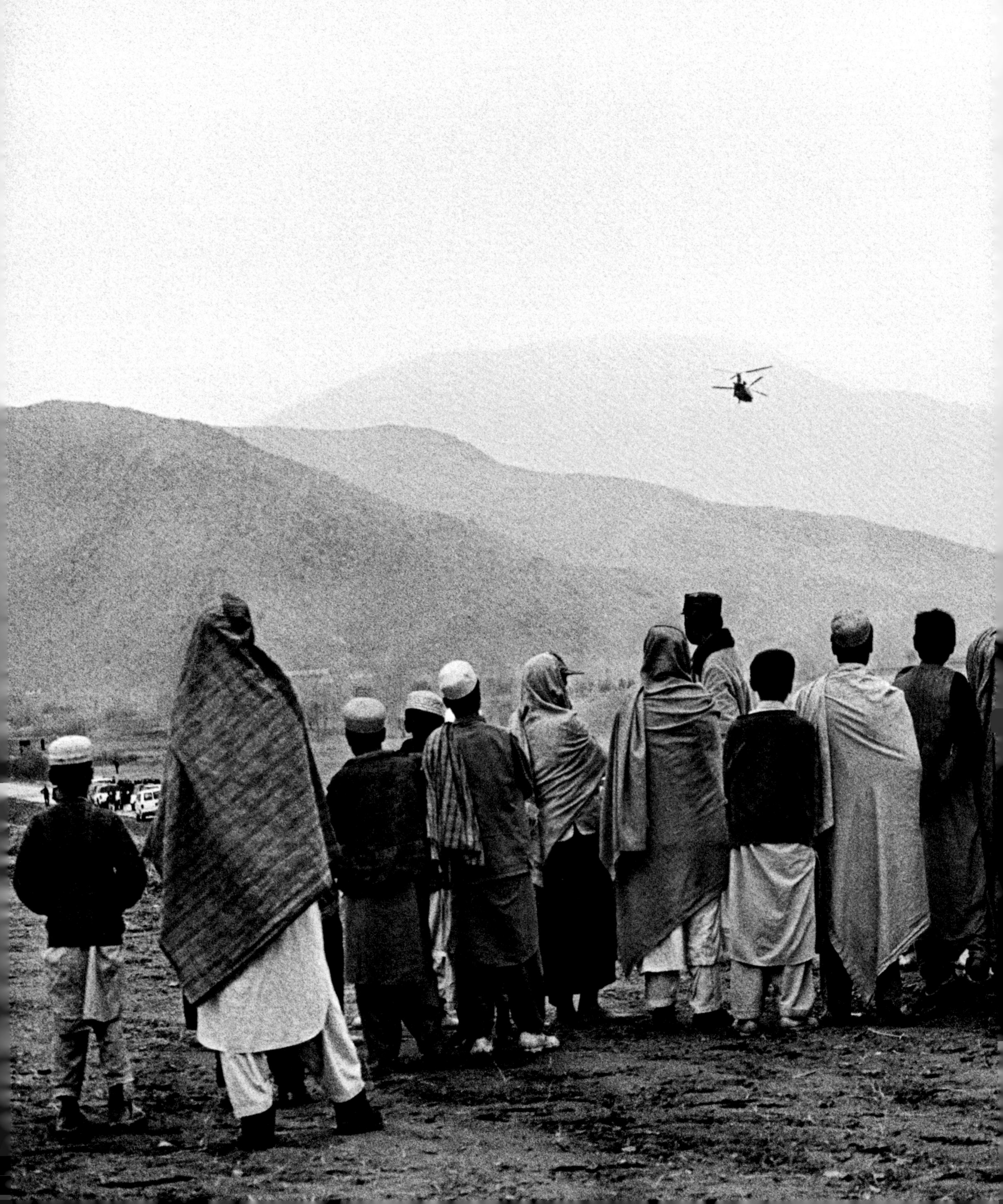

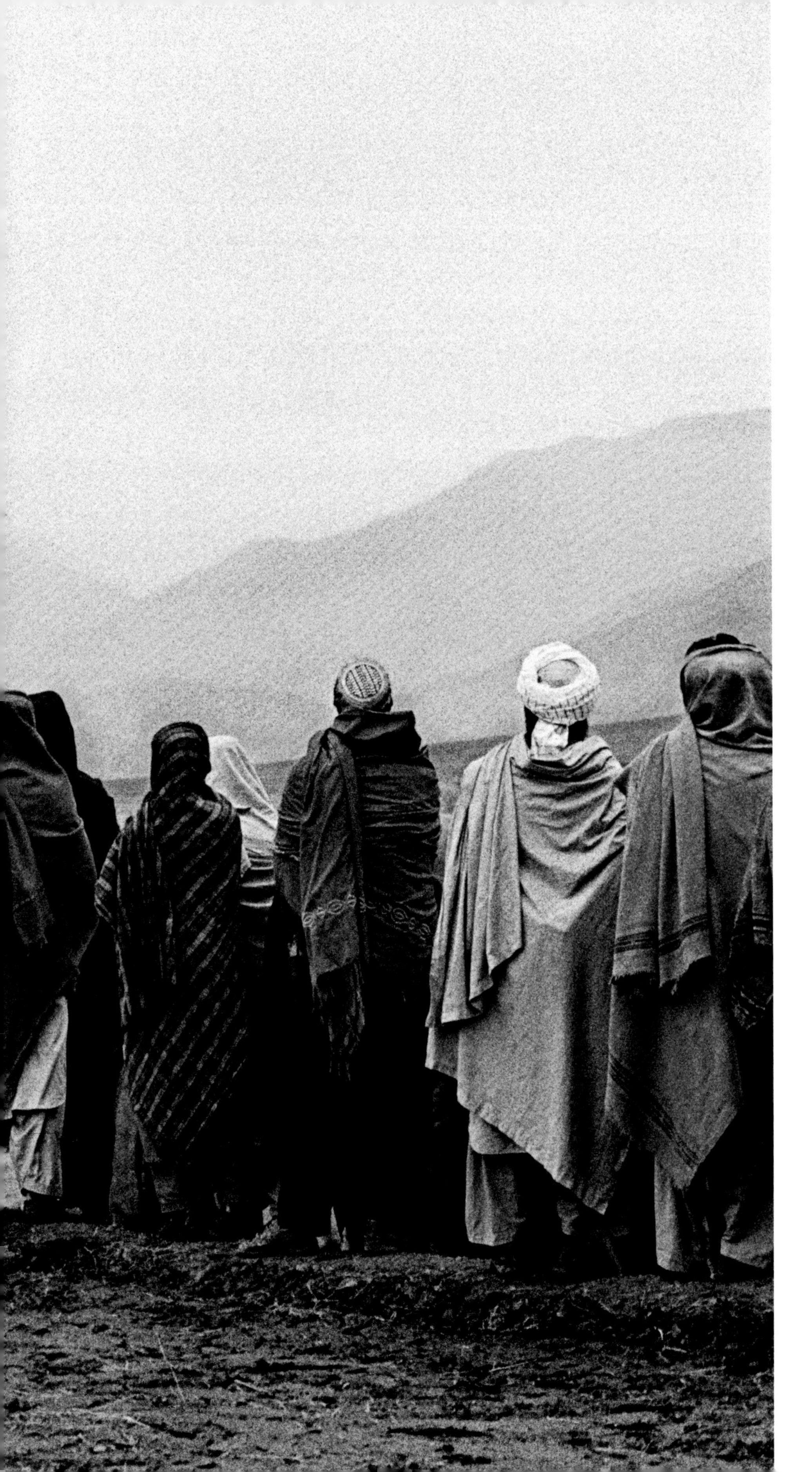

Villagers watch President Karzai return home to Kabul. The President had led a ceremony to inaugurate the beginning of construction of the Kabul to Kandahar Highway.

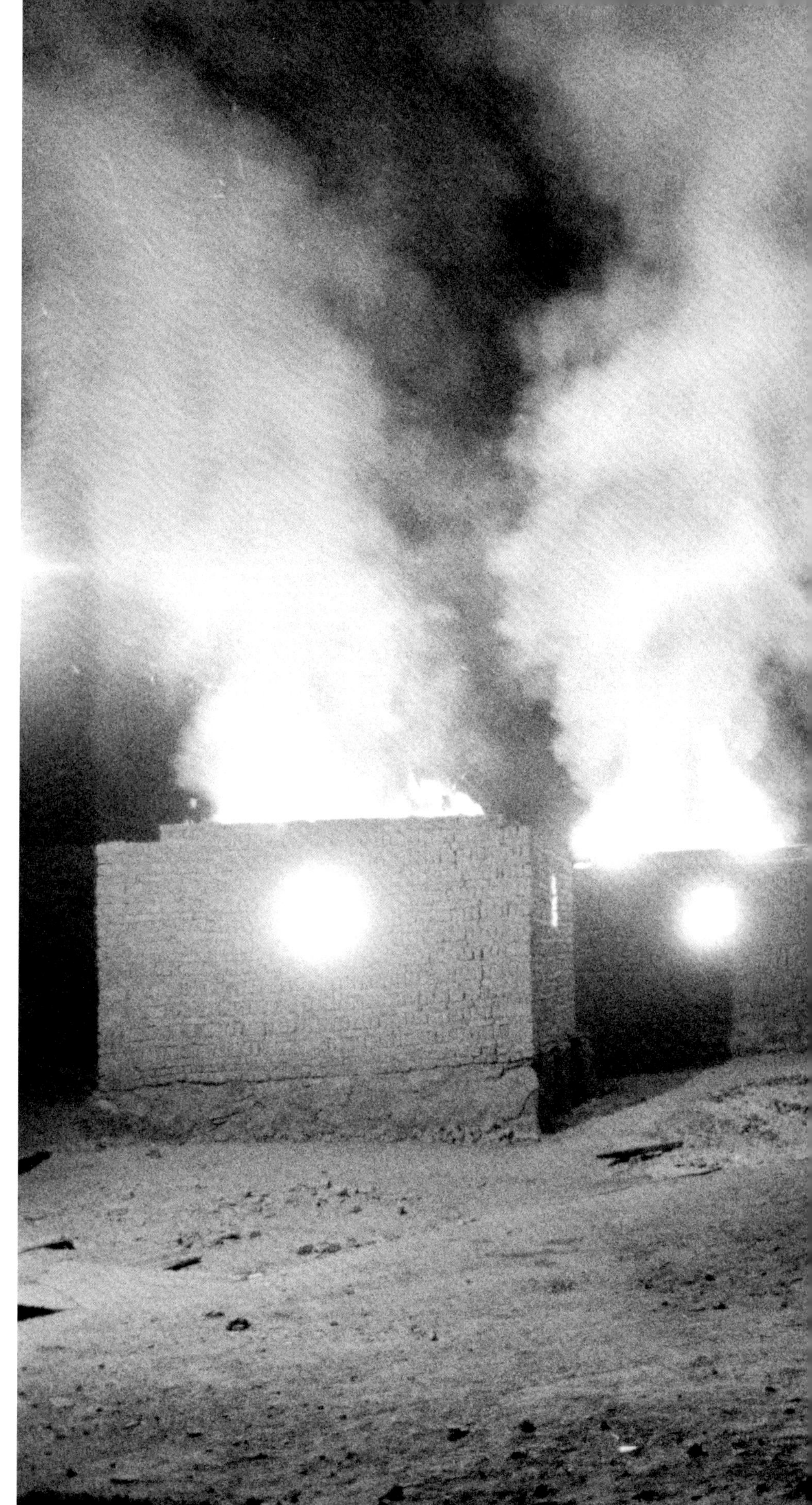

KABUL: NOVEMBER 2002
The burning of old Afghan currency prior to the
introduction of new notes.

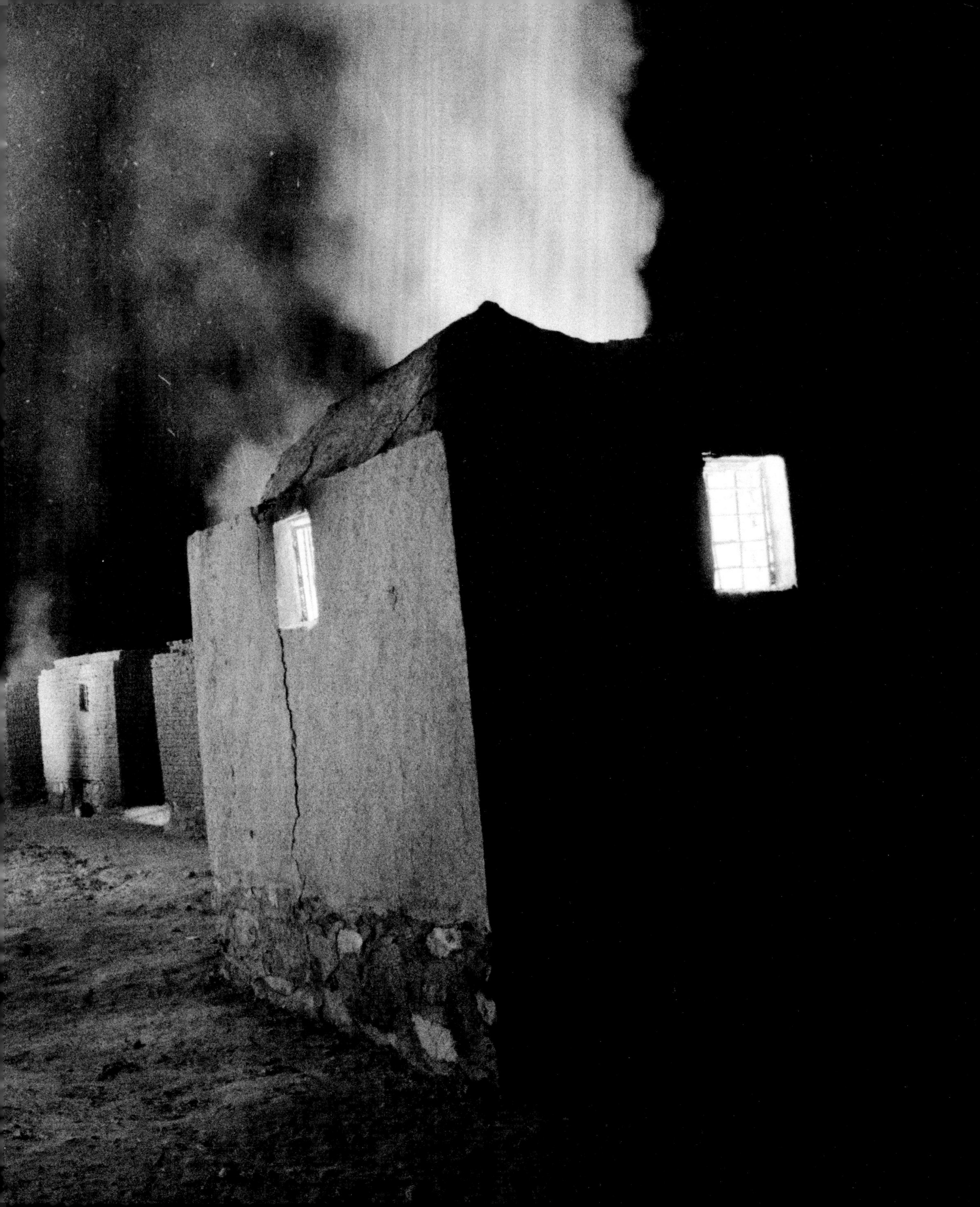

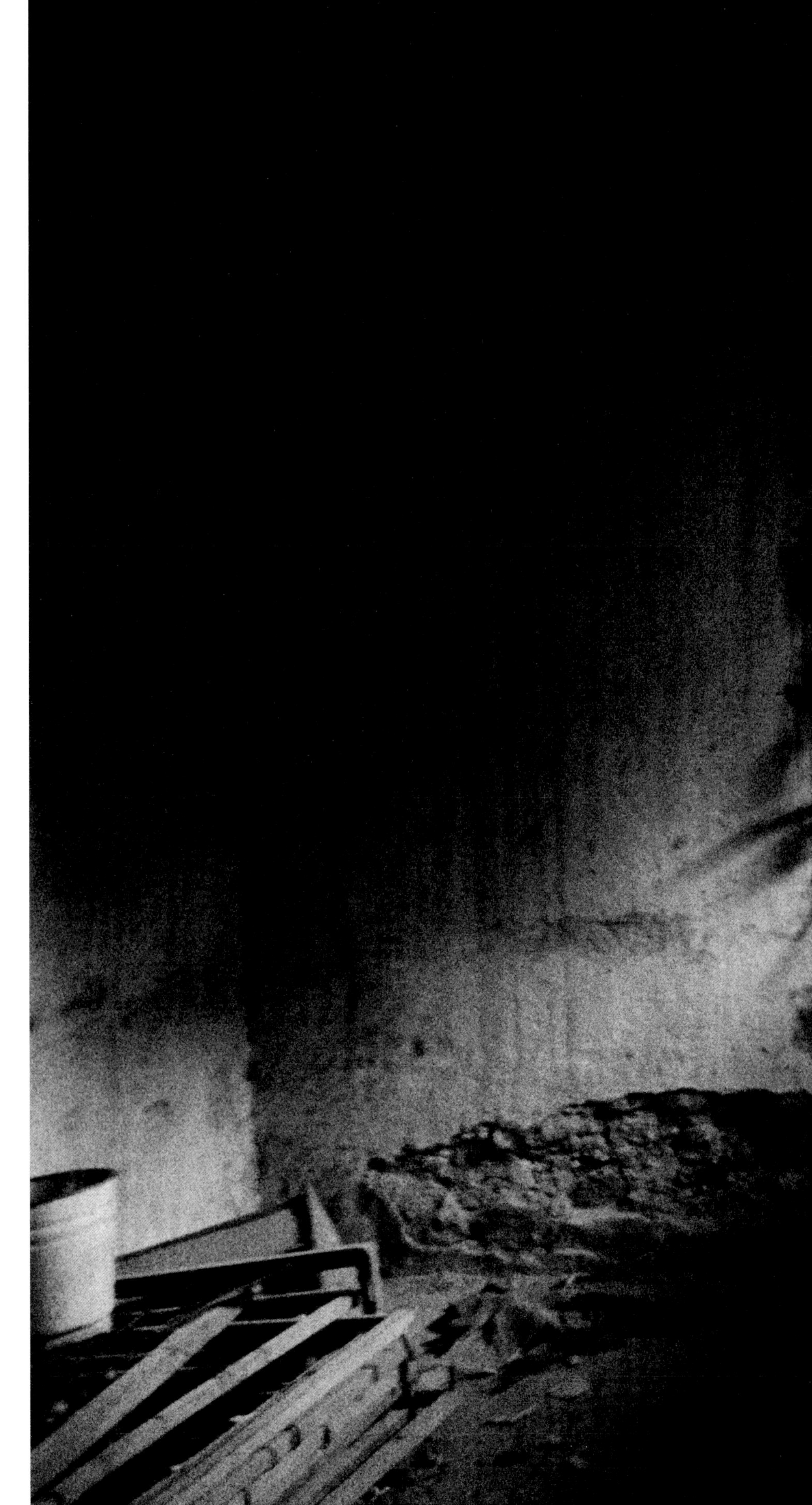

Kabul: 13 November 2001
A woman searches desperately for her sister in the cells of the Taliban Intelligence offices. Hours earlier the Taliban had abandoned their administration, abducting women as they fled the city.

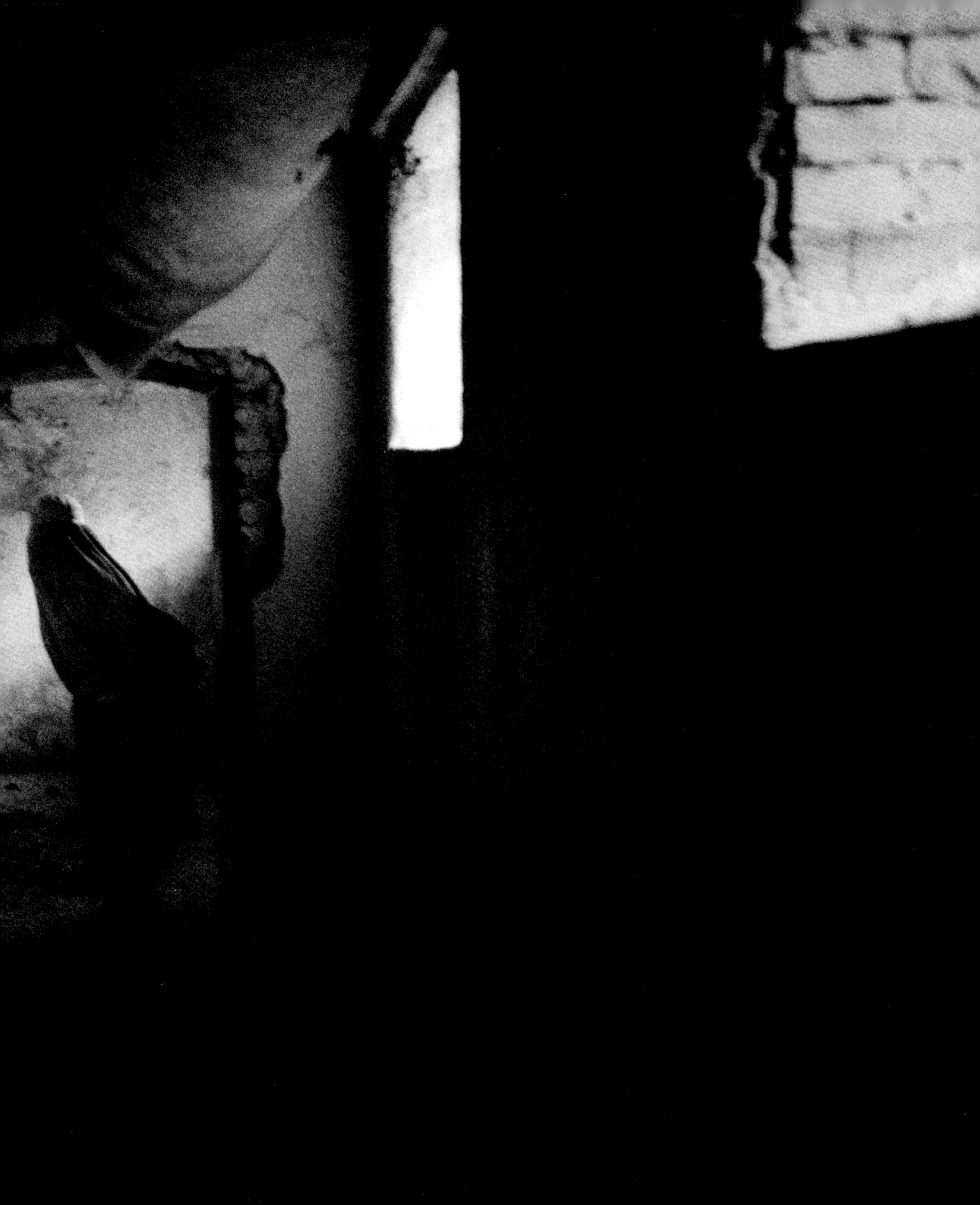

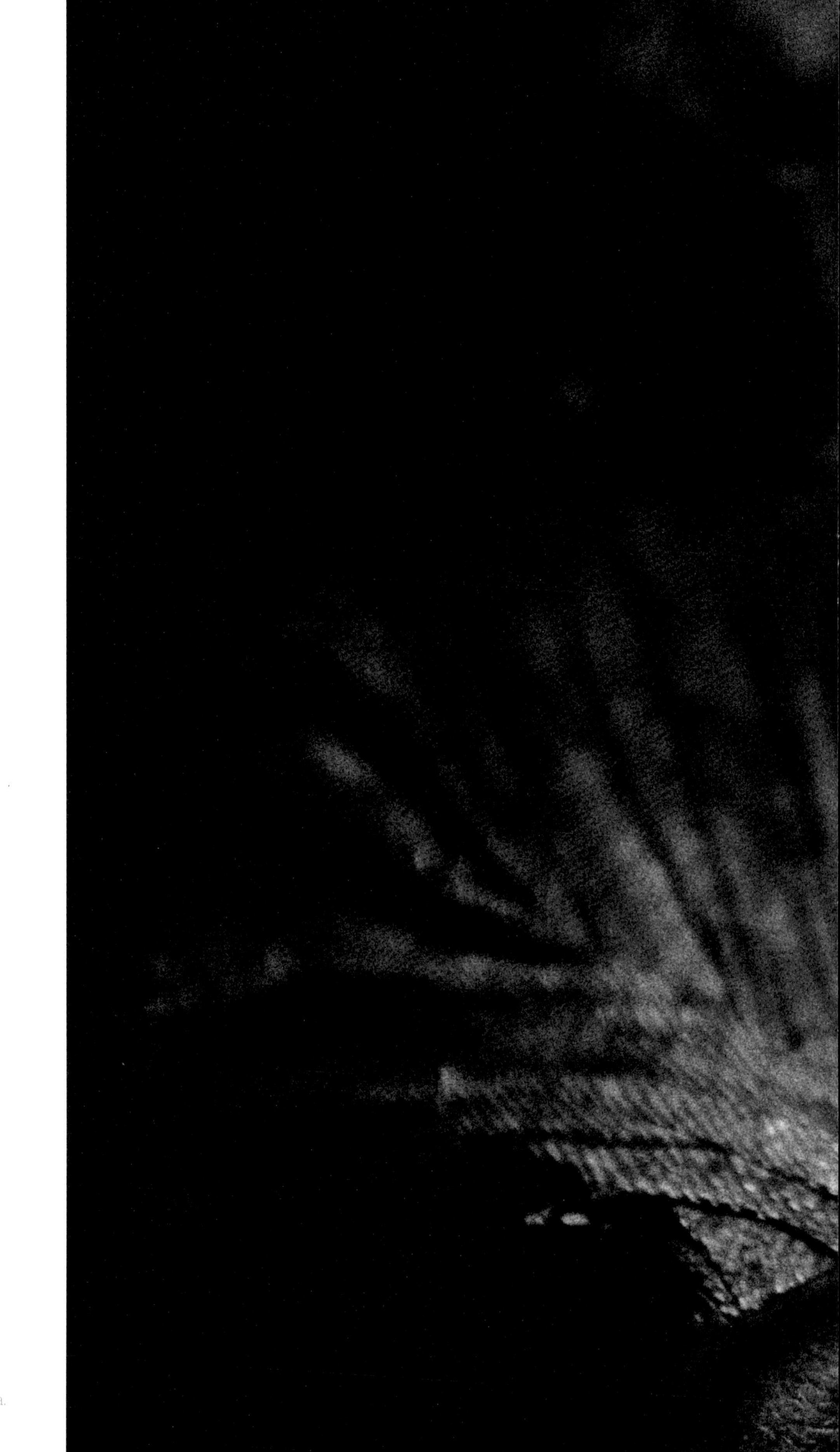

GAZASTAN, TAKHAR PROVINCE: NOVEMBER 2004
A miner working in a coal mine. Gazastan is
inhabited by Afghan Arabs, who are reputed to
have arrived centuries earlier from Saudi Arabia.

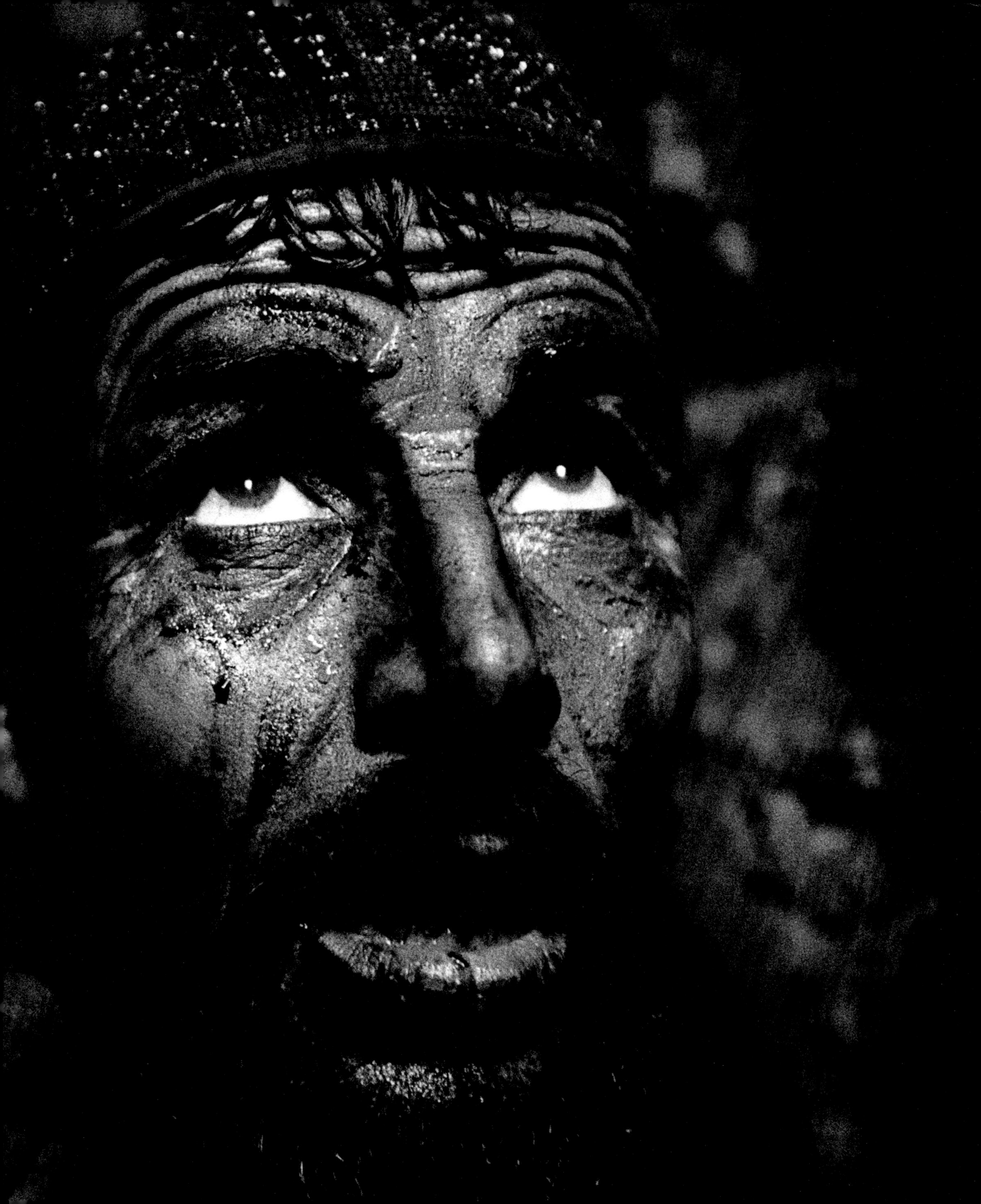

HISARAK, BALKH PROVINCE: NOVEMBER 2004
The entrance to the village mosque at prayer time.

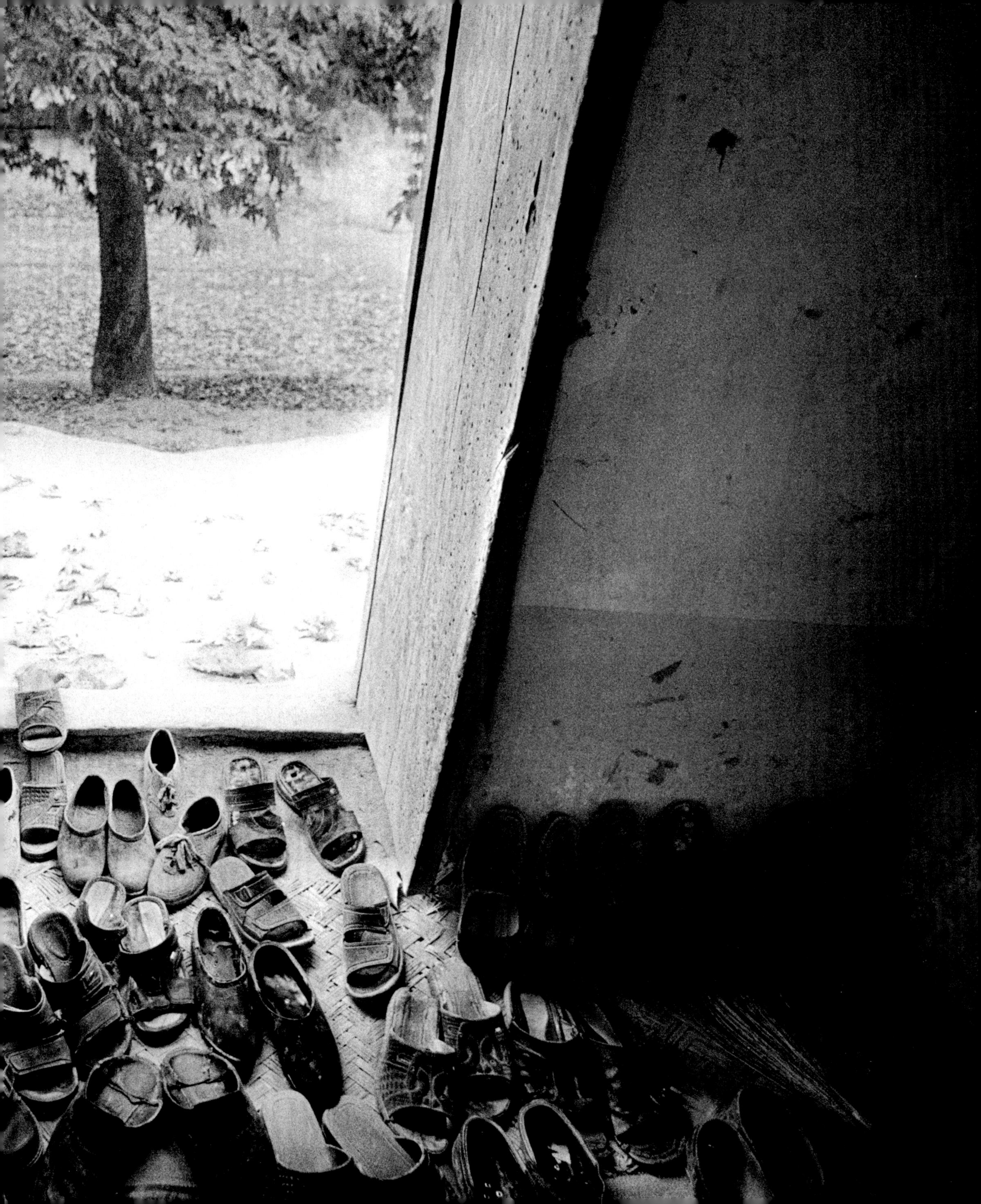

In the autumn of 2000 there was fighting on a distant frontline in northern Afghanistan. Murphy wasn't sure what he would find there. For a day he travelled by jeep over a featureless desert. The desert ended on the banks of a wide, turbulent river.

The bridge was blown so he left the jeep and hired a horse. The horse swam beside him as he spun downstream across the river on a raft made of inflated cow carcasses. On the far bank he began to ride. The horse suddenly reared up. He fell off. It was a hard fall and for a moment he lay stunned and speechless. "My cameras!" he shouted finally. But his cameras were undamaged. He remounted.

Dusk fell as he neared a village. He spent the night there on an earthen floor, as sounds of the fighting reverberated down the valley walls towards him. At dawn he rode onward on the horse. At first the ground rose in a series of low orange foothills, devoid of foliage. Then it climbed steeply. Finally it was so high that he saw a group of bored mujahideen shoot at an eagle flying far below him.

Eventually he reached the front itself, a succession of parallel bunkers facing each other along a narrow ridgeline that ascended one side of the Ibar Mountain. A Taliban raid had just been repelled and half a dozen corpses lay sprawled in the dust. Standing over the bodies of their enemy, a group of mujahideen laughed and joked and pointed as they relived their small victory. Murphy photographed them, and then turned southward to shoot the Ibar.

"It looks like Mars," he remarked, looking around at the mighty wilderness as occasional staccato bursts of gunfire rippled across the vista. He seemed content to be in that remote, unearthly place, as if merely getting there with his cameras capturing the images he had witnessed along the route had itself been vindication of the effort required.

It was. No event was needed. In the forefront of his photograph *Ibar, Takhar Province: November 2000* lies a black-shadowed foothill. Three mujahideen sit on its peak. Beyond them further ridges mount and merge in lessening degrees of shade to reach the Ibar itself, brooding beneath the pale light of the sky. Those three tiny figures, so dwarfed by the immensity of rising rock and plunging ravine, by the darkness and light of that faraway and forgotten front, guilelessly encapsulate both the title of this book and the essence of Murphy's work in Afghanistan.

Afghanistan's darkness lies not in wrongdoing or war, but in the shroud of ignorance that cloaks our understanding of the country, a blindness that has reduced it to little more than a backdrop of stale statistics, hackneyed images and Great Game clichés, against which play the momentary news stories of the world's press.

In countless ventures over fourteen years to illuminate Afghanistan's wilderness, both human and geographic, Murphy has breached this myopic vision to reveal the places and faces of a people, a war and a life that we would otherwise never see. Much of his work I have been fortunate to witness at first hand. Some trips into the hinterland, such as his journey to the Ibar, have lasted just a few days. Others have involved weeks of Spartan trek, drive, raft and ride.

The achievement of his enduring single-mindedness and patience is an account rarely attempted and seldom gained. Far greater than being just the skilled record of a people, time and place, his work has charted something much deeper and more ethereal, and has succeeded in rendering that most difficult of all revelations: a country's spirit.

Recently Afghanistan has become a subject of huge interest to picture editors and their audiences. The terrorist attacks of September 11th have brought the country to the forefront of Western consciouness. The subsequent involvement of coalition and NATO troops in Afghanistan, their fight with al Qaeda and the Taliban, and the hunt for Osama bin Laden ensure that interest continues, for the while. Afghanistan's destiny is now linked to the future security of lives in Europe and America. In the West political leaders and senior military commanders openly admit that the conflict there will be a defining experience in deciding both the outcome of their war with fundamentalist Islamic forces worldwide, and the very fate of NATO itself. Such implications make the country an obvious destination for a photographer. But it was not always so.

There was little suggestion of any such evolution in the Afghan war when Murphy first arrived in Kabul. It was 1994. Afghanistan was in the grip of a full-blown civil war so extensive and violent as to have imploded the nation's entire infrastructure. Utterly wracked, reduced and ruined, central authority no longer existed. Power lay instead in the gun and the mind of the man carrying it. There was no sense of any imminent change in the situation. The West's involvement with Afghanistan had ended the moment the last Russian soldier was withdrawn five years before. It was a hole, a vacuum, a darkness. And it was quite unimaginable either then, or beside the Ibar a few years later, how the everyday lives of the Afghans could ever again be of concern to the West.

Murphy kept returning to Afghanistan, long before it became the focus of renewed attention or editorial appetite, for reasons far simpler than those of professional investment. For all its hardships, misfortunes and cruelties, he liked the place and empathized with its people, finding attractive in the Afghans the qualities of stoicism, contradiction, belligerence, humour and hope that so define them.

"If too much time passes without having been there I suddenly realise how much I miss it, and know it's time to go back," he once remarked to me in the late nineties, as if that were all the explanation required for another Afghan assignment at a time when so few people cared.

Since 2001, countless other photographers have been drawn to the country. Yet the specific newsworthy events that now lure in these individuals remain of abstract significance to most Afghans, whose day-to-day life is geared to the simple, raw requirements of survival. Similarly, Murphy's work has been largely devolved from Afghanistan's news agenda. Foreign soldiers appear as fleetingly in his photographs as they do in Afghan lives and Afghan history. And when he has concentrated on figures of leadership, he has exposed them in the reality of their existence rather than the trappings of their status. Ahmad Shah Massoud, the Northern Alliance's famed commander, appears here peering out from a bunker – just another Afghan fighter with war on his mind – and again, in humility, with his face pressed to the desert floor in prayer (the only iconographic portrait of Massoud is of an official poster, shot with telling irony through a passing car window, three years after his assassination). Likewise President Hamid Karzai seems dwarfed by the opulence of his Palace, incongruous even, as he makes his weekly radio speech, a large crack showing beneath the wallpaper behind him. More powerful than both men is the gaze of the nameless father holding his sick daughter in a clinic in Takhar province.

The truth of Afghanistan lies in the Afghan people, and Murphy allows them their magnificence. In his diligent, evocative pursuit across so many years to reach this heart of the matter, Murphy does not shy away from Afghanistan's war. He can't. War is as enmeshed in the Afghan experience as the seasons, the mountains and weather. The country is home to millions of war tales, merging together with history into

ne long war story. But no war story is ever an account of anything more than a person or people, their
ilings, weaknesses and strengths, and their struggle to continue life and maintain dignity in the face of
he extreme challenges posed by conflict. Murphy knows this. He understands it. And the essential
umanity of this wisdom, combined with his natural engagement with his subject, is reflected throughout
is work. In his photographs, Afghans are always greater than that part of their lives that is war.

here is not another photographer with whom I would have preferred to work during the many times
e have shared together in Afghanistan. As with many dedicated, driven men, he has a profoundly
eveloped sense of humour and a lateral mindset. He knows when to wait for the moment, and when
o move in the hunt of it. This book is the consolidation of his many qualities both as an individual and
hotographer. Long after the last foreign soldier has gone and Afghanistan slides again from the world's
:age, I am sure he will be there, near the Ibar or some other forgotten region, making darkness visible.
count on it.

Anthony Loyd

Tashakur. Manana. Thank You.

owe a huge debt of gratitude to the mostly nameless Afghan people
who appear in these pages. Photographers are thieves. In order to get
the picture we rob or sometimes borrow without paying back. It's done
from necessity, and Afghans seem to understand this. I found myself in
some remote, desolate and lethal places. Yet aside from those times
when I was shelled or shot at for being the enemy on the other side
of a line in the dust, I was always made to feel at home. This sense of
humanity comes from their natural propensity for tolerance, and is
that fuels the hope that Afghanistan will eventually find harmony.

The photograph on the cover of this book, along with many others
exist on these pages thanks in part to some enterprising mujahideen
Charikar. On 13 November, 2001, they robbed my broken Leica and
mobile phone while I photographed the fall of Kabul. Happily they saw
no value in a knotted black plastic bag stashed in the same bag that
held their loot, along with some filthy clothes and a couple of books.
Brave warriors, I salute you! The plastic bag you flung to the corner of
the room was full of rolls of black and white film from the previous
months living on the Shamali frontline. Instead of being an important
constituent of this book and a record of the last days of Taliban rule,
the film would likely have enjoyed the attention of some curious goats,
nuzzling the bag amongst the rotting vegetables and rubbish. Over time
they would have been buried in the Shamali Plain, along with the bones,
tales and whispers of that fecund soil. Hope you got a good price for
the Leica.

This book has taken hostage many people's loyalty, energy, intelligence,
patience and goodwill. There isn't space to do justice to all the
generous contributions made over the years in bringing this work to
print. So in the manner of a Catholic confession, I beg forgiveness for
those deserving of thanks but not credited, and for all other such sins
of omission.

Special thanks to:
The Times Saturday Magazine, Newsweek Magazine, The New
York Times Magazine, Outside Magazine, the Massoud Foundation
and Afghanaid.
Everyone at Saqi, in particular: Mitch Albert, Ashley Biles, Lara Frankena,
Andre Gaspard, Mai Ghoussoub, Rebecca O'Connor and Anna Wilson.

Personal thanks to:
Anthony Loyd, a great and loyal friend since my second trip to
Afghanistan in 1996 and responsible for much that is of worth in
this book.
Nancy Hatch Dupree, who within days of my contacting her delivered
an essay that captures the sweep of Afghanistan history, giving an
invaluable insight into the country beyond its wars.
Steven Coleman, whose contributions are felt throughout the book and
whose passion for the project never waned.
Mark Edwards for his magical picture editing, and who managed to
fortify and energize the book when it was most needed.
Henrietta Molinaro for bringing elegance and clarity to the book
with her design.
Jocelyn Bain Hogg for his extraordinary well of ideas, energy
and generosity.
Susan Olle for single-handedly organizing a major exhibition of the
work at the Oxo Gallery in London in 2004.
Thomas Rees for being Doubtless Thomas.
Marcus Bleasdale for finding solutions.
Jamie Wellford at Newsweek for being The Virginian.
Graham Wood at The Times Saturday Magazine for consistently and
without fuss aiding my efforts. Also Simon Hills, Lyndsey Price and
Gill Morgan.
Ahmad Wali Massoud.
Philip Jones Griffiths and Tom Stoddart for sharing their wisdom.
Smita Tharoor for love, strength and more.

And to:
Glen Brent, Nigel Coleman, Marie Colvin, Marina Elmi, The Frontline
Club, Eliza Griswold, David Hall of Bluesky Images, Reggie Hastings,
Peter Juvenal, Abdul Karim of Afghan Travel Centre, Sean Langan,
The Librarian RJ, Paul Lowe, Angus MacKinnon, Dave Mather, Denise
Meredith, David Orr, Ramazam, Joe Regal, Kathy Ryan, Marcel Saba,
Mariana Sanchez, Rasool Sekandari and his trusty Toyota,
Charlie Sennott, Mohammed Sharif, John Simpson, Pranvera Smith,
Vaughan Smith, Patrick Symmes. And the tearaways of Poplar Road.